Social Studies in Elementary Education

Tenth Edition

WALTER C. PARKER

JOHN JAROLIMEK

UNIVERSITY OF WASHINGTON
SEATTLE

Merrill, an imprint of Prentice Hall
Upper Saddle River, New Jersey   Columbus, Ohio

Library of Congress Cataloging-in-Publication Data

Parker, Walter.
    Social studies in elementary education/Walter C. Parker and
John Jarolimek.—10th ed.
      p. cm.
    Jarolimek's name appears first on the earlier edition.
    Includes bibliographical references and index.
    ISBN 0-13-470015-5 (hardcover)
    1. Social sciences—Study and teaching (Elementary)—
United States.   I. Jarolimek, John. II. Title.
LB1584.J3   1997
372.83'044'0973—dc20

96-3433
CIP

Editor: Bradley J. Potthoff
Production Editor: Julie Anderson Peters
Text Designer: STELLARViSIONs
Production Manager: Laura Messerly
Design Coordinator: Julia Zonneveld Van Hook
Cover Designer: Tom Mack
Photo Researcher: Dawn Garrott
Electronic Text Management: Marilyn Wilson Phelps,
    Matthew Williams, Karen L. Bretz, Tracey Ward

This book was set in Transitional 511 by Prentice Hall
and was printed and bound by R.R. Donnelley & Sons
Company. The cover was printed by Phoenix Color Corp.

© 1997 by Prentice-Hall, Inc.
Simon & Schuster/A Viacom Company
Upper Saddle River, New Jersey 07458

Earlier editions © 1993, 1967, 1963, 1959 by Macmillan Publishing Company, and © 1990, 1986, 1982,
1977, and 1971 by John Jarolimek.

Printed in the United States of America

10 9 8 7 6 5 4 3

ISBN: 0-13-470015-5

Prentice-Hall International (UK) Limited, *London*
Prentice-Hall of Australia Pty. Limited, *Sydney*
Prentice-Hall of Canada, Inc., *Toronto*
Prentice-Hall Hispanoamericana, S. A., *Mexico*
Prentice-Hall of India Private Limited, *New Delhi*
Prentice-Hall of Japan, Inc., *Tokyo*
Simon & Schuster Asia Pte. Ltd., *Singapore*
Editora Prentice-Hall do Brasil, Ltda., *Rio de Janeiro*

Photos by: Scott Cunningham/Merrill/Prentice Hall,
pp. 13, 60, 65, 106, 116, 128, 133, 216, 230, 243, 260,
272, 296, 310, 324, 352; Courtesy of the Institute of
Texan Cultures, p. 92; KS Studios/Merrill/Prentice
Hall, p. 195; Anthony Magnacca/Merrill/Prentice Hall,
pp. 2, 15, 180, 186, 372; Barbara Schwartz/ Merrill/
Prentice Hall, pp. 35, 79, 124, 161, 275, 354; Anne
Vega/Merrill/Prentice Hall, pp. 47, 154, 264, 305, 322;
Tom Watson/Merrill/Prentice Hall, p. 26; Todd Yarring-
ton/Merrill/Prentice Hall, p. 344.

The color maps insert and Summary of the U.S. Constitution insert are courtesy of Macmillan/McGraw-Hill
School Division. The U.S. Landforms and Cross-Section
maps and the Summary of the U.S. Constitution are
from *United States and Its Neighbors*, © 1995, from the
World Around Us series and the World Political map
and Dictionary of Geographic Terms are from *United
States*, © 1997, in the *Adventures in Time and Place*
series. Reproduced with permission of The McGraw-
Hill Companies.

COVER ARTIST

Loretta Sherwood, a thirteen-year-old eighth-grader at Heritage Middle School in Westerville, Ohio, won our cover illustrator contest for *Social Studies in Elementary Education*, 10th edition. Not only do designers and editors at Prentice Hall think Loretta is quite accomplished as a young artist, but also they have learned that Loretta is a talented flute player and pianist. Loretta's favorite activities, however, are sailing and swimming, so she is torn between seeking a future career as a marine biologist or making a name for herself in the advertising field.

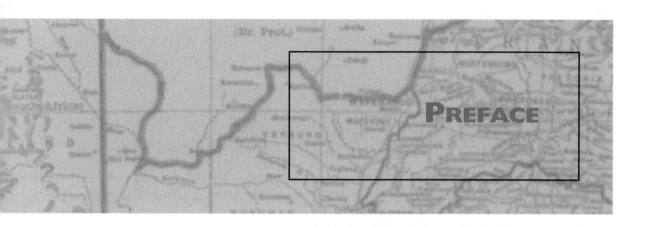

PREFACE

The purpose of this book is to introduce new teachers to the world of social studies teaching and learning in elementary and middle schools, and to help them unleash their creativity on this vitally important subject area. The social studies curriculum is a great collection of ideas and tools—a garden of delights—without which children are ill-equipped for both private life and public life in a fast-changing world. When children are empowered by skillful teachers with the facts, ideas, skills, values, questions, and dispositions that compose the social studies curriculum, their judgment is dramatically improved. Consequently, they are better able to help solve community problems, reason historically, appreciate diversity, cultivate civic life, protect the environment, and, with deep understanding, empathize with the hopes, dreams, and struggles of people everywhere.

The children in today's classroom are even more diverse than in the past, which translates into new challenges for teachers. The challenges are not entirely new, of course, but today's diversity is of a greater scale and range. The terms *majority* and *minority* are rapidly making less and less sense: Already in the nation's largest school districts, "minorities" are "majorities." Teachers cannot, therefore, attend only to yesterday's familiar categories of differences among children: development and ability. Educationally sound responses are needed as well to ethnic, linguistic, gender, and racial differences among children. Attending creatively to these differences *without lowering expectations* is one of the great pedagogical challenges facing today's teachers. Even teachers of very young children cannot sidestep this mandate, for it is in these early years that key foundations are set in place. If girls are not challenged to think as rigorously or called upon to participate as vigorously as boys, this will have consequences in their later school and life achievements. If poor and nonwhite children are taught mainly skills while children of the mainstream culture are taught skills *and* powerful ideas, this, too, will have consequences.

At the same time that classroom diversity is increasing and the commitment to hold *all* our children to high standards of achievement intensifies, teachers must redouble their efforts to nurture our common ground—that which binds us together in a civic and moral community. Diversity is no threat to this civic unity. "We the people" created the government of the United States in part to protect this diversity; indeed, the freedom to choose one's path is a standard against which democracies are measured. Educating children in such a way that they will not only exercise their freedom but take on the responsibilities of democratic citizenship—honoring diversity and caring for the community—is the great mission of social studies education. There is much that teachers of even the youngest children can do, as readers will see in this text.

New to This Edition

Instructors who used the previous edition of this text will find the present edition both familiar and new. Recent developments, such as numerous curriculum standards projects, the resurgence of interest in curricular integration, the revolution in assessment, and the presence of a highway—the "information superhighway"—in many of today's classrooms are all addressed. More influential even than these on today's teachers' professional development, however, are the demographic changes sweeping through the classrooms of North America. "Times have changed," we write in one of the new chapters, "The Children We Teach." "Today's teachers cannot get by on yesterday's teachers' knowledge and skills."

Numerous structural changes were made in the text that should make it easy to read, use, and reuse over the years. It is laid out in a way that readers should find very straightforward. There are three parts: The first orients readers to the mission of social studies education and the children we teach; the second concentrates on the curriculum—*what* we try to teach; the third on instruction—*how* we try to teach it. There are twelve chapters overall, reduced from fifteen in the prior edition, which should help instructors and readers alike deal with this material within a single term. Considerable pruning and reorganization made this possible at the same time that new material was added.

Explanatory footnotes have been inserted to provide additional information about many issues in the text. Endnotes, on the other hand, appear at the end of each chapter to refer readers to the original source of information presented in the text. Footnotes are marked with an asterisk (*) and endnotes are numbered sequentially beginning with 1.

Acknowledgments

I am grateful to my coauthor, John Jarolimek, for the invitation to assume responsibility for this book. Professor Jarolimek authored the first edition of this book in 1959. He was then on the faculty of San Diego State College (now San Diego State University); I was ten years old and a fifth-grader at Lowell Elementary School in Englewood, Colorado. John joined the faculty of the College of Education at the University of Washington in Seattle in 1962; I did likewise in 1985.

That first edition in 1959 was followed by seven meticulously crafted revisions. With the 1993 revision, I joined the project as John's coauthor, and with the present edition, the tenth, I moved into the driver's seat, so to speak. John and I planned this revision with the assistance of our editor at Merrill/Prentice Hall and a number of reviewers who provided extremely thoughtful evaluations of the ninth edition.

The authors are indebted to a number of individuals who assisted in procuring photographs, artwork, and other material. We wish to express our sincere thanks and appreciation to them: Sharon Pray Muir, Oakland University; Michael Simpson, National Council for the Social Studies; Judy Glickman, Macmillan/McGraw-Hill School Division; Kristin Palmquist, California Department of Education; Joseph A. Braun, Jr., Illinois State University; Allen Glenn and Diana Hess, University of Washington; and David Harris, Oakland County, Michigan, Public Schools.

We wish to express our gratitude and appreciation as well to a number of persons who gave generously of their time, whether reading drafts, offering suggestions, or otherwise challenging our thinking. These include James A. Banks, Sheila Valencia, Sam Sebesta, Sam Wineburg, Theodore Kaltsounis, Ilene Schwartz, Tom Lovitt, Carole Kubota, Gene Edgar, Barbara McKean, Brenda Weikel, Bruce Larson, Terry Beck, Bernadette Cole Slaughter, Akira Ninomiya, Patricia Avery, John Cogan, Roland Case, Ken Osborne, Chanita Rukspollmuang, Michael Hartoonian, Margaret Branson, Mary McFarland, Gloria Ladson-Billings, Barry Beyer, Jean Craven, Gloria Contreras, Valerie Ooka Pang, Paula Fraser, Doug Selwyn, Nathaniel Jackson, and the reviewers who evaluated the previous edition of this book and offered helpful suggestions for the current edition. These reviewers are: Jo Anne Buggey, University of Minnesota; Morris L. Lamb, Southern Illinois University at Carbondale; Jay Monson, Utah State University; Kenneth C. Schmidt, University of Wisconsin–Eau Claire; and Jan Waggoner, Southern Illinois University at Carbondale.

We are grateful, too, for the caring attention and commitment of our editors, Brad Potthoff, Linda Montgomery, Julie Peters, and Beth Dubberley.

Walter C. Parker
Seattle, Washington

BRIEF CONTENTS

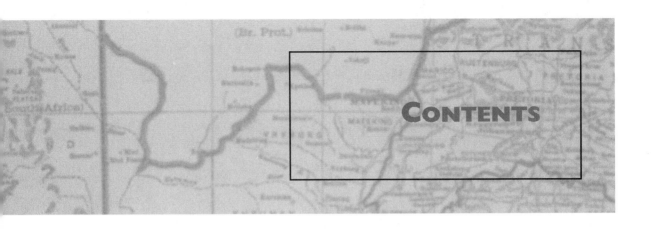

CONTENTS

PART I

ORIENTATION TO SOCIAL STUDIES EDUCATION   1

1 SOCIAL STUDIES EDUCATION: WHAT AND WHY   2

2   THE CHILDREN WE TEACH   26

PART 2

THE SOCIAL STUDIES CURRICULUM   59

3   CITIZENSHIP EDUCATION AND DEMOCRATIC VALUES   60

4 HISTORY, GEOGRAPHY, AND THE SOCIAL SCIENCES   92

PART 3

PLANNING AND TEACHING SOCIAL STUDIES   185

7   STRATEGIES FOR TEACHING SOCIAL STUDIES SUBJECT MATTER   186

8 PLANNING UNITS, LESSONS, AND ACTIVITIES   230

9 ASSESSING STUDENT LEARNING   264

10 COOPERATIVE LEARNING   296

11   READING TO LEARN SOCIAL STUDIES   322

12   SOCIAL STUDIES AS THE INTEGRATING CORE   352

LESSON PLANS

SPECIAL LESSON PLANS

GLOSSARIES

SCORING RUBRICS (SAMPLES)

PART

I

Orientation to Social Studies Education

CHAPTER 1
Social Studies Education: What and Why

CHAPTER 2
The Children We Teach

SOCIAL STUDIES EDUCATION:

WHAT AND WHY

OVERVIEW

The Social Studies Vision

**The Context for Teaching Social
Studies Today**
Trend 1: Teaching All Our Children
Trend 2: Higher Standards for
Learning
Trend 3: Character Education

**Goals for the Social Studies: Social
Understanding and Civic Efficacy**
Ideas and Information Goals
(Knowledge)

Attitudes and Values Goals
Skills Goals

Curriculum Scope and Sequence
Thinking Conceptually
Unit Topics

Plan of the Book

As they come into class, the kindergarten children are excited to find a large strip of paper going down the middle of the classroom floor. Their teacher, Jacob Stern, tells them to hang up their coats and come sit beside the paper strip. The strip, he tells them, is a highway connecting two distant towns. Mr. Stern takes a toy car and starts driving it along the highway. "What might happen as someone drives along?", he asks. The children suggest a number of possibilities: running out of gas, getting tired, being hungry. "What services might be necessary for people as they drive from town to town?" Tanisha suggests a gas station. A milk carton is placed along the highway and named "Tanisha's Gas Station."

Following an incident in which a student at a local high school threatened another student with a handgun, Janet Morton's fifth graders begin collecting news reports about other incidents in schools involving weapons. An attorney is invited to class to answer questions the students have raised regarding laws governing minors and weapon possession and use. Learning that there is no law prohibiting youth from carrying handguns, in or out of school, the class creates a plan to lobby their state legislature for tougher laws governing minors and weapons. They are successful: their bill passes both houses of the state legislature.[1]

Such simple, yet brilliant creativity is characteristic of good elementary and middle school teachers. "I love to teach," said one. "I do my best teaching around social studies because that's where the kids' future is. I can challenge my students to really think about the world. I want them to leave my class feeling good about themselves and about the fantastic future that can be theirs."

The Social Studies Vision

Elementary and middle school teachers need to have a vision of the future for the children they teach. This gives purpose and direction to their instructional decision making and lends passion and drive to their work with children. Readers of this book will be teaching the children who will be shaping the future for the next six to eight decades. Seated in the classrooms of today's teachers are children who, as senior citizens, will help this nation—the world's oldest constitutional democracy—celebrate its three hundredth anniversary in 2076. This, of course, assumes there actually will be such an event. Whether this nation survives that long depends in no small measure on how well today's school children are taught the ideas and information, the skills and habits, and the rights and responsibilities of democratic citizenship.

When the public school movement developed momentum in the 1840s, the motivating vision was of a citizenry that could meet the challenge of self-government, which is the defining attribute of democracy. The people *themselves* are expected to be the rulers, solving problems and making policy, appreciating diversity, and protecting the liberty of people to express even unpopular views. It was widely understood back when this nation was a little younger that democracy was a fragile social and political experiment. Many people in the United States take democracy for granted these days, it appears, but school teachers cannot afford to do so. In this respect, teachers must be civic leaders. They need to understand that an undereducated public cannot maintain a democracy, for democracy is a *path*, and it is not such an easy one to walk.

Democracy is not a "machine that would go of itself," but must be consciously reproduced, one generation instructing the next in the knowledge and skills, as well as in the civic character and commitments required for its sustenance.[2]

Democracy, freedom, and diversity are intimately related. Democracy is the only widely accepted path yet to have been invented for societies that are heterogeneous with respect to religion, race, ethnicity, social class, and national origin *and* that are committed to protecting and honoring this diversity. The democratic ideal, in addition to self-governance, insists on individual liberty, toleration, and respect for differences. It gives no quarter to repression or discrimination. Democracy, then, is much more than a political system; *it is a way of life*—a way of being with one another, whether in the city hall, the shopping mall, or the classroom. It is certainly not a perfect path; in fact, it is frustrating, contentious, and often exasperating. The only thing worse than democracy, the saying goes, is all the alternatives. If democracy is to be the vision that holds this diverse society together, then the people must be educated for it. There can be no democracy without democratic citizens.

The public school was considered by reformers the chief vehicle for the job. Public schools were to be free (i.e., supported through tax revenues rather than tuition payments), they were to have a common curriculum, and they were to serve all children. The establishment of the public school system in this country was a clear statement that the nation believed that a quality education is the key to this society's future and to the future of individuals within it. Without the collective intelligence afforded by a rigorous school curriculum, the chances are slim that the United States can remain on the democratic path and solve its myriad social problems, reduce the number of its children who live in poverty, retain (or regain) its competitive edge, or contribute in wholesome ways to the planet's future.

The Context for Teaching Social Studies Today

A teacher begins his or her teaching career always within the particular circumstances of time and place—that is, within a unique historical and geographic setting. The effects of this context on one's thinking and behavior as a teacher will be significant and, probably, long lasting. Human beings change and make choices, of course, but we also are products of our environments and creatures of habit. Accordingly, it makes a difference whether one begins teaching in a suburban community in southern California in the 1950s, an inner-city school in Chicago in the 1990s, or a rural Alaskan village during the Gold Rush.

Teachers beginning their careers now, at the turn of the twentieth century, and here, in contemporary United States society, will notice that educators are being asked to take the vision of the public school more seriously than ever before: Offering high-quality education to *all* children, raising the standards for student achievement, and paying more attention to the education of civility as well as knowledge and skills are each now a part of the expectation for new teachers. During an interview for a teaching position, a candidate most likely will be asked about these trends. We address them throughout this text and introduce them briefly at this point.

Trend 1: Teaching All Our Children

The public school movement was geared to getting all our children into schools and, once there, providing them with a common, high-quality curriculum. The racial segregation of schools dealt a huge blow to the common school vision early in its history and introduced an institutional habit that has been difficult to break: providing different curriculum and instruction to different groups of children. This phenomenon, called *curriculum differentiation* or *tracking*, is in direct violation of the vision of a high-quality curriculum for all children.

The U.S. Supreme Court ruled in 1954 that the segregated school system was failing to provide equal education for all children, and communities were forced to integrate their schools. Yet, the curriculum standards to which African-American children were held and the instructional support they were provided in the integrated schools sometimes were, and still are, lower than those for white children. Socioeconomic status complicates the picture: Poor children are often held to lower standards, and minority children are disproportionately from poor families.

This problem has not yet been solved. Today's teachers are expected to work diligently to educate the diverse children of today's classrooms *and to create more successful ways of doing so than have been developed thus far*. Today's teachers are expected to acknowledge and root out their own prejudices and stereotypes and, thereby, recognize the intelligence and potential in each child. They are expected to set challenging expectations and provide a strong and supportive instructional environment for students. As we shall see in Chapter 2, "The Children We Teach," this not only means examining one's own attitudes about racial and cultural differences, but also learning about the home cultures of the children, which can be quite different from the culture of the school. In addition to gaining this knowledge, it means building bridges across the gaps—becoming multicultural. This in turn requires teachers to reflect on their own ethnic group membership and understand how this can shape their interaction with children and parents.

Much can be done, but a fervent commitment to teaching every child who appears at the classroom door is necessary. Without this commitment—this *conviction* that "each one of my children is bright and will learn"—it is unlikely that teachers can overcome the old institutional habit of low expectations for some children and high expectations for others.

Trend 2: Higher Standards for Learning

In addition to this concern that children be given equal educational opportunities, there is concern today that children across the board—children of *all* races, classes, and cultures—may not be sufficiently challenged by the school curriculum. The general consensus across the country is that the quality of education that most children receive is not as high as it might be. This belief is coupled with the conviction that a more vigorous and substantive education is fully within our reach. Why then is it not being provided?

The most commonly identified reason is that low achievement standards have crept into schools and become accepted as the normal state of affairs. The first alarm was sounded in a widely read report of the National Commission on Excellence in Education in 1983, which asserted that our education standards—our expectations for student learning—had fallen so low as to make this "a nation at risk." Numerous social forces had contributed to the lowering of standards, but the one that received the most attention is this: Schools had been distracted by what was known as the "minimum competencies" movement in the 1970s and 1980s. Itself a response to the public's perception that achievement criteria had fallen too low (that students were not learning even the "basics" of the school curriculum), this movement caused principals and school boards to pressure teachers to pay nearly obsessive attention to drilling their students on lists of reading and math "skills." Lost in the process were the powerful ideas, abilities, and challenging issues that these skills were supposed to help children engage.

Since the commission's report, the effort to conceptualize "world-class standards" has become the major education project of the 1990s. The attention now is on both skills *and* powerful ideas, abilities, and issues. The new consensus is that we cannot afford the former without the latter and that educators must work to help children learn both in conjunction with one another.

A number of national standards committees in a variety of subject areas were convened across the nation, some funded by the federal government, others by organizations of educators, some by both. Their task was to develop higher standards for K–12 schooling—standards that answer one of the great, controversial questions of all time: *What should our children know and be able to do?* Of course, people disagree over the answer to this question; accordingly, they disagree over the answers these committees produce. With a question like this, it could not be otherwise.*

Elementary and middle school teachers will want to read and ponder the several sets of national standards that have been developed recently. The simple fact that they offer advice to teachers on which subject matter should be taught makes them intriguing and valuable resources, difficult to dismiss out of hand. Add to this the fact that some very knowledgeable and committed individuals served on these committees. The combination, in our judgment, makes these works deserving of our careful consideration. Like any advice, it can be considered without necessarily being taken. Four sets of standards are especially relevant to the field of social studies:

Geography (One Book)
Geography for Life: National Geography Standards 1994. Available from National Geographic Society, P.O. Box 1640, Washington, DC 20013–1640. Call toll-free 1-800-368-2728. Cost: $9.

---

* In 1995, the curriculum standards for the field of history were met with much criticism by talk show hosts and U.S. senators alike, who charged they were written by a "secret group" of "ultra-feminist" historians. For a criticism of these standards, see John Fonte's "The Naive Romanticism of the History Standards," *The Chronicle of Higher Education* (June 9, 1995), A48. For a defense, see Gary B. Nash and Ross E. Dunn, "History Standards and Culture Wars," *Social Education*, 59 (January 1995), 5–7.

History (Three Books)
National Standards for History, Grades K–4. Available from National Center for History in the Schools, University of California, Los Angeles, 10880 Wilshire Blvd., Suite 761, Los Angeles, CA 90024–4108. Cost: $7.95.

National Standards for United States History, Grades 5–12. Same address. Cost: $18.95.

National Standards for World History, Grades 5–12. Same address. Cost: $18.95.

Civics/Government (One Book)
National Standards for Civics and Government. Available from the Center for Civic Education, 5146 Douglas Fir Rd., Calabasas, CA 91302–1467. Call toll-free 1-800-350-4223. Cost: $12.

Social Studies, Integrated (One Book)
Curriculum Standards for Social Studies. Available from National Council for the Social Studies, c/o Whitehurst & Clark, 100 Newfield Ave., Edison, NY 08837. Call toll-free 1-800-683-0812. Cost: $15; $12.75 for NCSS members.

In the chapters that follow, especially in Chapters 3–5, we highlight each of these sets of standards. A "sampler" of the last set listed, the integrated social studies standards developed by the National Council for the Social Studies, accompanies this text. An order form can be found inside the *Sampler* so that interested readers may obtain the entire 178-page document. The *Sampler* lists at two grade levels what students should know and be able to do and provides readers with a sense of what the various standards documents attempt to accomplish.

Social Studies Standards

The NCSS standards identify ten overarching curriculum themes. From culture to civic ideals and practices, the ten themes attempt to capture the wide scope of the social studies curriculum. Each thematic statement begins with the phrase, "Social studies programs should include experiences that provide for the study of [*theme*]." As you examine the standards, note the performance expectations that are given for the early and middle grades. (A third level of proficiency—high school graduation expectations—are included in the standards, too, but not in the accompanying *Sampler*.) These spell out the specific ideas, skills, perspectives, and dispositions that students should be able to exhibit as a consequence of the curriculum experiences identified in the thematic statement.

Take time to read the teaching vignettes as well. The two vignettes at the beginning of this chapter are from these standards. Each vignette describes a situation in which an elementary or middle school teacher is providing instruction that is aimed at one or more of the ten standards. In the *Sampler* that accompanies this text, one teaching vignette was selected for each set of elementary and middle school performance expectations.

State and Local Standards

In addition to these national standards projects, there are curriculum framework development projects in each of the 50 states. This is not a new development entirely. Constitutionally, education in the United States is a responsibility of the individual states, not the federal government. What the states are doing now, however, reflects the national trend to raise standards beyond the minimal requirements, called *minimum competencies*, that most states had set before. Most states view the national standards documents as resources, with teachers reading and pondering them, perhaps, but not adopting them wholesale. According to most reports, "few states feel any obligation to use them."[3] One official in Texas put in bluntly: "If there is a conflict between the Texas standards and the national standards, this is Texas. And, by God, we would choose Texas standards."[4]

Most states delegate a good portion of curriculum decision making to the local school district. Within some districts, curriculum authority is decentralized still further to site councils. The committees are usually composed of representatives of a single school's faculty and parents, led by the principal.

As readers can see, teachers today face no shortage of advice on the key curriculum question, What should our children know and be able to do? First, there are the numerous sets of recent national standards. Also, there is the curriculum framework of the state in which one teaches, one or more school district curriculum guidelines, and perhaps a curriculum policy developed at the building where one teaches.

Trend 3: Character Education

Observers of this society have long been impressed by Americans' "habits of the heart." This was Alexis de Tocqueville's term over a century ago for the civic-mindedness he saw everywhere in the United States: people caring for neighbors, joining service clubs, gathering food for the hungry, creating all manner of groups in which citizens step outside their families—outside their private lives—and associate with strangers to solve problems, undertake projects, and engage in hobbies of common interest. This sort of activity indicates the civic health of a society, which in turn makes democracy possible. This activity still describes Americans, but there is evidence that it is in decline. Add to this the rise in juvenile crime, the uncontrolled influence of commercial media on children (not to mention adults), the persistence of racism, and the general perception that manners, civilized dialogue, and public decency are on the wane.

In response, schools across the nation are rapidly developing character education programs. Indeed, there is a national movement to this effect that involves conservatives and liberals, religious and civic leaders, members of all races, rich and poor. Former Secretary of Education William Bennett's *The Book of Virtues: A Treasury of Great Moral Stories* (Simon & Schuster, 1993) has become a national best seller. Educational psychologist Thomas Lickona's *Educating for Character: How Our Schools Can Teach Respect and Responsibility* (Bantam, 1991) is now widely read by educators. Former school superintendent Henry A. Huffman's *Developing a Character Education Program: One School District's Experience* (1994) was recently mailed to school principals and curriculum developers throughout the United States. Huffman writes:

Teachers and administrators must help parents understand that values-free classrooms and schools do not exist. Thus, the question is not "Should schools teach values?" but "How should schools teach values?" Would parents prefer that teachers carry out their responsibilities as character educators without any planning or direction? Or would they prefer an approach that was developed by the professional staff with community input and was reflective of a set of values and broad community support?[5]

Certain social phenomena are combining to create a deeply disturbing sense that society and its children are changing for the worse. The influence of mass media, children's access to a new and unbridled "cyberspace," the high rate of divorce and children without responsible fathers, the increasing number of sexually active children, the persistence of drug abuse and poverty, the upsurge in violence committed by children, the cynicism of many adults toward social institutions—these changes, in Lickona's words, "are reflected not just in the violent extremes of teenage behavior but in the everyday speech and actions of younger children as well."[6]

At the heart of any character education program are the moral values that children are expected to develop and that teachers will be expected to encourage and model. Often these are drawn from the values that underpin the "rule book" of our society, the Constitution of the United States. Deriving the values from this source helps a planning committee focus on *public* values necessary for the common good in a pluralistic society, rather than private or personal values that might be meaningful only to a particular religion, ethnic group, family, or individual. No broad agreement could be reached on private values, and, at any rate, none is needed in a democracy. (Totalitarian systems, on the other hand, reach deeply into the private values and family lives of citizens, banning all or some religions and, basically, punishing diversity.)

As we shall see in Chapter 3, public values are the *citizenship* values that bind us together as one people. Without public values, we are a diverse array of individuals and cultures without a "glue"—a common identity—on which cooperation and civic life can be based. The Baltimore County, Maryland, Schools, to take one example, selected 24 public values[7]:

Compassion	Objectivity
Courtesy	Order
Critical Inquiry	Patriotism
Due Process	Rational Consent
Equality of Opportunity	Reasoned Argument
Freedom of Thought and Action	Respect for Others' Rights
Honesty	Responsibility
Human Worth and Dignity	Responsible Citizenship
Integrity	Rule of Law
Justice	Self-Respect
Knowledge	Tolerance
Loyalty	Truth

Because the core values of a character education program typically are citizenship values, and because the mission of social studies education is citizenship education, it becomes the special responsibility of the social studies program to attend carefully to these values and their cultivation. Granted, citizenship education is the responsibility of the whole curriculum, but in fact it falls mainly to the social studies. As we shall see in Chapter 3, "Citizenship Education and Democratic Values," this is a good fit, and there is much that teachers can do from kindergarten on up.

Summary

These three trends—teaching all our children, aiming higher, and educating character—are not the only contextual forces converging on the beginning teacher today. Others of note are, first, the computer technology that is bringing more information resources into the classroom along with worldwide electronic communication. So rapidly has this technology developed that beginning teachers are expected in many school districts to be computer literate *before* enrolling in teacher education programs. Second, the psychological theories of *constructivism* and *multiple intelligences* have made their way from academic journals to mainstream educational thought. Third, a revolution in educators' conception of student assessment and evaluation has occurred recently, and, fourth, interest in curriculum integration has surfaced again.

These trends are important, to be sure, and they are dealt with explicitly in the chapters that follow. The three detailed earlier, however, are the more inclusive and powerful trends. They determine for which children, for what purposes, and to what standards such things as computer technology, contemporary learning theory, assessment procedures, and integrated curriculum will be put to use.

Goals for the Social Studies: Social Understanding and Civic Efficacy

According to the National Council for the Social Studies (NCSS), social studies education can be defined as follows:

Social studies is the integrated study of the social sciences and humanities to promote civic competence. The primary purpose of social studies is to help young people develop the ability to make informed and reasoned decisions for the public good as citizens of a culturally diverse, democratic society in an interdependent world.[8]

This statement is like a two-sided coin. On one side is the material that is studied: the content or subject matter of social studies. This includes essential information, ideas, skills, issues, and inquiry procedures drawn from the array of fields called the social sciences: history, geography, civics and government (political science), economics, sociology, and anthropology. Ethics, literature, music and the visual and performing arts, religion, and archaeology are involved as well. These fields of study or disciplines serve as *resources*: The social studies curriculum draws on them, blending and integrating them as needed to provide children with meaningful learning experiences. But to what ends? What are the goals?

On the other side of the definition is the purpose, which we introduced earlier as the vision of social studies instruction: citizenship education. It is important to understand that citizenship education includes both the knowledge of people and places that is gradually constructed as a consequence of studying material from history and the social sciences, and the civic competence that results from studying and practicing constitutional democracy.

A vision statement developed recently by NCSS elaborates on these two interdependent goals. "Powerful social studies teaching helps students develop social understanding and civic efficacy," it states.[9] *Social understanding* is knowledge of human beings' social worlds. *Social* here is used broadly to include economic phenomena, time (history), space (geography), group life, culture, religious and political institutions, and so forth. We want children both to know about and experience a deep sense of appreciation for the peoples and places on earth, their relationships, the similarities and differences among them, the problems they encounter, and social trends that likely will shape the future. *Civic efficacy* is "the readiness and willingness to assume citizenship responsibilities."[10] These responsibilities include more than voting. They include educating citizens to be civic-minded, to be just and lawful, tolerant, and self-disciplined; to be able to participate in and lead discussions of public issues; to influence public policy—in general, to be able and willing to walk the democratic path.

These two goals typically are broken down into three dimensions of learning—*knowledge, attitudes and values*, and *skills*. More specific goals are listed under each heading. When readers examine their state and local social studies curriculum guidelines, they will most likely find that the guidelines take this form or one that is similar. Of course, there are numerous ways to list the contents of each category.

Ideas and Information Goals (Knowledge)

The first, knowledge goals, could appear as a set of thematic statements, such as those in the *Curriculum Standards for Social Studies* shown in Figure 1–1. Or they may take the form of a topical listing, such as the following.

Students should know about:
1. The history, geography, and cultures of the world.
2. The history, geography, and cultures of the United States.
3. The history, geography, and cultures of the neighborhood, community, and home state; how they are similar to and different from other places in the world; how people live and work there; how they depend on each other to meet their basic needs.
4. The foundations and principles of American constitutional democracy.
5. The legal and political systems of the local community, state, and nation.
6. The world of work, earning and saving, production and consumption, and an orientation to jobs and careers.
7. Basic human institutions, such as the family, education, religion, government, and the economy.
8. Human-environment interaction.
9. Current events and enduring public issues.
10. Men and women who have made a difference in their communities and beyond.

Attitudes and Values Goals

The second category, attitudes and values, is directed less at rational knowledge and more at the affective domain, that is, the realm of emotion, feeling, loyalty, and commitment. Attitudes and values, also called dispositions, virtues, and character traits, are essential to democratic citizenship. Without them, self-governance and civic life would

Figure 1–1

Ten Themes from *Curriculum Stan-dards for Social Studies*

Social Studies programs should include experiences that provide for the study of:

I. Culture

II. Time, Continuity, and Change

III. People, Places, and Environments

IV. Individual Development and Identity

V. Individuals, Groups, and Institutions

VI. Power, Authority, and Governance

VII. Production, Distribution, and Consumption

VIII. Science, Technology, and Society

IX. Global Connections and Interdependence

X. Civic Ideals and Practice

Source: National Council for the Social Studies (Washington, DC: Author, 1994).

be impossible. The following are typical examples of what readers will find listed in state and local curriculum guidelines in this category. Current revisions of these documents are including greater attention to this category due in large part to the character education movement discussed earlier.

1. Developing a reasoned commitment to the public values of this society as suggested in its historical documents, laws, court decisions, and pledges (e.g., "liberty and justice for all"). Note that the Pledge of Allegiance is made not to a person but to a form of government.
2. Being able to deal with value conflicts that arise when making decisions about the common good.
3. Knowing the basic human rights guaranteed to all citizens and the role of government in protecting those rights.
4. Developing a reasoned loyalty to this nation.
5. Developing a feeling of kinship to human beings everywhere.
6. Treating oneself and others with respect; taking responsibility for oneself and the good of the community, fulfilling one's obligations to others and the natural environment.

Skills Goals

The third category, skills, identifies what students should be able to *do*. Of course, doing involves knowing; skillful behavior is skillful to a great extent because of the knowledge that supports it. A child is skillful at something because he or she *knows* how to do it well. Accordingly, the first and third categories are closely related. We find that this category often is subdivided as follows:

Costumes and props add depth to children's understandings.

I. Democratic Participation Skills
  A. Participating in group discussions of public issues (classroom, community, international) with persons with whom one may disagree; leading such discussions; mediating, negotiating, and compromising.
  B. Listening to, questioning, and expressing opinions and reasons.
  C. Participating in classroom, school, and community decision making.
  D. Working cooperatively to clarify a task and plan group work.
  E. Accessing, using, and planning community resources.
II. Study and Inquiry Skills
  A. Using and making time lines, maps, globes, charts, and graphs.
  B. Locating, gathering, organizing, and analyzing information from various resources such as books, electronic media, newspapers, and the library.
  C. Writing reports and giving oral reports.
  D. Reading social studies materials for a variety of purposes, such as to get the main idea, to get facts, to research a public issue, to detect author bias.
  E. Forming and testing hypotheses.
III. Intellectual Skills
  A. Identifying and clarifying problems and issues.
  B. Drawing analogies from other times and places and inferring cause-effect relationships.

    C. Drawing conclusions based on evidence.
    D. Determining the strength of an argument or conclusion (critical thinking); distinguishing between fact and opinion; detecting propaganda.
    E. Reasoning dialogically (arguing both for and against one's position on an issue).

Curriculum Scope and Sequence

Although most elementary and middle schools include history and the social science disciplines in their social studies programs, they do not ordinarily conduct separate courses in geography, history, economics, political science, or the other social science disciplines. The usual organizational format is one that combines components from more than a single field to form an interdisciplinary or integrated study around some topic of interest. Significant subject matter from related disciplines is *infused* in the instructional program. For example, a sixth grade class might study the topic "Crossroads of Three Continents—The Middle East." In such a study, geography would be essential, as would history, economics, and government. Doubtless, too, religious concepts would be included because this area of the world was the birthplace of three of the world's major religions.

Most schools are introducing basic concepts from history and the social sciences and related disciplines in the early years of the elementary school although they may not always be labeled as such. When children are studying the local landscape and learning how to map it, they are dealing in a simple way with geography. When they learn about the need for rules and laws, they are beginning to understand ideas from political science; and when they study about life in early times, they are having their first brush with history. It is not the purpose of the elementary school to teach the social science disciplines apart from their relevance to social reality. They should be taught in ways that will help children build understandings of the social and physical world in which they live.

The social studies program should be built on what the child already knows. This means that, in introducing topics or units for study, the teacher will need to explore with the children the extent of their prior knowledge of the subject. Some knowledge will come from their experiences outside of school through television, movies, peers, travel, and contact with adults. Some will come from school experiences in earlier grades. Social studies programs should take advantage of that background of knowledge, using it to help the children make sense of the new material specified in the curriculum. In this way, the social studies curriculum is made meaningful to the child, and the child is introduced to new ideas, information, values, and skills. Teaching, therefore, is not child-centered *or* curriculum-centered; it is *both*. The legendary teachers depicted in books and films throughout this century, whether in Japan, South Africa, Australia, England, Los Angeles, or New York, have managed to make this connection.

Each year there will be study units and topics that are consistent with the emphasis suggested by the district curriculum for that grade. Ordinarily, topics that have a concrete and familiar focus for the child such as homes, schools, families, neighborhoods, and communities are placed in the primary grades. Topics that are more remote in space and time, such as the home state, the nation, and regions of the world, appear as

Dramatizations with simple sets bring geography to life.

focal points in the middle and upper grades. It must be emphasized, however, that this *does not* mean that first-graders spend a year studying *their* families, or that second-graders study only the local neighborhood or third-graders only the local community. Rather, a compare-and-contrast approach should be used. Children should quickly learn how local houses and apartments are similar to and different from homes long ago and far away. The same is true for families, neighborhoods, and communities. Contemporary social studies textbooks typically provide the necessary information for helping children make such comparisons: Families and Friends in Mexico, Island Homes and Desert Homes, and America's First Communities are representative of such units of study in the primary grades, and they commonly appear in textbooks and other social studies curriculum materials.

Teachers may begin a study by focusing on aspects of a topic that are familiar to the children, such as their own homes, schools, and families; then the study is expanded to include those same institutions long ago and far away. The movement from things that are close to those that are distant, either in time or place, and back again is common in social studies programs today. Doing so helps to build a firm foundation for later learning. An NCSS position statement on early childhood social studies instruction makes this point clearly:

One of the most important conclusions one can draw from the available research on early learning in social studies is the critical importance of the elementary years in laying the foundation for later and increasingly mature understanding. *There is reason to believe that teachers who miss these crucial opportunities to build interest, to introduce concepts from history and the social sciences, and to develop social perspectives and civic understanding may make it more difficult for citizens of the 21st Century to cope with their future.*[11]

Curriculum specialists often talk in terms of the "scope and sequence" of a social studies program. The scope of the program refers to the substantive content—the information, ideas, skills, values, and attitudes that the program is to include. The sequence has to do with the order in which the various components are to be presented. In recent years there has been a revival of interest in scope and sequence documents at the state and local levels. The National Council for the Social Studies has published a planning document that can be useful to local schools in building their social studies programs. It includes guidelines for the social studies curriculum, criteria for excellence in social studies, questions for reviewing and evaluating the social studies curriculum, and three model scope and sequence statements. The following is one of the scope and sequence models included in the council's document:

Recommendations of the NCSS Task Force on Scope and Sequence

Kindergarten—Awareness of Self in a Social Setting

Grade 1—The Individual in Primary Social Groups: Understanding School and Family Life

Grade 2—Meeting Basic Needs in Nearby Social Groups: Neighborhoods

Grade 3—Sharing Earth-Space with Others: Communities

Grade 4—Human Life in Varied Environments: Regions

Grade 5—People of the Americas: The United States and Its Close Neighbors

Grade 6—People and Cultures: The Eastern Hemisphere

Grade 7—A Changing World of Many Nations: A Global View

Grade 8—Building a Strong and Free Nation: The United States

Grade 9—Systems That Make a Democratic Society Work: Law, Justice, and Economics

Grade 10—Origins of Major Cultures: A World History

Grade 11—The Maturing of America: United States History

Grade 12—One-year course or courses required; selection(s) to be made from the following:

      Issues and Problems of Modern Society

      Introduction to the Social Sciences

      The Arts in Human Societies

      International Area Studies

      Supervised Experience in Community Affairs

      Local options[12]

Now, recall the ten themes identified in *Curriculum Standards for Social Studies* (see Figure 1–1 and the accompanying *Sampler*). How might such themes be used with a scope and sequence plan of this kind? It is important to note that the ten themes are ideas or, more precisely, concepts. Furthermore, as the *Curriculum Standards for Social Studies* make clear, these themes are recommended as the basis for instruction in kindergarten through the twelfth grade. What the teacher can do, then, is select a grade level from the scope and sequence list above, or the one provided by a local school district, and then use the ten themes to help plan units and lessons. For example, let us select the grade 3 emphasis, communities, and think of some focus questions to engage children with each of the themes.

GRADE 3, SHARING EARTH SPACE WITH OTHERS: COMMUNITIES

1. **Culture**.   How do the ways of life of people living in our community differ from those of the people living in our sister cities in Japan and Russia?
2. **Time, Continuity, and Change**.   What were the turning points in our community's history?
3. **People, Places, and Environments**.   Why is our community located where it is, and how would our lives be different if it was located on the edge of the sea, in a desert, on an island, or high in the mountains?
4. **Individual Development and Identity**.   How does learning in school differ from the learning that takes place elsewhere in our community—on the job, on the playing field, at home, at a city council meeting?
5. **Individuals, Groups, and Institutions**.   What after-school clubs do kids belong to in our community, and how do they differ from those in our sister cities?
6. **Power, Authority, and Governance**.   Judging from the amount of newspaper coverage, what are the chief controversies people in our community face today over rights and responsibilities?
7. **Production, Distribution, and Consumption**.   What things do people in our community want that they don't really need? How are these different from the wants and needs in our sister cities?
8. **Science, Technology, and Society**.   How do our values influence the use of buses and cars in this community?
9. **Global Connections and Interdependence**.   What three products are imported in the greatest quantities to our community from other nations? Who are the workers in those nations that produce these goods? What are their cultures?
10. **Civic Ideals and Practice**.   Who is eligible to vote in this community? What percentage of them voted in the last presidential election and the last election for local officials? What can our class do to encourage eligible voters to vote? And, can our class sponsor a mock election for the school?

Thinking Conceptually

We encourage readers to create similar examples for other grade levels in order to gain experience in thinking conceptually about the social studies topical emphasis of a given grade level. For example, the same process can be repeated for the fourth-grade emphasis, geographic regions, or the fifth-grade emphasis, United States history. This is one of the most important curriculum-planning habits any teacher could develop. Without it, the teacher may not even think to identify key concepts for instruction, let alone help children to systematically build them "inside their own heads." Instead, the teacher will be limited to covering only the thin surface of a topic, taking students across numerous facts about the topic, perhaps, but not helping them to organize the facts into powerful ideas. Thinking conceptually is a planning skill that distinguishes more and less proficient teachers. Chapter 7 instructs readers on this key professional skill.

Unit Topics

The lists in "Examples of Unit Topics for Each Grade Level" on the following pages offer examples of topics and units taught at the grade levels indicated in schools across the nation. The examples should *not* be construed as a model curriculum. What is represented here will not be precisely the same as that found in any specific school program; in providing these examples, our intention is to help readers gain a better idea of what subject matter may actually be taught at different grade levels. Because of state-to-state, district-to-district, and school-to-school variation, the teacher will need to consult local curriculum resources to determine what is required.

Plan of the Book

This text has twelve chapters in three parts. The parts are sequenced so that readers are provided first with an *orientation* to the social studies and the children we teach, then with an examination of the social studies *curriculum*, and then with an examination of powerful *instruction* in social studies, including planning, teaching, and assessing student learning.

Orientation

The two chapters in Part I introduce readers to the the social studies curriculum and the children in today's classrooms. Chapter 1 introduced the what and why—the content and rationale—of the social studies. It also discussed three social forces or trends that are shaping schools and teachers today. Chapter 2 examines the diversity in today's classroom. Good teachers have always tailored instruction to individual children and endeavored to provide developmentally appropriate instruction, not aiming the subject matter or teaching method too high or too low. But the diversity in the classroom is now of a different kind—more varied and complex—and becoming more so at a breathtaking rate. Developmental differences among the children in a class cannot be the only concern for today's teachers; linguistic, cultural, ethnic, racial, and socioeconomic diversity are critically important, too. Today's teachers cannot get by on yesterday's teachers' knowledge of children.

Curriculum

Part II delves into the subject matter of the social studies curriculum—what we want children to know and be able to do. Because the vision and rationale *(continued p. 22)*

EXAMPLES OF UNIT TOPICS FOR EACH GRADE LEVEL

Kindergarten

Kindergarten programs ordinarily deal with topics that help to familiarize children with their immediate surroundings. The home and school provide the setting for these studies. With some kindergarten children it is possible to include, in a simple way, references to the world beyond the immediate environment.

Learning About Myself	Rules for Safe Living
Continents and the Globe	People Change the Earth
Working Together at School	Learning How My Family Buys Goods and Services

Grade One

Grade-one studies are based in the local area, such as the neighborhood, but provision is made to associate the local area with the larger world. A major criticism of first-grade units in particular and primary units in general has been that they have tended to be too confining and that their content has been thin. Units should provide for easy transition from the near-at-hand to the far away and back again at frequent intervals—when it is established that the backgrounds of children warrant such movement. Neighborhood and community services can be stressed in this grade.

Where We Live	Families at Work
Great Americans	A Japanese Family (comparative study)
Scarcity and Demand	Families Around the World
Families and Their Needs	Dividing the Work

Grade Two

The grade-two program provides for frequent and systematic contact with the world beyond the neighborhood. Through the study of transportation, communication, food distribution, and travel, the children begin to learn how their part of the world is connected to other places on earth.

Holidays in Other Countries	Transportation and Communication: Our
Rural and Urban Communities	Links to the World
People Work Together in Communities	Where and How We Get Our Food
We the People	How Neighborhoods Change
Discovering Our Past	

Grade Three

The grade-three program often emphasizes the larger community concept: what a community is, types of communities, why some communities grow and others do not, how communities provide for basic needs. Many programs include outside communities for purposes of comparison. Schools are giving a great deal of attention to the large, urban community at this grade level.

Our City's Government
How Communities Change
Life in Early American Communities
Washington, D.C.: Our Country's Capital
Beijing: China's Capital

Food for the Community
Communities at Home and Abroad
    (comparative cultures study)
Why a City Is Where It Is

Grade Four

In grade four the geographic regions of the United States are often stressed. Home-state studies are also popular in grade four; often they are included to meet legislative requirements. Comparative studies are recommended.

Historical Growth and Change of the Home State
The Pacific Northwest (regional study)
The Southwest, Midwest, Northeast, and Deep South (other regions)
Deserts of the World (regions)
Kenya and Its African Neighbors (comparative study)
India, a Society in Transition (comparative study)
Regions Make a World

Grade Five

Almost everywhere the fifth-grade program includes the geography, history, early development, and growth of the United States. The program may focus on the United States alone, on the United States and Canada, or on the United States, Canada, and Latin America. The latter option makes the fifth-grade program a heavy one. The fifth-grade emphasis should be coordinated with the eighth and eleventh grades in order to revisit difficult concepts (e.g., democracy, pluralism).

The American Land
European-American Encounters
Slavery and the Civil War
The Industrial Revolution
One Nation; Many Heritages

The Native Americans
Independence and Democracy
An Early American Mining Community
Civil Rights and the American Dream

Grade Six

The sixth-grade program may include the study of Latin America and Canada or of cultures of the Eastern Hemisphere. Both of these patterns are in common use. A major limitation of sixth-grade programs is that they attempt to deal with too many topics. Often this results in a smattering of exposures without developing significant depth of understanding. The same criticism applies to the seventh grade. Stronger programs emerge where teachers carefully select a few units that are representative of basic concepts that have wide and broad applicability. For example, a class need not study all the Third World nations in order to gain some understanding of the problems of newly developing countries.

Western Hemisphere Emphasis

Cooperation in the Americas
Three Incan Countries
The Organization of American States

The Prairie Provinces
The Saint Lawrence Seaway and Its Effect
    on Canadian Growth

Eastern Hemisphere Emphasis

The Birthplace of Three Religions
Southeast Asia Today
Empires and Revolutions
The People's Republic of China

Ancient, Classical, and Medieval Civilizations
The Renaissance and Reformation
The Holocaust: Causes and Consequences
Eastern Europe in Recent Times

Grade Seven

The nature of the seventh-grade program depends on the content of grade six. Either Latin America or culture regions of the Eastern Hemisphere are popular choices for this grade. Some schools are developing exciting programs in anthropology in grade seven. World geography is also included in some districts, as are studies of the home state.

Rise of Modern Civilization
Africa: Yesterday, Today, and Tomorrow
Public Issues of our Times
The Home State: Democracy and Pluralism
World Resources: Who Has Them? Who Uses Them?
The Age of Technology: Its Effects on People
Environmental Problems
Themes of Geography
The Future of Life on Earth

Grade Eight

The study of the United States and of the American heritage is widespread in grade eight. The program usually stresses the development of American political institutions. The approach typically consists of a series of units arranged chronologically. The fifth and eleventh grades also include elements of American history. Defining the emphasis for each of these grades and differentiating appropriately among them in terms of content and approach is necessary in order to ensure depth and breadth of understanding. A biographical approach effectively integrates social studies and language arts.

Mapping the Americas
Creating a Democracy
Birth of an Industrial Giant
Hot and Cold Wars

Natives and Colonizers: Cultures and Conflicts
A Divided Nation
Immigration and the American Dream
The United States in the World Today

for social studies is tied so closely to the democratic ideal, Chapter 3 deals directly with teaching the core elements of democratic citizenship: democratic ideas, values, and dispositions; discussion and decision-making ability; and community service opportunities. Chapter 4 examines the primary disciplinary resources for the social studies curriculum other than civics: history, geography, economics, sociology, and anthropology. The work of recent curriculum standards projects is featured, numerous teaching suggestions are provided, and notable children's literature is identified.

Chapter 5 gives readers a chapter full of teaching ideas related to key tools children need if they are to capably explore the social world: time lines, maps, globes, charts, and graphs. Each allows children to make sense of time and space, comprehending peoples, events, and places near and far and now and then. Chapter 6 focuses on current events and public issues. The daily newspaper comes to life as an important resource for social studies instruction, and children learn to deliberate with one another, as budding democratic citizens, about the public's problems—for example, poverty and homelessness, pollution and prejudice, war and juvenile crime.

Instruction

Part III turns to powerful methods of planning, teaching, and assessing student achievement of the social studies curriculum. Methods for helping children build flexible and usable understandings of concepts, generalizations, issues, skills, and a critically important kind of higher-order thinking, the inquiry process, are presented in Chapter 7. The art of asking good questions is introduced, and resources for teaching—from computer technology to field trips—are explained. Chapter 8 presents unit- and lesson-planning methods. Readers are given instruction on designing powerful learning activities that incorporate higher-order thinking, simulation games, music, role playing, and drama.

Chapter 9 will help readers plan assessment *as part instructional planning*, not as an afterthought. Exciting new scoring rubrics, performance tasks, and social studies portfolios are featured, and they capture what assessment activity too often misses: the learnings we value the most. Chapter 10 takes readers into the world of cooperative learning. Business leaders, government leaders, and psychologists are eager for children to learn to work well in teams and discuss issues with persons who are similar to and different from themselves. This chapter presents the methods and principles of cooperative learning in social studies and extends the common treatment of this subject by addressing another supremely cooperative form of citizenship action: discussion.

Chapters 11 and 12 suggest several ways the social studies can be the integrating core for other subjects in the elementary and middle school curriculum. Teaching reading in a way that is integrated with social studies learning is the focus of Chapter 11; integrating writing instruction and the social studies is the focus of Chapter 12. The use of biographies as a teaching/learning tool is featured in Chapter 12, but with an intriguing twist: Children do not only read biographies of key persons in the curriculum, but they write, with the help of teammates, original biographies of these people. Also in Chapter 12 is an exemplary program from a Colorado school district for integrating science and social studies learning.

We hope this book will serve you well.

Discussion Questions and Suggested Activities

1. What are your memories of social studies curriculum and instruction from your elementary school years? Middle school years? Share these memories with classmates.

2. Interview two or three teachers in the school where you are student teaching. Find out what they regard as the most important themes and topics in the social studies curriculum for their grade levels. Also, share with them the list of ten themes in the accompanying *Sampler* of the *Curriculum Standards for Social Studies*. Do they believe such themes are relevant to any grade level? Only to certain grades and topics?

3. Descriptions of two teaching activities or vignettes from the *Curriculum Standards for Social Studies* opened this chapter. To which of the ten themes from these curriculum standards (Figure 1–1 or the *Sampler* that accompanies this text) do you believe these teaching activities are best suited?

4. Do you believe it is true, as stated in this chapter, that "many people in the United States take democracy for granted"? What evidence would support (or contradict) this claim? Relevant categories of evidence might be voter turnout, membership in voluntary associations, and school efforts at citizenship education.

5. Which of the three major trends discussed in this chapter do you believe is the most likely to affect curriculum and instruction in the schools today? What is the difference between trends 1 and 2—between teaching all our children and raising the standards for all children?

6. Determine which of the standards documents listed in this chapter are located in your university curriculum library: Social Studies, Civics and Government, Geography, and History (three books). Before getting to the planning and teaching chapters of this book in Part III, skim each of these standards documents to get a basic understanding of their contents and format so that you might use them effectively as resources.

7. Locate a copy of the state social studies curriculum framework for the state in which you reside or to which you plan to move. Examine carefully the organization of the framework. Is the goal statement divided into knowledge, attitudes and values, and skills, as predicted in this chapter? Is the curriculum scope and sequence similar to what was presented in this chapter? If not, in what ways do they differ?

8. "Legendary teachers," it was asserted, are able to bring the curriculum to the child and the child to the curriculum, thereby overcoming the false dichotomy between child-centered and curriculum-centered teaching. Do you agree with this statement?
(a) List examples of such teachers depicted in books and films.
(b) Plan a series of Saturday morning videos about such teachers. You could start with *Twenty-four Eyes* from Japan, *My Brilliant Career* from Australia, and *Stand and Deliver, Dangerous Minds*, or *Dead Poets Society* from the United States.

9. In "Grade 3, Sharing Earth Space with Others: Communities," the ten conceptual themes in the *Curriculum Standards for Social Studies* were cross-referenced to the NCSS Task Force sample scope and sequence plan that preceded it. The grade 3 emphasis, communities, was featured. With a partner, select another grade and cross-reference its emphasis with the same ten themes. For example, you could select grade 4, regions, or grade 5, U. S. history.

10. With a partner, re-read the definition of social studies education given at the beginning of the chapter and the analysis that follows it. In your own words, distinguish between the two goals, *social understanding* and *civic efficacy*, then quickly sketch a lesson plan that targets one or both of these.

Notes

1 National Council for the Social Studies. *Curriculum Standards for Social Studies* (Washington, D.C.: Author, 1994), 54, 105.

2 *Report of the Task Force on Civic Education, The Second Annual White House Conference on Character Building for a Democratic, Civic Society* (May 1995), 3.

3 Lynn Olson, "Standards Times 50," *Education Week*, special report (April 12, 1995), 15.

4 Ibid.

5 Henry A. Huffman, *Developing a Character Education Program: One School District's Experience* (Alexandria, VA: Association for Supervision and Curriculum Development, 1994), 6.

6 Thomas Lickona, *Educating for Character: How Our Schools Can Teach Respect and Responsibility* (New York: Bantam, 1991), 4.

7 Huffman, *Developing a Character Education Program*, 17.

8 National Council for the Social Studies, *Curriculum Standards*, 3.

9 Task Force on Standards for Teaching and Learning in the Social Studies, *A Vision of Powerful Teaching and Learning in the Social Studies: Building Social Understanding and Civic Efficacy* (Washington, DC: National Council for the Social Studies, 1992). Reprinted as a supplement to *Curriculum Standards for Social Studies*, p. 157.

10 Ibid, 157.

11 National Council for the Social Studies, *Position Statement on Social Studies for Early Childhood and Elementary School Children Preparing for the 21st Century* (Alexandria, VA: Author, 1989), 19–20.

12 National Council for the Social Studies, *Social Studies Curriculum Planning Resources* (Dubuque, IA: Kendall/Hunt, 1990), 25–29.

Selected References

Bellah, Robert N., Richard Madsen, William M. Sullivan, Ann Swidler, and Steven M. Tipton. *Habits of the Heart*. New York: Harper & Row, 1985.

Bragaw, Donald H., and H. Michael Hartoonian. "Social Studies: The Study of People in Society." In *ASCD Yearbook*, edited by Ronald S. Brandt. Alexandria, VA: Association for Supervision and Curriculum Development, 1988.

Callahan, William T., Jr., and Ronald A. Banaszak (eds.). *Citizenship for the 21st Century*. Bloomington, IN: ERIC Clearinghouse, 1990.

Gagnon, Paul, ed. *Historical Literacy*. New York: Macmillan, 1989.

Jenness, David. *Making Sense of Social Studies*. New York: Macmillan, 1990.

Lickona, Thomas. *Educating for Character: How Our Schools Can Teach Respect and Responsibility*. New York: Bantam, 1991.

National Commission on Excellence in Education. *A Nation at Risk* (U.S. Department of Education, 1983). Reprinted in *Education Week*, April 27, 1983.

Noddings, Nel. "Social Studies and Feminism." *Theory and Research in Social Education* 20 (Summer 1992): 230–41.

Oakes, Jeannie. *Keeping Track: How Schools Structure Inequality*. New York: Yale University Press, 1985.

Parker, Walter C. *Renewing the Social Studies Curriculum*. Alexandria, VA: Association for Supervision and Curriculum Development, 1991.

Parker, Walter C., and John Jarolimek. *Citizenship and the Critical Role of the Social Studies*. Washington, DC: National Council for the Social Studies, and Boulder, CO: ERIC Clearinghouse for Social Studies/Social Science Education and the Social Science Education Consortium, 1984.

Ravitch, Diane. *National Standards in American Education: A Citizen's Guide*. Washington, DC: The Brookings Institution, 1995.

de Tocqueville, Alexis. *Democracy in America*. Edited by J. P. Mayer, translated by George Lawrence. New York: Doubleday, 1969.

THE CHILDREN WE TEACH

OVERVIEW

In 2026, we will have the exact inverse of student population as we knew in 1990, when white students made up 70 percent of our enrolled K–12 student body.[1]

The children in today's classrooms are similar in so many ways. They like to play and pretend, they will sit transfixed for a good story, cartoons enchant them, and they are hurt when teased or excluded from other children's games. They keenly observe the subtlest details in other children and are quick to recognize when they are treated unfairly. They scribble before printing and print phrases before paragraphs, and they will not master the five-paragraph essay for many years. Anyone who has spent time with young children knows they often talk to themselves while at play, and as they grow a little older this speech shifts to the "inside." (By the time they are young adults, they will know this inner chatter all too well!) Their physical, personal, social, and cognitive development progresses in fairly orderly ways, gradually, and always in ways that are unique. Like snowflakes, children have much in common, yet no two are alike.

As recently as a generation or two ago, an elementary or middle school teacher would quite probably face a classroom in which the children were remarkably similar in *appearance*, too. Children were required to attend their neighborhood elementary school, and because neighborhoods were not racially integrated, neither were schools. Neighborhoods tended to be segregated along social class lines as well, resulting in a consistent similarity among the children of people who lived there. Children with learning disabilities, physical challenges, and mental retardation often were not a part of the regular classroom. They were placed in special education classes. The resulting appearance of homogeneity masked differences among the children who remained to such an extent that researchers had a difficult time convincing teachers that they still needed to be concerned about student differences.

All of this has changed dramatically in recent years. Federally mandated racial desegregation of schools, busing, immigration, changing birth rates, increased integration of housing, and inclusion of students with disabilities are among the causes of the changing demographic pattern in the nation's schools. So completely have these changes transformed our classrooms that today it would be difficult to find a classroom anywhere in America that is wholly homogeneous with respect to the ethnic, racial, cultural, linguistic, and religious backgrounds of its students. Today's classrooms are lively aggregates of children that are incredibly diverse, and this diversity translates into new challenges for teachers.

In one sense, the challenges are *not* new. Good teachers have always tailored instruction to individual children, not ignoring but recognizing differences and providing appropriate learning experiences. But the diversity in the classroom is now of a different kind, number, and range. Today's teachers cannot get by on yesterday's teachers' knowledge and skills. Times have changed.

Diverse Classrooms

We turn now to changes, some demographic and some individual, that are challenging today's teachers in new ways.* We focus first on ethnicity, race, and culture; then we turn to gender, language, social class, the changing family, and, finally, children with special needs. Later in this chapter, we suggest the implications of these changes for successful teaching in today's classrooms.

Ethnicity, Race, and Culture

A child's ethnic group membership and identity, like an adult's, matters. Ethnic groups, after all, have different values and ways of seeing the world. Children from different ethnic groups do not behave in the same ways and do not necessarily learn in the same ways. Have you thought about the difference your own ethnicity makes in the ways you act and believe? The Mexican-American children in your classroom generally are exposed to traditional family values and role models; the Portuguese- and Nicaraguan-American children, however, may have experienced a more "modern" home life. This difference is due to the culture and politics of each homeland. African-American girls often have more self-esteem than their European-American counterparts. Filipino and Japanese immigrant children may have seen vastly different sex-role behavior—more gender equity in the Philippines, less in Japan.

Although teachers must be aware of ethnic differences, they must also be careful not to over-generalize on the basis of ethnicity. Asian-American children clearly are not all alike, as any one who has had Hmong-American and Chinese-American children in class will tell you. Nor are European-, African-, or Arab-American children alike. Differences in religion and social class can have an enormous impact in the behavior and values of children who share a similar ethnic background. Middle-class whites often share more cultural characteristics with middle-class blacks than with poor whites, for example. Native American children raised in families that emphasize acculturation to the mainstream American lifestyle, which is heavily influenced by European-American ethnicity, may view classroom and playground situations very differently than those who have been encouraged to maintain traditional values.

Let us define a few terms. A *culture* is the values, beliefs, and customs—in brief, the way of life or life style—shared by a group of people or society. Culture is learned. One can belong to many groups, each with distinct cultural characteristics. For example, one is a member of a gender group (women), regional group (southerner), racial group (black), religion (Baptist), occupational (school teacher), social class (lower-middle), ability (hearing impaired), and ethnic group (southern, rural black). The cultural characteristics of each of our several affiliations overlap, always making for a complex cultural identity.

An *ethnic group* is a particular kind of culture group. All Americans are members of one or more ethnic groups. Members of an ethnic group share a common history, a sense of peoplehood and fate, and values and beliefs. Moreover, "members of an ethnic

---

* *Demography*: the study of characteristics of human populations, especially with reference to size, growth, migration, vital statistics, and living conditions.

group usually view their group as distinct and separate from other cultural groups within a society."[2] More broadly, an ethnic group is a group distinguished by race, religion, or national origin. There are many, many ethnic groups in the United States, more than in most other nations. There are, for example, Vietnamese Americans, Anglo Americans, Mexican Americans, German Americans, African Americans, and Native Americans (e.g., Lakota Sioux). Irish Catholics are sometimes considered an ethnic group, as are Mormons, Midwesterners, Southern Baptists, and West Texans. The Pilgrims and Puritans of American colonial times were ethnic groups, as were the native groups they encountered.

An *ethnic minority group* in any nation has characteristics, usually both physical and cultural, that make its members easily identifiable to other groups. Very often, ethnic minorities suffer discrimination and subordination within a society. Arab Americans, Filipino Americans, Jewish Americans, and African Americans are examples.

Race refers to genetically transmitted physical characteristics that are innate and immutable. Race and ethnicity are often confused because in some cases they overlap. For example, the Japanese have physical characteristics that identify them as an Asian racial group. At the same time, the Japanese people have a language, tradition, common heritage, and history that give them an ethnic identity. A blond European baby boy who, at the moment of birth, was adopted and raised by a Japanese family would as an adult be ethnically Japanese in spite of the physical (racial) characteristics that he inherited from his European ancestors. Perhaps it would be difficult for such an individual to be fully assimilated by the Japanese society because of clearly differing physical characteristics. This is because negative social values are being associated with physical characteristics. This is an obvious illustration of *racism*, which is the practice of attaching nonphysical characteristics to physical qualities of human beings. It should also be obvious that this practice has been and continues to be quite common in the United States. *Race and racism are problems not because of the reality of physical differences between human beings but because there are social values attached to those differences.*

During the past three decades, there have been dramatic changes in the racial, ethnic, and cultural composition of school populations. Immigration, changing birth rates, and school desegregation are the paramount reasons. Looking at Table 2–1, you can see that in the last full decade, the 1980s, immigrants entered the United States at a record rate: a 63 percent increase over the prior decade. Comparing the first and third columns, you can see that 12 percent of all immigrants over the past seventeen decades arrived in the 1980s. Most immigrants in the 1980s came from countries close by: 1,655,843 from Mexico alone. The Philippines ranked second to Mexico in number of immigrants coming to the United States, followed by China, then Korea and Vietnam.

These numbers add up to a United States population that is extraordinarily diverse ethnically, culturally, and linguistically, perhaps more so than any other society on earth. Inside our classrooms, as in U.S. society generally, the term *minority group* is quickly becoming factually inaccurate. Traditionally the term has been used loosely to refer to nonwhite and Hispanic people in the United States, but in just three more decades the *numerical minority* will be the *numerical majority*. In the largest school districts in the nation, this is already the case.

Think about this: By 2026 the nonwhite and Hispanic student enrollment in U.S. schools will grow from 10 million (in 1976) to 45 million, comprising 70 percent of the

Table 2–1
Immigration to the United States

Region of Origin	1820–1990	1971–1980	1981–1990
All regions	56,994,014	4,493,314	7,338,062
Europe	37,101,060	800,368	761,550
Asia	5,019,190	1,588,178	2,738,157
North America	13,067,548	1,982,735	3,615,255
Central America	819,628	134,640	648,088
South America	1,250,303	295,741	461,847
Africa	334,145	80,779	176,893

Source: *Special Report on Immigration.* U.S. Census, (Washington, DC: Government Printing Office, 1992).

nation's students. According to the U.S. Department of Education, "In 2026, we will have the exact inverse of student population as we knew it in 1990, when white students made up 70 percent of our enrolled K–12 student body."[3]

Gender

In August 1920 the Nineteenth Amendment to the Constitution became the law of the land, and thereby women were given the right to vote, a right enjoyed by most white free men since the founding of the Republic. The discrimination against women, however, did not end with the Nineteenth Amendment. The evidence is clear that women have not achieved full status with men in the business and professional worlds, in education, in political affairs, or in any field that has been traditionally dominated by men. For a variety of reasons, the traditional roles of men and women in society have undergone great changes in the second half of the twentieth century, resulting in the emancipation of women. The independence of women, which without question is one of the most significant social developments of our time, has many implications for social studies education in the elementary and middle schools.

Many believe that school programs of the past actually contributed to discrimination against women because they reinforced conventional sex roles that emphasized male superiority. Where this can be studied with a degree of objectivity, as, for example, in analyzing school textbooks, the evidence is overwhelming that males had a clear advantage. They have been consistently represented in positions of greater prestige and as being more courageous, more clever, more witty, and more skillful than women. Women tended to be represented in subservient positions and most generally in social-service roles or in roles that require serving men, as, for example, secretarial service and nursing. Thus, discrimination against women became institutionalized in that both boys *and* girls came to believe in the superiority of the male. Much of such blatant sexist portrayal does not now appear in recently published textbooks and other instructional material.

Gender Bias

Nevertheless, during the pre-school, elementary, and middle school years, students continue to experience gender bias. Though sex-role stereotyping in curriculum materials has diminished significantly, children's interactions with one another and especially the teacher's interaction with them remains a serious problem. For more than two decades researchers have confirmed that gender bias is a serious problem from pre-school right up through adult education. Three aspects of gender bias are especially serious and were recently documented in a study conducted by the American Association of University Women (AAUW) called *How Schools Shortchange Girls*:

- Girls receive significantly less attention from classroom teachers than do boys.
- African-American girls have fewer interactions with teachers than do white girls, despite evidence that they attempt to initiate interactions more frequently.
- Sexual harassment of girls by boys—from innuendo to actual assault—in our nation's schools is increasing.[4]

Doonesbury

Sadker and Sadker have provided a wealth of examples of the ways in which gender bias actually works in classrooms in their popular book, *Failing at Fairness: How America's Schools Cheat Girls*.[5] The Doonesbury cartoon on this page gets right to the point—that interaction among students and between teacher and students in the elementary classroom is markedly different for boys and girls. The classroom consists of "two worlds," the Sadkers observe: one of active boys, the other of inactive girls.

Male students control classroom conversation. They ask and answer more questions. They receive more praise for the intellectual quality of their ideas. They get criticized. They get help when they are confused.[6]

Consider this example from a fifth-grade classroom that is getting out of hand. The teacher quiets down the commotion, then reminds students of the rule to "raise your hand." She reminds her students of the reason for the rule: "There are too many of us here to all shout out at once." Order is momentarily restored. Soon, Stephen shouts out:

Stephen:	I think Lincoln was the best president. He held the country together during the war.
Teacher:	A lot of historians would agree with you.
Mike (seeing that nothing happened to Stephen, calls out):	I don't. Lincoln was okay, but my Dad liked Reagan. He always said Reagan was a great president.
David (calling out):	Reagan? Are you kidding?
Teacher:	Who do you think our best president was, Dave?
David:	FDR. He saved us from the depression.
Max (calling out):	I don't think it's right to pick one best president. There were a lot of good ones.
Teacher:	That's interesting.
Kimberly (calling out):	I don't think the presidents today are as good as the ones we used to have.
Teacher:	Okay, Kimberly. But you forgot the rule. You're supposed to raise your hand.[7]

As a result of interactions like these, boys often receive more instruction and better instruction than girls. When boys are praised, for example, it is more often for the kind of learning and thinking they are doing at the moment; consequently, it serves as valuable feedback that will affect achievement. When girls are praised, it is often with less feedback. Compare these two interactions:

Teacher to boy: "Good job, William. I like the way you're thinking it through."
Teacher to girl: "Good job, Marissa"

The "good job" response is well intentioned, but it is not nearly as helpful as the additional and more precise feedback given to William. Because of the feedback, William is likely to repeat his "thinking it through" behavior, but Marissa has not learned *what* if anything to repeat.

Furthermore, when girls are praised or criticized in a more helpful, specific way, they are twice as likely as boys to receive it for following or breaking the rules of interaction, form, and appearance, as Kimberly was, rather than for the substance of their thinking and their work. "I like how quiet you are" is one message the girls get. "You are so neat" is another. "I love your margins" is another, according to the Sadkers' research.

Major Goals of Gender Equity in Education

One major goal of gender equity in the classroom is equal opportunity to learn. Sex discrimination prevents children from having an equal chance to get attention, praise, constructive criticism, needed correction—in general, feedback. Over the years, this lack of helpful attention adds up. By one estimate, girls receive 1,800 fewer hours of instruction than boys between pre-school and college. This matters! At the risk of stating the obvious, let us be clear about the effect of instruction: Generally speaking, it works. Children are much more likely to learn the knowledge and skills of the social studies curriculum if they are taught these things than if they are not. The main theme of the classroom interaction studies is that girls are taught less often and less constructively than boys.

A closely related goal of gender equity in classrooms is to help stem the well-documented decline in self-esteem experienced by girls as they move out of the early elementary grades into the intermediate elementary grades and middle school.[8]

The self-esteem gap between boys and girls as they enter adolescence is very wide. Though as spunky and self-reliant as boys in the early grades, once they make it through middle school, girls are less likely than boys to say, "I like most things about myself" and "I am good at a lot of things." They are more likely to agree with the statement, "I wish I were somebody else." There are many reasons for this self-esteem drop, and researchers have not put the puzzle together, but the relative lack of attention and instruction in school probably plays a key role. If girls were taught as vigorously as are boys, if they were given more opportunities to express themselves and reason aloud in class, if they were given as much helpful praise and constructive criticism, their view of themselves as capable and articulate persons should match more closely that of boys.

Language Differences in the Classroom

Another kind of difference that matters greatly for children and their teachers is linguistic diversity. Over 100 distinct language groups are present in the United States (see Table 2–2).[*] In the late 1980s, one-third (three million) nonwhite and Hispanic children in school came from homes where English was not the first language; by the year 2000, this number is expected to double. By 2026, the figure will approach 15 million students, or about 25 percent.

When children come to school in most communities in the United States today, they find that most of the adults and classmates speak one language at school, English, and that one dialect, standard English, is preferred. Depending on whether their home language matches the school's, students might face an awesome communication and learning barrier. If the match is perfect, however, the effect is like having a red carpet rolled out for them. Many of the directions and explanations given in classrooms and on the playground are verbal; most reading materials are in English; and a child's social contacts with peers, which are crucial for social development, depend heavily on linguistic expression. The impact on a child who speaks little or no English can be enormous. Consider this reflection by a Chinese-American student:

I started to hate myself when I failed to answer the teacher's questions . . . because I couldn't express my answers in English. Then I began to hate everything in the world, including my parents because they took me to this country.[9]

Certainly not all limited-English-speaking children react this way. Some take eagerly to the task of learning the new language, have a relaxed attitude toward the difficulties that inevitably arise, and make good progress learning English *and* academic content and skills. Such children most likely are those who are provided content-based instruction in their home language, supplemented with English lessons and practice. The children who do especially well often are those whose command of the home language is excellent for

---

[*] You should be able to obtain information on your state by calling your state education office. Also, you might interview a school district official or school principal about local language diversity.

Table 2–2

Common languages in the United States

Here are the twenty-five most commonly spoken languages in the United States after English. The number of persons speaking that language is given along with the state with the highest *percentage* of speakers of that language.

Language	Number of Speakers	State with Highest % of Speakers
1. Spanish	17,339,172	New Mexico
2. French	1,702,176	Maine
3. German	1,547,099	North Dakota
4. Italian	1,308,648	New York
5. Chinese	1,249,213	Hawaii
6. Tagalog	843,251	Hawaii
7. Polish	723,483	Illinois
8. Korean	626,478	Hawaii
9. Vietnamese	507,069	California
10. Portuguese	429,860	Rhode Island
11. Japanese	427,657	Hawaii
12. Greek	388,260	Massachusetts
13. Arabic	355,150	Michigan
14. Hindi	331,484	New Jersey
15. Russian	241,798	New York
16. Yiddish	213,064	New York
17. Thai/Lao	206,266	California
18. Persian	201,865	California
19. French Creole	187,658	Florida
20. Armenian	149,694	California
21. Navajo	148,530	New Mexico
22. Hungarian	147,902	New Jersey
23. Hebrew	144,292	New York
24. Dutch	142,684	Utah
25. Mon-Khmer	127,441	Rhode Island

Source: U.S. Census (Washington, DC: Government Printing Office, 1992).

their age, who are highly motivated to learn the new language, whose family support for second language acquisition is warm and unambiguous, *and whose teachers do not confuse the lack of proficiency in the new language with a learning disability.* Some of these children's parents and teachers may themselves be multilingual and move smoothly between languages and dialects, depending on the social situation.

It takes time, effort, and good opportunities to learn a second or third language.

Already, we are running into many specialized terms. It is necessary to understand several that are used by experienced school personnel when talking about the language diversity among children. *Limited English Proficiency (LEP)* refers to students of all backgrounds, both native born and immigrants, whose primary (home) language is not English. Such students may be referred to as *language-minority* students. The information given in the opening lines of this section can now be read as follows: By the year 2026, approximately 25 percent of U.S. school enrollments will be language-minority or LEP children.

English as a Second Language (ESL) refers to educational programs for language-minority (LEP) children in U.S. schools. The object of these programs is mainly to teach English to children for whom English is not their first language. This is not a strange idea. Some native-English-speaking readers of this book may have taken a year or two of "foreign language" in middle or high school. Perhaps it was French, in which case these readers had, in effect, a French as a Second Language course. They were learning the rules of standard French speaking and, perhaps, writing. They may have learned a little about French culture and history as well. The same idea applies to ESL.

If these readers studied hard and practiced a lot, they may have become *bilingual*—speaking two languages fluently. *Bilingual education* is a difficult and hotly debated term that has two quite different meanings. Sometimes it is used synonymously with ESL education; that is, LEP students are taught English as a second language so that they will become bilingual and, therefore, able to learn from teachers who provide instruction in English. Most times, however, it means that students are provided instruction in their home language until they become fluent in English. If you visited an elementary or middle school with such a program, you would see LEP students gathered together for part or most of the day for instruction on social studies, math, and science topics and for reading and writing instruction. This instruction would be provided in the children's first language by a bilingual teacher. The rationale is that children who are required to learn content and skills in a language they barely understand are going to fall farther and farther behind their *language-majority* classmates. Recall the feelings of the Chinese-American student quoted earlier. Or listen to this child:

I just sat in my classes and didn't understand anything. Sometimes I would try to look like I knew what was going on, sometimes I would just try to think about a happy time when I didn't feel stupid. My teachers never called on me or talked to me. I think either they forgot I was there or else wished I wasn't.[10]

Research shows that it takes about two years to learn a second language well enough to engage in face-to-face conversation (*BICS*: basic interpersonal communication skills). But it takes three times as long, often longer, to develop the skills needed to learn subject matter (*CALP*: cognitive academic learning proficiency).[11] Readers of this book who are themselves bilingual will know well this distinction. It is one thing for, say, French-as-a-Second-Language students to engage in conversational French with a classmate or a waiter in a cafe, but quite another to go to a French school where it is necessary to comprehend texts written in the French language and develop conceptual understandings from lessons delivered in French.

Finally, we arrive at the term *dialect*. A dialect is a variation of a language spoken by members of a regional or ethnic group. Each variation has somewhat different rules of speech and meaning. Educators disagree on how best to deal with dialect variations in the classroom. Most seem to agree that speakers of nonstandard dialects should learn to speak standard English.[12] The reason is that social rewards, such as higher paying jobs and higher status, generally will follow. However, teachers should encourage students to *retain and use* the home dialect as well. The point is not to replace it. Like a first language, it should be regarded as a strength, not a deficiency. Teachers and children who are bilingual clearly have an advantage in a modern, diverse society; the same can be said for those who are proficient in more than one dialect.

Education Policy

Education policy for language-minority students in the United States is deeply divided. Some people hold to the belief that the best policy for LEP students is to immerse them in English-only programs. Others cite the large body of research that concludes it is more effective to teach language-minority children content and skills in their first language *while* they are learning English. As one bilingual educator put it, "The fact is, it takes time to learn English. We cannot forego learning other content areas while they're in the process of acquiring English."[13]

The state of California's *Bilingual Education Handbook* sums up the matter clearly: Most language-minority students will learn the functional, conversational level of English with or without school programs. However, this is not the pressing problem for teachers and school officials; rather, it is helping students move toward a more empowering level of language proficiency—beyond basic skills to rich engagement with meaningful academic subject matter. In social studies, this means the ability to comprehend and produce historical narrative, to read and understand primary documents such as Sojourner Truth's "Ain't I A Woman?" speech and Jefferson's Declaration of Independence, to engage in persuasive speech, to participate in civilized discussions of class-room and community problems, and to construct charts, graphs, and maps. This is one of the clearest messages of modern educational research: A watered-down curriculum devoid of rich content does no one any good, neither the language-minority child nor the English-proficient child. As the California *Handbook* says,

The school reform movement has gone beyond basic skills as the proper measuring stick of academic success. Educators of limited-English-proficient students should raise their goals, as well. Instead of teaching merely functional English, they should lead students to a much more demanding and rewarding control of empowering English.[14]

Social Class

In 1964 President Lyndon B. Johnson's War on Poverty legislation was enacted, yet more people in this country are poor today than when the Johnson antipoverty program went into effect. According to a report issued by the *Phi Delta Kappan* in 1990, "nearly 20% of all children under the age of 18 are poor."[15] For preschool children the figure is nearly 25 percent, which means that the number appears to be increasing for the school-age groups of the future. Because these data are based on the nation as a whole, the number in specific areas or pockets of poverty may be as high as twice or three times the national average. For example, over 50 percent of the people living on some Native American reservations are poor. And rural poverty continues to outrun inner-city poverty; in fact, twice as many children in poverty live outside large cities as inside them.

Ethnicity and race are powerful predictors of social class. Though about two-thirds of poor children are white, the percentages are greater for nonwhite and Hispanic children. These children who are living with two parents are more than twice as likely to be poor as white children living with two parents.

It is nearly impossible to overstate the debilitating effects of a life style of poverty on young children. Poverty generates feelings of destitution, helplessness, and despair. Associated with a life of poverty are such other social problems as crime, child abuse, delinquency, drug addiction, alcoholism, gang life, prostitution, unemployment, and social alienation. Poverty has been described as a cyclical phenomenon because it extends and recycles from one generation to the next. Recent research indicates that (1) brain growth is enhanced if stimulated by interacting with a rich environment;[16] and (2) children who suffer extended malnutrition during prenatal and early years may suffer long-term and perhaps irreversible intellectual deficiencies. Children of poverty are in jeopardy on both counts. Moreover, a child cannot function normally in school if he or she is hungry, cold, sick, or frightened much of the time.

Changing Family Life

In a recent article, the Director of the Center for Demographic Study, Harold Hodgkinson, makes the astounding assertion that "the 'Norman Rockwell' family—a working father, a housewife mother, and two children of school age—constitutes only 6% of U.S. households today."[17] He goes on to point out that every kind of "atypical" family increased in number during the 1980s, whereas married couples with children declined. The situation is such that *almost half* of the nation's children will spend some time being raised by a single parent before they reach age eighteen. Frances Smardo Dodd reports on two national surveys conducted in 1988 and 1990 indicating that as many as 15 million children representing 20 percent of the elementary school-age population are what have come to be called "latchkey kids"—children who are on their own before and after school until an adult returns home from work.[18] In 1990, for every male head of a single parent household, there were 4.32 female heads, a figure slightly higher than in 1980.

The realities described in the foregoing paragraph have a great impact on the home life of children. Very often single-parent households have limited disposable income. The amount and quality of time available for child-parent interaction is necessarily shortened, especially during school days. Housing options are ordinarily limited for a single parent, especially if that parent is a female. The pressure to meet basic day-to-day needs adds to the stress—and often guilt—experienced by the parent in such circumstances.

Children with Special Needs

Let us consider now those children whose abilities and problems are exceptional—beyond the usual. Educators and parents often believe these children require what is traditionally called "special education," the purpose of which, simply, is to help these children reach their potential.

Gifted and Talented Children

Even though each child is in her or his own way unique or exceptional, some children are singled out as *more* exceptional. Gifted and talented children have a remarkable degree of general ability and/or extraordinary specific abilities. Furthermore, they display advanced creativity and are highly motivated to achieve in the areas of their ability and talent. They will often persevere on a problem far beyond the point where other children lose interest or give up. Gifted children in the elementary grades usually handle subject matter easily because of their capacity to use language and understand abstract relationships. Their work is sometimes "over the top"—very advanced for their age. Here is the gifted pianist or poet in the fourth grade, and the third-grade child who not only plants kernels of corn in milk cartons at the plant table, but, captivated by the fact that beans are an inexpensive and plentiful source of protein, brings to class the next week a well-worked-out plan for cultivating beans in greenhouses attached ingeniously to homeless shelters. She has attended to the details of light and moisture, researched the necessary building permits, and is asking how to raise the funds.

Recognizing giftedness is not always this easy. The state department of education or the local school district establishes criteria that teachers and administrators are asked to use. They usually are derived from a child's school achievement history, teacher observations, and scores on intelligence tests. Sometimes schools define as gifted any child who scores in the top 2 or 3 percent of their age group. Guidelines may be distributed to teachers with questions such as these: Who among your children has an extraordinary vocabulary? Who is remarkably (and perhaps annoyingly) observant? Who seems to know about many things the other children do not? Who tackles problems that other children do not even see?

Children who are identified as gifted may qualify for school-funded enrichment programs. Although federal and state legislation require schools to make provision for children with disabilities, as we shall see, such mandates often do not apply to gifted children. Regardless of the availability of special programs for gifted children, the regular classroom teacher will need to make provisions for them. Social studies is a curriculum area that is ideally suited to make such adjustments because of its open-ended subject matter. All children will be learning to understand and make maps, for example, but the teacher may ask the gifted child to examine the mapping problems faced by cartographers (map makers) working in the field today, perhaps in space or on the ocean floor.

Challenged Children

Harvard psychologist Howard Gardner notes that we are all gifted and challenged simultaneously.[19] Perhaps you are a gifted violinist, but when your Chevrolet breaks down on the highway you are utterly mystified and do not even bother to look under the hood. Or you are mechanically gifted but cannot carry a tune. Some people, however, are exceptionally challenged. In America's elementary and middle schools are children who are mildly and profoundly *mentally retarded*, children who have *physical disabilities* (e.g., epilepsy, hearing impairment, cerebral palsy), *emotional and behavioral disorders*, and *communication disorders* (e.g., delayed language development, stuttering). Other children (sometimes the same ones) will have *learning disabilities (LD)*. Learning disabilities pose challenges in specific aspects of functioning, for example, reading, writing, or thinking abstractly. Dyslexia is one well-known learning disability.

Learning disability is a much overused term, dangerously so. No doubt too many children are made to endure this label. For example, LEP students do not have a "learning disability"; they just do not know the second language well enough to understand their teacher. Children who belong to ethnic minority groups, especially African-American boys, are disproportionately labeled learning disabled. This was especially true before a federal law was passed that prevented this sort of segregation, but it persists today. Some African-American parents have created separate schools for their children to protect them from racist practices like these.

Let us emphasize two cautions. First, learning challenges are not disadvantages unless the child is in a situation where the disability or disorder gets in the way. A child with a hearing impairment, for example, is not necessarily at a disadvantage when making a map of the classroom or playground. The violin-playing Chevrolet driver above, the one with a "mechanical disability," is not disadvantaged when he or she is eating dinner with friends.

Second, it should be obvious after working through the thicket of specialized terms in the above paragraphs that educators' conversations about exceptionality are loaded with labels. This is a double-edged sword. On the one hand, labels can help educators speak precisely about teaching and learning; on the other, labels can be attached to children and "stick." When that happens, children may not be helped to achieve their potential, which, recall, is the purpose of special education. Rather, the label may be used as an excuse by teachers, administrators, and parents to not bother teaching children what they actually may be quite capable of learning. This is precisely what has happened to many children, especially Mexican-Americans who have been labeled LEP and African Americans who have been labeled behaviorally disordered.

Legislation

The Congress of the United States enacted two pieces of legislation during the 1970s that had a profound effect on the education of persons with disabilities. The first of these was Section 504 of the Vocational Rehabilitation Act of 1973. This law deals largely with the removal of discriminatory practices. Although it is basically a law that protects the civil rights of persons with disabilities, it has a number of implications for education. It guarantees that an individual may not be denied access to education solely on the basis of a disability. As a result, Section 504 brought some greater extension of employment, training, and promotion opportunities to individuals with disabilities.

Perhaps the most important contribution of Section 504 was its mandate to remove barriers in architecture and in transportation. The law requires that all *activities* (not all areas or spaces) must be accessible to participants and spectators with physical disabilities. This meant that substantial structural modifications in existing school buildings had to be made to bring them into compliance. New structures must make provisions for these antidiscriminatory requirements in their design. Section 504 was instrumental in establishing barrier-free environments in schools.

In 1975 two congressional subcommittees held hearings in various parts of the country to determine what, if any, additional legislation was needed to accommodate the educational needs of the disabled. Some of the findings of these hearings were astounding: Over 1.75 million children with disabilities were being excluded *entirely* from receiving a public education solely on the basis of their disability. Over half of the estimated eight million children were not receiving appropriate services. Many children with disabilities were being placed in inappropriate educational environments because their disabilities had not been detected. As a result of these findings and as a result of concurrent judicial intervention, the 142d piece of legislation passed by the 94th Congress was the Education for All Handicapped Children Act, otherwise known as PL 94-142. It passed both Houses of Congress by very wide margins—probably because the issue had already been settled by the courts. The bill was signed into law by President Gerald Ford on November 29, 1975, to go into effect in 1977, with no expiration date.

PL 94–142 was amended in 1990 by the Individuals with Disabilities Education Act (IDEA). Changes to the law included the substitution of the word *disabled* for the word *handicapped*. In the same year, the Americans with Disabilities Act (ADA) recognized the civil rights of disabled persons.

This legislation is one of the most lengthy and complex ever enacted by Congress. Its main points, however, are easily summarized. The law requires:

1. The availability of a free appropriate public education for all children with disabilities between the ages of three and twenty-one, unless inconsistent with state laws; school districts are obliged to search for and identify such children.
2. The maintenance of an Individualized Education Program (IEP) for all disabled children, prepared in cooperation with the parent or guardian, the teacher, and the school principal.
3. The guarantee of complete due process procedures.
4. The provision of special education and related services as needed in the "least restrictive" environment.
5. Nondiscriminatory testing, evaluation, and placement.
6. The placement in regular public school settings with nondisabled peers to the maximum extent appropriate and feasible.

PL 94–142 is based on a philosophy of *inclusion* rather than *exclusion*. It embraces the "zero-reject" principle. It frowns on the segregation and labeling of human beings. It shatters long-held assumptions about who is educable.

Multiple Intelligences

We conclude this survey of today's children by taking a closer look at a fascinating idea mentioned earlier: Each person is simultaneously gifted and challenged. Howard Gardner's theory of multiple intelligences recently has become popular with many teachers across the nation who are eager to tailor instruction to each child. Gardner proposes that intelligence is not a singular or general phenomenon, of which any one of us has more or less. Rather, there are seven intelligences, and each of us has all of them to one degree or another: linguistic, musical, spatial, logical-mathematical, bodily-kinesthetic, interpersonal understanding, and intrapersonal understanding. Most people eventually develop all the intelligences to a fairly competent level, but some people are exceptional in one or more areas. There are many ways to be intelligent in each category.

Table 2–3 describes each intelligence very briefly and suggests related learning activities in which children might participate. Readers surely can add to the list of suggested possibilities. Two points need to be made, however. First, such activities should be closely related to a lesson's objectives, otherwise they are not *learning* activities. This distinction quickly distinguishes average teachers from excellent teachers. An activity may be fun, but if it is not helping children know and be able to do important things—that is, if it is not helping them learn important subject matter—then precious instructional time has not been used as well as it might. Second, the purpose of gearing activities to multiple intelligences is to tap into *all* children's current strengths and also to encourage them to develop strength in new areas. Traditionally, activities emphasizing linguistic and logical intelligence have predominated in many classrooms. As a consequence, children with these strengths may have been advantaged while other children were not given opportunities to display their knowledge.

By broadening their repertoires of instructional tools, teachers can help more children achieve curriculum objectives. The third-grade child who loves to dramatize can be put in charge of a short play about the first meeting of Spaniards and Pueblo Indians in what is today New Mexico. And the child who has not participated much in dramatics can be encouraged to take a role. Another child can head the team that writes the script. Second-graders assembling the classroom store can be measuring, writing, counting, and planning the grand opening ceremony, complete with songs and interviews with local officials played by classmates. As one advocate has written, multiple intelligence teaching "encompasses what good teachers have always done in their teaching: reaching beyond the text and the blackboard to awaken students' minds."[20]

Conclusion: Rewards of Teaching in Diverse Classrooms

In this section, we examined the children in today's classrooms by focusing on ways they might differ from one another: ethnicity and culture, gender, language, social class, family life, exceptionality, and intelligences. Our view is that you are fortunate if you already are teaching in a school with a rich array of children or will be one day.

Table 2–3
Multiple intelligences

Intelligence	Characteristics	Learning Activities
Linguistic	sensitivity to words, their meanings and functions	read and write about it, discuss it
Musical	appreciation of musical expression and ability to produce music	sing or hum it, drum it out or rap it, listen quietly to it, compose it
Spatial	keen perception of the visual-spatial world and ability to change initial perceptions into other forms	map it, draw it, visualize the whole procedure
Logical-mathematical	sensitivity to and ability to perceive logical and numerical patterns	quantify it, identify the lines of reasoning used, classify it
Bodily-kinesthetic	sensitivity to one's body movements and ability to control them	dance it, get your hands in it, build it, dramatize it
Interpersonal	sensitivity and capacity to respond to other persons' ways of being (feelings, moods)	tutor someone, collaborate with others on it, talk about it
Intrapersonal	access to one's own feelings and moods and the ability to discriminate among and draw on them	write about it in a response journal, find personal analogy to it.

Source: Adapted from Howard Gardner, *Frames of Mind: The Theory of Multiple Intelligences* (New York: Basic Books, 1983).

Why? If you respond well, your teaching knowledge and skills will improve dramatically. As the old saying goes, "May you live in interesting times."

When teaching in a diverse classroom, you will face interesting challenges and be called upon to use more of, and add continually to, your professional knowledge and skills. As a result, your work should be more rewarding and fulfilling. You will be stimulated to learn more and more about your children *and yourself*. If you are open and curious, your conversations with children, colleagues, and parents will be fascinating and instructive. Your children will benefit because they have a skillful and knowledgeable teacher who genuinely appreciates them, who does not shy away from their cultural and individual differences and has high achievement expectations for *all* of them; at the same time, *you* will learn continually and, we are confident, enjoy insight after insight. This makes for a satisfying professional life. Indeed, it is just the sort of thing people are leaving other kinds of work to find.

Implications for Teaching Social Studies

Because children come from a wide variety of home and community environments, because they are diverse ethnically and in their ability to communicate and learn in English, and because they differ as much as they do in their abilities and motivations, they cannot possibly benefit equally from identical exposures to educational experiences. If everyone is treated the same, we simply institutionalize and perpetuate inequality. Why? Because of the red-carpet effect we mentioned earlier, some individuals and some groups are better able to take advantage of some school experiences than others. For some children the cultural match between their home and school experiences will be a good one; for others it will not. Identical instruction for unidentical children is not the best course. Gloria Ladson-Billings, a prominent African-American scholar whose book *The Dreamkeepers* details the work of successful teachers of African-American children, puts it this way: "Different children have different needs and addressing those different needs is the best way to deal with them equitably."[21]

Two Extremes

Well-intentioned teachers have disagreed on this matter, and from two different vantage points. At one extreme is the belief that it is best to ignore differences among children. "I don't really see color, I just see children," we have often heard. Or, "I don't care if they're red, green, or polka dot, I just treat them all like children."[22] Teachers holding this belief may sincerely understand that children are, after all, children and alike in so many ways. But these teachers often are uncomfortable talking about cultural differences and race and may have little or no knowledge about such concepts as ethnic group, culture, and second-language acquisition. On the other side are teachers who are so knowledgeable about and sensitive to individual and cultural differences that they are nearly paralyzed in their role as teacher. They shy away from teaching core subject matter to the whole class, partly due to anxiety about choosing which content and skills all children should learn and partly due to anxiety about selecting appropriate instructional strategies. "Who am I to choose?" we have heard such teachers say. "I just let the children choose. That seems the safest route."

A middle way is needed. Good teachers walk a sensible and flexible path between ignoring diversity and being paralyzed by it. They see both similarities and differences among the children in their classroom, and they hold high learning standards for *all* of them—both boys and girls, native born and immigrant, gifted and challenged, Asian American, black, and white.

Individualized Instruction

This middle way is *individualized instruction*. Individualized instruction means that children are provided with personally meaningful learning experiences that will help them to achieve the goals of the curriculum. Traditionally this has meant that learning experiences should be tailored to each child's *capabilities*. This definition emerged in an era when educators were concerned mainly with ability, developmental, and intelligence differences among white, European-American children of the majority language and culture. They paid little attention to other kinds of differences among children such as all those discussed earlier. The contemporary definition of individualized instruction encompasses not only children's capabilities but also the array of cultural differences they bring to class due to their diverse group memberships—ethnic, racial, social class, gender, religious, and linguistic.

Accompanying this definitional change is a shift in the way educators view cultural differences. It is a shift from the cultural *deprivation* (or deficit) model to the cultural *differences* (or pluralistic) model. For decades, children who were culturally different were thought to be culturally "deprived." Their diverse languages, values, behaviors, and beliefs were viewed as less developed, less important, and less attractive when compared to the cultural attributes of the majority culture. Culturally different children were thought to be culturally disadvantaged. Teachers might make comments such as, "If only we didn't have to send the children home at night" and "What can we expect of kids with parents like that?" This is not a helpful attitude, Bennett observes, "because it focuses on where our students *aren't*, and blinds us to where our students *are*."[23]

The cultural differences model, by contrast, assumes that schools need to be ready and able to teach children of all groups. This is part of the "American dream" that has attracted people to the United States from all over the world. It means that people of all cultures and creeds are free to be themselves while getting the best education possible. Rather than arguing that culturally diverse children are unready for school, the cultural differences position argues that schools too often are unready for children—that it is the schools' responsibility to teach, and teach effectively, all children. In a polycultural society, schools cannot be monocultural and expect to help all children learn. Teachers need to view cultural differences as strengths, not deficits, and be always on the lookout for ways to incorporate and build on those strengths.

Guidelines for Teaching

Here, now, are a few guidelines for teaching in ways that respect all the children in the class and help all of them to succeed. Each of the following chapters in this book is mindful of the diverse children we teach; accordingly, we will not attempt to say everything in this one section. Instead, we suggest some general directions for today's teachers, followed by examples.

Culturally Responsive Instruction

Teach in ways that bridge the gap between children's home cultures and the school culture. Learn about the cultural and linguistic characteristics of the children in your class and adapt instruction accordingly. The purpose of culturally responsive instruction is to help children maintain their cultural identities while learning the school curriculum. Doing so helps them learn what you want them to learn because they are not required to hide or feel badly about who they are. Teacher and researcher Kathryn Au, who works with Native Hawaiian children at the Kamehameha Elementary Education Program (KEEP), writes that the "approaches teachers use to work with students of diverse backgrounds should allow students to retain and feel pride in their own ethnic and cultural identity. . . . Too often, students of diverse backgrounds find themselves in the position of having to choose between school success and their cultural identity."[24] This is an unfair choice for any child in a democratic, pluralist society, and it systematically stunts the academic growth of nonwhite and Hispanic students.

- Native Hawaiian students often are raised in families that practice sibling caretaking. At school, they might feel just as comfortable learning from peers as from an adult teacher. Accordingly, their teachers often pair them for practice and for teaching one another the meaning of what they are reading.
- A fifth-grade teacher begins her unit on the U.S. Constitution by asking students what they know about the bylaws and articles of incorporation of local churches to

which they belong. African-American children in particular, who may be the most deeply involved in church activities, "learn the significance of such documents in forming institutions and shaping ideals while they also learn that their own people are institution-builders."[25]

- A third-grade teacher learns to say "please," "thank you," and "good morning" in the home languages of each of her language-minority children. He publicly praises these children for being already at work on another language. He often uses the phrases he has learned when working individually with the children.
- A fourth-grade class is planning their classroom newsletter, which will be sent home to parents and to a fourth-grade classroom in another school. Their teacher brought in copies of weekly newspapers from local ethnic minority communities to serve as models.

Teachers also should consider the following steps to learn more about their students' communities:

1. Collaborate with the ethnic minority communities in your area. Volunteer at youth centers and adult literacy programs.
2. Ask the parents of immigrant children if their children are attending a Saturday language and culture school. Volunteer to share maps and other curriculum materials.
3. Find out what your students' older brothers and sisters do for fun, then refer to these activities.
4. Find out what churches, mosques, and temples your children attend. Ask them about this. Go to an open house, choir concert, or picnic.

Knowledge of Your Own Cultural Identity(ies)

Study your own family history—its cultural and ethnic characteristics, language, dialect, religion, social values, gifts, and disabilities. As leading multicultural educator James A. Banks said, "Teachers are human beings who bring their cultural perspectives, values, hopes, and dreams to the classroom. They also bring their prejudices, stereotypes, and misconceptions. Teachers' values and perspectives mediate and interact with what they teach and influence the ways that messages are communicated and perceived by their students. A teacher who believes that Christopher Columbus 'discovered' America and one who believes that Columbus came to America when it was peopled by groups with rich and diverse cultures will send different messages to their students when they study European exploration of America."[26]

- Research and make your family tree and narrate a family history. Share this with other teachers who have done the same. Contemplate and talk about how your own ethnicity shapes your interaction with your students.
- Visit culturally different neighborhoods in your own town or city and, if you can, in other nations. Such experiences provide a reflective mirror in which you can better see your own customs and values.
- Read the histories of American ethnic groups and compare them to your own.[27]

Multimedia

Provide variation in the ways children acquire information, think about and manipulate it, and express what they are learning. The intake of new information is an essential requirement of social studies education. The conventional information sources have been the textbook, other children's literature, and the teacher. It is important to broaden the array of information sources: computer software, films, videos, recorded songs and speeches, paintings and photographs projected on the overhead projector, interviews, class discussions, and so forth. Similarly, the ways in which children are asked to manipulate and express the information they have gathered need to be expanded: Children can transfer information heard in a film to bar and pie graphs, organize information on charts, write plays and songs about it, draw and role-play.

- Teach children how to make and read charts and graphs depicting information they have gathered.
- Teach children how to re-tell a section of the textbook as a play or song.
- Create self-contained learning centers that feature multimedia presentations on an important topic: hospitals in our community, Washington D.C., goods and services in our community, regions of the United States, the U.S. Constitution.

High Expectations for Learning Important Subject Matter

Expect, assist, and cajole all students to achieve the curriculum. Children tend to perform according to the expectations of their teachers. Teachers in the past often have expected less achievement from girls, LEP students, African-American and Hispanic children, children with learning disabilities, and poor children. Sometimes they have lowered curriculum standards for these children or created altogether different curriculum for them, thereby teaching them less important subject matter (*curriculum differentiation* or *tracking*). Often these lowered expectations are based on prejudices and stereotypes.

Attached to a teacher's low expectations are behaviors, such as praising girls for neat work and praising boys for thoughtful work, drilling LEP students on skills while helping language-majority children develop important understandings in geography, civics, and history, or expecting Asian-American children to do well in math and expecting African-American children to misbehave. *Teachers need to communicate to each child that that they sincerely believe he or she can and will learn.*

- Call on girls as often as boys. Praise them for intellectual work—their reasoning and understanding—and provide constructive criticism. Be attentive to the misbehavior of both boys and girls. Use a checklist to help keep track of your feedback patterns. Ask a colleague to videotape your interaction, then return the favor.
- Make every effort to teach LEP children the academic curriculum, not merely language skills. Expect them to learn it. Use drama, art, construction, and music activities to remove some of the language burden on these children.
- Try not to change the curriculum to meet students' needs; rather, change the way you teach—the activity, the way information is presented, the way children are to think about or practice with this information, or the way they are to express their knowledge. For LEP students and poor urban children, "too often a watered-down version

Students tend to perform according to the expectations of their teachers.

of the curriculum has been offered with a heavy dependence on the remedial drilling of basic skills to the virtual exclusion of more engaging, significant content."[28]

- Genuinely *care* whether your students learn, and know them well enough so that you effectively can help them learn. Children notice this care for learning and the extent to which their teachers help them learn, and they will remember it long enough to talk about it when they are grown. Both are expressed in this Native Alaskan teacher's statement: "If there's someone who doesn't understand what I'm teaching, I try to understand who they are." Similarly, an African-American teacher remembered his own experience: "My instructors knew what you knew because they talked to you. They knew the students. . . . Teaching is all about telling a story. You have to get to know kids so you'll know how to tell the story."[29]

- Monitor carefully your nonverbal behavior. Act warmly to each child; speak warmly and firmly, as needed, with each child. Do not shy away from culturally different children.

Multicultural Curriculum

Help children understand key concepts, events, issues, and historical figures from diverse perspectives. Paying attention to *how* we teach is an important dimension of teaching in diverse classrooms. Paying attention to *what* we teach is another. Teachers should enrich their students' learning of social studies topics by including multiple viewpoints or perspectives. Children in the fifth grade should examine the American Revolution from the perspectives of loyalists as well as rebels, men and women, and slaves and free persons. They should study the westward movement of the European immigrants from the viewpoints of Native American groups as well as pioneer families.

When setting up a classroom store, help third-grade children plan for employees and customers who have disabilities and religious and language differences.

- Take care not to teach *only* the Anglo-American perspective on United States history. European conquerors came from Spain as well as England, and their history involves the American southwest more than the northeast. Asian immigrants came through San Francisco while European immigrants were lining up on Ellis Island in New York City. The popular term *westward expansion* refers specifically to the Anglo-American immigrant movement from the northeast toward the already occupied lands to the west. *Northward expansion* would capture the movement of Spanish-speaking immigrants from the south. Native American groups fought with both.
- When teaching about the children's neighborhoods and communities, emphasize both the cultural diversity *and* the laws and political structures that bind us together as one people. This is important. We may be culturally many, but we are politically one (our constitutional democracy). Talk with children about the classroom rules, such as listening carefully to one another and respecting one another's property, that "make us all one people."

Flexible Grouping

Group children in various ways, and change the groups often. During social studies instruction, groupings of children should be temporary and task-oriented. Often these groups are formed on the basis of a common interest—for example, working together on a display, construction project, play, or report. Other groups are formed on the basis of a common need. For instance, a teacher may work with a small group in reading their text, discussing a controversial issue, developing a map skill, or showing them how to use the materials in a learning center while other children are working independently. What should be avoided are fixed groups in which children are separated permanently for whatever reason, such as reading ability, prior knowledge, or behavior.[30]

- Use whole-class grouping when children should have a shared experience—a class discussion of a classroom problem, for example, hearing a story about Abraham Lincoln, or being introduced to time lines or different kinds of maps, charts, and graphs.
- Needs-based groups should be used sometimes to remediate students who need this kind of assistance but generally to help students achieve *beyond* what they normally do. This applies both to children with specific disabilities as well as gifted children. This kind of assistance is called *scaffolding* because it lifts children to a higher level of competency than they could get to on their own.[31]
- Use cooperative pairs when you want children to practice with information they have heard, give one another explanations, share responses to a reading, or test one another over material that has been studied. Pairs also can be used to teach one another by learning to ask good questions: questions that seek clarification, elaboration, a summary or prediction. Pairs are easier to form and disband than small groups.
- Use peer-tutoring pairs when a student who is more knowledgeable will help a student who is less so.
- Use cooperative small groups of three to five children for tasks that are complex and require some division of labor and group planning. Examples include making differ-

ent kinds of maps of the same play area, writing a multi-chapter history of Mexico or Canada, or creating a model of a village. These groups should mix children of different abilities, social status, and ethnicity.

Individualizing for Children with Special Needs

Traditionally, elementary school teachers dealt with children with disabilities by referring them to special education classes. As we have seen, this type of arbitrary exclusion is no longer socially or legally acceptable. Today the teacher can expect one or more children with varying types of disabilities to be present in most elementary school classrooms. This practice, known popularly as *mainstreaming* or *inclusion*, is the school's response to the mandate that such children must be educated with their nondisabled peers to the maximum extent appropriate.

What the teacher can and will do depends on the child's disability and the kinds of support services provided. It is important, if at all possible, that disabled children are not further disadvantaged by being denied access to the school district's curriculum. Like language-minority children, too many disabled children fall behind their classmates because they are not being taught the same academic curriculum as their same-aged peers. One way teachers are attempting to include these children in the regular curricular activity of the classroom is by providing them with additional support. One technique is to envision children with disabilities in regular curricular activities, doing the same tasks on the same subject matter with the same materials. Then, imagine how the materials might be changed. If the child still is not successful, an aide or more

Children prepare for a mock newscast.

capable student might be asked to assist, and, if necessary, the task itself might be changed. Only as a last resort, however, should the curriculum objective be changed. This way, all children are helped to attain the curriculum.[32]

It is quite clear that a child who is physically challenged but intellectually gifted will be taught differently from one who is physically normal but mildly or severely mentally retarded. In this context, the Individualized Education Program makes good sense because the learning needs of children vary greatly from one to another. Likewise, what the teacher does or does not do will depend on how much technical assistance and support service is available. If the classroom has the services of an interpreter-tutor who can work with the child for part of the time in a one-on-one setting and who works with the teacher on a cooperative basis, it becomes easier for the regular teacher to integrate children with disabilities into the day-to-day life and activities of the classroom.

In the case of a child who is severely disabled, the chances are good that a teacher trained in special education will prepare the Individualized Education Program. The classroom teacher may be responsible for only a small part of the implementation of the IEP. On the other hand, if the teacher has a child in the class with mild mental retardation, that teacher may have full responsibility for the preparation and implementation of the IEP. Even in cases of children who are not severely disabled, the regular classroom teacher may have available the assistance of a special education teacher in preparing the IEP. In those cases in which the child is attending both regular and special education classes, ordinarily the IEP goals and objectives will focus on compensating for the child's disability, and it is the special education teacher who attends the IEP meeting. The regular classroom teacher, the special education teacher, and other support personnel must, of course, collaborate to ensure a coordinated program of instruction for the child.

The Individualized Education Program must take into account the child's present level of attainment or development. In other words, a learning needs assessment must be made and the current status established. Based on that information, the IEP stipulates the long-range goals that are to be met by the end of the year and the short-term objectives to be achieved in order to attain the long-range goals. The short-term objectives should be listed in the sequence in which they are to be achieved. Although the regular teacher may exercise some initiative in preparing the IEP, the program planning and development *must* include, on a firsthand basis, the principal or other school representative and the child's parent or guardian. Teacher-prepared IEPs that are sent to the child's parent or guardian for signature are not acceptable in terms of federal legislation.

The actual format of the IEP will vary from district to district although the substance of what is included will remain pretty much the same. The sample form provided in Figure 2–1 illustrates a standard IEP that includes components required by federal regulation.

Common Ground

When we look at an American classroom in a public school, one thing we can be sure of is that the children do not share a common ethnic identity, home language, or a common set of abilities and talents. At parent night, we do not encounter families (continued p. 54)

PIEDMONT PUBLIC SCHOOLS
INDIVIDUALIZED EDUCATION PROGRAM

Standard Form

Student _____

Birthdate _____
C.A. _____

Address _____ (include zip)

Lives With _____ Relationship _____ Home Phone _____ Work Phone _____

Home School _____ Grade _____ IEP Conference Date _____ Projected Review Date _____

Teacher _____ Program _____ School _____ Date Enrolled _____ Terminated _____

I. SUMMARY OF PRESENT LEVELS OF PERFORMANCE
(Include statements of progress in each area from last reporting period)

ACADEMIC:

PHYSICAL:

SOCIAL:

II. ANALYSIS OF ASSESSMENT DATA
(Report of significant changes since initial IEP)

ELIGIBILITY CRITERIA: _____

PLACEMENT OFFICE ONLY:

Program Assigned _____ / Building _____ / Teacher _____ / Date Enrolled _____

PROGRAM AND/OR REPLACEMENT CHANGE:	
Team Leader: _____	Date: _____
Parent: _____	Date: _____

PROGRAM RECOMMENDATION:	
Psychologist: _____	Date: _____
Parent: _____	Date: _____
	Date: _____

Figure 2–1
Sample IEP form

51

III. STUDENT GOALS & OBJECTIVES

Academic Year _____

Special Classroom Teacher _____

Support Services _____

(Specify Service)

Name of Student	B.D.	Grade	Program	Building	Teacher	Date Enrolled	

Goals:	Initial Objectives:	Evaluation Criteria & Progress Notes (include pre-test, post-test data, and grades)	Date Started	Date Completed

_____   _____
Signature of person or persons responsible for reporting   Parent Signature   Date
progress on goals and objectives

Figure 2–1, *continued*
Sample IEP form

Student: _____   Projected I.E.P. Review Date _____

IV. RELATED SERVICES

Regular Education Program:

	Estimated Time/Week	Anticipated	
		Start	End

Support Services: (Speech-language, P.E., Voc. etc.)

Regular P.E. ☐   Adaptive P.E. ☐

My rights and responsibilities have been explained to me in a manner which I understand.

I have had the opportunity to participate in the development of this Individualized Education Program.

I understand all programs and services listed above and give my permission for my child/ward to participate in these programs/services.

I have been informed that the objectives listed on this form are initial objectives and that the person(s) responsible for implementing the objectives will revise and/or add objectives in keeping with the student's progress toward the stated goals.

Parent Signature: _____

Date: _____

V. I.E.P. Committee Members:

Name	Position

The School District shall provide the parent (or the adult student) a copy of the individualized education program.

53

with a common set of political party preferences, religions, or experiences. Ours is not a Christian nation, an Islamic nation, or Jewish or Buddhist nation. This is the United States, where the people created a government that would protect their liberties, not force a common way of life on them. Many immigrants—from the Pilgrims to the Jews and Cambodians—have come to this nation precisely for the purpose of escaping governments that refuse to protect individual freedom and, instead, force people into a common mold.

"With Liberty and Justice for All"

The chief way members of this diverse society are alike—our common ground—is our shared commitment to the values and principles of American democracy. First among these are the freedoms of religion, speech, and press and the commitment to equality and fairness. Most Americans also share a commitment to the ideal of *rule by law.* They believe that everyone should obey the law and that no one—not even the president—is above the law. They also believe that each person should take responsibility for the well-being of his or her community. This is often called civic-mindedness or civic virtue. Without it there could be no democracy. After all, it is not enough that we look out for our *own* rights and liberties; democratic citizens must insist on *one another's* rights and liberties. This is the essence of mutual respect, without which kindness and cooperation across our differences is not possible.

Teachers are among society's most important stewards of democracy. Educating children in such a way that they will themselves grow to nurture democracy is a major purpose of social studies education. Many educators believe this is its primary mission. Thus, in social studies, children are taught what the democratic ideal is, and they learn to practice it in their daily lives. In the next chapter, we suggest numerous ways in which elementary and middle school teachers are accomplishing this.

• •

Discussion Questions and Suggested Activities

1. Compare and contrast the *cultural deficit* and *cultural differences* approaches. How might they influence teaching? Learning? Curriculum planning?
2. Make a glossary of the specialized terms introduced in this chapter. Work with a classmate to develop definitions in your own words that make sense to both of you.
3. What are your memories of gender bias in your elementary classrooms when you were a child? What kinds of gender bias might you observe in classrooms today? Similarly, what are your memories of language differences and ethnic diversity?
4. Call your state department of education and one or two school districts to get demographic data on issues that concern you, for example:

   a. The home languages of students in your state.
   b. The number of immigrant children.
   c. The number of children living in poverty.

5. Record your understanding of and your position on the following ideas.

   a. "Here is a magic trick. Treat language differences as *gifts*. If you already speak one language and are trying now to learn another, and you are only a six- or seven-year-old child, that is fantastic! I will treat you as one of my gifted children."

    b. A watered-down curriculum devoid of rich content does no one any good, neither the language-minority child nor the English-proficient child.

    c. Rather than arguing that culturally diverse children are unready for school, the cultural differences position argues that schools too often are unready for children—that it is the school's responsibility to teach, and teach effectively, all children.

6. According to some researchers, educators over the years have narrowed the definition of what is considered "normal," thereby expanding the number of people considered different or disabled. Do you agree? And if so, what are the implications for your teaching?

7. "I don't care if they're red, green, or polka dot, I just treat them all like children." What might be the possible effects on children's learning of this teacher's belief?

8. Explain how a teacher's expectations can affect a child's achievement. Give two or three examples.

9. Develop a floor plan of a room that would lend itself to flexible grouping and multimedia learning activities.

10. List the procedures for individualizing (adapting) instruction that might be used in classrooms that have:

    a. a high percentage of poor readers.

    b. many LEP students.

    c. several gifted children.

    d. both mildly mentally retarded children and children with learning disabilities.

● ●

Notes

1 Eugene E. Garcia and Rene Gonzalez, "Issues in Systemic Reform for Culturally and Linguistically Diverse Students," *Teachers College Record* 96 (Spring 1995): 420.

2 James A. Banks, *An Introduction to Multicultural Education* (Boston: Allyn & Bacon, 1994), 101.

3 Garcia and Gonzalez, "Issues in Systematic Reform," 420.

4 American Association of University Women, *How Schools Shortchange Girls*, Executive Summary (Washington, DC: Author, 1992).

5 Myra Sadker and David Sadker, *Failing at Fairness: How America's Schools Cheat Girls* (New York: Charles Scribner's Sons, 1994).

6 Ibid., 42.

7 Ibid., 43.

8 Lyn Mikel Brown and Carol Gilligan, *Meeting at the Crossroads: Women's Development and Girls' Development* (Cambridge, MA: Harvard University Press, 1992), and Barbara Kerr, *Smart Girls, Gifted Women* (Columbus, OH: Ohio Psychology Pub., 1985).

9 Herbert Grossman, *Special Education in a Diverse Society* (Boston: Allyn & Bacon, 1995), 145.

10 Ibid., 189.

11 Ibid.

12 See, for example, Lisa Delpit, *Other People's Children: Cultural Conflict in the Classroom* (New York: New Press, 1995).

13 Grossman, *Special Education*, 186.

14 California Department of Education, *The Bilingual Education Handbook: Designing Instruction for LEP Students* (Sacramento: Author, 1990), 9–10.

15 Sally Reed and R. Craig Sautter, "Children of Poverty," Kappan Special Report, *Phi Delta Kappan* 71 (June 1990): K3.

16 Renate Nummela Caine & Geoffrey Caine, *Making Connections: Teaching and the Human Brain* (Alexandria, VA: Association for Supervision and Curriculum Development, 1991), 27–29.

17 Harold Hodgkinson. "Reform Versus Reality," *Phi Delta Kappan 73*, (September 1991), 10.

18 Reported in *Education Week*, October 16, 1991, p. 12.

19 Howard Gardner, *Frames of Mind: The Theory of Multiple Intelligences* (New York: Basic Books, 1983).

20 Thomas Armstrong, *Multiple Intelligences in the Classroom* (Alexandria, VA: Association for Supervision and Curriculum Development, 1994), 50.

21 Gloria Ladson-Billings, *The Dreamkeepers: Successful Teachers of African American Children* (San Francisco: Jossey-Bass, 1994), 33.

22 Ibid., 31.

23 Christine I. Bennett, *Comprehensive Multiculural Education: Theory and Practice*, 3rd ed. (Boston: Allyn & Bacon, 1995), 223–24.

24 Kathryn H. Au, *Literacy Instruction in Multicultural Settings* (Orlando: Harcourt, 1993), 12–13.

25 Ladson-Billings, *Dreamkeeper*, 19.

26 "Teaching Multicultural Literacy to Teachers," *Teaching Education* 4 (Summer/Fall 1991), 139–140.

27 See James A. Banks, *Teaching Strategies for Ethnic Studies*, 5th ed. (Boston: Allyn & Bacon, 1991).

28 California Department of Education, *Bilingual Education Handbook*, 2.

29 Delpit, *Other People's Children*, 120.

30 See Marguerite C. Radencich and Lyn J. McKay, *Flexible Grouping for Literacy in the Elementary Grades* (Boston: Allyn & Bacon, 1995).

31 Roland G. Tharp and Ronald Gallimore, *Rousing Minds to Life: Teaching, Learning, and Schooling in Social Context* (Cambridge: Cambridge University Press, 1988).

32 Sharon Freagan, Rhonda Best, Jennifer Sommerness, Ruth Usilton, Julie West, Kathryn Cox, and Pamela Reisling, "Inclusion of Young Learners with Disabilities in Social Studies," *Social Studies and the Young Learner* 7 (March/April 1995): 15–18.

Selected References

Alleman, Janet Elaine, and Cheryl L. Rosen. "The Cognitive, Social-Emotional, and Moral Development Characteristics of Students." In *Handbook of Research on Social Studies Teaching and Learning*, edited by James P. Shaver. New York: Macmillan, 1991, 121–33.

Allen, K. Eileen, and Ilene S. Schwartz. *The Exceptional Child: Inclusion in Early Childhood Education*, 3rd ed. Albany, NY: Delmar, 1996.

American Association of University Women. *How Schools Shortchange Girls*, Executive Summary. Washington, DC: Author, 1992.

Armstrong, Thomas. *Multiple Intelligences in the Classroom*. Alexandria, VA: Association for Supervision and Curriculum Development, 1994.

Au, Kathryn H. *Literacy Instruction in Multicultural Settings*. Orlando: Harcourt, 1993.

Banks, James A. *An Introduction to Multicultural Education*. Boston: Allyn & Bacon, 1994.

Bennett, Christine I. *Comprehensive Multicultural Education: Theory and Practice*, 3rd ed. Boston: Allyn & Bacon, 1995.

Brown, Lyn Mikel, and Carol Gilligan, *Meeting at the Crossroads: Women's Development and Girls' Development*. Cambridge, MA: Harvard University Press, 1992.

California Department of Education. *The Bilingual Education Handbook: Designing Instruction for LEP Students*. Sacramento: Author, 1990.

Curtis, Charles K. "Social Studies for Students At-Risk and with Disabilities." In *Handbook of Research on Social Studies Teaching and Learning*, edited by James P. Shaver. New York: Macmillan, 1991, 157–74.

Delisle, James R. "Gifted Students and Social Studies." In *Handbook of Research on Social Studies Teaching and Learning*, edited by James P. Shaver. New York: Macmillan, 1991, 175–82.

Delpit, Lisa. *Other People's Children: Cultural Conflict in the Classroom*. New York: New Press, 1995.

Gardner, Howard. *Frames of Mind: The Theory of Multiple Intelligences*. New York: Basic Books, 1983.

Grossman, Herbert. *Special Education in a Diverse Society*. Boston: Allyn & Bacon, 1995.

Harvey, Karen D., Lisa D. Harjo, and Jane K. Jackson. *Teaching About Native Americans*, Bulletin No. 84. Washington, DC: National Council for the Social Studies, 1990.

Ladson-Billings, Gloria. *The Dreamkeepers: Successful Teachers of African American Children*. San Francisco: Jossey-Bass, 1994.

Pang, Valerie Ooka. "Asian Pacific American Students: A Diverse and Complex Population. In *Handbook of Research on Multicultural Education*, edited by James A. Banks and Cherry A. McGee Banks. New York: Macmillan, 1995, 412–24.

Radencich, Marguerite C., and Lyn J. McKay. *Flexible Grouping for Literacy in the Elementary Grades*. Boston: Allyn & Bacon, 1995.

Sadker, Myra, and David Sadker. *Failing at Fairness: How America's Schools Cheat Girls*. New York: Charles Scribner's Sons, 1994.

Sleeter, Christine E., and Carl A. Grant. *Making Choices for Multicultural Education: Five Approaches to Race, Class, and Gender*, 2nd ed. New York: Macmillan, 1994.

Social Studies and the Young Learner, Vol. 7, No. 4, March/April 1995. The articles in this issue are on the theme, "Diverse Learners in the Social Studies Classroom." Included is a provocative article on "diversity taboos" (e.g., sexual orientation), by Rahima Wade.

Sunal, Cynthia Szymanski. "The Influences of the Home on Social Studies." In *Handbook of Research on Social Studies Teaching and Learning*, edited by James P. Shaver. New York: Macmillan, 1991, 290–99.

CITIZENSHIP EDUCATION AND DEMOCRATIC VALUES

OVERVIEW

We the people . . .

—Constitution of the United States

We march in the name of the Constitution.

—Martin Luther King, Jr.

After lots of talk, we decide on our rules.

—Gretchen Calkins, third grader

Citizenship education aims to prepare children for a particular relationship to one another and to the political community. While the children in a classroom will identify with diverse cultural and ethnic groups, religious beliefs, and family backgrounds, they share one political identity. This common political identity exists alongside the multiple cultural identities. It is called *democratic citizenship*, or simply *citizenship*. In American constitutional democracy, citizens are members of the nation (the United States), a state (e.g., Colorado), and local jurisdictions (Adams County; City of Northglenn; School District #12). According to the Constitution of the United States, where the legal definition of citizenship can be found, citizens are persons who were born in the United States, or who were born elsewhere and become citizens through a procedure called *naturalization*, and who are "subject to the jurisdiction thereof."

The U.S. Constitution is usually placed in fifth-grade social studies textbooks. While many teachers incorporate the Constitution into their teaching and classroom management systems long before the fifth grade, it is often during the fifth grade that children systematically study the entire Constitution. In American constitutional democracy, the Constitution is the citizen's handbook and the nation's "rule book." Typically, a summarized and paraphrased version of the Constitution is presented so that children more easily can comprehend it. One appears as the first color insert in this text following page 76. Readers should note that it contains all the parts: the preamble, seven articles in which are written the rules by which citizens agree to live, and twenty-six changes or additions, called amendments. The first ten amendments, recall, are together called the Bill of Rights.

In one's role as citizen, one owes allegiance to the nation and is entitled to its protection. Citizens enjoy rights and liberties, such as freedom of religion, press, and speech. They also have responsibilities and obligations, which range from paying taxes and voting in elections to monitoring public officials, influencing public policy, working with others to change laws when they are wrong, and perhaps even sacrificing one's life for the state or nation as a police officer or soldier.

Why Citizenship Education?

It may seem obvious that education for democratic citizenship is a worthwhile educational goal. Indeed, most school districts in the United States include it in their mission statements. Yet, it often gets overlooked amid the tremendous pressure to increase students' math and reading scores. Also, it is sometimes assumed that the knowledge and skills citizens need are by-products of the study of other school subjects. Alas, this is wishful thinking.

Democracy is a fragile system of living together. The knowledge, character, and skills citizens need for it do not emerge without education. In a talk to teachers some years ago, writer and social critic James Baldwin warned that if children are not educated to live democratically, then they may well become apathetic or worse: They could become the next generation of people to sponsor a Holocaust such as the one in Germany in the 1930s and 1940s. The perpetrators of that crime against humanity had been very well educated and knew a great deal about reading, writing, literature, math, and science. They may have been *smart*, but they were not *good*. They used their knowledge and skills to build not only great works of art and architecture, but concentration camps and human incinerators. In spite of all that education, they could not live democratically. Instead, they swore allegiance to a tyrant and committed great, unimaginable atrocities against humanity. "The boys and girls who were born during the era of the Third Reich," Baldwin said, "when educated to the purposes of the Third Reich, became barbarians."[1]

Democracy requires that we educate children to the purposes of democracy, and those purposes require of citizens great character and civility: the ability to reason in principled ways, for example; the possession of a deep appreciation of democratic values such as liberty, the common good, justice, and equality; the ability to think critically, to resolve disputes in nonviolent ways, to stay informed on issues of the day; the disposition to insist on other people's rights, not only one's own rights, to cooperate with persons with whom one may not want to cooperate, to tolerate religious and political views different from one's own and, indeed, to insist on the free expression of those views, as in the great democratic slogan attributed to French writer Voltaire, "I disapprove of what you say, but I will defend to the death your right to say it."

That's a tall order! What can elementary school teachers do? *They can do plenty, and it is surprisingly easy.* As Polly Greenberg writes in *Young Children*, "Democracy is full of problems waiting to be solved." Teachers can encourage children continually to solve small problems. They can form the habit of saying to a cluster of young children, "How can we solve this problem?" "What should we do?" "What's your idea?"[2] Such questions nurture cooperative discussion, decision making, and individual responsibility which, together, are *the* basic practices of democracy. Each primary grade classroom should have "the rug." The rug, according to elementary school principal Ethel Sadowsky, is "a spot where children gather on the first day of school to formulate the rules that will govern the classroom."[3] The rug is also used throughout the year as a place to discuss current problems and concerns. These may be children's complaints about one another's behavior ("She wouldn't let me play with them."), teamwork problems ("He never lets anybody else talk!"), or fairness issues ("It's not right that the row closest to the door always gets to the playground first!").

Citizenship Education Approaches

There is general consensus in constitutional democracies that citizens need to be educated to understand and participate in majority rule, respect minority rights, seek the common good, protect one another's freedoms, and limit the size and scope of government. Still, wide leeway is left to teachers: Some teachers conceptualize the citizen role mainly as one of voting and compliance with authorities. Accordingly, they teach and reward these behaviors, equating courteousness and obedience with good citizenship. Other teachers define the role in broader, more active and participatory terms. They teach students how to deliberate public policy, join in civic decision making, and engage in public service.

We recommend the second approach (see Figure 3–1). In the early elementary grades, this means bringing children to the circle or "the rug" (some teachers call it *community meeting* or *town meeting*) to discuss common problems and concerns and to help decide on the rules by which they will agree to live in the classroom and the school. Also, it means providing children with opportunities to cooperate with others in order to help care for the broader community; that is, to become *civic-minded*. Canned food drives, as simple as they are, give children the opportunity to care for people they do not know, yet to whom they are related as members of the same community. Within the classroom, committees of children can decide how to welcome new students and orient them to the playground, lunchroom, bathrooms, library, and bicycle racks.

Alongside these basic participatory practices must go three more key ingredients of democratic citizenship education: knowledge, democratic values, and character traits, also known as virtues or dispositions. Without these, children's participation will be less effective and could even do more harm than good. We turn now to each of these elements of citizenship education.

Figure 3–1
Elements of democratic citizenship education.

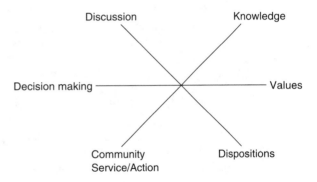

Discussion

Discussion is one of the most important foundations of democratic citizenship. Contrary to old sayings such as "Talk is cheap" or "Actions speak louder than words," discussion should be appreciated as a wonderful and constructive alternative to violence. When children learn to talk through their disagreements on the playground and in the classroom—explaining, negotiating, compromising, forgiving—then they are making significant progress toward democratic citizenship. The ancient Greeks, who first experimented with democratic living, were in awe of the power of discussion. Athenian leader Pericles said, "Instead of seeing discussion as a stumbling block in the way of action, we think it an indispensable preliminary to any wise action at all." Discussion is not merely better than fighting; *discussion leads to wise action.*

Discussion skills do not necessarily develop on their own; they need to be taught and learned. Teachers can let children know that when they are brought to the rug, they need to practice the skills of good discussion. These can be posted—listen as well as talk; encourage others to participate; criticize ideas rather than people; back up opinions with information and reasons. Such skills can be taught using a good skills-teaching procedure involving instruction and role-playing, such as the one in Chapter 7.

Rather than posting skills, some teachers prefer to elicit them from students. Tarry Lindquist, for example, an elementary teacher in the Seattle area, describes her method of elicitation:

I often start out in September by asking the class to brainstorm all the things we could do to make our classroom a terrible place, a place where no one would want to come, a place where we could guarantee no learning would occur.

As we list the surefire ways to kill a classroom, each suggestion more outrageous than the last, we begin to build a community. Eventually, when we have exhausted our efforts, most sincere and many hilarious, I ask the class to picture a room like the one we've just described. I ask them, "What would you know if you stayed in a classroom like that one all year? What would you be able to do? How would you feel?" After that discussion, it doesn't take long to reverse the list, identifying what needs to happen to make our classroom a place of joy where all students want to be and where all students can learn.[4]

Mrs. Lindquist goes on to create with her students a sort of mini-constitution—a rule book or what she calls an action plan for a "peaceful classroom." After much discussion and decision making, the plan is finalized. Each child signs it, as does Mrs. Lindquist. She sends a copy home. When misbehavior occurs, she can communicate with children, and parents, with the rule book in mind. "Do you recall the action plan we signed at the beginning of the year?" she might say to parents. "I am concerned that Nancy doesn't seem to be able to help the class reach this goal. Specific things about Nancy's behavior that have prompted my concern are. . . . " Mrs. Lindquist can now describe the behavior problem with reference to specific agreements written in the plan, such as "we are respectful of others" and "we listen and pay attention."

Another mentor on the art of conducting rich discussions with even the youngest children is Vivian Paley, who teaches kindergarten in Chicago. Mrs. Paley's approach is sometimes to *post* a rule for interaction, sometimes to *elicit* it from students, but most

This teacher helps young citizens search for more viewpoints to enrich their discussions.

often to *pose* a rule. She tells her children of a rule that she is considering, not one she has decreed, then engages them in an ongoing inquiry about the rule, perhaps lasting for months, and focusing on two questions: Will the rule work? Is it fair? These questions are compelling ones for the children. They have memories and opinions immediately.

Our favorite example of this process is when Mrs. Paley informed her class that she was considering a new classroom rule. She put up a poster that read, YOU CAN'T SAY "YOU CAN'T PLAY." It was greeted with disbelief, she recalls. "Only four out of twenty-five in my kindergarten class find the idea appealing, and they are the children most often rejected. The loudest in opposition are those who do the most rejecting. But everyone looks doubtful . . . "[5]

Mrs. Paley's approach to classroom discussion about rules strikes us as an elegant combination of two techniques: (1) She brings her children to the circle often for a discussion of a new rule she is planning. (2) She interviews older children to ascertain their views, then brings these views back to her kindergartners who, of course, are terribly impressed that *their* issues are of such interest to the older children.

Mrs. Paley began one discussion with her children this way. "I just can't get the question out of my mind. Is it fair for children *in school* to keep another child out of play? After all, this classroom belongs to all of us. It is not a private place, like our homes."[6] Notice here how clearly Mrs. Paley communicates that the classroom is a civic or public place and that how we conduct ourselves in such a place is somehow different. In public places, we have to be concerned with the *common good*, not just private interests. We are obliged to act with civility, to be civic-minded. "The children I teach are just emerging from life's deep wells of private perspective: babyhood and family," she says. Selfishness and jealousy are natural to both conditions. "Then, along comes school. It is the first real exposure to the public arena."[7]

Indeed, this is why discussion is important. Discussion is a *civic* practice that introduces children to the ways of behaving that are imperative if we are to have, as the Constitution calls it, "domestic tranquility" or what Mrs. Lindquist's class calls, simply, "peace."

Mrs. Paley:	Should one child be allowed to keep another child from joining a group? A good rule might be: "You can't say you can't play."
Ben:	If you cry people should let you in.
Mrs. Paley:	What if someone is not crying but feels sad? Should the teacher force children to say yes?
Many voices:	No, no.
Sheila:	If they don't want you to play they should just go their own way and you should say, "Clara, let's find someone who likes you better."
Angelo:	Lisa and her should let Clara in. . . .[8]

Soon, Mrs. Paley trades classes with a second-grade teacher for a little while. She asks those children's opinions about her class's plan. "I've come to ask your opinions about a new rule we're considering in the kindergarten. . . . We call it, 'You can't say you can't play.'" These older children know full well the issue she is talking about. Examples and some vivid accounts of rejection spill from their mouths. They are fully engaged in the discussion because it is a problem that they both recognize and feel. Many children believe it *is* a fair rule, but that it just will not work: "It would be impossible to have any fun," offers one boy.

Later, while interviewing a fourth-grade class, she gets the hunch that girls believe that exclusion is primarily *their* problem. The boys listen intently as the girls give examples, Mrs. Paley observes, "their eyes moving from speaker to speaker. I point to one of the boys and ask, 'Do you think rejection is more of a girl's problem?' 'No, I don't,' he says."[9] He gives examples of his own. The discussion continues. Eventually the fourth-graders conclude that it is "too late" in their lives to give them such a rule. "If you want a rule like that to work, start at a very early age," declares one fourth-grader. "Yeah, start it in kindergarten," someone says. "Because they'll believe *you* that it's a *rule*. You know, a law."[10]

Mrs. Paley takes these views back to the discussion circle in her own classroom. Her children listen, enthralled, to her retelling of the older children's thinking. They often revise their opinions as a consequence of hearing one another's arguments. In the Socratic spirit, gently, Mrs. Paley is forever challenging them to develop opinions of their own, to support their views with reasons, and to listen carefully and respond to the reasoning of other children, classmates and older children alike.

Listening to Diverse Views

This last detail is important: listening carefully to the reasoning of other children. Why does this matter? Sadowsky reminds us that "children learn from peers who are thinking in different ways and at different levels."[11] This is the miracle of a good discussion about an engaging problem *with a diverse group of children*. Research has shown that discussion stimulates growth in children's reasoning in important ways, and it is more likely to have this effect if each child encounters and listens to reasoning that is somewhat different from his or her own.[12] Therefore, teachers should encourage all children to speak during discussions, giving both opinions and reasons, and help all children to listen carefully to one another's opinions *and reasons*. Asking children regularly to paraphrase what others have said is a good way to build the listening habit. "Brandon, what was Neetha saying to the group?" "Jamal, were you listening as Myrna gave her reasons? Restate them for us, please." Also, when two children share the same opinion but have different reasons, help the class notice this: "You two seem to agree, but for different reasons. Who else agrees, but for yet a different reason?"

Discussions of this sort help children develop their capacity to reason about moral issues, especially issues of fairness. This is extremely important, because democratic life requires a well-developed sense of justice. To treat others as one wishes to be treated, which is hailed as a supreme level of moral maturity in the world's great religions, is an extraordinary human accomplishment representing the highest levels of character development. One way to help children move in that direction is to engage them in discussions of fairness issues of all sorts, especially those involving rules that are going to be binding on all members. Within these discussions, teachers can help children listen to and grapple with reasoning that is different from their own. This is the kind of discussion that, in Pericles' words, produces "wise action."

Assessing Discussion

We devote an entire chapter to assessment later in this book, but it should be helpful to look at this matter now. As teachers think about how they will find out what students have learned about a topic or skill, they must think about levels of proficiency or the *criteria* by which a performance can be judged. These criteria then serve as the objectives of instruction.

Social studies educators in Oakland County, Michigan, have done some very careful thinking about this and developed a guide for assessing the quality of a child's participation in discussions of civic issues.* A civic issue, recall, is a *public* issue—an issue that "we the people" face in common. Public issues range all the way from "How shall we behave toward one another in our classroom?" and "Shall we have a rule that you can't exclude classmates from your play?" to the major policy issues that confront our communities today: Who is responsible for the poor? Are affirmative action policies fair? Should our students be tested for drug use before they can play team sports? What can be done about hate crimes? Teenage suicide? Teenage pregnancy? The epidemic of homelessness?

---

* David Harris is the social studies curriculum coordinator for the Oakland County, Michigan, schools. A full description of this scoring guide appears in his chapter in *Handbook on Teaching Social Issues*, edited by Ronald Evans and David Saxe (Washington, DC: National Council for the Social Studies, in press).

The Oakland County assessment emphasizes two dimensions of discussion. The substantive dimension refers to the content of children's contribution to the discussion—the knowledge and information they bring to it, their ability to support opinions with reasons and analogies, and so forth. The procedural dimension includes the ways children participate—whether they invite others to contribute, for example, or make negative statements that inhibit others from participating. Figure 3–2 lists the substantive and procedural guidelines, and Table 3–1 arranges these into four levels of quality. An unacceptable performance in a discussion would mean that, on the substantive dimension, a child remained silent or made only irrelevant comments, and, on the procedural dimension, the child made no comments to help the conversation along or made statements that lacked civility—they were negative in character.

A highly skillful contribution to the group discussion, on the other hand, is characterized by making no comments that inhibit other students' participation, *and* the child intervenes if others do this. Moreover, the child engages in sustained dialogue with others, both talking and listening. On the substantive side, this child weighs multiple perspectives and considers what is best for everyone—the common good. Moreover, this child uses higher-order participation skills, such as drawing analogies and summarizing what has been said.

Teachers use this scoring guide to assess their students' current discussion abilities and, just as important, to help them plan instruction. Perhaps a teacher will decide to

Figure 3–2

Performance criteria for discussing public issues.

Source: David Harris, "Assessing Discussion of Public Issues," in *Handbook on Teaching Social Issues*, ed. Ronald Evans and David Saxe (Washington, DC: National Council for the Social Studies, in press). Reprinted by permission.

THE SUBSTANTIVE DIMENSION
+ States and identifies issues
+ Brings knowledge to the discussion
+ Specifies claims or definitions
+ Elaborates statements with explanations, reasons, and evidence
+ Recognizes values or value conflict
+ Argues by analogy

THE PROCEDURAL DIMENSION
Positive
+ Acknowledges the statements of others
+ Challenges the accuracy, logic, relevance, or clarity of statements
+ Summarizes points of agreement and disagreement
+ Invites contributions from others

Negative
− Makes irrelevant, distracting statements
− Interrupts
− Monopolizes the conversation
− Engages in personal attack

Table 3–1
Scoring guide for assessing students' participation in discussions of public issues.

	Exemplary (3)	Adequate (2)	Minimal (1)	Unacceptable (0)
SUBSTANTIVE	Weighs multiple perspectives on a policy issue and considers the public good; or uses relevant knowledge to analyze an issue, or employs a higher order discussion strategy, such as argument by analogy, stipulation, or resolution of a value conflict.	Demonstrates knowledge of important ideas related to the issue, or explicitly states an issue for the group to consider, or presents more than one viewpoint, or supports a position with reasons or evidence.	Makes statements about the issue that express only personal attitudes, or mentions a potentially important idea but does not pursue it in a way that advances the group's understanding.	Remains silent, or contributes no thoughts of his or her own, or makes only irrelevant comments.
PROCEDURAL	Engages in more than one sustained interchange, or summarizes and assesses the progress of the discussion. Makes no comments that inhibit others' contributions and intervenes if others do this.	Engages in an extended interchange with at least one other person, or paraphrases important statements as a transition or summary, or asks another person for an explanation or clarification germane to the discussion. Does not inhibit others' contributions.	Invites contributions implicitly or explicitly, or responds constructively to ideas expressed by at least one other person. Tends not to make negative statements.	Makes no comments that facilitate dialogue, or makes statements that are primarily negative in character.

teach the difference between positive and negative comments, followed by a lesson on how to encourage other children to participate and how to respond constructively to ideas they offer. Assessment guides of this sort, called *scoring rubrics* or *rating scales*, can be enormously helpful in planning instruction.

A much simpler discussion rating scale is shown in Figure 3–3. Teachers in the primary grades may wish to use this guide. Likewise, teachers in the intermediate grades may wish to use it until they become more adept at talking with children about the more ambitious discussion guidelines used in Oakland County. Discussion is important to democratic citizenship. Accordingly, teachers should use assessment procedures that will ensure high standards for their children's discussions.

Figure 3–3
Rating scale for discussion.

(Primary Grades)	Always	Sometimes	Not Often
1. Helps make plans			
2. Listens to what is said			
3. Takes turns			
4. Gives own ideas			
5. Considers what others have said			

Decision Making

For many teachers, it is enough to engage students in discussions of classroom rules and problems as well as community and world events. These discussions naturally revolve around decisions: Which rule? Which plan of action? What should we do? We recommend going further, however, to include teaching the decision-making process directly.

There are three reasons for this. First, as we saw in Chapter 2, teachers must provide explicit instruction on the topics and skills they expect their students to demonstrate. Direct instruction on the decision-making process can enable all children to "hold the office of citizen" and care for the community.

Second, the decision-making process offers many opportunities for higher order thinking. When children ferret out all the alternatives for a particular decision and predict the consequences of each alternative, they are engaged in several important intellectual processes that will enable them to be more thoughtful citizens.

Third, the decision-making process offers opportunities for values education as well. Groups and individuals choose an alternative typically because they value its consequences more than the others; similarly, conflicts can arise when values differ. Budding citizens in a diverse society need many opportunities to examine and wrestle with value conflicts, for they are an inevitable part of democratic life.

Teaching Decision Making

Children can be taught the decision-making process in four phases. Older children probably will not need to begin with the first phase.

First, the teacher helps children become aware of decisions and decision making. The children themselves make many decisions each day, as does their teacher. Decisions are being made throughout the school and community. Some of the decisions are *political*—that is, decisions about rules and laws by which "we the people" agree to live. Others are *social*, concerning fund raising for charities or welcoming new students to school. Still others are *personal*: What shall I wear? How should I spend my allowance?

Second, the teacher helps children "crawl inside" a decision, so to speak, in order to make a visual representation of it—a decision map. Decision maps show all the parts of a decision in relationship to each other: the occasion for the decision (usually called the problem), the array of alternatives that could be considered, and the consequences of each alternative.

Third, the teacher models good decision making for children. Standing in front of a decision map sketched on the chalkboard, the teacher can talk about how he or she decided on the next unit of study, for example, or how to handle a difficult class problem. In this way, children see a decision being made thoughtfully.

Fourth, the teacher can provide opportunities for students to practice decision making. The opportunities are too numerous to list here, but key areas are decisions about classroom rules and issues; decisions about classroom management (clean-up, play time, cooperative group work, work habits); and decisions about subject matter: Which reference resources will be best for this project? Will you use the tools to build a tower or a bridge? Will you make a model of Mt. Everest or Pikes Peak? Will you write about Harriet Tubman or Susan Anthony?

Lesson Plan 1 is geared to the first and second phases of decision-making instruction. Notice that it teaches the design of basic decision maps while building children's awareness of the decisions they and others make.

When it comes time in the second phase to introduce children to the skill of predicting consequences, two focus questions are helpful for organizing the lessons.[12] First, what might be the consequences (effects) of each alternative on all the persons involved? This question focuses students' attention on each alternative and its possible consequences. It challenges students to think in terms of everyone's interests, not just their own. Second, will the alternative help or hinder the realization of democratic values, such as liberty, the common good, and fairness? *This question asks students purposefully to bring the ideals of democracy into the heart of decision making.* These values can act as powerful screening tools, causing children to reject an alternative because it curtails someone's liberty unnecessarily or unequally, or because it fails to take the welfare of the whole community into consideration.

Student teams can be created to do this work on each alternative. Team 1 is asked to work with Alternative 1, Team 2 with Alternative 2, and so on. As readers can see, decision making is challenging intellectual work, especially when students take seriously the task of predicting consequences. A more elaborate decision map in the form of a decision tree is shown in Figure 3–4. Notice that it includes positive and negative consequences for each alternative.

Community Service and Action

The real test of a social studies program comes in the out-of-school lives of children. If the school has provided them new insights, improved skills, and increased civic-mindedness, such learning should be apparent in their out-of-school behavior now as children and later as adults. One way to help bridge citizenship learning in school with citizenship experiences in the community and the world is through community-service activities.

This kind of participation can be social or political in nature. If children are concerned with vandalism of school property, for example, they might volunteer to clean up and repair some of the damage. This is social action. But if they propose new rules

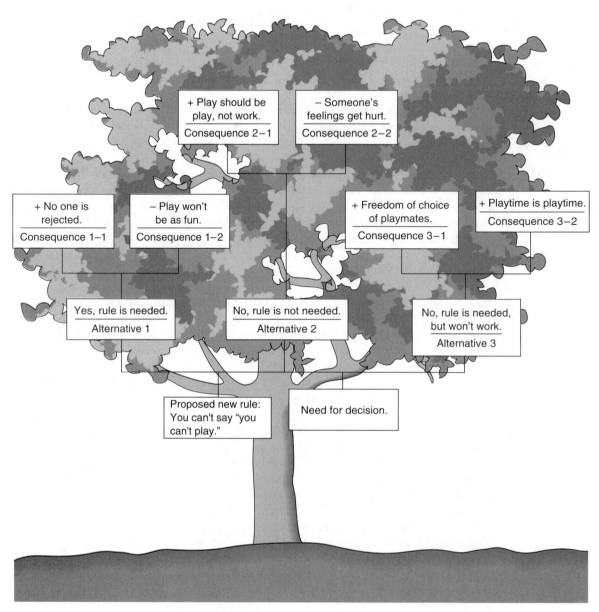

Figure 3-4
A decision tree sample.

to officials or request stronger enforcement of existing rules, this is political action. Both social and political action by citizens are important for the health of democratic communities. As Supreme Court Justice Louis Brandeis said early in this century, "The greatest menace to freedom is an inert people."

Community service activities can be spontaneous and short-lived, such as when the children learn of a fire at a nearby house and collect canned goods and clothing for the family. Activities can also be planned systematically and sustained over a longer period of time, such as the adoption of a creek or a section of the school grounds.

Lesson Plan 1

Making a Decision Tree

Grade
1–3

Time
One class period

Objectives
Children will become aware of the numerous decisions they make every day and the alternatives that are considered in each decision. They will learn a way to "map" such decisions.

Interest Building
Remind students of a lively discussion they had recently about a rule, such as deciding on a rule for sharing books or playground equipment. Ask them to recall what was decided. Help them remember the alternatives (choices, options) that were considered. As they recall the alternatives, record them on the chalkboard using a "decision map" such as this:

Lesson Development

1.   Ask students to think of all the decisions they have made so far today. Help them recall some: Whether to get up early or late; whether to have cereal, toast, or something else; what to wear; what to do upon arriving at the school building; whether to get to class early or just when the bell rang, and so forth. Record these on butcher paper and post.

2.   Explain that decision making means choosing among alternatives. Select a few decisions that will not invade anyone's privacy, such as what to do upon arriving at school and whether to get to class early. Have the class help you map one of these decisions on the chalkboard, similar to the way you did this in the introduction. Then put children in pairs and ask them to map one or two more of these decisions. Ask the pairs to share their maps with the class.

Assessment

3.   Because you have been using the terms up to this point in the lesson, most children should by now have some understanding of their meaning. Check those understandings now. Ask several children for a definition of *decision* and *alternative*. Ask several others to suggest examples. Provide explanations as necessary.

4.   Build awareness of decisions that others make. Ask one pair of children to make a list of the decisions they think the school principal might make in a typical day; ask another pair to list the decisions the mayor might make; to other pairs, assign community helpers: the librarian, the curator of a museum, an athletics coach, an orchestra

conductor, a police officer, a doctor, a firefighter, an ambulance driver, a health inspector, a newspaper delivery person.

Summary and Assessment

Ask each pair to decide on one decision to share from step 4 above. As each pair shares, listen for any misunderstandings and provide explanations as needed. As they share, diagram each decision on a decision map. Post these on a bulletin board called "Decisions in Our Community."

Follow-up

Ask the children to tell brief stories about *courageous* decisions that someone has had to make. Probe for the alternatives that person may have considered. Make decision maps for the decisions and alternatives. As the weeks go by, have children make more decision maps based on material they are studying in math, science, and literature, as well as social studies.

Materials

Posters and marker for decision maps in summary. Also, if children have difficulty coming up with stories of courageous decision makers, you may want to have some ready. You can draw on current news stories, literature the children are reading, and exciting historical examples: Harriet Tubman's decision to continue the underground railroad despite great dangers, the Pilgrims' decision to sail for America, Jefferson's decision to write the Declaration of Independence.

Examples of Community Service

The following projects have been done by real kids in real communities. Note that some are social, some are political, and some are both.

Saving a Creek

The children at an elementary school near Everett, Washington, decided to do something about a dirty little stream named Pigeon Creek. The children were alarmed that Pigeon Creek had become so dirty that salmon stopped coming there to lay their eggs, so they "adopted" it.

The first thing the children did was to get an aquarium for their classroom. They raised thousands of salmon eggs. Meanwhile, they worked with people in their community to clean up the creek. Litter was removed and the children put up "DON'T DUMP" signs. When the eggs hatched, the students released them in Pigeon Creek and monitored the creek to keep it clean.

Getting Out the Vote

"Do you know that a lot of adults are numb? They're numb from filling out forms, balancing checkbooks, changing diapers, and changing tires. In the process, many have forgotten the principles our country was founded upon. Many don't think their votes count for anything.... Imagine what could happen if kids attacked their communities in a campaign to shake adults out of the mothballs." This is what Barbara Lewis, a Salt Lake City elementary school teacher, tells her students. Ms. Lewis wrote a book for children about social action, *The Kid's Guide to Social Action: How to Solve the Social Problems You Choose, and Turn Creative Thinking into Positive Action.*[*]

Children can be *very* influential participants in get-out-the-vote campaigns. Distributed door to door, their flyers can read: "We can't vote yet. You can. Please do." By urging adults to register and vote, children can learn about voting eligibility, voting rates, and the role voting plays in representative democracies. Hopefully, the experience will help them become regular voters themselves.

---

[*] The book is available from Free Spirit Publishing, Inc., Minneapolis, 1991. Barbara A. Lewis also wrote *The Kid's Guide to Service Projects: Over 500 Service Ideas for Young People Who Want to Make a Difference* (Free Spirit, 1995).

Teaching Senior Citizens about Computers

Clare Devine teaches at North Dover Elementary School in Toms River, New Jersey. Her students had learned about computers in the school's computer lab. They realized that many adults around them, especially older people, are nervous about working with these machines. Mrs. Devine and the children decided to offer a series of classes to seniors. Significant cooperative group work and planning were involved—both good opportunities for citizenship learning. In the computer classes, the students showed *their* "students" how to write to their grandchildren using word processing programs and how to communicate on the Internet, and they shared some of their favorite computer games.

Mrs. Devine liked how the project brought the two groups together. Did the seniors like the classes? "Yes, I think so. This year at the last class," reported Mrs. Devine, "they bought ice cream for everyone."*

Giraffes Stick Their Necks Out

Members of the Giraffe Club in LaConner Elementary School in LaConner, Washington, make this vow: "I promise to stick my neck out to make a difference. I will help people, animals, and my environment to make the world a better place to live."[14] The little giraffes do all manner of things to help people. (The address of the Giraffe organization and other resources appear in Figure 3–5.) One service they perform is gathering donations of food for people at Friendship House, a shelter for homeless people.

Other Projects

The following categories of community service projects for children have passed the test of time and can be arranged rather easily. It is important to remember that service projects require skillful behavior on the part of students. It is a good idea, therefore, for the teacher to assess children's skill levels and determine what instruction and practice is needed. Some basic skills for service projects are telephoning, letter writing, interviewing, giving speeches, conducting surveys, getting signatures on petitions, making proposals to community officials, and raising funds.

Good Neighbor Club

Middle-grade students formed a Good Neighbor Club to help elderly residents in the neighborhood with yard work and errands.

Peer Tutoring for Citizenship

Your children can help welcome new children from other lands, not only into the classroom social system, but into the processes of democratic citizenship, too. An immigrant child can be paired with an especially good citizen in your classroom—or one who needs to learn to be a better citizen. This "tutor" helps the new student learn to participate in class discussions and consider all alternatives when making a decision. Ask a resourceful

---

* Many aspects of life in Toms River are described as part of a community study conducted by the third-grade children at Toms River's Walnut Street Elementary School. The impressive community study is described in detail in the Macmillan/McGraw-Hill social studies program for grades K–7, *Adventures in Time and Place* (New York, 1996).

Summary of the
Constitution of the United States

PREAMBLE

We, the People of the United States, in Order to form a more perfect Union, establish Justice, insure domestic Tranquility, provide for the common Defense, promote the general Welfare, and secure the blessings of Liberty to ourselves and our Posterity, do ordain and establish this Constitution for the United States of America.

This is the meaning of the Preamble:

The people of the United States made the Constitution for the following reasons: (1) to set up a stronger government and a more united nation than the one that existed under the Articles of Confederation; (2) to ensure peace and justice among the people; (3) to defend the nation against enemies; (4) to help ensure the well-being of all the people; and (5) to make sure that the people of this nation will always be free.

ARTICLE 1
LEGISLATIVE BRANCH
Section 1: The Congress

The legislative branch, or Congress, makes the nation's laws. It is made up of two houses—the Senate and the House of Representatives.

Section 2: The House of Representatives

Members of the House of Representatives are elected for two-year terms. A representative must be at least 25 years old, a citizen of the United States for at least 7 years, and live in the state he or she represents.

The number of representatives a state has depends on the state's population. In order to find out how many people live in each state, the government must do a count of the population every ten years. This count is called a census.

Section 3: The Senate

The Senate is made up of two senators from each state. Each senator is elected for a six-year term. A senator must be at least 30 years old, a citizen of the United States for at least 9 years, and live in the state he or she represents.

The Vice President of the United States is in charge of the Senate but may vote only if there is a tie.

Sections 4–6: Rules

The houses of Congress set their own rules for their members. Each house must keep a record of its meetings and how each member voted.

To make sure that there is complete freedom of discussion in Congress, senators and representatives cannot be arrested for things they say while doing their jobs.

Section 7: How a Bill Becomes a Law

A suggested law, or bill, becomes a law when both houses of Congress agree to it by a majority vote and when the President signs it. If the President vetoes, or rejects, the bill, it can still become a law if both houses of Congress approve it again by a two-thirds vote.

Section 8: Powers of Congress

The powers of Congress include the power to: collect taxes; borrow money; control trade with other countries and among the states; decide how foreigners can become citizens; coin money; set up post offices; set up courts; declare war; set up an army and a navy; make all laws necessary to carry out powers granted to the government.

Sections 9–10: Powers Denied to Congress and the States

There are certain powers that Congress and the states do not have. Congress cannot, for example, spend money without telling how the money will be spent. The states cannot make treaties with other countries or coin money.

ARTICLE 2
EXECUTIVE BRANCH
Section 1: President and Vice President

The President and Vice President head the executive branch. Along with the people who work with them, their job is to carry out the laws made by Congress. They are elected for four-year terms.

The President and Vice President must be natural-born citizens and at least 35 years old, and must have lived in the United States for at least 14 years.

Sections 2–4: Powers and Duties

The President's powers and duties include: commanding the armed forces; appointing government officials; reaching agreements with other countries; and pardoning crimes. At least once a year, the President must tell Congress how the nation is doing. This is called the President's State of the Union message.

A President who commits a serious crime may be removed from office.

ARTICLE 3
JUDICIAL BRANCH
Section 1: Federal Courts

The judicial branch is made up of the Supreme Court and all other federal, or United States, courts. Federal judges are appointed for life.

Section 2: Duties

The judicial branch has the power to decide the meaning of the Constitution. It may decide if the actions of the other two branches are unconstitutional, or go against the Constitution.

Federal courts have a say in many cases, such as those having to do with the Constitution, federal laws, or disagreements between citizens from different states.

Section 3: Treason

Treason is a crime committed when a citizen of the United States betrays the country, especially in wartime.

ARTICLE 4
THE STATES
Sections 1–4: Dealings Among the States

All states must accept the actions, records, and court decisions of other states. When citizens visit another state, they must be given the same rights as citizens of the state they are visiting.

New states may be added to the United States. The United States government promises to protect the states from enemies.

ARTICLE 5
AMENDMENTS

The Constitution may be amended or changed, if Congress and three fourths of the states agree.

ARTICLE 6
SUPREME LAW, OATHS OF OFFICE, DEBTS

The Constitution of the United States is the supreme law, or the highest law, in the nation. Government officials must promise to support the Constitution. In addition, the government promised to pay back all debts owed before the Constitution was adopted.

ARTICLE 7
APPROVING THE CONSTITUTION

The Constitution was to become law when 9 of the 13 original states ratified, or approved, it. Special conventions were held for this purpose, and the process took nine months to complete.

AMENDMENTS TO THE CONSTITUTION
(The first 10 are called The Bill of Rights.)

AMENDMENT 1
Freedom of Religion, Speech, Press, Assembly, and Petition (1791)

Congress cannot make a law setting up an official religion. It cannot stop people from practicing any religion they choose. Congress cannot take away freedom of speech or of the press. Congress cannot stop groups from assembling, or meeting together, peacefully.

It cannot stop people from petitioning, or asking the government, to end an injustice.

AMENDMENT 2
Right to Keep Arms (1791)

The people have the right to keep and carry arms, or weapons.

AMENDMENT 3
Quartering Soldiers (1791)

During peacetime, people cannot be forced to quarter soldiers, or let them stay in their homes.

AMENDMENT 4
Search and Seizures (1791)

People's homes and other property cannot be searched and seized unless the police have a search warrant.

AMENDMENT 5
Rights of Accused Persons (1791)

People who are accused of a crime cannot be forced to testify, or give evidence, against themselves. Their lives, freedom, or property cannot be taken away from them unfairly. The government may take a person's property for public use only if the person is paid for it.

AMENDMENT 6
Jury Trial in Criminal Cases (1791)

People accused of crimes have the right to a public and speedy trial with a jury. They have the right to be told the charges against them. They have the right to have a lawyer.

AMENDMENT 7
Jury Trial in Civil Cases (1791)

In most civil, or noncriminal, cases, people have the right to a jury trial.

AMENDMENT 8
Excessive Bail or Punishment (1791)

Bail must be reasonable for people accused of a crime. Punishments may not be cruel and unusual.

AMENDMENT 9
Other Rights of the People (1791)

The people have rights in addition to those listed in the Constitution.

AMENDMENT 10
Powers of the States and the People (1791)
Powers that are not granted to the national government and not forbidden to the states are left to the state governments or to the people.

AMENDMENT 11
Suing the States (1798)
A state government can be sued only in its own courts.

AMENDMENT 12
Election of President and Vice President (1804)
Electors vote for President and Vice President on separate ballots.

AMENDMENT 13
Abolition of Slavery (1865)
Slavery is abolished, or made illegal, in the United States.

AMENDMENT 14
Rights of Citizens (1868)
Every citizen of the United States is also a citizen of the state in which he or she lives. No state may pass a law limiting the rights of citizens or take away a person's life, liberty, or property unfairly. Every person must be treated equally under the law.

AMENDMENT 15
Voting Rights (1870)
No person may be denied the right to vote because of race.

AMENDMENT 16
Income Tax (1913)
Congress has the right to tax people's incomes.

AMENDMENT 17
Direct Election of Senators (1913)
United States senators are elected directly by the people of their states.

AMENDMENT 18
Prohibition (1919)
The manufacture or transport of liquor is prohibited, or banned, in the United States.

AMENDMENT 19
Women's Voting Rights (1920)
Women cannot be denied the right to vote.

AMENDMENT 20
Terms of Office (1933)
The President and Vice President take office on January 20. Senators and representatives take office on January 3.

AMENDMENT 21
Repeal of Prohibition (1933)
Amendment 18 is repealed, or ended.

AMENDMENT 22
Two-Term Limit for Presidents (1951)
A President may serve only two terms in office.

AMENDMENT 23
Presidential Elections for District of Columbia (1961)
People who live in Washington, D.C., have the right to vote for President and Vice President.

AMENDMENT 24
Poll Tax (1964)
No citizen may be made to pay a tax in order to vote for President, Vice President, senator, or representative.

AMENDMENT 25
Presidential Succession and Disability (1967)
If a President leaves office before the end of term, the Vice President becomes President. If the Vice President leaves office, the President suggests a person to fill the job and Congress must approve. If the President becomes too ill to do the job, the Vice President becomes Acting President until the President recovers.

AMENDMENT 26
Voting Age (1971)
Citizens who are at least 18 years old have the right to vote.

AMENDMENT 27
Congressional Salaries (1992)
Congress cannot change its salary until after the next congressional election.

Figure 3–5
Community service resources.

These national resources can help teachers plan community service projects. Just as helpful are local resources. Teachers can find out about them from local officials, the local chamber of commerce, and local chapters of the 4-H, Camp Fire, Kiwanis, Rotary Club, and League of Women Voters.

American Bar Association, 541 N. Fairbanks Ct., Chicago, IL 60611–3314. Phone: (312) 988-5522.
American Red Cross, Program and Services Department, 431 18th St., N.W., Washington, DC 20006. Phone: (202) 639-3039.
American Society for the Prevention of Cruelty to Animals, Education Department, 441 E. 92nd St., New York, NY 10128. Phone: (212) 876-7700.
Boys and Girls Clubs of America, 771 First Ave., New York, NY 10017. Phone: (212) 351-5900.
Center for Civic Education, 5146 Douglas Fir Rd., Calabasas, CA 91302. Phone: (818) 591-9321.
Center for Living Democracy, RR #1 Black Fox Rd., Brattleboro, VT 05301. Phone: (802) 254-1234.
Close Up Foundation, 44 Canal Center Plaza, Arlington, VA 22314. Phone: (800) 765-3131.
Constitutional Rights Foundation, 601 S. Kingsley Dr., Los Angeles, CA 90005. Phone: (213) 487-5590.
Educators for Social Responsibility, 23 Garden St., Cambridge, MA 02139. Phone: (617) 492-1764.
Giraffe, P.O. Box 759, Langley, WA 98260. Phone: (360) 221-7989.
Habitat for Humanity, 121 Habitat St., Americus, GA 31709. Phone: (912) 924-6935.
Keep America Beautiful, Inc, Mill River Plaza, 9 W. Broad St., Stamford, CT 06902. Phone: (203) 323-8987.
Kids Against Pollution (KAP), Tenakill School, 275 High St., Closter, NJ 07624, Phone: (201) 768-1332.
National Association for Advancement of Colored People, 4805 Mt. Hope Dr., Baltimore, MD 21215-3297. Phone: (301) 358-8900.
Volunteers of America, Inc, 3813 N. Causeway Blvd., Metairie, LA 70002. Phone: (504) 837-2652.

parent to obtain a copy of the citizenship test preparation booklet from the federal court-house. The peer tutor can go over the items with the new student, explaining ideas, people, and places (e.g., national and local elections, representatives, and Washington, D.C.).

Adopt a Part of the School

Frustrated by vandalism and litter on school grounds, fifth-grade children surveyed other students in the school to determine how many regarded this as a pressing problem. Results in hand, they wrote a proposal to the principal. Upon its approval, the children divided up the grounds by the number of classrooms in their school. Then they mounted a campaign to persuade each class to adopt one section of the school grounds as its own, regularly picking up the litter and painting over vandals' marks.

Civic Letter Writing

On a walk around the school, a second-grade class noticed that a main sidewalk was so badly damaged that children on their way to and from school had to walk into the street to avoid it. The class had practiced writing five kinds of letters: letters of support, letters giving information, letters requesting something, letters disagreeing with an action or opinion, and persuasive letters. They debated which kind was best for the current situation, eventually deciding to draft a letter to the city council *informing* it of the problem and *requesting* a repair.

Public Information Campaigns

Students can create posters and flyers for the school and neighborhood. These should be informational in nature, educating the reader about a problem and suggesting possible or proven solutions the students think others should know about. Possibilities are fire safety in the home and at camp grounds, poison products in the home, and pet safety.

One group of fourth-graders was studying pollution problems in each region of the United States as part of their U.S. geography curriculum. One student brought to class an article from the newspaper about the things that can pollute their front yards—weed killers and chemical fertilizers. Children playing in the yard and pets rolling in the grass can come into contact with these chemicals and track them into the house. They may develop rashes and become ill. These students produced a flyer that described the problem, listed information resources, and suggested remedies:

1. Water the lawn once a day for two days before allowing people or pets on it.
2. Take your shoes off before entering the house.
3. Don't use "weed and feed" products, which spread weed killer even where there are no weeds. Instead, pull weeds or use a spot sprayer.

The children printed the flyers and distributed them to the houses or apartments near their homes. Children, of course, should never to go door to door without an adult supervisor. When this poses a difficulty, teachers rely on the classroom newsletter to get the word out to parents, school board members, and others on the class's mailing list.

Knowledge

We have examined three categories of participatory democracy: discussing common concerns, making decisions, and taking action in the community. If children learned to be good discussants, decision makers, and community servants, that would be terrific. But there is something better: knowledgeable discussants, knowledgeable decision makers, and knowledgeable community servants. When participants possess a rich storehouse of knowledge about democracy, their discussions and decisions are more

Citizens gather information about the issue at hand, then revise their positions as needed.

intelligent and their service projects more effective. As James Madison, fourth president of the United States, wrote in 1788, "A people who mean to be their own governors must arm themselves with the power knowledge gives."

Informed participants have a keen respect for the facts. They are disposed to listen to facts rather than to prejudices, stereotypes, or the first thought that comes to mind. Moreover, they have learned ideas, examples, and analogies from their studies of other peoples' experience—people who may have lived long ago and far away. History is one of democracy's best teachers. Knowing, for example, that other democracies have collapsed into hatred and tyranny when the people became apathetic is powerful information. Knowing only this much will motivate some children to mount a voter registration campaign in the school neighborhood.

The field of history is not the only source of subject matter for democratic citizenship. Geography, economics, sociology, and anthropology provide much relevant material, too. We deal with these in the next few chapters, so let us here concentrate on the core knowledge of democratic citizenship: knowledge of civic life, politics, and government.

We are *not* saying that this knowledge of democracy needs to be learned first, before democratic participation experiences begin. As anyone who spends time with young children knows, this would never work, even if it were a good idea. Children need to "learn as they go," experientially: identifying problems, discussing and debating them, defining them further; doing research and listening to stories to answer questions that were raised; then returning for more discussion, then more learning, and so on. In the midst of decision making, for example, when children realize they can identify only two alternatives, they are driven to do more research until they can describe several alternatives and how each affects various people in a diverse society. Participation skills and knowledge go hand in hand.

Key Citizenship Ideas

Ideas, or what we shall know more precisely as *concepts* and *generalizations* in Chapter 7, are the cornerstones of social studies education generally and democratic citizenship in particular. *Democratic* is an idea, as is *citizenship*. Ideas are the basic mental tools that human beings think with and about. Without them, problem solving, reflection, and living could not proceed. Imagine going to the grocery store without the benefit of such ideas as *nutrition, cost,* or *fresh*.

Identifying the key ideas that children should develop for a life of citizenship is a task to which teachers need to devote a good deal of time. Fortunately, good advice is available. As we saw in Chapter 1, several sets of curriculum standards have been published. One of these, published by the National Council for the Social Studies,[15] includes *civic ideals and practices* as one of ten subject-matter themes for the social studies curriculum. Examining the expectations for the early grades related to this theme, we can see that emphasis is given to several ideas:

- democratic government
- relationship of public policies to stated ideals of democratic government
- common good
- actions that can influence public policy
- rights and responsibilities of citizens

Another helpful source of citizenship ideas is the book of curriculum standards for civics and government.[16] Among the ideas to which this resource gives emphasis are those listed in the citizenship glossary in Figure 3–6. Teachers can help children develop these ideas by providing examples of them drawn from children's literature, the newspaper, and the social studies textbook, then helping children see the similarities among the examples. This teaching procedure, called *concept formation*, will be explained in Chapter 7.

Citizenship Values

Children need to understand that democratic ideas and practices as they have developed in the United States rest on a foundation of democratic values. Values are a unique kind of idea. They are ideas about the worth of some behavior, person, place, or thing. Values define for us what is worth striving for, what is right and desirable, what is important, what is preferred, what constitutes worthy life goals, what may be worth sacrificing one's life for. Like other ideas, values are abstract conceptions and, therefore, cannot be observed directly. Democratic values include the individual rights to life, liberty, and the pursuit of happiness; the public or common good; justice; equality

Figure 3–6

A glossary for democratic citizenship.

Bill of Rights. First ten amendments to the Constitution. Ratified in 1791, these amendments limit governmental power and protect basic rights and liberties of individuals.

Citizenship. Status of being a member of a state; one who owes allegiance to the government and is entitled to its protection and to political rights.

Civil rights. Protection and privileges given to all U.S. citizens by the Constitution and Bill of Rights.

Civil rights movements. Continuing efforts to gain the enforcement of the rights guaranteed to all citizens by the Constitution.

Common or public good. Benefit or interest of a politically organized society as a whole.

Constitutionalism. Idea that the powers of government should be distributed according to a written or unwritten constitution and that those powers should be effectively restrained by the constitution's provisions.

Democracy. Form of government in which political control is exercised by all the people, either directly or through their elected representatives.

Due process of law. Right of every citizen to be protected against arbitrary action by government.

Equal protection of the law. Idea that no individual or group may receive special privileges from nor be unjustly discriminated against by the law.

Founders. People who played important roles in the development of the national government of the United States. *Framers* are delegates to Philadelphia in 1787 who wrote the Constitution.

Freedom of expression. Refers to the freedom of speech, press, assembly, and petition that are protected by the First Amendment.

Freedom of religion. Freedom to worship as one pleases.

Government. Institutions and procedures through which a territory and its people are ruled.

Justice. Fair distribution of benefits and burdens, fair corrections of wrongs and injuries, or use of fair procedures in gathering information and making decisions.

Limited government. Constitutional government; a government created by the people to protect their individual rights and promote the common good. The opposite is *totalitarian* government.

Loyal opposition. Idea that opposition to a government is legitimate; organized opponents to the government of the day.

Politics. Process by which a group of people, whose opinions and interests are divergent, reach decisions that are binding on the group and enforced.

Representative democracy. Form of government in which power is held by the people and exercised indirectly through elected representatives who make decisions.

Rule of law. Principle that every member of a society, even a ruler, must follow the law.

Separation of powers. Division of governmental power among several institutions that must cooperate in decision making.

Suffrage. Right to vote.

Source: Adapted from *National Standards for Civics and Government* (Calabasas, CA: Center for Civic Education, 1994): 151–156. Reprinted by permission.

of opportunity; diversity; and responsibility. There is general agreement among the people of American society that such things are valuable. They are judged positively and are widely believed to be worth nurturing in our children. We saw in Chapter 1 that the Baltimore County schools selected 24 democratic values as the core of their character education program.

Democratic values are *public* or *general* values. They are expressed in our great public documents, such as the Declaration of Independence, the Constitution of the United States, the Bill of Rights, and the speeches of Martin Luther King, Jr., Abraham Lincoln, and many others. Individuals who lead exemplary lives that reflect these general values are extolled as national heroes.

If children are to be socialized in accordance with these general values of society, they must be provided with examples of behavior that illustrate these values in action. That is, young people need to have encounters with idealized types—persons who illustrate by their way of life the values that society rewards and likes to see in its citizens. It is because these general values are internalized by the majority of citizens that orderly social life can take place. We expect our fellow citizens to behave in ways that are predictable and consistent with the basic premises inherent in those values on which there is general consensus. Law enforcement agencies are provided to protect society from the minority of persons who cannot or will not live in accordance with the general values embraced by the majority. But no police force could possibly monitor the behavior of all citizens if they were not willing to comply voluntarily with the accepted rules of the society.

These voluntary ways of being were called *virtues* by the framers of the Constitution. If there is no virtue in the people, James Madison believed, then no amount of law, government, or police power will protect them from one another.

Lesson plan 2, dealing with symbolic values, provides a good example of a lesson based on public or general values. These values are promoted through social studies in the following ways:

1. Daily life in the classroom that stresses consideration for others, freedom and equality, independence of thought, individual responsibility for one's actions, and the dignity of individual human beings.
2. The study of the history and development of this country stressing the ideals that inspired it and showing that a continuing effort is needed to move reality closer to those ideals.
3. The study of biographies of individuals whose lives reflect the general values of the nation.
4. The study of law, the justice system, and the U.S. Constitution.
5. The celebration of holidays that reinforce values and ideals associated with the holiday (Veterans Day, Fourth of July).
6. Thoughtful analysis of the meaning of such statements as the Pledge of Allegiance, the Preamble to the Constitution, and the Bill of Rights.
7. Building awareness of situations that are not in accord with values to which this society is committed.
8. Cross-cultural studies to illustrate differences in values from one society to another.

Lesson Plan 2

Symbolic Values

Grade
6

Time
One class period

Objectives
Children will deduce certain information about a country from symbols placed on its coins. Children will relate the symbols to basic values of that country.

Resources
At least one coin for each child, preferably coins or facsimiles of coins, from several different nations.

Lesson Development

Teacher: Boys and girls, for the past few days we have been studying the use of signs and symbols. At the close of our discussion yesterday we came to an important conclusion. What was it?

Child: We said that we could tell what people considered to be important to them by the symbols and signs they use on their buildings.

Teacher: Yes. Now today you will have a chance to test that idea in a slightly different way. Each of you will be given a coin to use. Study the coin carefully and see how many things you can tell about the country just from what you see on the coin.

Coins are distributed to the class. After they have had time to make their observations, ask the children what they have concluded. As these are presented, write them on the chalkboard. Have each child tell *why* the conclusion was made. Pass the coins about for other children to inspect. Items such as the following may surface in this discussion:

These people believe in God.

They want (or believe in) liberty.

They are able to read their language.

Men must be more important than women in this country.

They construct large buildings.

They speak more than one language.

It is an old country.

They have a queen (or king).

They are a peace-loving people.

They are proud of their wars and war heroes.

They want people to be courageous.

Assessment

Imagine that the United States is planning to issue a new coin and there is a contest to get the best design. You decide to enter the contest. The rules are these:

1. Write down two ideas that best describe what people in our country think are important to them.
2. Think of and draw symbols that could be used on a coin to show these two qualities.

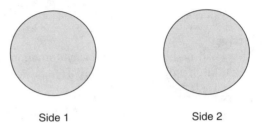

Side 1   Side 2

As we move from public values to *personal* values, the role of social studies becomes considerably different and, to some extent, less clear. Personal values are those values that influence the decision making of individuals in their own personal lives. To some extent they represent individual interpretations of general values, that is, the integrating of general values in the personal life of each individual. However, they also refer simply to what individuals like or want to do—preferring films to television, blue to yellow, bicycling to jogging.

Modern life in affluent, industrialized societies involves an incredible amount of choice making: how to spend our time, what career to choose, what clothes to buy and to wear, where to live, what brand products to buy, what hobbies and leisure-time activities to pursue, and how to spend our money. The list could go on and on to include literally every facet of our lives. Each of these decisions is an expression of individual preferences. This is really what personal values are all about—decision making concerning our personal lives.

Citizenship Dispositions: Character

Dispositions or character traits are closely related to values. They are a person's habits or inclinations that, in a way, summarize a person's behavior and values. One may value honesty and courage, for example, but only rarely behave honestly and courageously. On the other hand, if we describe a person as honest and courageous, we mean that generally he or she exhibits these traits or is inclined to behave these ways. Such behavior has become a *habit*, or part of this person's character.

Teaching children in a way that helps them develop positive dispositions is what many today call *character education*. Others call it *moral* or *values education*, terms often used interchangeably. Whatever we call it, it is a long-standing tradition in Amer-

Figure 3–7
Traits of democratic character.

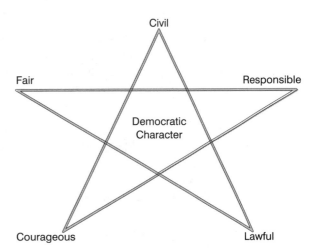

ican education (Figure 3–7). Edward A. Wynne calls it the "great tradition" and points out that "the transmission of moral values has been the dominant educational concern of most cultures throughout history."[17]

What character traits are important to democratic citizenship? Perhaps the most important are individual responsibility and civility. Individual responsibility is the habit of fulfilling one's obligations to family, friends, teachers, and other citizens in one's community and nation. Civility is the habit of treating other persons courteously and respectfully, regardless of whether one likes them, agrees with their viewpoints, or shares their cultural or religious beliefs. *Un*civilized behavior is summed up by such terms as *rude, bigoted, ill-mannered, criminal*, and *hateful*. The willingness to listen generously to others, asking for clarification and elaboration, especially to persons one may not know well or want especially to be friends with, is a hallmark of civility. If people are to walk the democratic path together, they must behave with civility toward one another.

Courage is another important democratic disposition. Courage is the habit of standing up for one's convictions when conscience demands. For young and older children alike, courage is required when "everybody is doing it," but one knows in one's heart that it is wrong. This applies to cheating, stealing, teasing, illicit drug use, lying—all the very real temptations of social interaction. Bringing children to the circle for a discussion of courage can be a wonder-filled event for the teacher who is curious about children's character development.

There are other democratic dispositions: Being lawful and fairminded, respecting the rights of others, being critical minded, and being patriotic—these are surely important. And no list of democratic dispositions is complete without honesty. "Honest Abe" Lincoln is an honored figure in American history, largely to due his reputation for truth telling; and whether or not George Washington actually chopped down that cherry tree, the famous line "I cannot tell a lie" resonates in the American citizen's value system. "Throw the rascals out" is not an uncommon American attitude toward elected representatives, bred by cases of dishonesty in office. The mere thought that a politician is corrupt or that the military academy cadet has cheated is sufficiently jarring to make the evening news. Teachers can help children develop the *habit* of honesty by exhibiting it themselves, pointing it out in those who model it, and giving children plenty of opportunities to discuss with one another, in the style of Mrs. Paley earlier in this chapter, the challenge of being honest when "nobody else was" or when it was easier to avoid punishment by lying or cheating.

Religion and the Social Studies

"The schools' silence on religion results in failure to tell students the whole story of human civilization," says a report of the Association for Supervision and Curriculum Development.[18] In keeping with the mandate of the First Amendment, the schools have been diligent in their effort to maintain a separation of church and state. Some observers believe that schools have been overly zealous in removing religion from the schools. As a result, religion is treated as though it does not exist as an important force in shaping the affairs of human beings and their cultures. The First Amendment prohibition is against teaching doctrinal religious beliefs; it does not disallow the *study* of religion as a salient phenomenon of history and culture.

Religion is always associated with the inculcation of values and with moral education. Thus, when schools engage in values and moral education, they are, to some extent, entering the domain of religious and family responsibility. Such teaching can easily become controversial because of what is presumed to be the ultimate source of truth and moral authority. Even though it is undoubtedly true that many—perhaps even most— public school teachers have deeply held religious convictions themselves, the public school is a secular institution. Thus, the extent to which it can teach that the affairs of human beings are somehow influenced by the hand of God or gods is limited. Schools do not and, by law, must not promote a religious belief system. Yet, when schools engage in problem-solving or thinking activities that are based on values such as human dignity and rationality, rather than on mandates from God, they are judged to be promoting a philosophy of *secular humanism*. Certain religious groups have taken schools to task for teaching "the religion of secular humanism," claiming that this is in violation of the First Amendment. School authorities take the position that schools are simply following a well-established system of validating knowledge using the methods of modern-day science.

The procedures used by schools to teach various aspects of thinking are almost always based on an empirical problem-solving model. Although the process did not originate with the prominent American philosopher and educator, John Dewey, he popularized it and brought it to American education through his writing and teaching. This helps explain why critics of the schools even today point to Dewey as the person most responsible for bringing secular humanism to the public schools. It was out of the Dewey book, *How We Think*, that have come the five basic components of problem solving: (1) problem identification; (2) hypothesis formation; (3) data gathering; (4) testing hypotheses in terms of evidence (or data); and (5) drawing conclusions based on evidence.[19]

Conclusions based on scientific problem-solving procedures are accepted tentatively on information available at the time the investigation is made. This leaves the door open to further refinement of explanations and conclusions—or even different explanations or conclusions—at a later time when more information may become available. This procedure stresses the *probability* of something's being true in terms of evidence rather than being true in the *absolute*, unchanging sense. This means that there are no areas closed to further investigation, obviously a point of conflict with those who embrace other ways of knowing.

Teachers cannot ignore the fact that a large segment of the U.S. population believes that revealed truth is a legitimate way of knowing—that is, that God revealed truth to human beings either through written accounts (such as the Bible or the Koran) or through holy persons who were especially commissioned to make these truths known to others. It does not matter in the slightest what the teacher's personal views on this matter are; the fact is that seated in the public school classrooms of this nation are hundreds of thousands, perhaps millions, of children who, to some extent, are taught the validity of revealed truth, and to fail to take this into account in school instruction is a mistake.

Where, then, does this leave the teacher who is serious about wanting to teach critical thinking and other intellectual skills to students? Does this mean that teaching for independent thinking must be done only passively or clandestinely and that it cannot be pursued affirmatively as an instructional goal? Certainly not; but the teacher needs to know that the matter remains an *issue* in education. This means that it is the context of the local school community that will govern the guidelines to be followed in teaching thinking and problem-solving procedures. The matter will continue to be discussed and debated by professionals and laypersons in the years ahead. Meanwhile, it is the responsibility of public school teachers to help children develop ways of thinking that characterize an educated and thoughtful citizenry. At the same time, teachers must be sensitive to the fact that there is so much about which we know so little; for many people, ways of knowing other than scientific problem solving appear to be more appropriate in dealing with those unknowns. The individual's right to embrace other paths to those unknowns must be respected.

Quite apart from the connection of religion with values and moral education, the study of religion as a social phenomenon constitutes a legitimate area of inquiry for social studies. Religion has had and continues to have a tremendous impact on history and human affairs. Children cannot possibly understand historical events, such as the European colonization of the Americas or the Civil Rights Movement, without understanding the role of religion. Nor can they appreciate the fact that democracy, with its guarantee of religious liberty and its insistence on religious tolerance, is so much better than the alternative: the religious warfare and persecution so common in nondemocratic societies. "Thanks in large measure to the Religious Liberty clauses of the First Amendment [to the U.S. Constitution], this country remains the boldest and most successful experiment in living with religious differences the world has ever seen."[20]

The challenge to teachers is to make religion a natural part of the social studies topics studied. Just as it is common to have children study the geography, government, and history of a selection of communities around the world, it should also be common for the children to gather information about the religions practiced in these communities. This means that teachers need to become knowledgeable about the religions of people studied and how the lives of those people are affected by their religious beliefs. Closer to home, today's teachers need to know more about the diverse religions embraced by the families of the children in their classrooms. As noted in the previous chapter, a teacher can display genuine respect for children's home cultures in many ways; attending a special event at a child's mosque, temple, or church is one way that is sure to be remembered by the child and the family.

. . . .

Discussion Questions and Suggested Activities

1. Prepare a list of decisions that could be made in your classroom in which children could legitimately participate. Also, make a list of decisions in which they would not participate. Develop, through discussion with classmates, a set of guidelines regarding the involvement of children in classroom decision making.

2. "Democracy is a fragile system of living together. The ideas, dispositions, and skills citizens need for it do not emerge without systematic education." Do you agree with this opinion? Reason dialogically about it: create a dialogue "inside your head" in which you argue in favor of this statement, then against it. Incorporate James Baldwin's argument about the education of "barbarians."

3. Compare the discussion/decision-making approaches of Ethel Sadowsky, Tarry Lindquist, and Vivian Paley. Then list some of the specific things they do that you might want to try. For example, Mrs. Paley has students *consider* a new rule and discuss its positive and negative consequences. She conducts an inquiry based on two questions: Will the rule work? Is the rule fair?

4. Select three terms from the Citizenship Glossary (Figure 3–6), such as citizenship, democracy, and rule of law. Ask your students what these terms might mean. Encourage them to guess. Try explaining these terms using only classroom (not community or national) examples. Treat this as an assessment experiment, and discuss your "results" with classmates.

5. Divide up the community service resources list (Figure 3–5) with five other students. Call or write to each. Explain that you are seeking advice on starting up community service projects with your class and request materials. Be sure to indicate the grade levels of the children. If writing, use school letterhead.

6. Examine the levels of proficiency in the two discussion scoring guides (Table 3–1 and Figure 3–3). Compare and contrast them, and skip ahead to Chapter 9 to the section on performance assessment. Design a scoring guide for a decision-making or a community-service skill.

7. In your own elementary and middle school social studies experiences, what values did your teachers stress? What activities do you remember that were particularly values oriented? Would such activities be worthwhile for today's children? Legal? Why or why not?

8. Examine report cards used by schools in your area. How do they report to parents on the learnings discussed in this chapter? If a checklist of learnings is used, what is included? Is emphasis placed on participatory processes such as discussion, decision making, and community service? How about knowledge of democratic values, dispositions, and concepts?

9. What is the relative value of democratic knowledge and democratic participation skills in the education of democratic citizens? Would you advise teachers to emphasize one more than the other?

10. Select a children's trade book that might be especially useful in illustrating a *public* or general value. Explain why you selected this particular book. Develop a set of questions related to this value that you would want children to respond to in connection with this book.

• •

Notes

1 James Baldwin, "A Talk to Teachers." In *Multicultural Literacy*, ed. Rick Simonson and Scott Walker (Saint Paul, MN: Graywolf Press, 1988), 4.

2 Polly Greenberg, "How to Institute Some Simple Democratic Practices Pertaining to Respect, Rights, Roots, and Responsibilities in Any Classroom," *Young Children, 47* (July 1992): 10–17.

3 Ethel Sadowsky, "Taking Part: Democracy in the Elementary School," in *Preparing for Citizenship: Teaching Youth to Live Democratically*, ed. Ralph Mosher, Robert A. Kenny, Jr., & Andrew Garrod (Westport, CT: Praeger, 1994), 153.

4 Tarry Lindquist, *Seeing the Whole Through Social Studies* (Portsmouth, NH: Heinemann, 1995), 35.

5 Vivian Paley, *You Can't Say You Can't Play* (Cambridge: Harvard University Press, 1992), 4.

6 Ibid., 16.

7 Ibid., 21.

8 Ibid., 18–19.

9 Ibid., 61.

10 Ibid., 63.

11 Sadowsky, *Preparing for Citizenship,* 153.

12 Thomas Lickona, *Educating for Character* (New York: Bantam, 1991).

13 Shirley H. Engle and Anna S. Ochoa, *Education for Democratic Citizenship* (New York: Teachers College Press, 1988), 75.

14 Giraffe, organizational brochure. Contact Giraffe, P.O. Box 759, Langley, WA 98260.

15 National Council for the Social Studies, *Curriculum Standards for Social Studies* (Washington, DC: Author, 1994).

16 Center for Civic Education, *National Standards for Civics and Government* (Calabasas, CA: Author, 1994).

17 Edward A. Wynne, "The Great Tradition in Education: Transmitting Moral Values," *Educational Leadership, 43* (December 1985/January 1986): 4. The most comprehensive resource book for character education is Thomas Lickona's *Educating for Character* (New York: Bantam, 1991).

18 *Religion in the Curriculum.* A Report from the ASCD Panel on Religion in the Curriculum (Alexandria, Virginia: Association for Supervision and Curriculum Development, 1987), 27.

19 John Dewey, *How We Think* (Boston: D.C. Heath, 1933), 106.

20 Charles C. Haynes, ed., *Finding Common Ground* (Nashville: The Freedom Forum First Amendment Center, Vanderbilt University, 1994), 1–2.

• •

Selected References

Anderson, Charlotte C., Arlene F. Gallagher, Gayle Mertz, Myra Zarnowski, Tarry L. Lindquist, and others contribute articles and a pull-out section on "Celebrating the Bill of Rights," a special issue of *Social Studies and the Young Learner, 4* (September/October 1991).

Bennett, William. *The Book of Virtues: A Treasury of Great Moral Stories.* New York: Simon & Schuster, 1993.

Dewey, John. *Democracy and Education*. New York: Macmillan, 1916.

Dillon, James T. *Using Discussion in Classrooms*. Philadelphia: Open University Press, 1994.

Engle, Shirley H., and Anna S. Ochoa. *Education for Democratic Citizenship*. New York: Teachers College Press, 1988.

Evans, Ronald, and David Saxe (eds.). *Handbook on Teaching Social Issues*. Washington, DC: National Council for the Social Studies, in press.

Gilligan, Carol. *In a Different Voice*. Cambridge: Harvard University Press, 1982.

Goodman, Jesse. *Elementary Schooling for Critical Democracy*. Albany: State University of New York Press, 1992.

Greenberg, Polly. "How to Institute Some Simple Democratic Practices Pertaining to Respect, Rights and Responsibilities in Any Classroom," *Young Children, 47* (July 1992): 10–17.

Haas, Mary, Barbara Hatcher, and Cynthia Szymanski Sunal. "Teaching About the President and the Presidential Election," *Social Studies and the Young Learner, 5* (September/October 1992): special pull-out section.

Huffman, Henry A. *Developing a Character Education Program: One School District's Experience*. Alexandria, VA: Association for Supervision and Curriculum Development, 1994.

Kohlberg, Lawrence. *The Psychology of Moral Development*. San Francisco: Harper & Row, 1984.

Leming, James S. "In Search of Effective Character Education," *Educational Leadership, 51* (November 1993), 63–71.

Lickona, Thomas. *Educating for Character*. New York: Bantam, 1991.

Mosher, Ralph, Robert A. Kenny, Jr., and Andrew Garrod. *Preparing for Citizenship*. Westport, CT: Praeger, 1994.

Paley, Vivian Gussin. *You Can't Say You Can't Play*. Cambridge: Harvard University Press, 1992.

Parker, Walter C., (ed.). *Educating the Democratic Mind*. Albany: State University of New York Press, 1996.

Patrick, John J., and John D. Hoge. "Teaching Government, Civics, and Law." In *Handbook of Research on Social Studies Teaching and Learning*, edited by James P. Shaver. New York: Macmillan, 1991, 427–36.

Walzer, Michael. *What It Means to Be an American*. New York: Marsilio, 1992.

Wilen, William W., and Jane J. White. "Interaction and Discourse in Social Studies Classrooms." In *Handbook of Research on Social Studies Teaching and Learning*, edited by James P. Shaver. New York: Macmillan, 1991, 483–95.

Wynne, Edward A., and Kevin Ryan. *Reclaiming Our Schools: A Handbook on Teaching Character, Academics, and Discipline*, 2nd. ed. Upper Saddle River, NJ: Merrill/Prentice Hall, 1997.

HISTORY, GEOGRAPHY, AND
THE SOCIAL SCIENCES

OVERVIEW

What children of this age need is rich food for their imagination, a sense of history, how the present situation came about.[1]

The subject-matter banquet table of the social studies curriculum in the elementary and middle school is loaded with offerings, each more tempting than the next. An entire curriculum could be built around history alone, or geography, political science, economics, sociology, or anthropology. Also, an exciting curriculum could result from a focus on problems and issues that people have tried to resolve in the course of making a common life together. Yet, history and geography traditionally have been the backbone around which most schools organize their social studies programs. Children typically are introduced to the history of their community, state, nation, and world in grades 3 through 6, respectively. Geography is integrated easily into these units, because historical narratives cannot be comprehended, nor historical investigations undertaken, apart from their geographical settings. Every history lesson needs maps.

We explore the fields of history and geography in this chapter, along with economics, sociology, and anthropology. These are the major sources of subject matter for social studies lessons and units. Political science, which is another subject-matter source, especially for citizenship education, is not addressed here because it was dealt with extensively in Chapter 3.

History and the Social Studies

Throughout most of the 20th century, the subject of history has been the jewel in the crown of the social studies curriculum in the United States. Indeed, for many teachers and parents alike, social studies means history. Nonetheless, the evidence suggests that citizens' knowledge of events that have been significant to this nation's history is so meager that it is a national embarrassment. To produce citizens with a better grasp of history, schools need to give more thought to the way the subject is taught.

Most important, however, is that it *is* taught, for children stand little chance of learning a subject if they are not afforded the opportunity. Add to a planned history curriculum a heavy dose of effective instruction, and the combined effect should be a most welcome increase in children's historical knowledge and skills. It is a genuine thrill for children to encounter a teacher who vigorously teaches history and who can make it come alive and seem more important than anything else the children could possibly want to study.

Purposes

Among the reasons why teachers should devote considerable time to history in the school day, the most important has to do with citizenship education. As the *National Standards for History* emphasize,

"Knowledge of history is the precondition of political intelligence." Without history, a society shares no common memory of where it has been, of what its core values are, or of what decisions of the past account for present circumstances. . . . Without history, one cannot move to the informed, discriminating citizenship essential to effective participation in the democratic processes of governance and the fulfillment for all our citizens of the nation's democratic ideals.[2]

We might summarize this first purpose as *judgment*. Knowledge of history and the ability to think historically improve one's judgment.

A second vital reason for history instruction is that it enlarges children's imagination and experience. In this way, history, like literature, is expanding and liberating: It takes children to far-away places and far-away times, even to unknown destinations close to home, introducing them to stimulating people, events, and ideas. These "experiences" in turn become part of who the children are. They are added to the inventory of knowledge children bring with them to new situations and problems. This is one reason why in Chapter 2 such emphasis was given to helping language-minority children gain access to the rich subject matter of social studies, rather than only "drilling and skilling" them in language lessons. Without the substantive subject matter, their growth and development is tragically and unnecessarily stunted. It is no different for the language-majority child, of course. Deprived of the enlarging effects of historical knowledge and inquiry, *any* child is disadvantaged.

A third, related reason is that history learning builds children's knowledge of the world's peoples and the inclination to empathize with their struggles and respect their humanity. Obviously, this is important for international peace and understanding. History teaching is therefore something very concrete that teachers around the world can do to help the world's peoples get along better. By learning about the diversity of the world's cultures and their histories, children see that some people live differently than they do, *and that their own way of life is "different," too*, at least from the perspective of other peoples. Respect for the tapestry of human differences is a virtue that can distinguish the intolerant bigot from the good neighbor who wants to be friends with people alike and different.

As readers can see, history learning has much to do with self-identity. Children learn that they share memories in common with others; they are *connected*. The heritage of the nation and of the children's home cultures both become part of the heritage of individual children. They learn that their histories and life styles are similar to many people and different from many others. With encouragement and good role models, they make their peace with difference, appreciating it and feeling enriched by it. Most powerfully, perhaps, they come to see that just as they have been shaped by the past, so will they shape the future for others. How will they shape it? Ask them this question often.

The History Curriculum

The teaching of history in the elementary and middle schools occurs within the context of the social studies curriculum and contributes substantially to it. It contributes topics and ideas for study, achievement standards for those topics, historical eras, themes, and skills of historical inquiry. Figure 4–1 lists eight curriculum topics suggested for study

Figure 4–1

Historical topics for study in the early grades.

1. Family life now and in the recent past; family life in various places long ago.

2. History of students' local community and how communities in North America varied long ago.

3. The people, events, problems, and ideas that created the history of their state.

4. How democratic values came to be, and how they have been exemplified by people, events, and symbols.

5. The causes and nature of various movements of large groups of people into and within the United States, now and long ago.

6. Regional folklore and cultural contributions that helped to form our national heritage.

7. Selected attributes and historical developments of various societies in Africa, the Americas, Asia, and Europe.

8. Major discoveries in science and technology, their social and economic effects, and the scientists and inventors from many groups and religions responsible for them.

Source: National Standards for History for Grades K–4: Expanding Children's World in Time and Space (Los Angeles: National Center for History in the Schools, 1994): 29–30.

in grades K–4 by the *National Standards for History*. For grades 5–12, this group suggests the chronological study of both United States and world history. Teachers of the intermediate and middle grades will find both documents to be tremendously useful resources, both for selecting topics and identifying levels of proficiency.*

Another blue-ribbon committee of historians and educators produced Table 4–1. This chart summarizes the knowledge on which fourth-, eighth-, and eleventh-graders are assessed by an agency of the the United States government.[3] What is interesting here are the eight suggested chronological eras, each of which might be explored for one month in a fifth- or eighth-grade class. Also specified are four themes, briefly described below.

1. *Change and Continuity in American Democracy*: The development of American political democracy from colonial times to the present. This includes basic principles and core civic ideas developed through the American Revolution, U.S. Constitution, and Civil War and the struggles over slavery and civil rights.

---

* Addresses for ordering the U.S. and world history standards are given in Selected References at the end of this chapter.

Table 4–1
U.S. history content outline.

Periods	Change and Continuity in American Democracy: Ideas, Institutions, Practices, and Controversies	The Gathering and Interactions of Peoples, Cultures, and Ideas	Economic and Technological Changes and Their Relation to Society, Ideas, and the Environment	The Changing Role of America in the World
Three Worlds and Their Meeting in the Americas (Beginnings to 1607)				
Colonization, Settlement, and Communities (1607 to 1763)				
The Revolution and the New Nation (1763 to 1815)				
Expansion and Reform (1801 to 1861)				
Crisis of the Union: Civil War and Reconstruction (1850 to 1877)				
The Development of Modern America (1865 to 1920)				
Modern America and the World Wars (1914 to 1945)				
Contemporary America (1945 to Present)				

Source: U.S. History Framework for the 1994 National Assessment of Educational Progress (NAEP) (Washington, DC: U.S. Department of Education, 1994): 18.

2. *The Gathering and Interactions of Peoples, Cultures, and Ideas*: The gathering of people and cultures of many countries, races, and religious traditions that have contributed to the American heritage and the development of American society.

3. *Economic and Technological Changes and Their Relation to Society, Ideas, and the Environment*: The transformation of the American economy from rural frontier to industrial superpower and its impact on society, ideas, and the environment. This includes the development of a market economy and the influence of geography, urbanization, and science and technology.

4. *The Changing Role of America in the World*: The movement from isolation to worldwide responsibility. This includes the impact of geography, resources, interests, and ideals on American foreign policy; relations between domestic politics and foreign affairs; and the influence of the American example on the rest of the world and of other nations on the United States.[4]

Historical Thinking

Passive absorption of this material is certainly not the point. For this reason, historical thinking is also an important part of the curriculum. The point is made well in the *National Standards for History, K–4*:

Real historical understanding requires that students engage in historical reasoning; listen to and read historical stories, narratives, and literature with meaning; think through cause-effect relationships; interview "old-timers" in their communities; analyze documents, photos, historical newspapers, and the records of the past available in libraries, local museums and historical sites; and construct time lines and historical narratives of their own.[5]

Two kinds of historical thinking are especially important. *Chronological thinking* means developing a sense of historical time—past, present, and future. Phrases such as "long, long ago" and "at the turn of the century" begin to make sense, and children can talk about conflicts and major inventions in terms of what happened before and after. This is important for the appreciation of history as a story well told—as a narrative account—and it is crucial if students are going to learn *why* things happen—to hypothesize causes of major events such as wars, social movements, revolts, famines, and migrations. This involves *historical inquiry*

Historical inquiry is a kind of thinking that involves formulating and testing hypotheses about what might have caused a conflict, weighing competing accounts and evidence, and wrestling with moral questions in history. The key questions for students are these:

What do you think might be the cause?

Which account should we believe?

Was what they did right (good; decent; compassionate)?

Mrs. Paley, the kindergarten teacher we met in the prior chapter, seems to do this effortlessly. Having been enthralled by her telling of the story of the Montgomery bus boycott—the incident involving Rosa Parks especially—her children were eager to retell it, dramatize it, and talk about the consequences. Consider this excerpt from a conversation in which her students are discussing the morality of separating the races and the movement led by Martin Luther King, Jr.:

> Wally: Martin changed all the rules.
> Lisa: All the *bad* rules.
> Fred: But not the one for the bathroom. The girls still have to separate from the boys.[6]

Clearly, these four- and five-year-olds are able to consider the moral questions; furthermore, they are able to draw the distinction between separations based on gender as opposed to race.

Teaching Suggestions

Chapter 7 presents numerous strategies for teaching ideas, skills, and the inquiry process. Here, we share a few other time-honored suggestions for engaging children in history.

Examine Objects of Historical Significance

Children love to examine historical objects closely and handle them. Arrowheads from a native group, a facsimile of a slave contract or auction announcement, an army recruitment poster, a spinning wheel or spittoon, a manual typewriter or rotary telephone, a quill pen or piece of fool's gold, photos, a piece of traditional clothing, an old family Bible, an old butter churn, rice steamer, or tortilla press—any of these might be related to the instructional unit at hand. If an item is brought from home and is highly valued, it is best for the adult owner to bring it to school to show the children and tell them of its significance.

Local museums often have permanent displays of historical materials significant to the local community, state, and region. Increasingly, they package materials in a "museum treasure chest" that is loaned to the school. A phone call should provide needed information about this service.

Oral History

Structured interviews or informal conversations with local persons of historical significance can be preserved as "oral history" by using cassette tape recorders. Children are fascinated when old-timers talk of their exciting experiences in the early community. They are surprised to hear that the person now speaking to them marched in the Civil Rights Movement, bicycled across a desert or mountain range, fought in Vietnam, or helped change a community rule. This procedure has the added value of involving children, firsthand, in gathering historical data. The taped interviews, therefore, need to be planned, with questions written out and practiced first with classmates.

Holidays

Holidays appeal to children and can be a wonderful vehicle for teaching history. Needed is a comparative perspective, where holidays are compared and contrasted to one another; a multicultural perspective, where Hispanic-American, Asian-American,

African-American, and European-American traditions are investigated; and a global perspective, where religious and civic holidays in various regions of the world are brought together for study. In the United States, Presidents Day, Columbus Day, Thanksgiving Day, Veterans Day, and Martin Luther King, Jr., Day provide terrific opportunities for history teaching and learning. A special issue of *Social Studies and the Young Learner* (November/December 1993) has many helpful ways of thinking about and teaching the holidays.

Role-Playing

Display a photo, painting, or other visual representation of a historical event to help children imagine *being there*, and read aloud a vivid description of the event from a piece of historical fiction, textbook, magazine, or encyclopedia. Assign children the roles of key persons in the scene. Coach them into the appropriate postures, expressions, and feelings. In this way, children can reenact Paul Revere's ride, Squanto's meeting with the Pilgrims, or a wagon train heading west. They can march for women's rights, conduct a sit-in at a segregated lunch counter, land on the moon, or surround Custer's troops at the Battle of the Little Big Horn. More ideas can be found in Vivian Paley's *Wally's Stories* (Harvard, 1981) and Douglas Selwyn's *Living History in the Classroom* (Zephyr, 1993).

Biographical Sketches

Chapter 12 explains how teams of children can compose biographies of courageous citizens, labor and business leaders, explorers, presidents, framers of the U.S. Constitution, women's suffrage and civil rights activists, heroes, villains, and other persons of historical significance.

Dramatizations and Speeches

There is perhaps no one activity more powerful for developing historical empathy than to dramatize an event. Have the children dictate or write the script. Involve speeches and poems that some children can memorize, and music and dance for others. Include all children in some capacity. Hold plenty of rehearsals. Invite an audience, such as another class.

National History Day

Children can participate in numerous ways. Each state has a National History Day coordinator from whom information may be obtained. Local competition is usually held in March and April, with state competition in May and nationals in June.

Song and Dance

Collect folk and patriotic songs and dances of various periods of history. Present "A Musical Pageant of American History."

Paint

Paint a mural of some aspect of the history of the local community or state.

Time Travel

Plan imaginative trips back and forward in time, complete with travel brochures and descriptions of places to visit.

Models

Make models of communities (the children's town as it looked fifty or one hundred years ago, Mesa Verde, Tokyo, Plymouth), shelters (hogans, igloos, highrises, and longhouses), transportation (oxcarts, prairie schooners, trains, ships, and canoes), and means of long-distance communication (pony express, telegraph, radio, television, telephone, and Internet).

Simulations

Classroom Curators (grades 4–6) can create a classroom museum displaying artifacts from their parents' and grandparents' lives. *Pilgrims* (grades 2–4) re-creates the Plymouth Colony in seventeenth-century Massachusetts. *Magellan's Shopping List* (grades 5–8) asks students to decide what supplies Magellan should have taken on his 1522 voyage.[7]

Children's Literature

The four themes and eight chronological periods of U.S. history shown in Table 4–1 may take some readers of this book aback. "I don't know this material very well," is likely the first reaction of some readers who themselves may not have taken a course in history since high school. Teachers must know the material they want to teach, and it is well documented that teachers' knowledge of a subject shapes their teaching of it, sometimes dramatically.

Nonetheless, it is true (and perhaps a well-kept secret of teaching) that teachers themselves sometimes learn much of the material they will teach as they plan it. The children's social studies textbook and its teacher's guide are major sources of information for teachers. Trade books written for children are another source. Encyclopedias, both print and electronic, are also helpful, and *Cobblestone*, the children's history magazine, should be on every elementary school teacher's nightstand, in addition to his or her desk at school. We examine such resources in later chapters (7, 11, and 12 especially). The children's trade book titles below, geared to the four themes in Table 4–1, suggest the range of possibilities:

Theme 1: American Democracy
Jump Ship to Freedom, James and Christopher Collier (Delacorte, 1981).

Thomas Jefferson, Father of Our Democracy, David Adler (Holiday House, 1987).

Shh! We're Writing the Constitution, Jean Fritz (J. J. Putnam & Sons, 1987).

Theme 2: Gathering of Peoples
Indian Chiefs, Russell Freedman (Holiday House, 1987).

The Pilgrims of Plimoth, Marcia Sewall (Macmillan, 1986).

Tales from Gold Mountain: Stories of the Chinese in the New World, Paul Yee (Macmillan, 1990).

Theme 3: Economic and Technological Change
The President's Car, Nancy Parker (Crowell, 1981).

African American Inventors, Patricia and Fredrick McKissack (Millbrook, 1994).

Living in a Risky World, Laurence Pringle (Morrow, 1989).

Theme 4: America in the World
Sarah Bishop, Scott O'Dell (Houghton-Mifflin, 1980).

My Daddy Was a Soldier, Deborah Ray (Holiday House, 1990).

The United Nations, Harold and Geraldine Woods (Franklin Watts, 1985).

Geography and the Social Studies

"Geography is a field of study that enables us to find answers to questions about the world around us—about where things are and how and why they got there." So begins *Geography for Life*, a book of curriculum standards published in 1994 for the field of geography.[8] Geography's vantage point as it looks out over the world is not so much historical as it is *spatial*. When we engage in geographical inquiry, we learn about the arrangement and interaction of people and places on earth's surface. Geography brings the physical (e.g., landforms, climate, glacial activity) and human (culture, migration, interaction) dimensions of earth's space together.

Purposes

There are many reasons why individuals need to understand the spatial settings of people and places on earth. The most basic reason is that people everywhere try to make sense of their lives: They want to know the nature of the world and their place in it. Great religions and literature grapple with this uniquely human need. "Humans want to understand the intrinsic nature of their home. Geography enables them to understand where they are, literally and figuratively."[9] There are also very practical reasons for having geographical knowledge and abilities: travelers, explorers, military leaders, and entrepreneurs in search of natural resources all would be at a great loss without geographical tools and information. All of us need geographical knowledge to get where we want to go, to know where we have been, to understand the wants and needs of people in different places, and to grasp daily events in relation to their settings—a picnic in July in Kansas, a flat tire in Minneapolis in February, a subsistence farmer on the horn of Africa, an earthquake in a Japanese port city. From a child's point of view, each of these practical reasons comes to life when his or her parents decide to move their home from one neighborhood to another.[10]

The Geography Curriculum

Children's geographic knowledge, like their knowledge of history, has suffered somewhat at the hands of numerous social phenomena. Here are three: the American public's concern over children's scores on reading assessments and the high rate of adult illiteracy (20 percent); elementary school educators' increased attention to teaching reading and writing "skills" at the expense of substantive content knowledge; teachers' lack of pedagogical knowledge required for effectively integrating reading and writing instruction with subject matter instruction (e.g., geography and history). A fourth phenomenon is that, in the past, geography instruction too frequently meant memorizing the names and locations of states, capitals, and landforms without *reasoning geographically* about them. This gave geography instruction a bad name compared to more popular instructional trends such as whole language and cooperative learning.

Five Themes

A tremendously helpful response to the nation's growing geographic illiteracy was a set of curriculum guidelines developed in the 1980s by the National Council for Geographic Education and the Association of American Geographers. Five *themes* were identified by this joint committee, and they have since provided teachers and textbook publishers with a meaningful framework for getting a handle on this otherwise sprawling field and for enriching geography instruction beyond memory work alone. The five themes of geography are:

1. **Location: Position on the Earth's Surface**. Absolute and relative location are two ways of describing the positions of people and places on the earth's surface.

2. **Place: Physical and Human Characteristics**. All places on the earth have distinctive tangible and intangible characteristics that give them meaning and character and distinguish them from other places. Geographers generally describe places by their physical or human characteristics.

3. **Relationships Within Places: Humans and Environments**. All places on the earth have advantages and disadvantages for human settlement. High population densities have developed on flood plains, for example, where people could take advantage of fertile soils, water resources, and opportunities for river transportation. By comparison, population densities are usually low in deserts. Yet flood plains are periodically subjected to severe damage, and some desert areas, such as Israel, have been modified to support large population concentrations.

4. **Movement: Humans Interacting on the Earth**. Human beings occupy places unevenly across the face of the earth. Some live on farms or in the country; others live in towns, villages, or cities. Yet these people interact with each other: that is, they travel from one place to another, they communicate with each other, or they rely upon products, information, and ideas that come from beyond their immediate environment.

   The most visible evidences of global interdependence and the interaction of places are the transportation and communication lines that link every part of the world. These demonstrate that most people interact with other places almost every day of their lives. This may involve nothing more than a Georgian eating apples grown in the state of Washington and shipped to Atlanta by rail or truck. On a larger scale, international trade demonstrates that no country is self-sufficient.

5. **Regions: How They Form and Change**. The basic unit of geographic study is the region, an area that displays unity in terms of selected criteria. We are all familiar with regions showing the extent of political power such as nations, provinces, countries, or cities, yet there are almost countless ways to define meaningful regions depending on the problems being considered. Some regions are defined by one characteristic such as a governmental unit, a language group, or a landform type, and others by the interplay of many complex features. For example, Indiana as a state is a governmental region, Latin America as an area where Spanish and Portuguese are major languages can be a linguistic region, and the Rocky Mountains as a mountain range is a landform region.

Ten years after the committee's report, the geography standards, *Geography for Life*, acknowledged the value of the five themes but endeavored to push geography learning toward yet more sophisticated understandings and abilities. Six themes called *essential elements* were identified that embraced eighteen curriculum standards. Time will tell whether these standards make more or less sense to elementary and middle school teachers than the five themes developed in 1984. Some observers worry that the new standards overshoot the mark, complicating rather than clarifying the field for teachers. What is your judgment?

Element 1: The World in Spatial Terms

Standard 1. How to use maps and other geographic representations, tools, and technologies to acquire, process, and report information from a spatial perspective.

Standard 2. How to use mental maps to organize information about people, places, and environments in a spatial context.

Standard 3. How to analyze the spatial organization of people, places, and environments on earth's surface.

Element 2: Places and Regions

Standard 4. The physical and human characteristics of places.

Standard 5. That people create regions to interpret earth's complexity.

Standard 6. How culture and experience influence people's perceptions of places and regions.

Element 3: Physical Systems

Standard 7. The physical processes that shape the patterns of earth's surface.

Standard 8. The characteristics and spatial distribution of ecosystems on earth's surface.

Element 4: Human Systems

Standard 9. The characteristics, distributions, and migration of human populations on earth's surface.

Standard 10. The characteristics, distribution, and complexity of earth's cultural mosaics.

Standard 11. The patterns and networks of economic interdependence on earth's surface.

Standard 12. The processes, patterns, and functions of human settlement.

Standard 13. How the forces of cooperation and conflict among people influence the division and control of earth's surface.

Element 5: Environment and Society

Standard 14. How human actions modify the physical environment.

Standard 15. How physical systems affect human systems.

Standard 16. The changes that occur in the meaning, use, distribution, and importance of resources.

Element 6: The Uses of Geography
Standard 17. How to apply geography to interpret the past.
Standard 18. How to apply geography to interpret the present and plan for the future.[11]

Teaching Suggestions

A thoughtful reading of *Geography for Life* and the five themes of geography will suggest many teaching possibilities. Teachers have used the following ideas successfully.

Local Land and Water

Have children observe firsthand in the school neighborhood various land and water forms—lakes, creeks, islands, hills, gullies, slopes. Younger children can draw these; older children can draw them to scale and locate them on maps they create themselves.

Moving

Every year, about 40 million Americans load their possessions into cars and trucks and move to new neighborhoods, near and far. A class can help orient a newly arrived classmate to the physical geography of the school grounds and community by creating maps, conducting guided tours, and preparing a "Welcome" brochure. Questions and answers in the brochure can be geared to geographic themes:

Location   Where is our school in our community? Why is it located there? Where is it relative to the park and city hall?

Place   What is it like here? What are this community's most notable natural and human-made features? What do kids do here for fun? What languages are spoken here? If you want to draw this place, what color crayons should you bring?

Movement   How did early settlers get to this place? How many newcomers arrive each year, and by what means of transportation? How many leave? Is there an interstate highway near?

Human-environmental interaction   What natural resources can be found here? How have people here changed the environment? Do we recycle anything? Where does our food and drinking water come from?

Region   What regions is our town a part of and what are the regions *in* our town? What things do nearby towns have in common? What kinds of jobs do people in this region have? What is the highest and lowest average temperature in this region?[10]

Making World Maps in 30 Seconds

Helping children get to the point where they can draw a world map from memory is, for them and their parents, a notable achievement. The task is not so difficult as it might seem, but the children must be provided ample opportunity to study world maps and to practice drawing their own. One helpful technique is to begin with circles (Figure 4–2).

Orienteering in the Library and Elsewhere at School

Have teams of children make maps of the library. They will learn where the card catalogue, the biography section, and the CD-ROM collections are located while symboliz-

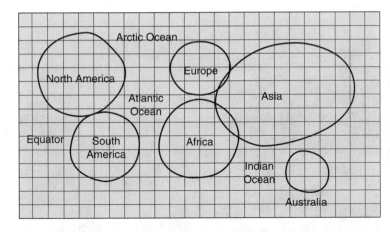

Six quickly sketched circles, roughly in the right places and in roughly proportionate sizes, make a working map of the continents. Asia is the biggest, Australia the smallest.

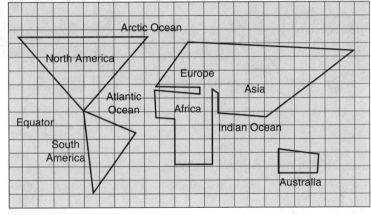

Turn the continents into squares, rectangles, and triangles. Remember that the Africa bulge is over the Equator, the Tropic of Cancer underpins Asia, and the Tropic of Capricorn cuts Australia in half.

Figure 4–2

Steps for drawing a world map

Source: Geography for Life: National Geography Standards (Washington, DC: National Geographic and Exploration, 1994) 65. Reprinted by permission.

ing them on the map and in the map key. Polar directions should be included, and the maps should be drawn to scale. Before this: map the classroom. Afterward: map the cafeteria, the playground, the school grounds.

Excavations

A primary-grade class can visit a nearby basement excavation for a new home. The children observe the various layers of soil, and the teacher calls their attention to the many roots found in the fertile topsoil. The class is able to obtain samples of the various strata of soil to take back to their classroom for an experiment in seeing how well plants grow in the various layers—an early beginning in the appreciation of soil conservation. The presence of earth-moving equipment suggests that human beings do things to modify the environment.

Construction activities build appreciation.

Weather and Climate

Weather and climate present another area of exploration. Children have viewed weather forecasts on television. The frequency of reference to weather in adult conversations indicates the degree to which weather and climatic conditions have an effect on the lives of people. In primary-grade classrooms, children will want to have their own charts on which they can record various weather data observed each day. The teacher reads the daily temperature, or the children report the official daily temperature that they have heard over an early morning radio broadcast. These temperatures can be shown graphically, thereby applying knowledge of numbers and graphs. Over a period of several weeks or months the graph will show the changes occurring in temperatures and seasons of the year. Children can also record data dealing with wind velocities, cloud formations, precipitation, and similar subjects. They can also make their own predictions based on the data they have collected. Sensitivity to weather changes will again call attention to the changes in native plant and animal life as well as to the adaptations people make to changing seasons. Here the teacher can apply another technique of the geographer: recording data and using simple charts.

Studying Regions

The study of specific communities and regions (e.g., desert people, mountain people, polar regions, and so on) presents difficult instructional problems no matter what system is used in selecting them. Too often they are treated in a superficial or romantic way. It becomes easy to make unwarranted value judgments about the people studied, to arrive at hasty and inaccurate generalizations, and to develop stereotyped ideas of people. The tendency has been to stress traditional or legendary aspects of a people's culture rather than coming to grips with their way of life in modern times. The need for accurate information and a proper instructional emphasis is essential if children are to develop valid understandings.

The geographic regions selected for study should be sufficiently different from one another to help the child learn the characteristic adjustments people make under varying conditions. These then may be compared with life in the local community, stressing the similarities in the basic requirements of life that people everywhere have to meet. Such a study should include historical and cultural elements as a natural part of geographic study.

Intensive studies of entire continents, with the exception of Australia, are usually not well suited for elementary school grades because the natural, cultural, and historical backgrounds of various regions are generally so diverse that it is difficult to select a unifying set of concepts for the study. Consequently, children often learn a number of facts about geographic features but fail to relate these to the people who inhabit the area. It is ordinarily better to select specific communities in representative regions of the world and study those intensively. At the beginning of the study of a community or a region, it is helpful, however, to make an overview of the continent on which the region is located. This places the area properly in its larger geographical setting.

Simulations

Caravans (grades 4–6) has students form caravans that compete to gather museum artifacts from around the world. *Flight* (grades 5–8) has students race in airplanes across the U.S. in teams, taking weather into account and keeping journals. *Southwest* (grades 4–8) explores the lands and peoples of what is now the southwestern U.S., culminating with a fiesta.[13]

Children's Literature

The five themes identified in the 1984 *Guidelines* document have been widely used as reference points for selecting children's trade books. The following sample suggests some possibilities.[14]

Movement
The Seekers, Eilis Dillon (Charles Scribner's Sons, 1986).

Hector Lives in the United States Now: The Story of a Mexican-American Child (HarperCollins, 1990).

Region
One Day in the Tropical Rain Forest, Jean Craighead George (HarperCollins, 1990).

Mojave, Diane Siebert (Crowell, 1988).

Human-Environment Interaction
Window, Jeannie Baker (William Morrow, 1991).

Roxaboxen, Alice McLerran (Lothrop, Lee & Shepard, 1991).

Location
My Place in Space, Robin and Sally Hirst (Orchard, 1990).
The Third-Story Cat, Leslie Baker (Little, Brown, 1987).

Place
Seeing Earth from Space, Patricia Lauber (Orchard, 1990).
Sarah, Plain and Tall, Patricia MacLachlan (Harper & Row, 1985).

Economics and the Social Studies

Economics is the study of the production, distribution, exchange, and consumption of goods and services that people need or want. In a modern industrialized society such as ours, wants and needs are great because individuals expect a high standard of living. Moreover, the processes involved in production, distribution, exchange, and consumption form an interrelated web of relationships. So directly are individuals enmeshed in it that almost everything they do is, in one way or another, related to our economic system. Economic education concerns itself with helping children achieve an understanding of some of the basic relationships between our economic system and our way of life, thereby enabling them to make informed decisions on economic matters. Another major purpose of economic education is to teach students a way of thinking about economics and economic issues.

These samples represent major generalizations from economics that have been used as organizing ideas in developing programs in economic education:

1. The wants of people are unlimited whereas resources needed to fulfill wants are scarce; hence, societies and individuals have to make choices as to which wants are to be met and which are to be sacrificed.
2. The interdependence of peoples of the world makes exchange and trade a necessity in the modern world.
3. Economic systems are usually mixed with both public and private ownership and with decisions made both by the government and by individual members of society.
4. Increased specialization in production has led to interdependence among individuals, communities, states, and nations.
5. In a modern industrialized society, the government plays an important role in the economy. Just how great a role it should play is an enduring public controversy, for *limited government* is one of the fundamental values of constitutional democracy.

Teaching Suggestions

The elementary and middle school program of instruction should be built around basic economic concepts such as scarcity, supply and demand, goods and services, needs and wants, production, consumption, exchange, and distribution. These in turn should be related to one or more generalizations of the type listed earlier. Each of these economic concepts can be developed in many of the topics included in the social studies curriculum. There may be times, however, when particular topics are selected because they have special usefulness in developing specific economic concepts. Units on the grocery store or the shopping mall in the primary grades are of this type and ordinarily focus on the distribution of goods and services.

Learning resources and teaching materials for economic education in elementary and middle schools are available in increasing quantities. The best sources of such instructional materials are the National Council on Economic Education, 1140 Avenue of the Americas, 2nd Floor, New York City 10036; the Foundation for Teaching Economics, 260 Russell Blvd., Suite B, Davis, CA 95616; and the home state council for economic education. From these sources the teacher can secure curriculum standards, sample units, scope and sequence charts, background information, and other teaching materials, as well as information concerning other resources for teaching economic concepts.

Learning activities such as the following can be used in developing economic concepts:

1. *Examine ways that people depend on each other* in their families, neighborhoods, and communities. Relate this to the need for many different kinds of jobs.
2. *Compare work roles* of today with those in colonial times to discover differences between cottage-industry procedures and assembly-line production.
3. *Study different types of advertising* (for example, cigarette ads) to learn how producers create consumer needs and wants.
4. *Compare wages* paid to workers in terms of such things as the (*a*) level of education required for the job; (*b*) extent to which the job requires highly developed skills; (*c*) length of the preparation or training program for the job; (*d*) amount of risk to the worker.
5. *Role play negotiations* between buyers and sellers; employers and employees in a salary dispute; a consumer with a complaint about a product and a retailer; a customer who has been overcharged and the person who did the repair work.
6. *Use newspapers* to compare prices of items among various retailers. Relate this to factors that affect pricing policies.
7. *Study the concept of seasonal employment* as it relates to employment patterns in different parts of the country.
8. *Study government regulation* of business operations in terms of consumer protection, quality control, and pollution.
9. *Familiarize children with local businesses* through the use of field trips and guest speakers.
10. *Study personal and family budgeting procedures* to illustrate the relationship between income and expenditures, the difference between wants and needs, and the necessity of choice making.
11. *Participate in simulation games* designed to teach economic concepts (see Chapter 8 for an example concerning assembly-line production). Others include *Candy Market* (grades 3–5), in which the class holds a candy auction, learning about supply, demand, and money; *Mini-Economy* (grades 3–6), in which students manage businesses, apply for jobs, and earn play money to spend at the classroom store; and *Kids' Town* (grade 3), in which students create a classroom economy using a salary schedule created by the class; jobs include tutors, carpenters, librarians, toymakers, and farmers.[15]

The World of Work

The world of work is a subset of economic education, and elementary and middle schools have for many years included it in their social studies programs. Units on family life, neighborhood relationships, workers in the community, transportation and communication, food, clothing and shelter, and ways of living in societies past and present are familiar subjects in elementary school social studies. Even though many changes have been made in the social studies program in recent years, these topics are still in the curriculum of most schools. These units and others like them stress work roles, jobs, the importance of work to the community and to the individual, interdependence, and simplified producer and consumer economics. In this context the social studies program is a natural vehicle to teach important ideas and attitudes relating to the world of work.

In teaching about the work world, a systematic, integrated approach is probably more effective than special units spaced throughout the grades. This, of course, does not preclude the possibility of having special units with a world of work focus, but simply suggests that such an approach is not in itself adequate. Teaching is strengthened when concepts from the work world are built into many of the existing units of the social studies program. Most who have been involved in curriculum work in this field suggest that *awareness building* should be a major goal of a program relating to the world of work in the elementary school. The major components of such a program follow.

Information About the World of Work

Persons are often uninformed about choices available to them when they decide on a vocation. They simply select from those few occupations they have learned about firsthand from a close relative or from a friend. This explains why some occupations seem to "run in families." Children should *not* be encouraged to make occupational choices when they are in elementary school. But they can begin to build a background of knowledge about a broad spectrum of occupations that will one day help them make an intelligent career choice.

Opportunity to Explore Work Values

Children need to see the connection between values that are stressed in school, such as responsibility, dependability, honesty, cooperation, trustworthiness, and the world of work. They need to develop a sense of appreciation for a job that is well done. They need to learn what it means to take pride in one's work.

Cooperative Learning

Part of awareness building for the world of work is learning to work cooperatively and productively with persons with whom one may not have chosen to work. This reflects the reality of most job settings. For this reason, an important attribute of the instructional method called cooperative learning (Chapter 10) is *teacher-assigned work groups*. In this way, children gain experience at working well and solving interpersonal problems with classmates who are not necessarily their friends.

Workplace Competencies

Assign children to small groups and ask each group to brainstorm a list of skills and dispositions that, if developed by the children, would help them get and keep the kind of work they want. Second, have the groups share their lists on butcher paper with the whole class. Third, share with the class two economic trends: the internationalization of production, distribution, and consumption, and the changing technological skills required on the job. Give examples to help the children understand the trends. Fourth, ask the groups to revise their lists as needed, based on these trends. Fifth, share with the class the list of workplace skills and dispositions shown in Figure 4–3. Developed under the direction of U.S. Labor Secretary Lynn Martin and published in a report nicknamed the SCANS report,[16] this list contains powerful categories and thoughtful workplace competencies.

Society and the World of Work

Children need to learn about the relationship of the individual to society *through* the world of work. What one does for a living does not simply have to be a job that has no purpose other than as a way of earning enough money to pay bills and stay alive. Work contributes to the life and health of the larger society. Society's need to have jobs performed and performed well can be learned by the youngest children. All of us depend on others to help us meet our basic needs. Social studies units that deal with so-called community helpers provide opportunities for learning outcomes of this type. Work is so important to society that individuals are often identified by others in accordance with what they do for a living: "He is a data analysis specialist," "He is a commercial airlines pilot," "She is a doctor in town," "She is the city manager at Augusta," and so on.

Many of the outcomes sought in career education are affective, dealing with attitudes, appreciations, and feelings. This means that children will need a broad exposure to the world of work and opportunities to respond to it in a variety of ways. Such experiences have feeling as well as knowledge dimensions. For example, children may want to express their own feelings about certain occupations, and the strength of those feelings should be

Figure 4–3
Workplace competencies.

Resources	Know how to allocate time, money, materials, space, and staff
Interpersonal Skills	Know how to work on teams, teach others, serve customers, lead, negotiate, and work well with people from culturally diverse backgrounds
Information	Know how to acquire and evaluate data, organize and maintain files, interpret and communicate, use computers to process information
Systems	Know how to understand social, organizational, and technological systems; monitor and correct performance; design and improve systems
Technology	Know how to select equipment and tools, apply technology to specific tasks, and maintain and troubleshoot equipment

Source: The Secretary's Commission on Achieving Necessary Skills (SCANS), *What Work Requires of Schools: A SCANS Report for America 2000* (Washington, DC: U.S. Department of Labor, 1991).

explored. Children should be encouraged to find out the attitudes of their parents toward the jobs they hold. Why do they like them or dislike them? Other ideas include:

Brainstorm a list of reasons why people might have selected particular occupations. This list should include such things as "It provides me with a chance to be my own boss" or "I earn a good salary." Have this list refined and duplicated, and then use it in a survey with working adults in your community. Have the adults choose three reasons from the list, and ask them to rank them in order of most important to least important.

Administer an interest inventory on possible career opportunities. Then invite adults from the community to come to talk to your class in the areas in which the most interest was expressed.

Education about the work world clearly must be sensitive to sex-role and ethnic stereotyping. Traditionally, women have been stereotyped along the lines of domestic roles and a certain limited number of occupational roles—elementary school teaching, nursing, secretarial services, food services, and so on. School programs have often reinforced these stereotypes, with the result that women have a much more restricted set of occupational choices than do men. Boys and girls need to learn that the traditional ideas about what is "woman's work" and what is "man's work" no longer apply and that people now have greater opportunities to do the things *they* want to do to lead self-fulfilling, productive lives. Much the same can be said in connection with ethnic stereotyping. Although a great deal has been done in recent years to eliminate such stereotyping in learning resources, the teacher still must be careful not to associate certain occupations with specific national, ethnic, or racial groups.

Activities for Studying the World of Work

Conduct interviews to find out how adults in the community earn money. Have the children compile a list of categories for their questionnaire such as these:

People Who Produce Things
People Who Fix Things
People Who Create
People Who Work with Ideas

Analyze these data in terms of different subpopulations in the questionnaire compilation, such as women and minorities. Other ideas include:

Brainstorm a list of occupations—say twenty-five to fifty. In groups have the children organize the data into four categories, using any system they wish to devise. Have each group explain its system.

To sensitize children to sex-role stereotyping, *have them generate lists of occupations* that are associated with males, those associated with females, and those that are neutral. Discuss these in terms of equality of job opportunity and whether or not a person's sex has anything to do with performance of the jobs listed in the male and female categories.

Analyze television commercials and newspaper and magazine advertisements to detect evidence of sex-role and racial stereotyping in certain occupations.

Use "classified ad" sections of local newspapers to discover the types of jobs that are most available. Relate this to a study of changing needs of the work world over a period of time; for example, what jobs are available now that were not available ten, twenty, fifty, or one hundred years ago?

Study the relationship between the number of producers and consumers and the growing demand for increased social services. Relate this to taxing policies and the increasing need for persons employed by various levels of government; that is, local, state, and federal.

Lesson Plan 3 illustrates how a primary-grade teacher developed the concept *division of labor* with a class.

Sociology and the Social Studies

Sociology is a broad social science that deals with the study of the structure of society and its groups, institutions, and culture. Sociological studies often focus on the diverse societal and cultural phenomena that influence the behavior of individuals and groups. Sociology is especially concerned with social organization and the way people organize themselves into groups, subgroups, social classes, and institutions. It is difficult to draw a sharp line between the content of sociology and some of the other social sciences because their areas of concern overlap.

Social psychology and sociology concern themselves with somewhat the same social phenomena. Whereas sociology focuses on groups, social psychology studies the individual in a social situation. Social psychology is particularly concerned with the effects of group life on the behavior of individuals. Studies in social psychology deal with the problems of the individual's role in groups; the development of the self-concept; the effects of group pressure on individual behavior, attitudes, and how they are formed; leadership; followership; and the origins and effects of social-class structure.

The following are samples of major generalizations from sociology that have been used as organizing ideas in developing social studies units with a sociological emphasis:

1. The family is the basic social unit in most cultures and is the source of some of the most fundamental and necessary learnings in a culture.
2. Social classes have always existed in every society although the bases of class distinction and the degree of rigidity of the class structure have varied.
3. Every society develops a system of roles, norms, values, and sanctions to guide the behavior of individuals and groups within the society.
4. All societies develop systems of social control; conflicts often arise between individual liberty and social control in societies where both are valued.
5. The social environment in which a person is reared and lives has a profound effect on the personal growth and development of that individual.

Lesson Plan 3

Division of Labor

Grade
2 or 3

Time
Two class periods

Objective
Children will form the concept *division of labor*.

Interest Building
Have children discuss jobs they know about in their family or neighborhood by responding to these questions:

Do *you* have a job at home? What do you do?

What is the difference between your job and the jobs of grownups?

Explain that during the next few days they are going to learn about different kinds of jobs in the community.

Lesson Development
Have the children make a chart with the following headings:

NAME OF JOB   REASONS FOR THE JOB
1. _____   _____
2. _____   _____
3. _____   _____

Instruct the children to take the chart home with them and complete it with the help of their parents, naming three different jobs in the community.

On the following day have the children compare and discuss their lists with each other.

Compile a list of as many different jobs as possible on the chalkboard. Children should pick one from their individual lists until everyone has had a turn to name one. Keep going as long as *different* jobs are named.

Have children discuss the need for a variety of jobs by responding to these questions:

Why do we have so many different jobs in our community?

Why couldn't each family do all these jobs itself?

Why do you suppose people in a community divide the work the way they do?

Do you mean that people who have these jobs have special skills? What do you mean?

Do you think people can do their jobs better when each person has a special job? Why do you think so?

Tell the children that when people divide work so that each one does something special, we call that *division of labor*. Write this term on the chalkboard. Discuss this term by having the class respond to these questions:

Does anyone know another word for *labor*? (Children suggest *work* as a synonym for labor. This is discussed and examples are provided.)

Can anyone tell us in his or her own words what division of labor means? (Children respond that "division of labor means dividing the work.") This is discussed and examples are elicited.

Assessment and Summary
Have children tell in their own words how they see the division of labor in these places

in their school	at the shopping center
in their families	in a hospital
in the supermarket	at the airport
at the post office	anywhere else they may have visited

Materials
No special materials are needed.

Teaching Suggestions

A considerable amount of content of the elementary school social studies is drawn from sociology. This is particularly true in the primary grades. One of the units studied in first grade is "The Family." Children learn about the structure of this basic group in our society and elsewhere, some of its functions, and the roles of various members. This is usually followed in the primary grades by units dealing with the neighborhood, community workers, community living, and community institutions. As children study the diversification of work that is done in a modern community, they begin to see how various groups are formed and learn of the purposes of these groups. Later, in the higher grades, students will learn that the interests of such community groups are often in conflict and that this sometimes results in problems and sometimes in progress.

Studies of various cultures should focus on basic social processes rather than on the quaint ways used by the group to achieve them; that is, all groups have systems of communication, worship, education, and government. Much of value can be learned by showing what factors tend to disrupt conventional ways of living and cause people to change to other ways. Students in the middle and upper grades can also learn the consequences that befall cultures that do not make necessary changes in their way of living as external conditions change.

A teacher can do wonders to help children make connections.

In units on the growth of the United States in grades 5 and 8, as well as in home-state units in the fourth grade, children should study the cultural, religious, and racial backgrounds of the people who live there. Such a study will show that the United States is pluralistic and has benefited from the contributions of a great many cultures of the world. Often it is possible for children to see concrete evidences of contributions of other cultures in the life about them in things such as the names of towns, cities, bodies of water, festivals, customs, language, and famous men and women in our history. A knowledge of, and appreciation for, the contributions of other cultures to our own can be a strong force in combating harmful aspects of ethnocentrism. Such studies provide a setting in which to deal realistically with pluralism and with the distinctive multiethnic and multicultural composition of the United States.

Certainly, a problem that will be receiving increasing attention in the social studies is that of population distribution. In its simplest form, the study of population might call for the examination of population centers. Which areas are densely populated? Which are more sparsely settled and why? In the upper grades, students can study more intensively some of the problems that develop in areas of high population density. They can trace the movements of peoples and discover why they move when and where they do. They can compare population trends and birth and death rates in several countries, and examine problems faced by countries with rapidly increasing numbers of people.

Simulations

Disabled Society (grades 2–6) encourages children to participate in situations that help them understand and empathize with disabling conditions. In *The Numbers Game* (grades 5–12), the class is distributed proportionally to North America, Latin America, Asia, Africa, and Europe based on world population data. Cookies and crackers are then distributed, but based on each area's resources.[17]

Anthropology and the Social Studies

Anthropology, with its several divisions, is often thought of as a unifying social science because it is by definition the study of human beings in their totality: their culture. Anthropology is concerned with the development of language, social institutions, religion, arts and crafts, physical and mental traits, and similarities and differences of cultures. Anthropological concepts become a part of the social studies in the culture studies that are made of human societies.

Anthropological studies are often comparative. Such comparative, cross-cultural studies show the wide range of capabilities of human beings: modern medical practice and the tribal Shaman; affluence and poverty; humanitarian behavior and cruelty and war; urban living and rural life; life in extremely cold areas and life in hot, desert regions. People are, therefore, contradictory creatures, highly adaptive in their behavior, capable of remarkable achievements, rational yet often acting in irrational ways. They can, within limits, control and shape their environment and build a culture. They rely on their ability to think, imagine, and innovate to solve problems of living. This characteristic results in great diversity among the people of the world in how they live, what they believe, and how they conduct their affairs. Nonetheless, people are all part of the human family; all are a part of humankind, and all have many common physical and social needs.

A considerable amount of interest has developed in the exciting possibilities for social studies programs with an anthropological orientation. This may be, in part, a result of the increased importance of the non-Western world in international affairs and the traditional interest of the anthropologist in non-Western cultures. The increased interest in anthropology may also stem from the concern of the discipline with concepts that are so closely related to the shaping of the human personality, human institutions, and the evolution of human societies.

The following are representative generalizations from anthropology that have been used as organizing ideas in developing social studies units:

1. Every society has formed its own system of beliefs, knowledge, values, traditions, and skills that can be called its culture.
2. Culture is socially learned and serves as a potential guide for human behavior in any given society.
3. Although people everywhere are confronted with similar psychological and physiological needs, the ways in which they meet these needs differ according to their culture.
4. The art, music, architecture, food, clothing, sports, and customs of a people help to produce a national identity.

Teaching Suggestions

Anthropological studies deal with the concept of culture from many different perspectives—cultural determinism, cultural relativity, cultural diffusion, cultural borrowing, and cultural change. Other concepts included in anthropological studies are environment, languages, tools, adaptation, technology, human variation, values, authority, institutions, socialization, and of course many others. These concepts cut across several of the social science disciplines. Thus, social studies units often contain a substantial amount of information that could be defined as anthropological even though it may not be made explicit in the curriculum. The point is that there is already much in the social studies curriculum of most schools that is anthropological in content. Indeed, the unified concept of social studies has a closer kinship to anthropology, in terms of its attempt to deal with the totality of social phenomena, than it does to any of the other social sciences.

Activities such as the following have been used by elementary and middle school teachers in studies having an anthropological emphasis:

1. *Trace the development and use of certain tools*; associate ways of living with the use of tools.
2. *Follow the development of language and communication* systems from early signs and symbols to modern information dissemination devices.
3. *Identify ways that inventions have changed civilizations.*
4. *Have children serve as participant observers* in groups of which they are a part, such as their families, play groups, and teams.
5. *Prepare data-retrieval charts* to compare the use of resources, tools, technology, or other variables by different groups.
6. *Use role playing and creative dramatics* for cross-cultural comparisons of human behavior.
7. *Use music and art* to gain insight into the culture of a people.
8. In the upper grades, *participate in a simulated archaeological dig.*
9. *Provide experiences in the exchange of goods and services*, such as a simulation game involving medium of exchange.
10. *Study artifacts from the local area* that provide traces of the early history of the community.
11. *Simulations. Nacirema* (grades 5–6) asks students to examine a supposedly alien culture that is really American (Nacirema spelled backwards) and compare it to the culture of the Bushmen of the Kalahari Desert. *Dig 2* (grades 4–8) is a simulation of an archeological dig. Competing teams create a culture and bury representative artifacts on the school grounds. Each team then excavates and analyzes the other team's artifacts, using them to reconstruct its culture.[18]

Discussion Questions and Suggested Activities

1. Examine the *Curriculum Standards for Social Studies Sampler* that accompanies this text. In particular, read the performance expectations and the teaching examples given for history (theme 2), geography (themes 1, 3, and 9), economics (theme 7), sociology (theme 5), and anthropology (theme 1).

2. Select one of the fields discussed in this chapter, or civics/government from Chapter 3, and find out what particular methods of inquiry are used by scholars in that field. Explain how—or if—any of these might be adapted for use with elementary and middle school children.

3. Examine a social studies textbook and its accompanying teacher's manual. Which of the social sciences are included? In what way are they included? Are they integrated or taught separately?

4. Request a copy of a school district's social studies curriculum guidelines. Ascertain how the various social sciences were incorporated. If possible, interview one of the committee members who developed the guidelines.

5. Secure copies of the national standards documents (1994) for history and geography. Then determine which of the ten themes in the *social studies* standards document address some of the same topics.

6. Dividing the labor with classmates, gather and evaluate the children's trade books suggested in the history and geography sections of this chapter.

7. Obtain a copy of Sharon Pray Muir's simulations bibliography referenced in this chapter. Dividing the labor with classmates, gather and evaluate those suggested here for history, geography, economics, sociology, and anthropology.

8. School librarians and media specialists frequently organize exhibits around selected social studies themes throughout the year. For example, Black History Month in February and Women's History Month in March provide opportunities for librarians to display relevant books and references. Visit an elementary school library. Ask the librarian or resource person about other special weeks or holidays during the year. How might these be tied to the social studies program?

9. How might all of the fields of study discussed in this and the prior chapter be integrated to help children examine and experience social roles such as *family member, producer, consumer, friend, worker, volunteer, member of social and civic groups,* and *citizen*?

10. A year-long program entitled MAN: A COURSE OF STUDY (MACOS) was an anthropology-based program developed during the 1960s for the fifth grade. It was widely acclaimed by scholars as a fine effort to build social science concepts into the social studies curriculum. Yet, this program was thoroughly rejected by many parents and religious groups as being secular humanist in its philosophy, that it promoted relativism in values education, and that it taught children to question the authority of their parents and church leaders. Disregarding the specific issues of this particular program, discuss what you believe should be the appropriate role of parents in deciding the subject matter and procedures used in teaching social studies at the elementary and middle school levels. Do you have the same view regarding their role at the high school level? Why or why not?

Notes

1 Bruno Bettelheim, quoted in Charlotte Crabtree, "Returning History to the Elementary Schools," in *Historical Literacy*, eds. Paul Gagnon and the Bradley Commission on History in the Schools (New York: Macmillan, 1989), 176.

2 *National Standards for History for Grades K–4: Expanding Children's World in Time and Space* (Los Angeles: National Center for History in the Schools, 1994), 1.

3 *U.S. History Framework for the 1994 National Assessment of Educational Progress* (NAEP) (Washington, DC: U.S. Department of Education, 1994), 18.

4 Ibid., vi–vii.

5 *National Standards for History for Grades K–4*, 6.

6 Vivian Gussin Paley, *Wally's Stories* (Cambridge: Harvard University Press, 1981), 112.

7 See Sharon Pray Muir, "Simulations for Elementary and Primary School Social Studies: An Annotated Bibliography," *Simulation and Gaming: An International Journal of Theory, Practice, and Research* 7 (March 1996):41–73.

8 *Geography for Life: National Geography Standards* (Washington, DC: Geography Education Standards Project), 9.

9 *Ibid.*, 23

10 *Moving with Children*, Thomas T. Olkowski and Lynn Parker (Littleton, CO: Gylantic, 1993).

11 *Geography for Life*, 34–35.

12 See "Kids' Questions About Moving," in *Moving with Children*, 37.

13 See Muir, "Simulations for Elementary and Primary School Social Studies."

14 See Belinda Y. Louie, "Using Literature to Teach Location," *Social Studies and the Young Learner* 5 (January/February 1993): 17–18, 22; and Robert Stremme, "Great Geography Using Notable Trade Books" in *Children's Literature and Social Studies: Selecting and Using Notable Books in the Classroom*, ed. Myra Zarnowski and Arlene F. Gallager (Washington, DC: National Council for the Social Studies, 1993), 12–15.

15 See Muir, "Simulations for Elementary and Primary School Social Studies."

16 The Secretary's Commission on Achieving Necessary Skills (SCANS), *What Work Requires of Schools: A SCANS Report for America 2000* (Washington, DC: U.S. Department of Labor, 1991).

17 See Muir, "Simulations for Elementary and Primary School Social Studies."

18 *Ibid.*

Selected References

General

Cobblestone, Cobblestone Publishing, Inc., 7 School Street, Peterborough, NH 03458, Phone: 800-821-0115.

Laughlin, Mildred Knight, and Patricia Payne Kardaleff. *Literature-Based Social Studies: Children's Books and Activities to Enrich the K–5 Curriculum*. Phoenix: Oryx, 1991.

Naylor, David, Bruce Smith, Ann Lockledge, Mary Franklin, and other contributors. "Rethinking the Holidays." *Social Studies and the Young Learner* 6 (November/December 1993).

Wronski, Stanley P., and Donald H. Bragaw, eds. *Social Studies and Social Sciences: A Fifty-Year Perspective*, NCSS Bulletin No. 78. Washington, DC: National Council for the Social Studies, 1986.

History

1994 Standards: *National Standards for History*, 3 volumes: K–4 general, 5–12 U.S. History, and 5–12 World History. *Write*: National Center for History in the Schools, University of California at Los Angeles, 10880 Wilshire Blvd., Suite 761, Los Angeles, CA 90024-4108.

Research: Downey, Matthew T., and Linda S. Levstik. "Teaching and Learning History." In *Handbook of Research on Social Studies Teaching and Learning*, edited by James P. Shaver. New York: Macmillan, 1991, 400–10.

Resources

Haas, Mary E., Sherry L. Field, Lynn Nelson, Cynthia Szymanski Sunal, Samuel Totten, and other contributors. "History and the Young Learner." *Social Studies and the Young Learner* 7 (November/December 1994).

Nelson, Jack L. "Charting a Course Backwards: A Response to the National Commission's Nineteenth Century Social Studies Program." *Social Education* 54 (November/December 1990): 434–37.

Ravitch, Diane. "The Plight of History in American Schools." In *Historical Literacy: The Case for History in American Education*, edited by Paul Gagnon. New York: Macmillan, 1989, 50–68.

Wilson, Suzanne M. "Mastodons, Maps, and Michigan: Exploring Uncharted Territory While Teaching Elementary School Social Studies." *Elementary School Journal* (in press).

Geography

1994 Standards: *Geography for Life: National Geography Standards. Write*: National Geographic Society, P.O. Box 1640, Washington, DC 20013-1640.

Research: Stoltman, Joseph P. "Research on Geography Teaching." In *Handbook of Research on Social Studies Teaching and Learning*, edited by James P. Shaver. New York: Macmillan, 1991, 437–47.

Resources

Association of American Geographers and National Council for Geographic Education. *Guidelines for Geographic Education, Elementary and Secondary Schools*. Washington, DC: Authors, 1984.

Louie, Belinda Y. "Using Literature to Teach Location." *Social Studies and the Young Learner* (January/February 1993): 17–18, 22.

Salter, Christopher L., and Cathy Riggs-Salter. "Five Themes in Geography and the Primary-Grade Learner." *Social Studies and the Young Learner* 1 (November/December 1988): 10–13.

Stremme, Robert. "Great Geography Using Notable Trade Books." In *Children's Literature and Social Studies: Selecting and Using Notable Books in the Classroom* edited by Myra Zarnowski and Arlene F. Gallagher. Washington, DC: National Council for the Social Studies, 1993.

Economics

Standards are being developed. *Write*: National Council on Economic Education, 432 Park Ave. S., New York, NY 10016.

Research: Schug, Mark C., and William B. Walstad. "Teaching and Learning Economics." In *Handbook of Research on Social Studies Teaching and Learning*, edited by James P. Shaver. New York: Macmillan, 1991, 411–19.

Resources

Joint Council on Economic Education. *Economics: What and When: Scope and Sequence Guidelines, K–12*. New York: Author, 1988.

Kourilsky, Marilyn L. "Children's Learning of Economics: The Imperatives and the Hurdles." *Theory Into Practice* 36 (Summer 1987): 198–205.

Sociology and Anthropology

Research: Nelson, Murry R., and Robert J. Stahl. "Teaching Anthropology, Sociology, and Psychology." In *Handbook of Research on Social Studies Teaching and Learning*, edited by James P. Shaver. New York: Macmillan, 1991, 420–26.

Resources

Barnes, Buckley R. "Using Children's Literature in the Early Anthropology Curriculum." *Social Education* 55 (January 1991): 17–18.

Boulding, Elise. *Building a Global Civic Culture: Education for an Interdependent World*. New York: Teachers College Press, 1988.

Cohen, Elizabeth. *Designing Groupwork*. 2d ed. New York: Teachers College Press, 1994.

Cole, Johnnetta, ed. *Anthropology for the Nineties: Introductory Readings*. New York: Free Press, 1988.

Little Soldier, Lee. "Making Anthropology a Part of the Elementary Social Studies Curriculum." *Social Education* 54 (January 1990): 18–19.

Civics/Government

1994 Standards: *National Standards for Civics and Government. Write*: Center for Civic Education, 5146 Douglas Fir Rd., Calabasas, CA 91302-1467.

Research: Patrick, John J., and John D. Hoge. "Teaching Government, Civics, and Law." In *Handbook of Research on Social Studies Teaching and Learning*, edited by James P. Shaver. New York: Macmillan, 1991, 427–36.

Resources

See Selected References, Chapter 3.

TIME LINES, MAPS, GLOBES, AND GRAPHICS: KEY TOOLS FOR THE SOCIAL STUDIES

Any subject can be taught effectively in some intellectually honest form to any child at any stage of development.[1]

The opening quote, taken from Jerome Bruner's landmark book, *The Process of Education*, has motivated two generations of teachers to empower children by teaching them the conceptual tools they need to succeed as reflective citizens, thoughtful workers, good neighbors, and friends of art and the natural environment. These concepts and skills too often are not taught, or not taught systematically and meaningfully. As we saw in Chapter 2, this is disproportionately the case for girls and for children from ethnic, racial, and linguistic minority groups.

This chapter examines a set of conceptual tools that are important if children are to make sense of time and place—that is, history and geography. We suggest numerous ways to teach them, and we are confident that readers will think of many more. These tools promote in students an attitude of thoughtfulness about historical and geographic information by requiring the organization and analysis of facts, rather than only their acquisition.

The social studies curriculum operates within a space-time matrix that might be represented very simply as follows:

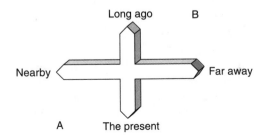

Experiences that could be charted at point A would be the least abstract and would usually be found in the primary grades. Experiences at point B would be more difficult to make concrete for children because they are remote not only in space but also in time. Because many children today have firsthand experiences that acquaint them with places beyond their immediate environment, it is not necessary to confine the social studies program to the local area. There can be some movement from the near at hand to the far away even in the early grades. This can be more difficult to do with the time dimension, however; hence the reliance on things that are known concretely—the family, the home, and community workers, for example—as vehicles for moving into the past. Examples include families now and long ago; homes the children live in today and the caves, castles, and manors of yesteryear; farmers and mail carriers now and then.

There are many instructional aids that can help one teach and learn about time and space. Time lines can make chronology more meaningful. Graphs and tables can make some types of quantitative relationships easier to comprehend: "half-way around the world," for example, or "four score and seven years ago," "soon thereafter," and "after a long journey." Globes and maps are indispensable tools for working with spatial phenomena. Refer to the color insert following page 140, which contains several types of maps that are used in elementary and intermediate schools. It is imperative, therefore, that the social studies program teach children how to use these tools.

Developing a Sense of Time and Chronology

Children, of course, learn much about time through ordinary living outside of school. Undoubtedly most children would learn how to tell time and the days of the week and months of the year, and they would become familiar with terms ordinarily used in referring to units of time, such as *noon, midnight, afternoon,* and *morning,* even if these were not taught in school. The school program can ensure that these are learned correctly, however, and can provide children the opportunity to practice using them with the guidance of the teacher and more capable peers.

Nonetheless, the main thrust of the school program should be on those aspects of time and chronology that are *not* likely to be learned outside of school. These include (1) the more technical vocabulary of time and chronology such as *century, decade, fortnight, fiscal year, calendar year, generation, score, millennium,* A.M., P.M., B.C., and A.D.; (2) placing events in chronological order; and (3) developing an understanding of the time spans that separate historical events. References to *indefinite* units of time—such as "many years ago," "several years had passed," and "in a few years"—need special attention because they are apt to mean almost any amount of time to young children. Definite references to time can be made meaningful by associating them with units of time that are known to the children: their own ages, the length of time they have been in school, when their parents or grandparents were their age, and so on. The teaching of these relationships can and should take place within the context of social studies units, especially those that focus on history, and in connection with current news stories.

The development of time concepts should begin with time situations that are within the children's realm of experience. Children should be given help in learning to read clock time and in understanding references to the parts of the day, days of the week, months, seasons, and the year. Even though primary-grade children make statements about things that happened "a hundred years ago," they have little comprehension of the real meaning of the expression and simply use it as a vague reference to something that happened in what seems to them a long time ago.

Time lines are often used to show how related events are arranged in chronological order and to show the relative amount of time that separates them. Teachers report success in helping children arrange events in proper sequence by using time lines. Using only a limited number of events that are clearly and saliently a part of the subject matter studied seems to enhance understanding.

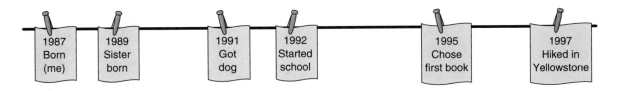

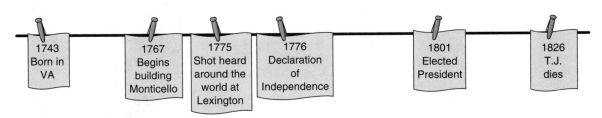

Figure 5–1
Times lines: Autobiographical and biographical.

Children can develop the concept of representing time on a continuum by first arranging events that they experience firsthand. They can make time lines that show things that happened to them yesterday, today, or are being planned for tomorrow. The amount of time included on the line can gradually be expanded to cover several months and then years. Time lines are more interesting to children if events are shown pictorially rather than simply as dots and dates. With upper-grade children, frequent use can be made of time lines in connection with historical studies of their home state and their nation. Such time lines need not stop with the present date but may be projected into the future, thus illustrating that time is continuous and that the present stands between the past and the future. Figure 5–1 shows two simple time lines, one of events in the child's own life and one of Thomas Jefferson's life.

Map and Globe Skills Essential to the Social Studies Curriculum

Maps and globes are vehicles for representing space symbolically. The essential features of all maps and globes are a grid, color, scale, symbols, and a legend that explains the symbol system used. The ability to read and interpret maps and globes, like conventional reading, is a summarizing skill in that it represents a composite of several subskills. These subskills can be inferred by making an analysis of the behavior of someone reading a map who is skillful at it. Fortunately, this will not be necessary

One good bulletin board speaks a thousand words.

because it has been done by specialists several times and always with somewhat the same results. One list that is available to school districts throughout the nation is published by the National Council for the Social Studies. According to this source, the essential map-reading skills include the ability to

1. orient a map and note directions,
2. locate places on map and globe,
3. use scale and compute distances,
4. interpret map symbols and visualize what they mean,
5. compare maps and make inferences, and
6. express relative location.[2]

Directional Orientation

To deal with directional relationships on maps and globes, the child must first understand them in reality. The easiest directions to use are those that express relative location, such as *close to, near, over here,* and *over there*. These can be learned in the primary grades. The *cardinal directions* are also learned in the primary grades by having them pointed out and by referring to places that are known to children as being north of, east of, south of, and so on. Placing direction labels on the various walls of the classroom helps remind children of cardinal directions. They can associate east and west with the rising and setting of the sun. They can learn how a compass is used to find direction. While on field trips, children should be given practice in noting directions, observing especially the directions of streets and roads. Gradually, they learn the purpose of the poles, the meridians of longitude, and the parallels of latitude in orienting a map and noting directions. When maps with unfamiliar projections are introduced, children should be taught how to establish correct directional relationships on them.

Using Map Scales

In making a map, the cartographer tries to reproduce as accurately as possible that portion of the earth being represented. Because globes are models of the earth, they can represent the earth more correctly than can maps. No map can altogether faithfully represent the earth simply because the earth is round and maps are flat. The flattening process inevitably results in some distortion.

Scaling is the process of reducing everything in the same amount. When one works with children in the primary grades, scaling should be done in the relative sense. Some things are larger or smaller than other things, and the maps should show their *relative size* as accurately as possible. For example, a fifty-foot-high tree in the schoolyard should be about five times larger than the ten-foot-tall playground set. On conventional maps, three types of scales are used:

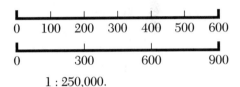

1. The graphic scale
2. The inches-to-miles scale
3. The representative fraction   1 : 250,000.

Of these, the graphic scale is the easiest to use and can be taught at about fourth grade. The inches-to-miles scale is more complex, but it can also be taught in the intermediate grades. The representative fraction is usually considered beyond the scope of the elementary school program.

As children become more global in their experiences, they will encounter map scales in metric measures. If metric measurement is used, the distance on a graphic scale would be recorded in kilometers. Likewise, rather than as inches to miles, the scale would show the relationship as centimeters to kilometers. The following graphic scale illustrates the same distance expressed in miles and in kilometers:

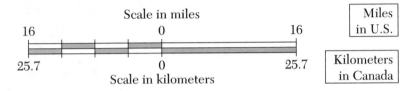

Locating Places

The ability to locate places on maps and globes comes with a familiarity with these devices cultivated over a period of several years. Children first learn to locate places that are known to them on simple maps and layouts that they make in the classroom. In the early grades, too, children can learn the names and shapes of some of the major geographic features, such as continents, oceans, the equator, and the poles. The commercially prepared maps and globes designed for the lower grades are quite plain, having only a few features shown. Gradually, children increase their repertoire of known places they can find on the map and globe because of frequent references to the location of important cities, countries, rivers, mountains, and other physical features.

In the intermediate grades, children are taught to use coordinates to locate places. Local highway maps are well suited for use in teaching this skill because they deal with an area familiar to the children. One set of lines of the grid—perhaps the north-south lines—is identified with letters; the other set of lines is numbered as is done in Figure 5–2. The teacher can have the children find several places located on or very near to a north-south line, say D. Then several places can be found on an east-west line, say 7. If the teacher is clever enough to pick two coordinates that intersect on a major point of interest, the children will discover that some city or other important feature is located at the point where D and 7 intersect. Figure 5–2 is an example of an exercise of this kind. This experience provides readiness for the use of meridians of longitude and parallels of latitude in locating places on wall maps and the globe. At this stage, children are mature enough to understand why reference points such as poles, the equator, and the prime meridian are essential in locating places on a sphere.

Reading Map Symbols

Maps use symbols to represent real things: Dots of varying sizes stand for cities of different populations; color is used to represent elevation; stars indicate capital cities; and lines are used to show boundaries, coastlines, and rivers. Naturally, the reader will not comprehend the messages of maps unless he or she knows what these symbols represent. Children begin to learn their meanings early in the elementary school social studies program. The development of this subskill closely parallels that of locating places on maps.

Figure 5–2

Intermediate-grade children can learn to use a grid in locating places by using road maps that have coordinates of the type shown on this map. Test your own memory of place locations by responding to these questions:

1.   What major city is located in square C2?

2.   What major city lies near the intersection of the squares D1, D2, E1, and E2?

3.   Describe the location of Savannah by using the coordinates provided on this map.

Check your answers by consulting a map of Georgia that shows cities.

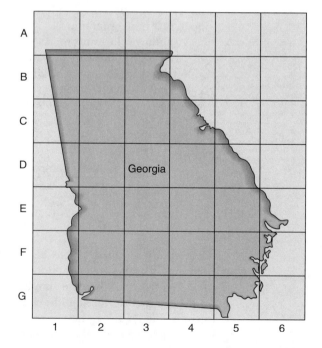

Map and globe symbols vary in their abstractness. Indeed, some simple maps for children in the primary grades use symbols that are pictorial or semipictorial. These symbols either look like the object being represented or provide a strong clue as to its identity, as shown in Figures 5–3 and 5–4. It would not take much imagination, for example, to differentiate water areas from land areas on a globe simply on the basis of their color.

The instructional sequence to be followed in teaching the symbol system of maps is to move gradually from pictorial and semipictorial symbols on maps made by children to the abstract symbols used on conventional wall maps, globes, and maps that are included in the textbooks of the middle and upper grades. It is essential that children learn to consult the map legend or key to confirm which symbols are being used. In most cases, children in the middle and upper grades will be dealing with maps that use conventional map symbols, but special-purpose maps such as those showing vegetation, rainfall, population density, and so on often use symbols that are unique to the particular map.

Figure 5–3
Children can be introduced to the concept of symbols through pictorial representations that they encounter in real life, such as the ones shown here.

Figure 5–4

Examples of standard symbols used on maps.

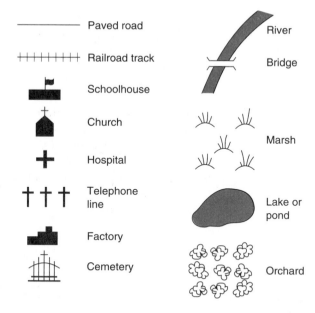

It is always a good idea to make generous use of photographs of the areas shown on a map in order to help the children associate the map symbol with what the place actually looks like. Similarly, when children go on field trips, they should be encouraged to observe carefully the appearance of landscapes, rivers, bridges, railroad tracks, and other features that are shown on maps. In time they will be able to visualize the reality that the abstract map symbols represent.

Understanding Relative Location

Understanding relative location is an interpretive skill that requires information beyond that provided by the map itself. It has to do with thinking about how places relate to each other in terms of political, cultural, religious, commercial, or historical perspectives. It has nothing to do with how close or how far away places may be in the absolute sense. For example, the non-Asian people—and even many Asians—of Hong Kong feel closer to Great Britain (10,000 miles away) than they do to the People's Republic of China (less than twenty miles away) because of political, economic, and cultural ties.

Relative location may also be thought of in terms of the amount of time required to get to a place using the kind of transportation available. This is commonly expressed nowadays in ordinary conversation and small talk as people say, "It takes me thirty minutes to get to work," or "I'm about two hours from Washington." Distances that now take two hours to traverse would have taken two days a hundred years ago and two weeks or even more at the time of the founding of the Republic. Increasingly, we reckon distances in terms of time. Consequently, places may be thought of as being remote or near in terms of how difficult it is to get to them. Air crash survivors stranded in the High Sierras in the dead of winter, no more than fifty miles from Fresno, California, might be as far away from civilization in the relative sense as they would be if they were in Antarctica.

Instructional Experiences with the Globe

Every social studies classroom should have a globe and use it often. In grades 1, 2, and 3 a simplified twelve-inch globe is generally recommended because small children find this size easier to handle than the larger sixteen-inch one. For primary grades, the globe selected should have a minimum amount of information on it. It should not use more than three colors to represent land elevation or more than two colors to represent water depth. Only the largest cities, rivers, and water bodies should be shown. In the intermediate and middle grades, a sixteen-inch globe is recommended because of its easy scale of one inch to 500 miles. Moreover, its larger size allows more detail to be shown without the globe becoming a confused collection of facts. Globes for intermediate and middle grade children will ordinarily use seven colors to represent land elevations and three colors to represent water depths.

The chief value of the globe in grades 1, 2, and 3 is to familiarize the children with the basic roundness of the earth and to begin to develop a global perspective. Parents speak of places in the news, and the children wonder where those places are. They hear of wars and famines and wonder about their location. Perhaps a girl has just joined the class; her family has recently moved to this country from another part of the world, and she wants to show the class the location of her former home. The teacher will use situations such as these—and hundreds more like them—to acquaint the young child with the globe.

The teacher should help children discover other things about the globe—differences between water and land areas and that these are represented by different colors; the line that separates the water and the land is called the seacoast. Children may be shown pic-

Globes invite inspection.

tures to help them visualize different kinds of coastlines. Similarly, the teacher extends their understanding of other concepts—oceans, cities, rivers, mountains. Children learn that most of the brown areas that represent land are on the half of the earth that has the North Pole and that it is here that the majority of the people of the world live.

In addition to the incidental references made to the globe, the teacher should make frequent use of the globe when teaching social studies and other subjects. For instance, in a reading lesson, children might find where their book friends "live." Thus, the globe can be used in a great variety of ways to lay a good foundation for more formal aspects of the teaching of these skills later on.

The following are examples of the *types* of learnings and experiences that can be planned with the globe for children in the lower grades:

1. Stress that the globe is a very small model of the earth. Good models look exactly like the real thing but are smaller. The globe is a good model of the earth.
2. Show the children how land areas and water bodies are represented on the globe. Have them find land areas and water bodies. Names of these need not be taught at this level, but children might already know the large water bodies such as the Pacific and Atlantic oceans. Similarly, they might be familiar with North and South America, Africa, or the Antarctic, and these can be pointed out. Explain that all water bodies and land areas have names.
3. Have children discover that there is considerably more water than land shown on the globe.
4. Show children the location of the North Pole. Explain that most of the land of the world is on the same half of the world as the North Pole. We call this the Northern Hemisphere or half.
5. Show children the location of the South Pole. Explain that most of the water areas of the world are on the same half of the world as the South Pole. We call this the Southern Hemisphere.
6. Explain that our earth is a planet.
7. Show children how they can find their country, their continent, their state, and possibly their city on the globe.
8. Use the globe to find places that are familiar to the children—places they have visited on vacations, places in the news, homes of book friends and visitors from other countries, or places in the world from which some circus or zoo animals are brought.
9. Encourage children to handle the globe and to find places on it themselves.
10. Answer questions the children ask concerning the globe in simple, nontechnical language.

Lesson Plan 4 is an example of a plan used by one teacher to familiarize primary-grade children with geographic concepts and skills using the globe.

As children move into the intermediate and middle grades, instruction in the use of the globe should take two forms. First, the teacher should take time from regularly scheduled unit activities to teach skills needed in reading and interpreting the globe. Second, in unit work and other classroom activities, there should be frequent reference to the globe and maps. Both of these aspects of instruction are important, and one

Using the Globe to Learn About Earth

Grade
1 or 2

Time
One class period

Objective
To develop a familiarity with concepts relating to the globe.

Interest Building
Give the children free time to manipulate a globe and explore it on their own.

Lesson Development
The teacher directs the following questions to the children:

What shape is a globe?

Can you find the North Pole? Place your finger on it.

Where is north on a globe?

Where is south on a globe?

Is south the opposite direction of north?

What divides the north from the south?

Have any of you lived near the equator?

Is the equator really a line?

How much of the globe is north?

How much of the globe is south?

What is half of a sphere?

Does anyone know what we call the northern half of the globe?

Does anyone know what we call the southern half of the globe?

How can we tell water from land on the globe?

Does anyone know what we call these large pieces of land?

Can you find a continent in the Northern Hemisphere?

Can you find a continent in the Southern Hemisphere?

Are there any continents that are in both hemispheres?

Summary and Assessment
How is the globe divided?

Can you name the parts of the globe we talked about?

Can you point to the Northern Hemisphere?

Can you point to the Southern Hemisphere?

Can you point to a continent?

Materials
As many globes as are available so that each child can easily explore and manipulate the globe.

should supplement the other. To hope that children will become skillful in the use of a globe or maps simply by making incidental references to them when the occasion presents itself is wishful thinking. At the same time, formal lessons in the use of these devices without application of the newly acquired skills in purposeful situations is equally ineffective. The best arrangement is to provide for systematic instruction in the use of map- and globe-reading skills as a part of unit activities, reinforcing this with direct teaching of these skills as the need arises.

Maps may be used to find distances between points only under certain conditions, but the globe represents distances accurately and true to scale at all points on the surface of the earth. It is easy to place a flexible ruler on the globe and measure directly the distance between two points in question, then refer to the scale and determine the actual distance between the two places. The air routes of the world use great circles because these are the shortest distances from place to place on the earth's surface. If nothing but flat maps are used, it is difficult to understand the concept of great circle routes and, therefore, of airplane routes. The globe can help clarify this concept (see Figure 5–5). In

Figure 5–5
Notice how differently the map and globe portray global relationships.

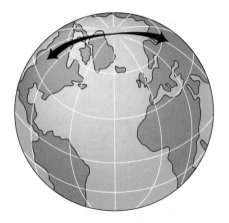

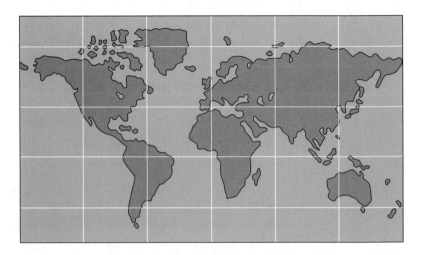

this connection, the slated globe (sometimes called the project globe) is useful because it is possible to write on the surface of it with a piece of chalk.

Globes are helpful, too, in establishing concepts of direction. It is not difficult to think of north as being in the direction of the North Pole when using a globe. On the other hand, this may be confusing if only a flat map is used. Furthermore, the relative direction of various parts of the earth can be better understood through the use of a globe. Many Americans are surprised, for example, when they learn that Great Britain lies in a more northerly latitude than do any of the forty-eight mid-continent states of our country; that Boston has nearly the same latitude as Rome; that our most westerly state is not Hawaii but Alaska; that our most southerly state is not Florida but Hawaii; that Moscow and Glasgow have approximately the same latitude, both being farther south than any city of Norway or Finland. These facts illustrate that one perceives the earth differently on a globe than on a flat map.

A definite advantage that globes have over maps is that they show the size and shapes of areas exactly as they appear on the earth's surface whereas maps cannot. The classical examples of distortions in the size and shapes of land areas are Greenland on the Mercator projection and Australia on the polar projection. On the Mercator projection, Greenland appears as a very large area—larger than South America. On a polar projection, Australia appears to have a greater east-west distance and a shorter north-south distance than is actually the case. Notice the different shapes North America takes on various maps as illustrated in Figure 5–6. A globe will show all these map shapes and sizes to be inaccurately represented. Therefore, a globe should be used with maps to prevent or correct misconceptions.

Instructional Experiences with Maps

A number of complex skills are involved in map reading and interpretation; therefore, early experiences with maps should be kept simple. This can best be done through the use of diagrams and maps that the teacher and the children make of their immediate vicinity. These experiences may take the form of a layout on the classroom floor, using blocks and other objects for houses, streets, trees, and public buildings. The layout can be done on a table, or the map can be drawn on a large piece of wrapping paper on the classroom floor. When the floor surface will permit, masking tape can be placed on the floor itself to represent boundaries, streets, or roads.

Opportunities to teach and apply these skills often arise in the everyday life of the classroom. For instance, children in one class learned about map direction when a new student joined the group. Soon after the child arrived, the teacher used a map to show the class the location of the child's previous home. They determined the direction the child's family traveled to reach their new home. The teacher then used a map of the local area and had the children discover the direction they travel in going from their homes to school each day.

Teaching Map Symbols

A fundamental skill in map reading is to learn that a symbol represents a real and actual thing. The symbol may be arbitrarily chosen and bear no resemblance to the object

Figure 5–6

A land area such as North America may take a variety of shapes on maps, depending on the projection that is used. Professional cartographers continually search for more exact ways to show the earth's surface on flat maps. In 1988, its centennial year, the National Geographic Society selected a new map projection that more accurately represents the earth than did earlier projections. The new projection was developed by Arthur H. Robinson at the University of Wisconsin-Madison. The Robinson projection replaces the Van der Grinten projection that had been used by the Society for its world maps for more than five decades.

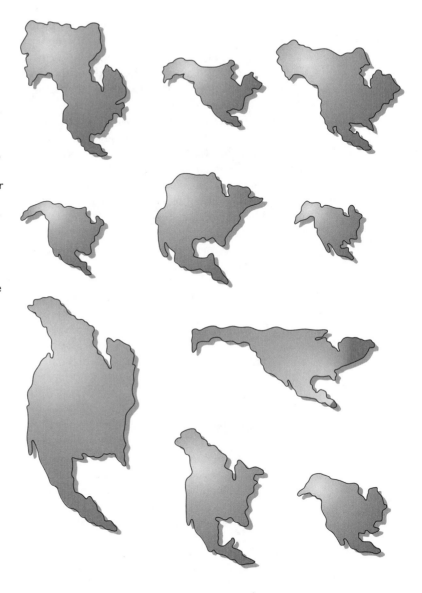

represented, or it may be one that would suggest to the reader what is intended. A school might be represented by a small circle or by a small square with a flag placed on top. It is easier to associate the flag and square with a school than to associate the circle with it. The flag and square are, therefore, less abstract. With young children, it is better to use pictorial or semipictorial symbols of this sort than to use completely abstract ones. In teaching map-reading skills, one must remember that both reading and interpretive skills are involved, and the interpretive skills depend heavily on maturity and background knowledge. Primary-grade children will do less with interpreting maps than they will with reading them.

DO-IT-YOURSELF MAP

This exercise can be used in the intermediate and middle grades for teaching or assessing map skills. The teacher can have everyone in class do the exercise as the directions are read, one step at a time. Directions can also be displayed with an overhead projector. When the maps are completed, the exercise should be discussed. Children can be invited to walk around the room to see maps drawn by their classmates. Maps can also be displayed on the bulletin boards.

Directions:
1. On a clean sheet of paper, draw an outline map of an imaginary continent. You may make it any shape you wish, but you must include at least one peninsula and one bay.
2. Show a scale of miles in your legend for the map.
3. Draw east-west and north-south lines on your map.
4. Draw a mountain range running east and west across your continent, but include at least one mountain pass. Place the symbol you use for your mountain range in your legend.
5. Show a city in the northern half of your continent and one in the southern half. Make each one a seaport.
6. Show a railway joining the two cities.
7. Show three rivers on your continent; show a lake and a swamp. Place all the symbols you use for cities, rivers, lakes, and swamps in the legend.
8. Place a third city somewhere on your map where you think a city should be. On the bottom of your map tell why you think a city should be where you have placed it.
9. Show boundary lines that divide your continent into three large countries and one small country.

The idea of objects representing other objects, people, or things is not new to the children; they have substituted symbols for the actual things many times in imaginative play. The teacher can begin by explaining that they are going to draw a map of the schoolroom, schoolyard, or some segment of the immediate vicinity. It is best if this can be done on the classroom floor, so the layout can be oriented exactly as it appears in relationship to the classroom; this sidesteps the matter of orientation to directions at this early stage. Trees, doors, playground equipment, parking areas, and other objects appear in relation to other objects, and only the major ones should be included. The purpose of this experience is simply to show that it is possible to represent space symbolically and that symbols stand for real things. Their maps should have a title and a key to tell what the symbols stand for. This is the first experience in the development of skill in comprehending the significance of symbols, and it will be continued and extended as long as maps are used.

As the children become ready for more abstract symbols, such symbols will be introduced, taught, and used, as will more conventional map symbols. As a part of this instruction in the intermediate and middle grades, it is important to make generous use of pictures and other visual aids that will help children visualize the area represented. It is helpful, too, to take children to some high point in the community where they can look down on an area and see what it actually looks like from above. In most localities it is possible to purchase inexpensive aerial photographs of the local community, and these can be used in studying map symbols and in making maps of the local area. The teacher also should take advantage of the many fine maps and photographs in social studies textbooks to acquaint children with the appearance of various areas, landscapes, surface features, land and water forms, and people-made things that are represented symbolically on maps.

Teaching Map Directions

For reasons of simplicity, orientation to direction may be avoided in the children's first attempts at making diagrams or maps. But the need to orient a map properly for direction will become apparent to them if their classroom map is rotated. Being able to note and read directions is a prerequisite to serious map study, and this skill should be introduced fairly early, perhaps in the second grade. Children can learn the cardinal directions by having the directions pointed out to them. They learn which wall of the room is north, south, east, and west because the teacher may have placed labels on the walls. They learn that if one knows the direction of north, the other directions can be determined; for if one faces north, the direction of south will be to one's back, east to the right, and west to the left. To extend their ability to orient themselves, children should be taken outdoors and the directions pointed out to them. If this is done at noon on a sunny day, the children's shadows will point in an approximate northerly direction. After the children have this basic orientation to direction, subsequent mapwork should include reference to direction and should become increasingly more complex.

Finding directions on conventional wall maps can be facilitated with the aid of a globe and perhaps should not be taught much below the fourth grade. When this concept is introduced, it should be done through reference to north-south and east-west grid lines. Children are taught that north is in the direction of the North Pole and that south is in the direction of the South Pole. The poles can be easily found by following the meridians of longitude. The east-west directions can be found by following the parallels of latitude. Generalizations such as "north is at the top of the map" and "south is at the bottom of the map" should *not* be taught because they are not correct and because they may be confusing when one uses a variety of different map projections. Similarly, references to north as "up" and south as "down" should not be taught in connection with either maps or globes. When we speak of the earth, the term *down* means toward the center of the earth and *up* means away from the center of the earth, and both terms should be taught only in that way. The matter of associating *up* with north introduces many instructional problems as children learn more of the geography of the earth. For example, if north is up, how can so many of the world's rivers flow north? The children will invariably ask why we say "way down South" or "the Land Down Under"; these can be explained as being colorful expressions and figures of speech similar to "way out West" or "out at sea" that have crept into our language but have nothing at all to do with direction itself. (See Figure 5–7.)

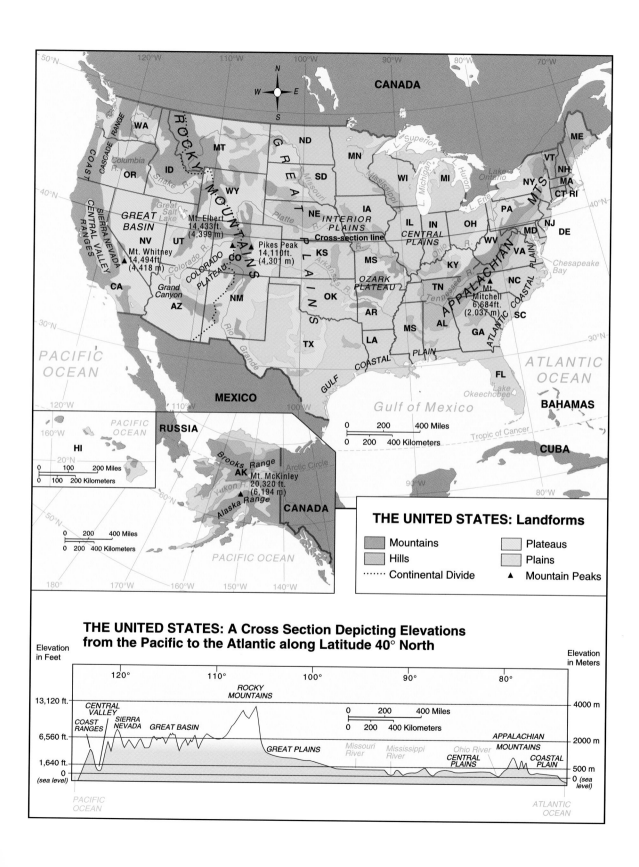

CANADA

WA
OR
ID
MT
ND
MN
ME
VT
NH
MA
CT RI
NY
SD
WI
MICHIGAN
OR
WY
NE
IA
IL
IN
OH
PA
NJ
DE
MD

ROCKY MOUNTAINS
CASCADE RANGE
GREAT BASIN
Columbia R.
Snake R.
Great Salt Lake
GREAT PLAINS

COAST RANGE
SIERRA NEVADA RANGES
CENTRAL VALLEY

NV
UT
CA
NM
AZ

Mt. Elbert
14,433 ft.
(4,399 m)
CO

Pikes Peak
14,110 ft.
(4,301 m)

Mt. Whitney
14,494 ft.
(4,418 m)

Grand Canyon

COLORADO PLATEAU

Colorado R.

KS
MO
OK
AR
TX

INTERIOR PLAINS
CENTRAL PLAINS
Cross-section line

Platte R.
Arkansas R.
Rio Grande

OZARK PLATEAU

KY
TN
MS
AL
GA
SC
NC
VA
WV

APPALACHIAN MTS
ATLANTIC COASTAL PLAIN

Mt Mitchell
6,684 ft.
(2,037 m)

Tennessee R.
Ohio R.
Mississippi
Missouri

L. Superior
L. Michigan
L. Huron
Lake Ontario
L. Erie

Chesapeake Bay

LA
MS
COASTAL
GULF
PLAIN

PACIFIC OCEAN

MEXICO

FL
Lake Okeechobee

Gulf of Mexico

ATLANTIC OCEAN

BAHAMAS

CUBA

Tropic of Cancer

0   200   400 Miles
0   200   400 Kilometers

RUSSIA

PACIFIC OCEAN

HI

Brooks Range
AK
Mt. McKinley
20,320 ft.
(6,194 m)
Yukon R.
Alaska Range
CANADA
Arctic Circle

0   100   200 Miles
0   100   200 Kilometers

0   200   400 Miles
0   200   400 Kilometers

PACIFIC OCEAN

THE UNITED STATES: Landforms

- Mountains
- Hills
- ...... Continental Divide
- Plateaus
- Plains
- ▲ Mountain Peaks

THE UNITED STATES: A Cross Section Depicting Elevations from the Pacific to the Atlantic along Latitude 40° North

Elevation in Feet

13,120 ft.

6,560 ft.

1,640 ft.
0
(sea level)

120°   110°   100°   90°   80°

ROCKY MOUNTAINS

CENTRAL VALLEY
COAST RANGES
SIERRA NEVADA
GREAT BASIN

GREAT PLAINS

Missouri River
Mississippi River
Ohio River

CENTRAL PLAINS

APPALACHIAN MOUNTAINS
COASTAL PLAIN

0   200   400 Miles
0   200   400 Kilometers

Elevation in Meters

4000 m

2000 m

500 m
0 (sea level)

PACIFIC OCEAN

ATLANTIC OCEAN

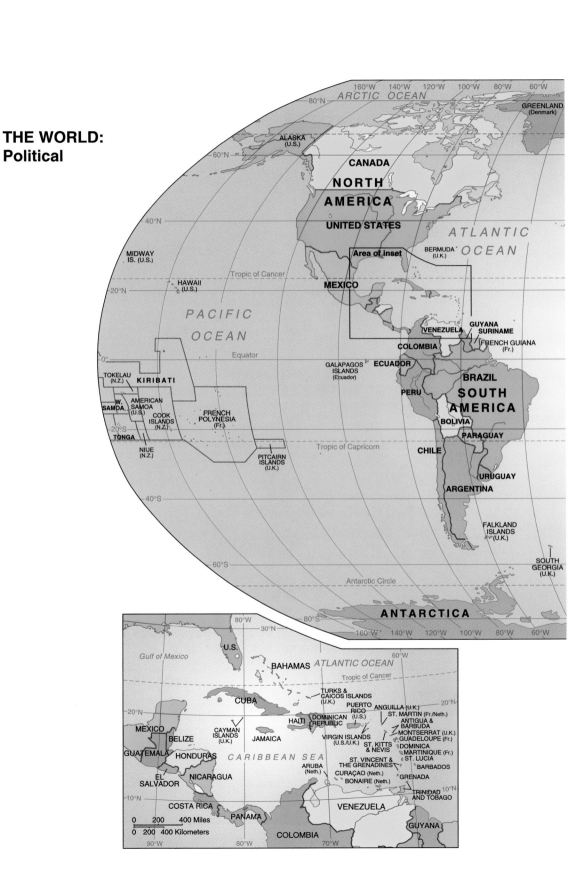

THE WORLD:
Political

ARCTIC OCEAN

160°W 140°W 120°W 100°W 80°W 60°W

80°N

GREENLAND
(Denmark)

ALASKA
(U.S.)

60°N

CANADA

NORTH
AMERICA

40°N

ATLANTIC

OCEAN

UNITED STATES

MIDWAY
IS. (U.S.)

BERMUDA
(U.K.)

Area of inset

Tropic of Cancer

20°N

HAWAII
(U.S.)

MEXICO

VENEZUELA

GUYANA
SURINAME

PACIFIC

COLOMBIA

FRENCH GUIANA
(Fr.)

OCEAN

Equator

0°

GALAPAGOS
ISLANDS
(Ecuador)

ECUADOR

TOKELAU
(N.Z.)

KIRIBATI

BRAZIL

PERU

SOUTH

W.
SAMOA

AMERICAN
SAMOA
(U.S.)

COOK
ISLANDS
(N.Z.)

FRENCH
POLYNESIA
(Fr.)

AMERICA

BOLIVIA

20°S

TONGA

PARAGUAY

NIUE
(N.Z.)

Tropic of Capricorn

CHILE

PITCAIRN
ISLANDS
(U.K.)

URUGUAY

40°S

ARGENTINA

FALKLAND
ISLANDS
(U.K.)

60°S

SOUTH
GEORGIA
(U.K.)

Antarctic Circle

80°S

ANTARCTICA

160°W 140°W 120°W 100°W 80°W 60°W

30°N

Gulf of Mexico

U.S.

BAHAMAS

ATLANTIC OCEAN

60°W

Tropic of Cancer

TURKS &
CAICOS ISLANDS
(U.K.)

20°N

CUBA

PUERTO
RICO
(U.S.)

ANGUILLA (U.K.)
ST. MARTIN (Fr./Neth.)
ANTIGUA &
BARBUDA

20°N

MEXICO

CAYMAN
ISLANDS
(U.K.)

HAITI

DOMINICAN
REPUBLIC

MONTSERRAT (U.K.)
GUADELOUPE (Fr.)

JAMAICA

VIRGIN ISLANDS
(U.S./U.K.)

DOMINICA
MARTINIQUE (Fr.)

BELIZE

ST. KITTS
& NEVIS

ST. LUCIA

GUATEMALA

CARIBBEAN SEA

ST. VINCENT &
THE GRENADINES

BARBADOS

HONDURAS

ARUBA
(Neth.)

CURAÇAO (Neth.)

GRENADA

EL
SALVADOR

NICARAGUA

BONAIRE (Neth.)

TRINIDAD
AND TOBAGO

10°N

COSTA RICA

PANAMA

VENEZUELA

GUYANA

0 200 400 Miles

0 200 400 Kilometers

COLOMBIA

90°W 80°W 70°W

Dictionary of
GEOGRAPHIC TERMS

STRAIT (strāt) A narrow waterway that connects two larger bodies of water.

PLATEAU (pla tō´) An area of elevated flat land.

GULF (gulf) Part of an ocean that extends into the land; larger than a bay.

DAM (dam) A wall built across a river, creating a lake that stores water.

RESERVOIR (rez´ər vwär) A natural or artificial lake used to store water.

MESA (mā´sə) A hill with a flat top; smaller than a plateau.

CANYON (kan´yən) A deep, narrow valley with steep sides.

BUTTE (būt) A small, flat-topped hill; smaller than a mesa or plateau.

DUNE (dūn) A mound, hill, or ridge of sand heaped up by the wind.

HILL (hil) A rounded, raised landform; not as high as a mountain.

VALLEY (val´ē) An area of low land between hills or mountains.

DESERT (dez´ərt) A dry environment with few plants and animals.

COAST (cōst) The land along an ocean.

BAY (bā) Part of an ocean or lake that extends deeply into the land.

ISTHMUS (is´m əs) A narrow strip of land that connects two larger bodies of land.

PENINSULA (pə nin´sə lə) A body of land nearly surrounded by water.

ISLAND (Î´lənd) A body of land completely sur-rounded by water.

Figure 5–7
This map illustrates why statements such as "north is at the top of the map" are incorrect. East-west lines or parallels of latitude have been omitted in order to draw attention to north-south directions. What questions might you pose to students studying this map?

Teaching Map Scale

Children can be helped to understand the need for map scales by indicating to them that maps must be small enough to bring into the classroom or carry around. We cannot make maps as big as the area we wish to show because that would make the maps so large they could not be used. A map must, therefore, be made smaller, and everything on the map must be made smaller in the same amount. Just as a photograph of the family shows everyone smaller in the same amount, so must the map; otherwise, it would not give a true picture. Children should learn that maps are precise and accurate tools.

In primary grades, the scaling is not done in the mathematical sense, but the reductions are correctly made in the relative sense. That is, lakes would be larger than houses; streets, longer than driveways; cars, smaller than business buildings; and so on. In intermediate grades, when children have had sufficient background in mathematics, they can deal with graphic reductions more precisely. They learn that wall maps have the scale printed on them and are taught how to read the various ways by which scale can be indicated. The experiences children have using map scales provide a good context in which to call their attention to distances between various places. Children can be helped to visualize these distances through an appreciation of the amount of time needed to traverse the distances in question by air travel. These times may be obtained in time tables from commercial airlines.

Teaching Map Interpretation

When children have learned the meaning of map symbols, are skillful in orienting a map to direction, and can recognize and use map scales, they are well on their way toward an understanding of the language of maps. This does not mean, however, that they find maps especially useful or that they regard them as a valuable source of information. The development of skills that deal largely with map language must be accompanied by associated interpretive skills. Proficiency in interpreting maps will vary considerably among the children. One who is skillful in map use has developed the ability to visualize what an area actually looks like when it is seen on the map. Looking at the map color, one in a sense "sees" the rugged Rocky Mountains of our West, the waving grainfields of western Montana, the rich farmlands of the Midwest, and the rolling countryside of Virginia. Because the child cannot visualize places not actually seen except in an imaginative way, the *generous use of additional visual material along with maps is suggested*. Good-quality pictures are especially important, and the class should see several pictures of an area to avoid fixing a single impression of the area in their minds. Filmstrips and slides can be used for the same purpose, and motion pictures and television are also excellent aids. As was previously noted, in the early stages of map reading, an excellent procedure is to have an aerial photograph of the local area as well as a conventional map. When these are placed side by side, the child can see how the area actually looks and how it is represented on a map. Stories and other narrative accounts also are helpful in assisting the child visualize areas represented on maps.

Activities such as the following can be used to relate the abstractions of maps to the reality they represent:

1. Observing local landscapes and geographical features, preferably from a high point.
2. Using pictorial and semipictorial symbols, especially at the lower grade levels.
3. Using three-dimensional models of the areas mapped; using blocks and models to represent buildings.
4. Making maps of the local area with which children are familiar.
5. Making generous use of pictures, films, and filmstrips of the areas shown on maps.
6. Relating aerial photographs (angle shots rather than perpendicular ones) to maps of the same area.

The types of information that can be read directly or inferred from map study can be classified as follows:

Land and water forms—continents, oceans, bays, peninsulas, islands, straits.

Relief features—plains, mountains, rivers, deserts, plateaus, swamps, valleys.

Direction and distance—cardinal directions, distance in miles or kilometers, relative distance, scale.

Social data—population density, size of communities, location of major cities, relationship of social data to other factors.

Economic information—industrial and agricultural production, soil fertility, trade factors, location of industries.

Political information—political divisions, boundaries, capitals, territorial possessions, types of government, political parties.

Scientific information—location of discoveries, ocean currents, location of mineral and ore deposits, geological formations, air movements.

Human factors—cities, canals, railroads, highways, coaxial and fiber optic cables, telephone lines, bridges, dams, nuclear power plants.

Comparing Maps and Making Inferences

Comparing different maps of the same place can be an insightful experience. In the fourth and fifth grades, teachers often have children compare vegetation maps with rainfall maps. They also have them compare maps showing the location of important resources, such as iron and coal, with maps showing the location of industrial centers, population densities, and so on. It is quite common to find special-purpose maps of the same region in the children's textbook, making comparisons easy. These provide excellent settings for critical thinking as the children can study the data presented on two or more maps, make predictions or hypotheses about these data, and then go on to the next step of verifying or rejecting their speculations.

Children in the intermediate and middle grades should study maps based on different projections and compare the shapes and sizes of known areas with those same areas as shown on the globe. This will familiarize them with the concept of distortion, which, in greater or lesser amounts, is present in all flat maps. Children should learn why distortion occurs and what cartographers have done to minimize its effect.

Teaching Map Color

The use of color has caused confusion for children trying to visualize elevations. Children seem to believe that all areas represented by one color are precisely the same elevation, not recognizing that there are variations in elevations that occur within the limits of the interval used by the color representation. (See Figure 5–8.) Moreover, children develop the mistaken idea that elevations occur abruptly where colors change. Conventional color symbols give no impression of gradual elevations or depressions and create the illusion that changes are abrupt. The use of a relief map helps show that changes in elevation occur gradually. Comparing colors of a wall map with elevations on a relief map helps children gain a better understanding of map color as used to represent elevations.

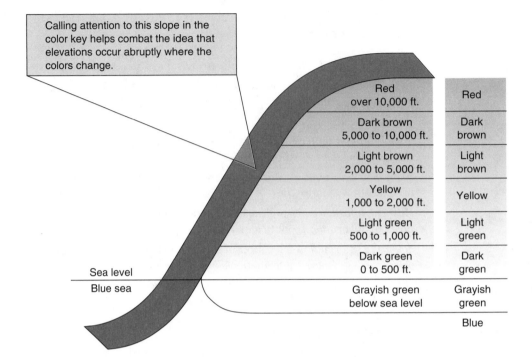

Calling attention to this slope in the color key helps combat the idea that elevations occur abruptly where the colors change.

Red over 10,000 ft.	Red
Dark brown 5,000 to 10,000 ft.	Dark brown
Light brown 2,000 to 5,000 ft.	Light brown
Yellow 1,000 to 2,000 ft.	Yellow
Light green 500 to 1,000 ft.	Light green
Dark green 0 to 500 ft.	Dark green
Grayish green below sea level	Grayish green
	Blue

Sea level
Blue sea

Figure 5–8
This diagram shows two methods of illustrating keys to colors, used to express elevations on class-room maps. Some teachers find it helpful to construct a three-dimensional papier-mâché model of the key to help students associate elevation with the color code.

Landform maps are often used in social studies textbooks. (See the color insert fol-lowing page 140.) The usual landforms shown are *plains, plateaus, hills*, and *mountains*; each is represented by a different color. Difficulty in using these maps arises when the child mistakenly thinks of the colors as representing elevations in absolute amounts. For example, there are high mountains and low mountains, yet on a landform map they may appear in the same color. Some high plateaus are actually higher in absolute eleva-tion than some low mountains. Some hills may be lower in elevation than plateaus and plains. Children need to learn that landform maps show only where the plains, plateaus, hills, and mountains are located, not how high they are above sea level.

Applying Map and Globe Skills

Map- and globe-reading skills are learned through direct teaching and by application in situations in which the skill is normally used. In many instances, these processes can be combined. Let us say, for example, that children in a fifth-grade class read that "Permafrost is a condition found only in high latitudes." The teacher can use this encounter with *high latitudes* to teach map reading in connection with that concept. That is, class time can be taken to teach the meaning of *high, low*, and *middle latitudes* on maps and globes, and the teaching would occur in what we refer to as a functional or authentic setting. Teachers are encouraged to teach as many map and globe skills as possible in this way rather than to

MAKING A TRIP MAP

The teacher showed children color photographs of several states and discussed the many interesting things that can be seen and done in the various states. Children shared some of their own travel experiences. The teacher provided the class with road maps of several different states and asked them to find places that might be of interest to someone visiting those states. These places of interest were discussed briefly. Children were then asked to think about and select a state they would enjoy visiting. Choices were to be made by the next day.

The following day the children made their selections of states they wanted to "visit." Using a road map of that state provided by the teacher and using references available in and outside the classroom, they were to plan a route of travel through the state of their choice, making at least five stops at places that would be interesting to a visitor. These places were to be marked with a large dot. A short narrative description was to be written to accompany the map telling about the travel route, state or national parks, natural areas of interest, historical landmarks, or other items of interest. If the children preferred, they could prepare a verbal rather than a written narrative by using the cassette recorder in the classroom.

The children responded to the teacher's encouragement to be creative in describing their imaginary trips, and several prepared travel brochures and recorded travelogs. They began a classroom exhibit of their trip maps and narratives, and in a week the room resembled a travel agency office. This generated a considerable amount of discussion and sharing of ideas and, of course, numerous opportunities to learn about maps. Also, through this activity the children acquired a great deal of information about their country, applied important skills (reading, research, writing, discussion, speaking), and developed an appreciation for the diversity and variety of their own country.

---

isolate the skills from their relevant subject matter. After direct teaching there must be a generous application and use of the skills if proficiency is to be developed and maintained.

Because these skills are *developmental*, one cannot expect to teach them once and assume that they have been learned. Most skills are introduced early in the grades and then are retaught, reviewed, or expanded later on. We expect that children will show increased proficiency and maturity in their use of these skills each year they are in school. Such development comes through continued teaching and use, not automatically through the natural process of maturation.

What follows is a list of map and globe activities that will provide the teacher with examples of the kinds of activities that can be used to stimulate interest and at the same time teach important concepts and thinking skills related to map and globe reading.

1. After an on-the-spot observation of the school grounds or the immediate vicinity, construct a three-dimensional floor map of the area.
2. Locate the place where stories about children in other lands take place or where news events are occurring.
3. Find pictures in magazines and the textbook that illustrate various landforms: plains, plateaus, hills, and mountains.

4. Make maps of the same area, such as the playground or local county, using different scales for each map.
5. Plan a pretend trip to a distant place. Locate the destination in relative and absolute terms. Have small groups each develop a different route, one group heading east, another going west, another south, another southeast and so on.
6. Develop a classroom exhibit of maps found in current newspapers and periodicals. Place captions under each that describe its unique features, errors, and projection.
7. Secure an outdated political map of the world and have the class compare it with a current one.
8. Make use of board games such as *Take Off* and computer software such as *Where in the World Is Carmen Sandiego?* to build and reinforce map and globe skills.
9. Develop an illustrated glossary of geographic concepts and terms.
10. Hold a regular "Monday Morning Geography Bee" using those concepts and terms. Teacher-assigned teams rehearse and compete, vying to spell and define the terms correctly. Figure 5–9 contains more than 50 terms. The teacher can select terms the children are ready for, and children can work on the definitions, using the textbook, dictionary, and other references, as they compile the illustrated glossary in item 9.

Regular social studies unit work and the current events program provide natural settings for teaching map and globe skills. Children can use maps to record their data or observations as they study unit topics. They can think through the significance of the relationships they detect in maps. They can use maps as a means of communicating ideas and findings to their classmates. It has been said that maps are the constant companions of geographers, and the same might be said about children as they engage in the social studies.

Teaching map and globe skills does require some special resources and equipment. Every classroom should have a globe along with wall maps appropriate to the curriculum content of the grade. In fourth grade and above, all classrooms should have a wall map of the world. Outline maps are needed, and it helps to have available a three-dimensional relief map of the United States and of the home state. Additional equipment might include charts showing conventional map symbols; slated maps and globe; and special-purpose maps showing vegetation, historical development, and natural resources. When children engage in map making, they will need to have available essential construction materials: boxes, blocks, butcher paper, black tape, tracing paper, colored pencils, pens or crayons, paints and brushes, papier-mâché, plaster, salt and flour, or other modeling material.

A Summary of Map and Globe Skills

Elementary- and middle-school children should develop map and globe skills associated with the following concepts and generalizations:

1. Primary grades

• A map is a drawing or other representation of all or part of the earth.
• On maps and globes, symbols are used to stand for real things.
• The earth is a huge sphere.

Figure 5–9
The Monday Morning Geography Bee.

Select easier or more difficult terms from this list as appropriate.

absolute location	forest	migration
artifacts	globe	monsoon
barrier island	groundwater	mountain range
bay	hemisphere	multinational organization
biosphere	hill	nonrenewable resource
cartographer	hurricane	plateau
climate	hydrosphere	pond
contour map	industrialization	population density
creek	infant mortality rate	rain shadow
culture	interdependence	region
deforestation	landform	relative location
desert	lake	river system
developing country	latitude	scale
ecology	legend (key)	settlement pattern
equator	longitude	sustainable development
ethnocentrism	map	terrace
fauna	map projection	urbanization
fertility rate	mesa	
flora	metropolis	

- A globe is a small model of the earth and is the most accurate representation of the earth.
- Half of the earth is called a hemisphere.
- The earth can be divided into several hemispheres. The most common ones are the Eastern, Western, Northern, and Southern Hemispheres; land hemisphere and water hemisphere; and day hemisphere and night hemisphere.
- Any part of the globe can be shown on a map.
- Large bodies of land are called continents.
- Large bodies of water are called oceans.
- Terms such as *left, right, near, far, above, below, up,* and *down* can be useful in expressing relative location.
- A legend or key on a map tells the meaning of colors and symbols used on the map.
- Directions on a map are determined by the poles; to go north means to go in the direction of the North Pole, to go south means to go in the direction of the South Pole.
- North may be shown any place on a map; north is *not* always at the top of a map.
- The North Pole is the point farthest north on the earth; the South Pole is the point farthest south.
- The scale on a map or globe makes it possible to determine distances between places.

- Maps are drawn to different scales; scale ensures that all objects are made smaller in the same amount.
- Maps and globes use legends, or keys, that tell the meaning of the symbols used on the map.
- The cardinal directions are north, south, east, and west; intermediate directions are northeast, northwest, southeast, and southwest.
- All places on the earth can be located on maps and globes. Different maps provide different information about the earth.

2. Intermediate and middle grades

- The larger the scale used, the larger each feature appears on the map.
- The same symbol may mean different things from one map to another; the legend tells what the symbols stand for.
- The elevation of land is measured from sea level; some maps provide information about elevation.
- Physical maps can be used to determine land elevations, slopes of land, and directions of rivers.
- Parallels of latitude can be used to establish east-west direction and are also used to measure distances in degrees north and south of the equator.
- All places on the same east-west line (parallel of latitude) are directly east or west of one another and are the same distance north or south of the equator.
- All places north of the equator are in north latitudes; all places south of the equator are in south latitudes.
- The Tropic of Cancer and the Tropic of Capricorn are imaginary lines of latitude lying north and south of the equator. The part of the earth between them is known as the tropics.
- The Arctic and Antarctic Circles are imaginary lines that define the polar regions.
- The low latitudes lie on either side of the equator; the high latitudes surround the poles; and the middle latitudes lie between the low and high latitudes.
- Parallels of latitude, parallel to the equator, get shorter as they progress from the equator to the poles.
- Knowing the latitude of a place makes it possible to locate its north-south position on the earth.
- Meridians of longitude can be used to determine north-south direction and are also used to measure distances in degrees east and west of the prime meridian.
- The zero or *prime* meridian passes through Greenwich, a suburb of London.
- Meridians of longitude are imaginary north-south lines that converge on both poles.
- Meridians of longitude are *great circles* because they divide the earth into two hemispheres.
- The shortest distance between any two places on the earth follows a great circle.
- West longitude is measured to the west of the prime meridian from zero to 180°; east longitude is measured to the east of the prime meridian from zero to 180°.
- All places on the same north-south line (meridian of longitude) are directly north or south of each other and are the same distance in degrees east or west of the prime meridian.
- The latitude and longitude of any place determine its exact location on a globe or map.

- Longitude is used in determining the time of day at places around the world. The earth rotates through 15° of longitude every hour; the earth is divided into twenty-four time zones.
- Globes give such information as distance, direction, relative and exact location, and sizes and shapes of areas more accurately than flat maps can.
- Maps and globes often use abbreviations to identify places and things.
- An imaginary line through the center of the earth, running from pole to pole, is called the earth's axis; the earth rotates on its axis from west to east.
- Night and day are the result of the rotation of the earth.
- Maps and globes provide data about the nature of areas by using color contour, visual relief, and contour lines.
- All flat maps contain some distortion because they represent a round object on a flat surface.
- Different map projections provide different perspectives on the sizes and shapes of areas shown.

Teaching Children the Use of Graphs and Charts

Because of the widespread use of graphs and charts in social studies and in printed material outside of school, it is imperative that children develop the skills needed to read and interpret them. Just leafing through a daily newspaper or weekly news magazine reminds one of how commonly these graphics are used. Citizens today are "digest" oriented. They do not have the time or the inclination to wade through a mountain of narrative that explains social events or conditions. They want to see these ideas in summary form and in stark relief. Besides, the complexity of social data, much of which is in statistical form, lends itself well to a graphic format.

Graphs

Graphs are used to illustrate relationships among quantities. These relationships may be spread over a period of time, thus showing trends. The most commonly used graphs are some variation of the *bar graph*, the *pie* or *circle graph*, and the *line graph*. Any of these graphs may include pictorial representations, thereby making them more interesting to young children and making the content less abstract. For instance, with primary-grade children, stick figures can be used to represent children in a bar graph showing the number absent from class each day. It is easy to visualize the relationships of the parts to the whole in a circle graph, but to construct one accurately requires the ability to compute percentages, usually not possible in the elementary school grades. Modern elementary school textbooks make liberal use of graphs in presenting data, but children need to be instructed in how to read and interpret them. Because graphs can be designed to present distorted pictures of data, children in the intermediate and middle grades should be taught how bias is introduced in a graph. (See Figures 5–11, 5–12, and 5–13.)

Children can learn much about graphs and how to read them by constructing their own graphs. Such learner-made graphs can be used in making oral or written reports and for bulletin board displays. In the making of graphs, accuracy in the presentation should be emphasized rather than artistic perfection (see Figure 5–10).

Number of days the sun was shining at noon for the first five months

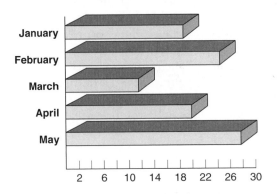

A class kept a record of the number of days the sun was shining at noon from the first of January through May. In January there were nineteen days when the sun was shining at noon; in February there were twenty–five; in March there were twelve; in April there were twenty; and in May there were twenty–eight days. These graphs show three different ways of showing these data. Graphs of this type can be constructed and used for study purposes by elementary schoolchildren. What inquiry questions might be based on these graphs?

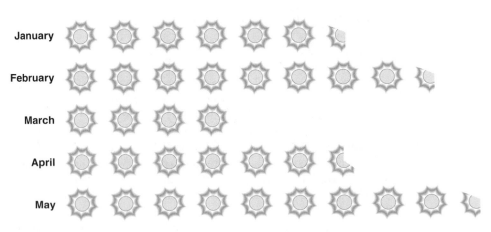

Figure 5–10
Examples of graphs and data suitable for use with elementary school children.

Figure 5–11

The drawing illustrates how the popular "pie" graph is sometimes used to create an incorrect impression. Because the sketch is shown in perspective, the sizes of the sections are distorted. Thus, sections that seem to be farthest from the viewer appear smaller than those in the foreground, although arithmetically they represent equal amounts.

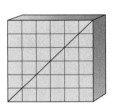 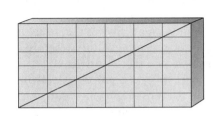 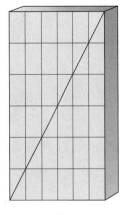

Figure 5–12

It is important for children to learn that graphs can create false impressions. In these line graphs, the same data were used on three different grids, resulting in varying steepness in the slopes of the lines. Consequently, although the facts are the same, the rate of change appears markedly different.

Figure 5–13

How much larger were profits in 1997 than in 1995? The chances are that you have said "about twice as large." This graph illustrates how wrong impressions are conveyed when pictorial graphs are improperly constructed. Careful examination of this graph will show that the 1997 profits are not even twice those of 1994. The basic error in this graph is that it does not show the first $500,000 of profit. A more accurate perception of the growth in profits can be made if the correct position of the baseline is established. Can you locate the place where the baseline should be?

Growth in profits over a four-year period

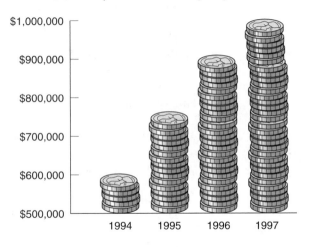

Charts

Like graphs, charts are widely used to present ideas in a vivid and forceful way. Charts are often designated as follows:

1. *Narrative chart*: Tells a story; shows events in sequence. (Examples: how ears of corn become tortillas, stages of the development of civilization, how to use a computer, or the construction of homes.)
2. *Tabulation chart*: Lists data in table form to facilitate making comparisons. (Examples: data placed in tabular form to show infant mortality rates, illiteracy rates, or per capita income among nations of the world.)
3. *Pedigree chart*: Shows events stemming from a common origin. (Examples: a family tree, the development of a political party, or the history of language.)
4. *Classification chart*: Groups data into various categories. (Examples: the various types of restaurants, types of personal services available, or different modes of transportation.)
5. *Organization chart*: Shows the structure of an organization. (Examples: the three branches of government, the structure of a corporation, or the organization of a city government or a school district.)
6. *Flow chart*: Shows a process involving change at certain points. (Examples: how raw materials are transformed into finished products or how scrap iron is converted into a usable raw material.)

The frequent use of charts in children's books provides a good basis for learning. In the process children not only learn how to read and interpret the chart, but also broaden their substantive knowledge and build their understanding of associated concepts.

. . . .

Discussion Questions and Suggested Activities

1. Make a time line showing six events in your life. One event should be your birth, shown at the far left end; another should be the making of the time line today, shown at the far right. Select four other events, and place them between these two. Be sure to show the relative amount of time between the events as in Figure 5–1.
2. Examine a current social studies textbook at a grade of your choice for its use of time lines and graphics. What are the different types of time lines shown?
3. Prepare a series of posters showing map symbols, and accompany each symbol with a photograph of the symbolized object.
4. Make a list of words or phrases related to the understanding of maps and globes that are misleading (for example, *up, down, outer space*). For each entry, suggest an alternate word that would be more accurate.
5. Secure a copy of the national geography standards, *Geography for Life*, and look in its glossary for definitions of the geographic terms given in Figure 5–9. Compare these definitions to those found in a dictionary. Skip ahead to Chapter 7 and read the section dealing with the teaching of concepts using the strategy called *concept formation*.
6. Develop an inquiry-oriented learning experience based on a map, globe, or chart. Arrange to teach it to your peers. Skip ahead to Chapter 7 to read about inquiry teaching.

7. Bring to class three wall maps of the world. These can be purchased for a few dollars at book stores and large drug stores, or borrowed from the campus map collection. Try to get three different projections: Mercator, Robinson, and Peters. Compare and contrast their distortions of land and water.

8. If you are teaching or have access to a class, try these activities.

   a. *Assessment.* Interview a class of children on the concepts *time* and *space*. Ask them for the meanings of such terms as *long ago, soon, century,* and *decade.* Then ask about *near, far, Southern Hemisphere,* and landforms such as *plateau, lake, bay,* and *mountain range.*

   b. *Proverbs.* Have the class think of as many popular expressions or proverbs as they can that have to do with time (e.g., "a stitch in time saves nine"; "time is money"). Conduct this activity for a period of days, and as phrases are suggested, place them on the bulletin board. Have children make drawings to illustrate them.

9. Make a chart or graph (your choice) to show how your time is spent during a school day.

Notes

1 Jerome Bruner, *The Process of Education* (Cambridge, Harvard University Press, 1960), 33.
2 National Council for the Social Studies, *Social Studies Curriculum Planning Resources* (Dubuque, IA: Kendall/Hunt, 1991), 36.

Selected References

Atkins, Cammie L. "Introducing Basic Map and Globe Skills to Young Children." *Journal of Geography* 83 (March 1984): 228–33.

Cochrane, Katherine. "China: A Case Study in Using Geography to Understand Culture." *Social Studies and the Young Learner* 4 (January/February 1992): pull-out feature.

Forsyth, Al, Jr. "Computer Simulation Games for Geography Basics." *Social Studies and the Young Learner* 1 (November/December 1988): 28–29.

Frazee, Bruce M. "Foundations for an Elementary Map Skills Program." *Social Studies* 75 (March/April 1984): 79–82.

Hatcher, Barbara. "Putting Young Cartographers 'On the Map.' " *Childhood Education* 59 (May/June 1983): 311–15.

Hicks, Sandye. "Mini-Units for Teaching Geography." *Social Studies and the Young Learner* 1 (November/December 1988): pull-out feature.

Miller, Jack W., Raymond Muessig, Linda S. Levstik, and Val Arnsdorf. Several articles related to building children's understandings of map skills. *Social Education* 49 (January 1985).

Muir, Sharon Pray. "Understanding and Improving Students' Map Reading Skills." *The Elementary School Journal* 86 (November 1985): 207–16.

Lacks, Cissy. "Sharing a World of Difference: International Education in the Early Years." *Social Studies and the Young Learner* 4 (January/February 1992): 6–8.

Rice, Gwenda H. "Teaching Students to Become Discriminating Map Users." *Social Education* 54 (October 1990): 393–97.

Sesow, F. William, David Van Cleaf, and Bob Chadwick. "Investigating Classroom Cultures," *Social Studies and the Young Learner* 4 (January/February 1992): 3–5.

Winston, Barbara J. *Map and Globe Skills: K–8 Teaching Guide.* Western Illinois University: National Council for Geographic Education, 1984.

CURRENT EVENTS AND PUBLIC ISSUES IN SOCIAL STUDIES

OVERVIEW

The things to do are the things that need doing.[1]

A ten-year-old named Michael wondered what to do with his life. Seeking advice, he wrote to Buckminster Fuller, the philosopher, map maker, architect, poet, and inventor of the geodesic dome. "Bucky's" response was direct:

Thank you very much for your recent letter. The things to do are the things that need doing; that *you* see need to be done, and that no one else sees need to be done.[2]

Bucky then tells Michael that doing what *he* sees needs to be done will naturally bring out his own, unique brilliance. He encourages Michael, closing the letter with this:

You have what is most important in life—initiative. Because of it, you wrote to me. I am answering to the best of my capability. You will find the world responding to your earnest initiative.[3]

The point of view in this chapter is that a program of teaching current events and social problems is a *must* in elementary and middle school classrooms. Such a program must be planned carefully and taught well. Without it, children are not likely to form citizenship dispositions that are critically important to the health of their communities, such as civic mindedness and initiative. Without it, they may not have adequate opportunities to see the things that need doing, to respond, and, in turn, to develop their own talents.

Included in the chapter are four strategies and several additional activities for teaching children about current events. As well, we address a sampling of the enduring social problems that make so many current events controversial: poverty, environmental degradation, crime, war and peace, and prejudice. When made appropriate to the ages and experiences of children and linked to social studies education, these events and problems can and should be taught in the elementary school.

Purposes

If this nation expects its adults to have an abiding interest in news and current developments and have a desire to keep informed, the ground-work for these attitudes, interests, and skills must be laid in the elementary school. The first major purpose of current events teaching at the elementary school level is, therefore, *to promote the habit of interest in current events and news developments.*

Intelligent analysis of current events requires the use of a variety of skills and abilities: (1) to read news materials, (2) to discriminate between important and less significant news items, (3) to take a position on issues based on a knowledge and a critical evaluation of the facts, and (4) to predict likely consequences in terms of present developments. *Promoting the growth of these skills and abilities represents the second major purpose of current events instruction at the elementary school level.* These skills evolve over several years through the study of current events under the direction and guidance of capable teachers. It is unrealistic to hope for an adult population that can exercise critical judgment regarding social problems and issues unless individuals have at their command the fundamental skills and abilities such action demands.

The third major purpose of current events teaching is *to help the child relate school learning to life outside school.* The constant reference to current events is good insurance against the separation of school activities from the nonacademic life of the child. Good teachers recognize that printed material begins to become obsolete shortly after it is written, and there is always a gap between the information contained in books and changing developments in the world. A generous use of current events materials helps to close this gap. Some encyclopedia publishers recognize the need for timely information and issue annual supplements that include changes that have occurred during the preceding year. Because textbooks and supplementary books usually are not revised each year, teachers must depend on such sources as newspapers and magazines for the latest information on some topics.

The Program of Current Events Instruction

The three most common methods of including current events in the elementary school program are (1) teaching current events in addition to social studies, (2) using current events to supplement or reinforce the regular social studies program, and (3) using current events as the basis for social studies units. A discussion of each of these methods follows.

Teaching Current Events in Addition to Social Studies

Ms. Hansen, who teaches fourth grade, plans to spend a few minutes each morning during the sharing period for the discussion of important news stories. She encourages children to bring news clippings from daily newspapers or from weekly magazines for the class bulletin board. Children are encouraged to bring news stories related to classroom work, and Ms. Hansen helps interpret these stories for the children by her comments and leading questions, such as

"Do you suppose the new highway will help our town?"
"What are the astronauts looking for on these expeditions?"
"Why do you suppose the animals died when they were brought here?"
"Can you show the class on the map the exact location of the explosion?"

Ms. Hansen uses a classroom periodical and plans to spend a half hour on it with the children each week. This consists of reading the material or portions of it, with a discussion following. She varies the procedure from week to week and uses the suggestions provided in the teacher's edition that accompanies the classroom periodical.*

This method has the advantage of providing a regularly scheduled time for news each day. Such periods can be useful in building interest in current events and in teaching skills of reading and interpreting news stories. It has the clear disadvantage of isolating current affairs from the remainder of the school program, most especially from the social studies. If current events teaching is handled as is done by Ms. Hansen in the example, time should be taken to relate news content to topics and units in social studies. This can be done by (1) interpreting news stories within the context of topics that have been studied or are under study; (2) extending the meaning of concepts developed in social studies; (3) applying social studies skills, such as map, graph, or chart reading, to the news stories; or (4) comparing and contrasting events in the news with events encountered in social studies units.

Using Current Events to Supplement Social Studies

Mr. Chung schedules his social studies period immediately following morning opening activities for his fifth-grade class. As a part of the beginning activities, he provides time for reporting of news and encourages children to report news items related to social studies. He and his class maintain a news bulletin board as well as a small table on which are placed news articles, magazines, current maps, or similar materials of a timely nature related to the social studies unit. He uses current events materials in this way to augment other instructional resources and as a means of reminding his class of the need for up-to-date information.

Mr. Chung often suggests parallels between events that happened long ago and events that are occurring today, thereby illustrating recurrent problems in the conduct of human affairs. For example, in the study of the struggle for freedom and independence in America, he used examples from present-day affairs to show that some people of the world are still struggling for the right to govern themselves. When the class studied early explorers, Mr. Chung related this study to present-day exploration.

The difference between this method and the one used by Ms. Hansen is that Mr. Chung is more explicit in making the connection between current events and social studies. He is concerned mainly with those news stories that can be related to his social studies program. He builds an awareness of the relationship between what is currently happening in the world and what the class is studying in social studies. He is using the affairs of the world as reported in the news media as a current information source for social studies. This method has the advantage of keeping the information base for social studies up to date. It has the disadvantage of restricting the range of news stories that are appropriate. Therefore, if this approach is used, the teacher should provide some opportunity to examine news items that are significant and timely, yet may not be directly related to the social studies unit under study at the time.

---

* *Scholastic News* is a newsweekly with different editions for grades K–8. For a sample, write Scholastic Inc., P.O. Box 3710, Jefferson City, MO 65102-9957.

Using Current Events as the Basis for Social Studies Units

Ms. Diaz likes to develop social studies units with her sixth-grade class around topics that are currently in the news. She schedules these between the regular units she is required to teach. During her years as a teacher, she has found that units of this type must be carefully selected because it is not always possible to find a sufficient amount of instructional material suitable for children that deals with topics in the news. Units that she has taught with success in this way in the past have dealt with gun control legislation; gangs; world organizations, such as the United Nations; meeting North America's energy needs, particularly oil; migration of the world's people; contemporary explorers; progress in science, medicine, and computer technology; and current elections. When Ms. Diaz selects the unit topics carefully, she finds it possible to include much of the subject matter ordinarily included in her social studies curriculum under other unit titles. She believes that the use of current news happenings as a starting point for units does much to stimulate interest and discussion in her class.

This method has the advantage of being highly motivating because it deals with subject matter that is of immediate interest. It also bridges school learning with life outside of school. It has the disadvantage of being difficult to plan because news events may not relate directly to the social studies curriculum. Also, news stories may not provide a continuing or sustaining source of information on topics, and, therefore, other sources would need to be available.

Any of the three current events programs described here can be used successfully. In good programs there will be time during the school day devoted to the study and discussion of current affairs that may be entirely unrelated to topics under study in the social studies units, and perhaps unrelated to any other curricular area as well. At the same time, in guiding unit work, the teacher will not ignore current events relating to the topic being studied but will, in fact, seek with enthusiasm the current events materials that will add strength to the unit. From time to time, too, the teacher and children can plan an entire social studies unit from current news developments. Units dealing with the topics of energy, environment, safety, intercultural relations, law and justice, housing, food, elections, discoveries in science, and items of local news may, and frequently do, grow out of current events. When the social studies program includes these three methods, the teacher and class will use any or all of the procedures described in the following sections.

Strategies for Teaching Current Events

Strategy 1: Daily Discussion of News

Children enjoy discussing the news and should be given the opportunity to do so within the school program. It is a fairly common procedure for classes to have a morning meeting or sharing period at the beginning of each school day, during which time the children can report news items. Children in the primary grades frequently report only news that affects them directly: Daddy took a business trip, the family has a new baby, the pet cat had kittens, or other similar items of "news." As children mature, they move away from news items that are of concern only to them personally to news of more general interest.

In reporting, discussing, and analyzing daily news occurrences, elementary school-children frequently report the sensational headline news that may or may not be particularly significant. Without guidance, children are likely to report murders or robberies or hold postmortems on the previous night's television programs. The teacher should help children evaluate the importance of news stories and teach them to discriminate between significant news and the sensational.

Use of Daily Newspapers

Some teachers in the intermediate and middle grades find a daily newspaper helpful in promoting the goals of current events instruction. In units dealing with aspects of communication, the newspaper is an important learning resource. Students will profit from classroom instruction on the use of the newspaper that focuses on items such as these:

1. The organization of newspapers, purposes of various sections, where to look for certain kinds of information.
2. The nature of news stories, why some appear on the front page and others elsewhere.
3. The purpose and use of headlines.
4. Newspaper illustrations: wire photos, maps, charts, graphs, cartoons.
5. The editorial page and its function.
6. Detecting bias in news stories.
7. How to read a newspaper.

From time to time the teacher can devise practice exercises such as those described in this chapter to help students develop their skills in using a daily newspaper.

Many teachers have found the Newspaper in Education (NIE) program sponsored by the Newspaper Association of America (NAA) to be a useful resource in teaching current events and, more specifically, in using the newspaper. For information about the NIE program and the several materials available through it, contact your local newspaper, or write to the NAA, 11600 Sunrise Valley Dr., Reston, VA 22091, or call 703-648-1000. The NIE program provides many teaching and learning resources; two that are especially recommended are (1) *The Newspaper as an Effective Teaching Tool*, and (2) *Bibliography: Newspaper in Education Publications*.

Use of Political Cartoons

Cartoons are an accepted form of social commentary. Through a dramatic visual format, the reader projects meaning into the visual by virtue of his or her own experience (Figure 6–1). Cartoons are often humorous because they exaggerate, subjects are presented in caricature, and the cartoons are designed to show all the vices or virtues associated with a particular character in our culture. Cartoons are especially effective in calling attention to the ironies that surround our lives. They use an amusing way to make a serious point.

Editorial cartoons are not necessarily humorous. Indeed, they are often biting in their comment on social issues. The techniques of symbolism, the use of familiar situations, exaggerations, satire, and caricature are used to present forcefully a single point of view. Political cartoons usually deal more with irony, hypocrisy, and cynicism than they do with humor. The cartoon does not allow the reader or the person portrayed in it an opportunity for rebuttal. Recognition of the fact that only one point of view is repre-

Figure 6–1
This cartoon is a good illustration of how much the reader must bring to such visuals if they are to have meaning. Ordinarily, we do not get new information from editorial cartoons. The artist relies on what we already know and provides a visual that places that information in a setting that conveys a powerful social, economic, and/or political message. (Reprinted with special permission of North America Syndicate.)

sented in cartoons is important in their interpretation. Older children need to be taught the general makeup of cartoons that deal with social and political problems and need the experience of evaluating their message critically. It is good for the children to present an opposite point of view from the one depicted in the cartoon.

Controversy

There can be no doubt that the social studies teacher has a responsibility to include controversial issues in the current events-social studies curriculum. In so doing, the teacher has a strong ally in the National Council for the Social Studies. According to an NCSS policy statement on the subject, it is the prime responsibility of the schools to help students assume the responsibilities of democratic citizenship. To do this, education must impart the skills needed for intelligent study and orderly resolution of the problems inherent in a democratic society. Students need to study issues upon which there is disagreement and to practice analyzing problems, gathering and organizing facts, discriminating between facts and opinions, discussing differing viewpoints, and

Making decisions includes getting the facts.

drawing tentative conclusions. It is the clear obligation of schools to promote full and free contemplation of controversial issues and to foster appreciation of the role of controversy as an instrument of progress in a democracy.

In teaching controversial issues, the teacher has a special responsibility to help children develop the disposition to be civil and open-minded, to evaluate sources of information, and to appraise the soundness of facts. Young children are impressionable, and the habit of insisting on getting multiple sides of a question before taking a stand can be taught to youngsters by the teacher's example. It is the teacher's responsibility to see that all sides of the issue being discussed are presented fairly and impartially and that the reasons underlying points of view are thoroughly aired. If the class requests the teacher's own views on an issue, it is clearly the teacher's right to express them and to state the reasons for the position taken. The professional obligation remains, however, not to attempt to impose a personal point of view on the children on issues that are unsettled and on which there may be honest differences of opinion among well-informed persons. In such cases, the teacher should encourage children to discuss the matter with other adults whom they respect whose views may be different. The child thus learns that there are honest differences of opinion among reasonable persons who consider problems in good faith. The children will respect the teacher who is willing to take a stand on issues, who gives reasons for the position taken, and who accepts and honors the differences in points of view of others.

Strategy 2: Decision Making on Controversial Issues

Daily discussion of the news is bound to expose students to controversial issues of all kinds. The news story found in Figure 6–2 is a good example of the types of controversial issues that can be found in nearly all communities, large and small. It is a *current event*, because it is happening now. But it also involves *enduring public issues*—in this case, protecting the natural environment and deciding how best to navigate the value conflict between individual liberty and the common good. Enduring public issues, also called *social concerns* or *social issues*, are what turn a current event into a controversial issue. By controversial, we mean that reasonable people will disagree over what needs to be done.

Not all current events are controversial. Many current happenings around the school and the community arouse little disagreement and debate: The school halls are swept nightly, the town garbage is picked up once each week, children go to school during the day, rice is eaten in many homes each evening, schools are closed for the summer, children are not allowed to run for the state legislature. Perhaps no one makes an *issue* of these humdrum events of daily life. Until someone does, they are not controversial issues. Once someone does, however, and someone else disagrees, then we have a controversial issue.

One of the best ways to teach current events is to select those that are controversial. In addition to the whale capture in Figure 6–2, here are several other current events that involve controversy:

- Establish city-wide curfew for persons under eighteen years of age
- Test athletes for illicit drug use
- Choose new equipment for the playground
- Allow animals to be used for medical research
- Whether to build a new orchestra hall, sports stadium, or jail
- Remove a park for a shopping center
- Remove a tree for a sidewalk
- Place metal detectors at school entrances
- Serve only low-fat foods in the school cafeteria
- Make gang membership illegal
- Cut off public assistance to teenage parents
- Cut off public assistance to large corporations
- Permit freeway construction through a residential area
- Require public school students to wear uniforms
- Permit organized prayer in schools
- Pass a dog leash ordinance
- Ban cigarette machines throughout the city
- Allow needle exchanges as an AIDS prevention measure
- Close public swimming pools to save water for farmers

These current events present good opportunities for teaching children how to deal constructively with controversy. We recommend the following decision-making procedure, which is based on the decision-making model presented in Chapter 3, Citizen-

Whale Capture Creates Wail

Seattle – Six killer whales are being held inside the Aqua Life, Inc. nets at Cook Inlet while Bill Holberg decides which ones, If any, will be kept for aquarium exhibits. Hundreds of people watched the capture from boats and shore yesterday afternoon.

The huge mammals swam slowly round and round inside two purse seine nets today, surfacing to "blow" for only moments. They stayed under for five minutes at a time.

GOVERNOR RECONSIDERING

Meanwhile, a political storm was gathering over the capture operation. The governor today interrupted her skiing vacation long enough to say that she was "reconsidering" the state's position on making the inlet a sanctuary for killer whales. The state's senior senator in Washington said that a declaration of support from the governor for a whale sanctuary would clear the way for protection of the sea animals. The senator also said, "Apparently this man [Holberg] had a valid permit. But there aren't going to be any more. This is the end!"

DEPTH CHARGES USED

Raul Santana, an assistant to the State Game and Fisheries director, watched the capture from about fifty feet away. Santana said Aqua Life, Inc. boats used "sonar, radar, and 'depth' charges" to drive the whales into smaller and smaller coves and finally into the nets. He said he watched three men in power boats racing across the water atop the whale school, "dropping 'depth charges' as fast as they could light them. I've never seen anything so disgusting in all my life," he said today. "This ought to be stopped right now."

A federal enforcement officer who supervised yesterday's operation said, "there is nothing in the permit that prohibits the use of such explosives."

USE OF CHARGES DENIED

Many citizens complained about the capture operation. An automobile dealer from South Harbor said he saw an airplane dropping "tomato can"-size cannisters that apparently exploded as the plane herded the whales. Sheila Moss, veterinarian for Aqua Life, Inc. said no such charges were used. She said the whale chasers used "firecracker"-type explosives thrown from boats to herd the whales. Holberg himself was aboard the Aqua Life, Inc. boat, KANDU, and was unavailable for comment.

COURT ACTION THREATENED

Environmentalists and others bitterly opposed the capture of the whales. Fred Russell, president of the state's largest environmental protection group, PROTEX, demanded that the whales be released. He said his group was prepared to take the matter to court if necessary to prevent Aqua Life, Inc. from keeping the creatures. "This is an outrage," he said, "and we are not going to sit by and let it happen."

Russell cited a Canadian biologist who found that only sixty-five killer whales remain in the Straits fo Georgia and Juan de Fuca and Puget Sound. Earlier data had placed the number of whales at about three hundred.

OVERLAPPING JURISDICTION

The power to create a whale sanctuary rests with the federal government, but federal law says the governor of a state that contains the sanctuary may veto its creation. This overlapping jurisdiction sometimes creates confusion or results in no action being taken.

Until today, federal officials thought the governor opposed creation of a killer whale sanctuary in this area. The governor's staff said that no record could be found of the governor's ever having opposed such a proposal.

Figure 6–2
A sample controversial issue in the newspaper.

ship Education and Democratic Values. Using a decision-making framework, teaching current events and social concerns serves a citizenship purpose: educating "we the people" to participate intelligently and constructively in community decision making. There are four parts to the procedure: learning the facts of the matter, identifying the controversial issues, deliberating on one of the issues, and dramatizing the issue.

1.   Have the children identify the *facts* of the case. In an examination of the captured whales news story in Figure 6–2, some of the facts are these:

- Six killer whales were captured
- The governor said she was reconsidering the state's policy
- Raul Santana said he saw three men dropping depth charges
- Sheila Moss said they used firecracker-type explosives
- The state and federal governments both have jurisdiction over whale sanctuaries

When identifying the facts, it is important not to confuse them with opinions. Though the distinction is often fuzzy, children can develop a working understanding of the difference between facts and opinions. In the whale story, one would need further documentation that the explosives were of the firecracker type and that they were thrown from the hunters' boats, not dropped from an airplane.

2.   Have students identify the *issues* in the case. Help them to identify a broad range of issues. Usually, issues involve conflicting values. In the whale case, the following are some of the issues. Notice that issues are stated as questions. People disagree on how to *answer* these questions, and this is why they are called controversial issues.

- Should the capture of wild animals for uses in aquariums, zoos, and circuses be permitted? If so, to what extent, and why?
- Should animal hunters be allowed to use explosives?
- Was Holberg's permit "valid"?
- Should the captured whales be freed?
- Should governments, state or federal, protect wildlife? Or does this violate the constitutional principle of limited government?

3.   *Select one of the issues* with the children. Make it an issue that requires a decision that the children can deliberate in the following way (see Chapter 3):
   a. Identify a range of *alternatives*.
   b. Predict the *consequences* for each alternative
   c. Engage in *discussion* about which is the best alternative.

There is no need to rush toward a decision: The process of identifying alternatives and consequences, discussing them, and learning more about the issue is the primary objective here. Indeed, slowing the children's inclination to "jump to a conclusion" (a decision about what the community should do) is precisely what is needed here. As discussed in Chapter 3, we want them to grow in their ability and disposition to be thoughtful and reflective citizens, not reckless, uncivil, or ill-informed.

   a. *Identify alternatives.* Let us assume that a group of children select the fourth issue above, Should the captured whales be freed? Using a decision tree (Figure

3–4), the children can then be helped to identify alternatives. One group suggested these:

- Free the whales immediately and arrest Holberg.
- Free the whales immediately and pay Holberg for them with public tax money.
- Make courts decide if Holberg was acting lawfully.

b. *Predict consequences*. After identifying alternatives, the teacher helps the children predict consequences for each. The following consequences might be suggested:

- Holberg takes "we the people" to court, claiming that he was acting lawfully.
- Whales return to open sea and live happily ever after.
- Zoos across America close down because no one will collect zoo animals after reading what happened to Holberg.

c. *Discussion*. After completing a decision tree on the issue, the teacher leads a discussion resulting in a decision about what should be done. The teacher might push students in the direction of a consensus, though this really is not necessary. The children may "agree to disagree" on the issue. (See Chapter 3 for suggestions on conducting discussions with children.) Roundtable discussions and panel discussions can be arranged in addition to whole-group discussions.

4.   Issues such as this lend themselves well to *role playing and dramatic play*. Children can play the roles of Holberg, the governor, the senator, Santana, the federal enforcement officer, the automobile dealer, Moss, and Russell. Doing this helps make the event and the issues more concrete and real for children. Additional questions will be raised (this is inevitable), and the information can be secured by the students from the point of view of the role they are playing. Children can gather this additional data from the community by interviewing individuals and reading local news stories.

Follow-Up Activities.

This decision-making strategy should not be limited to the use of newspaper articles. It is equally useful when the current event is a classroom or playground incident on which a decision is needed. As well, it is useful when children are considering the adoption of a new rule, such as Mrs. Paley's "you can't say 'you can't play' " rule (see Chapter 3).

When a decision-making procedure is used to examine a current event, a great deal of student interest may be generated. The teacher may wish to channel this enthusiasm into follow-up activities. These learning activities need to be related to the same event, yet they should expand the learning outward to incorporate additional ideas and skills. Several categories of follow-up activities are widely applicable. Below we exemplify each category with reference to the whale capture event.

Biography.   Study the lives of individuals who have dedicated themselves to the preservation of wildlife and other aspects of the natural environment: Rachel Carson, Jack Miner, John Muir, and local environmentalists.

Organizations.   Find out about the purposes and activities of organizations concerned about protecting the environment such as the Sierra Club, the National Wildlife Federation, the Environmental Protection Agency, and Greenpeace.

Government/Jurisdiction.   Study the authority of federal, state, local, and voluntary associations in relation to the current event. In the whale capture event, this should lead students to local and state regulations concerning wildlife, conservation, and hunting.

Community Service/Action.   Use the event to build interest in developing a community service or action project, in this case dealing with ecology or conservation.

Strategy 3: Teaching About Kinds of Disagreements

Discussions of controversial issues foster healthy disagreements, which in turn foster more discussion, more higher-order thinking, and more effort to apply what one knows. Consequently, disagreements should not be discouraged; rather, students should be prepared to take advantage of them—to learn more about the topic and one another and to practice reaching a consensus. An extremely helpful way to teach intermediate- and middle-grade students to learn from disagreements is to teach them occasionally to stop for a moment in the middle of a disagreement and to identify the *kind* of disagreement they are having. Doing so creates some cool distance from the disagreement, provides an opportunity to analyze the issue at hand, and to suggest what is to be done. The three most common kinds of disagreements, together with suggested methods for dealing with them, follow.

Factual Disagreements

These are disagreements over the facts of the case. Sometimes they are called *informational disagreements* or *disagreements over the data*. Children may disagree about what Holberg was planning to do with the whales, whether depth charges were actually used, and so on.

Methods.   To help children deal with factual disagreements, they can be taught to (1) re-read the source of information, searching for relevant facts; (2) go to a reference resource, such as an almanac or encyclopedia; and (3) ask a credible authority for a judgment (ask the teacher, call the journalist who covered the story, ask the librarian).

Definitional Disagreements

These are disagreements over the meaning of a term. Even these can be quite heated. Children might disagree about whether Holberg was a "hunter," for example. Some children will argue that animal hunters kill whales for food or sport, whereas Holberg was searching for whales in order to sell them to an aquarium. When discussing homelessness, water pollution, welfare, crime, and other social problems, children will disagree over basic terms.

Methods.   To help children deal with definitional disputes, they can be taught to (1) get a dictionary, (2) agree to accept the dictionary definition, or (3) tentatively agree to define the term in a particular way. Called *stipulation*, this last method is used in everyday situations when someone suggests, "Let's say that (*a term*) means (*a definition*)," and the others involved in the conversation agree.

Value Disagreements

These are disagreements about what is most important, right, best, or worthwhile. Typically, value conflicts arise as children (and adults) are trying to decide the question, What *should* the community do? In the captured whales example, value disagreements will arise as children discuss which alternative course of action is best.

Methods.   To help children deal constructively with value disagreements, they can be taught to: (1) Clarify the values at stake, which involves asking one another questions such as, "What do you mean?" and "What is important to you in this issue?" (2) Children also can be taught to give reasons for arguing that one alternative is more valuable than another. (3) "Agreeing to disagree" means that the children realize that there is a disagreement and that it has not yet been settled. Nevertheless, everyone involved will continue to be friendly and civil toward one another. Citizens in a community or nation often disagree and must not become hateful or ill-mannered toward those with whom they disagree.[4]

Strategy 4: Writing About Issues

Controversial issues present many authentic opportunities to improve children's writing. Writing letters to the editor in the classroom, school, or community newspaper is one good way to work with children on writing brief, persuasive essays. Another way is to write to local and national officials (the mayor, the school principal, a senator) presenting an analysis of an issue along with a suggested course of action. Nowadays, letters can be sent conventionally or by electronic mail.

Perhaps our favorite writing technique for helping children think more deeply and creatively about current events and social problems is called the *dialogical essay*. As the name implies, the writer creates a dialogue about the choices that need to be made. This dialogue occurs inside the writer's mind, but only after he or she has explored the issue orally with the class using the decision-making strategy above. Writing in this way helps the child sort out the opposing arguments on a controversial issue. This is far better than merely giving one's own opinion again and again, for it encourages one to examine the multiple perspectives on the issue.

One short-essay format has been found especially effective for this purpose.[5] Most children in the intermediate grades will have the necessary writing skills to compose such an essay, but clear directions are needed. The essay format, with directions, follows:

- *Paragraph 1.* Tell your reader that you are going to write an essay on this issue. Then tell your reader your position on the issue. Do not give any reasons yet.
- *Paragraph 2.* Give your reasons for your position. In other words, give good arguments that support your position.
- *Paragraph 3.* Give good reasons *against* your position. In other words, give good arguments that support the opposing position on the issue.
- *Paragraph 4.* Come to a conclusion. Now that you have thought about the reasons for and against your position, what is your position?

Other Activities

Many learning activities can be used profitably to study current affairs.

Viewing CNN

If a television monitor is available to the classroom, have the class watch one of the news summaries that are aired at the top of each hour. Keep track of CNN's coverage of an event that the children also are following in the daily newspaper or a weekly news magazine. Have the children compare the two, and then hypothesize the causes of the different coverage. Keep a news bulletin board of this event. If CNN is not available, another television news source will do. (Note: This comparative approach is especially effective for dealing with a breaking news story or crisis with which the children and community are intensely concerned.)

Viewing Telecasts of Special Events

Reports on inaugurations, visits of foreign dignitaries, dedications, and other newsworthy programs can be used for in-school viewing in the elementary school. Children can also be encouraged to view news programs out of school and report on these to their classmates.

Making Charts, Maps, Graphs

Show increases in school population, steps in an event that led to a crisis, decline or increase in employment, the number of highway accidents over a holiday weekend, the route of a recent air flight of importance, and so on.

Constructing Posters, Murals

Emphasize safe living, progress in preventive medicine, changes in air travel, progress in space, and other topics.

Keeping scrapbooks of news stories or pictures

Clip and keep the headlines from the evening paper for several weeks. This helps children to distinguish between news stories that are of continuing interest and those that are transitory in nature. Collections of news clippings can be a valuable resource if the topic selected is one that is likely to be in the news for a period of several weeks or months. Careful selection of articles in the scrapbook will allow the class to follow the development of the news story.

Drawing Cartoons to Illustrate News

This can be used effectively with older children. Care must be taken to avoid having children draw cartoons that might be offensive to individuals or groups.

Giving Reports

This is a widely used technique for handling current affairs by having individuals report news items to the class.

Conducting Television News Programs

Use from time to time to dramatize news stories. Children can take turns as reporters; variety can be obtained by using a tape recorder and playing the recorded "broadcast" for the class.

Dramatizing News Events

Some events lend themselves to dramatization. Not all do, but items dealing with festivals, meetings, conferences, and negotiations can be used.

Forecasting the Consequences of Trends

This is an exciting way to examine current events in greater depth while engaging students in higher-order thinking: forecasting. Have students think about whether particular events are part of a *trend*. Lesson Plan 5 describes a lesson that concludes with each student mapping the projected consequences, both positive and negative, of a trend of personal interest.

Teaching Enduring Public Issues

We turn now to a few of the enduring public issues that turn current events into controversial issues on which "we the people"—the public—must engage in public decision making. As we have seen, children can learn to deliberate these issues—discussing them, making decisions, planning service/action projects, and sending their advice to officials. The purpose of developing these deliberative habits in children is to prepare them to hold the "office of citizen."

Public issues do not appear, nor are they solved, within the confines of one discipline or another. Consider the worldwide problem of industrial pollution, for example. Concepts, generalizations, and methods of study drawn from economics, sociology, history, and geography all will be crucial if progress is to be made and the environment prevented from ruin. Furthermore, no era of American or world history, no region of the United States, and no society on the planet can be understood fully without exploring the multiple dimensions of social life: government, power, location, culture, social class, labor, the distribution of goods and service, roles and rites of passage, religion, and so on. Imagine trying to understand the early civilizations of Africa and China without peering through the lenses of history, geography, and all the social sciences. The very term *social studies* was coined, in part, to emphasize the need to draw on the various social sciences and history and geography.

Issue-centered, also known as problem-centered, unit planning has been one of the most popular approaches to social studies education in the 20th century. The central focus of an issue-centered unit is an authentic public issue. It should be an issue that has challenged people throughout history and in many cultures, for example:

1. *Poverty*: Who is responsible for the poor?
2. *Human-environment interaction*: How much environmental harm should be allowed for the sake of human economic productivity? How much pollution should be permitted for the sake of providing jobs?
3. *Justice*. How should society punish lawbreakers? Are there better responses than "an eye for an eye"?
4. *Peace*. How can war be prevented? What can individuals do to increase peace and harmony among people?

Lesson Plan 5

Futuring

Grade
6

Time
Four or five class periods

Objectives
Children will develop the concept *trends* and cooperatively forecast future consequences of current trends.

Interest Building
Suggest that the class has gathered together in the year 2025 for a reunion. Have them speculate on what their lives will be like then. Define *trends*, and have the students list current trends (e.g., electronic communication, increasing gun ownership, popularity of democracy around the world).

Lesson Development
With the students working in groups of three, have them choose one of the current trends and brainstorm all the consequences of that trend, such as the decrease of pen-and-paper correspondence in the case of the electronic communication (e-mail) trend. Ask the students to organize their ideas for sharing with the class.

Summary
In the next class period, have the groups (1) share their ideas with the class and (2) identify consequences that they believe are negative and positive.

Assessment
As homework, ask the children to search news magazines and newspapers for a trend of personal interest. Have them forecast the positive and negative consequences of the trend and display this on a poster. Ask each child to make a brief oral report, using the poster as a visual aid. Prompt them to clearly title the poster, using the word *trend*, and label the positive and negative consequences.

Materials
Butcher paper or construction paper and markers.

5. *Diversity/unity.* How can we keep our individual and cultural differences *and* be one people? How can we achieve *e pluribus unum*?

Note that the issues are stated as questions, and the questions are mighty. They apply to many times and cultures. They are *recurring* issues: People have grappled with them for years but never answered them once and for all. And, one of the responsibilities of being a member of "the public" is to tackle such problems. They are, of course, the sort of questions on which reasonable people will disagree; they lend themselves, therefore, to discussion and decision making.

With such a question as the unit's centerpiece, the teacher plans learning activities that inform the children's discussion and writing. This, then, is the instructional goal: to have children discuss and write and read on the problem, and to *inform* these activities through study. Discussion without study, while not worthless (at least it activates prior knowledge), has none of the power and depth of discussions to which participants bring information, judgment, competing viewpoints they have read elsewhere, and the like. Consequently, the problem-centered unit moves through iterations of discussion, study, and writing. In this way, not only are the social sciences and history integrated, so are reading and writing instruction.

Let us consider an example using the focus question, Who is responsible for the poor? Figure 6–3 shows that the children will endeavor to gather information from various disciplines to inform their decisions on this matter. The suggested procedure in Who Is Responsible for the Poor? can be altered considerably to suit a teacher's knowledge of the problem and related curriculum materials. Its focus can be shifted, for example, from U.S. to state, community, or world history. Its essence, however, is discussion. There should be plenty of discussion. There also needs to be ample opportunity for students to reflect on the quality of their discussions.

Figure 6–3
Issue-centered units.

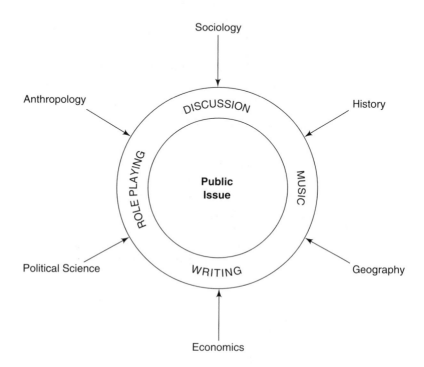

WHO IS RESPONSIBLE FOR THE POOR? (AN ISSUE-CENTERED UNIT)

1. *Initial discussion* of the unit question followed by writing on the question in a "discussion journal" or "learning log."
2. *Instruction* on the characteristics of good discussion (see Chapter 3).
3. *Historical study*: Using a time line that has been drawn on the board, the teacher describes for children several historical eras in which poverty was a problem and who did what about it.
   a. poor African slaves living on plantations
   b. poor immigrants
   c. poor unemployed during the Great Depression
   d. a current, local example (rural or inner-city poverty; homelessness)
4. *Additional data gathering*: The class is divided into four committees. Each is assigned to one of the four examples. The committee's job is to find out more about its example and, to give children a sense of the era, interesting facts about society at that time.
   Option. If the children are too young to conduct small-group research, the teacher can provide the additional information on each example using the same material the small groups would—films, stories, guest speakers, the textbook, primary documents, and references.
5. *Second discussion* of the question, now informed by historical information. Discussion followed by reflection on the quality of the discussion.
6. *Second writing in journals* on the unit question. Revise and share with peers.
7. *Additional data gathering*. Again using a small-group research format (option: teacher provides the data), the children divide among group members the four social sciences: economics, sociology, anthropology, and political science. Each is given study questions and works with others from the other groups assigned to the same topic.[*] Study questions should be designed with the capabilities of students and available curriculum materials in mind. For example:

Economics:	For two or three of the examples, describe (a) who else in society was poor, and (b) who was rich?
Sociology:	For two or three of the examples, find out (a) what conflicts occurred? (b) how were families affected by poverty?
Political Science:	For two or three of the examples, find out (a) did government help the poor? if so, how? (b) who else helped?
Anthropology:	For two or three of the examples, describe (a) how the life style of the poor people—their culture—was different from the nonpoor and (b) an example of poverty in another nation.

8. *Third discussion* of the unit question, informed by the additional data.
9. *Third writing in journals* on the unit question. Share, revise, and publish.

[*] This technique, called "Jigsaw," is explained in Chapter 10.

Human-Environment Interaction

Another enduring public issue, and one for which children have much natural concern, can be stated something like this: How can humans best live with the natural environment? Human consumption, especially in the affluent nations of Europe and North America, has already overwhelmed many ecosystems, and the developing nations of Asia, South America, and Africa are close behind. At the present rate, earth will be overwhelmed by its human residents in the not too distant future.

One of the essential characteristics that distinguishes a modern, economically developed nation such as the United States from a less well-developed nation is its use of and dependence on various forms of energy. Modern nations have taken burdens off the backs of human beings and animals and have substituted inanimate sources of power and energy. The dependence on various forms of such energy—and in huge and escalating amounts—is absolute in modernized nations. Their economic systems cannot survive without it. They could not sustain their present standards of living if their energy sources were curtailed. Perhaps no topic is related more directly to the day-to-day lives of citizens than is energy.

Energy is, of course, related to the environment. The relationship occurs at all stages of the energy production–delivery–consumption sequence. Extracting energy sources such as coal, gas, and oil from the earth either scars or pollutes the environment. Processing the raw materials of energy into usable forms and delivering the finished products also do violence to the environment. Similarly, the consumption of energy in most instances has some environmental impact. Thus, one of the major profound social issues of our time is that of providing for the vast energy needs of our modern industrial society while at the same time preserving an environment that can sustain human and other forms of life at an acceptable level of quality.

When European settlers first came to North America, the incredible vastness and abundance of resources they found produced no concern in their minds for the environment. There was fresh water aplenty. Forests and trees were in such abundance that they were perceived as obstacles to land use. There was no shortage of places to dispose of solid wastes. There were no internal combustion engines or other devices creating large quantities of harmful hydrocarbons to pollute the air. The forests and streams were well stocked with wildlife and fish. What happened in the 300 years that followed provides us with a shocking case study of unbelievable exploitation and waste and an almost total lack of concern for the consequences of this behavior. All this is now too-familiar history.

Serious efforts to reverse this trend got under way about three decades ago. National and state leadership, combined with publicity in the popular press and, most importantly, concerned citizen groups, raised the consciousness of the general public to the violence being perpetrated on the ecosystem. More than that, these forces were successful in securing state, national, and local legislation that slowed the pace of environmental abuse. Scientific data relating to the use of certain energy-producing fuels raised the frightening possibility that the planet could experience something in the way of an "eco-catastrophe" in the foreseeable future. The most significant danger signals seemed to be those associated with (1) the use of fertilizers and pesticides, (2) the disposal of solid wastes, (3) air pollution, (4) water pollution, (5) radiation and radioactive substances, and (6) overpopulation.

Energy and environmental studies are, of course, not the sole province of the social studies. The subject is such a comprehensive one that it can be studied from many perspectives. It can be approached from the standpoint of science education, for, clearly, much of our polluted environment is a direct consequence of science and technology. Likewise, the subject is appropriate for health education because research has established relationships between air pollution and respiratory ailments such as asthma, emphysema, lung cancer, and bronchitis. Certainly, energy and environmental studies have geographical, esthetic, sociological, economic, and even political dimensions. Thus, the broad topic is highly appropriate for social studies programs because of its implications for human societies and human life. It is an ideal subject for interdisciplinary studies.

As with the study of poverty and other social concerns, a program of energy and environmental studies should concern itself with three types of broad goals:

1. **Knowledge**. It should provide children with an opportunity to develop a basic understanding of the dimensions of problems surrounding energy and the environment, the causes and consequences of ecological disaster, the remedial measures now under way, the need for additional corrective legislation and action, *and* similar inputs of information that affect these important topics.

2. **Concern**. It should help children develop an attitude of responsible concern for energy use and the quality of the environment. It should leave them with the feeling that they have a personal investment in their natural surroundings—that energy and environment truly are everybody's business.

3. **Action**. It should provide children with the opportunity to do something themselves about improving the environment. That is, if goals 1 and 2 are concerned with knowledge, thinking, and valuing, this goal constitutes the action dimension of the program.

In Chapter 12, we present an exemplary interdisciplinary environmental studies unit that is used by third-grade teachers and children in the Northglenn, Colorado, schools. Readers may wish to read ahead at this point. In the following exercises, however, we provide simple learning activities, not whole units, that are related to energy and environmental issues. Beginning teachers have used these successfully with elementary school children.

POPULATION

1. Use a checkerboard or other similar squares and kernels of corn, and try doubling the number of kernels in each square, starting with one. How many kernels can be used before there is no longer room to double again? Discuss how this relates to population growth and its implications.

2. Encourage children to suggest problems that would be caused by an increase of twice as many persons in their environment.

3. Make a chart comparing the present-day population of a selected area with its population twenty years ago, 100 years ago, 200 years ago.

4. Using a map and reference books, compare the populations of various parts of the United States. Why do people live where they do? What areas have the fewest people? Could people be moved to those areas? Why or why not?
5. Construct a map showing areas of heavy population in the city, state, nation, or world. Identify sparsely populated areas. Have children give reasons for both conditions.

AIR POLLUTION

1. Construct a map of the local region showing places of highest pollution. Explain why these areas have a high level of pollution.
2. Discover the major sources of air pollution. Present these on charts.
3. Relate air pollutants to health problems.
4. Have class gather data associating smoking with lung cancer and other respiratory ailments.

WATER POLLUTION

1. Discover major sources of water pollution in the local area. Prepare a chart showing those sources. Discuss. Present the chart to local government officials.
2. Make a map of a specified area through which a large river flows. Find out if or to what extent the river becomes polluted as it flows.
3. On a map of the United States, identify water bodies that once were contaminated but that have been rehabilitated.
4. Select a water body in the local area that is not available for recreation because of contamination. Plan a strategy to have it rehabilitated. Present the plan to local officials. Begin a movement to mobilize public opinion in support of such an action.

ENERGY USE

1. Through discussion, establish the relationship between increasing wants and needs and increased energy consumption. Find pictures from magazines to illustrate points.
2. Develop a class project to encourage energy conservation in the children's homes (turning off lights, turning down thermostats, shutting off TV and appliances not in use, and so on).
3. Prepare a bulletin board display of energy-related news stories. Through discussion, establish the importance of energy to the everyday lives of everyone.
4. Make a survey of their homes to identify energy uses that would not have been in homes fifty years ago, 100 years ago. Discuss in terms of new demands on energy resources.

Crime and the Rule of Law

Children need to learn to be lawful citizens. They also need to construct in their own minds the constitutional *idea* of the rule of law. Furthermore, as citizens they will need to decide how to cultivate lawfulness in other citizens and what to do with persons who break the law.

Americans—adults and children alike—are more afraid of crime than ever, recent polls show. Seventy-three percent of parents and 56 percent of children are worried that a family member will be a victim of violent crime. Are these fears exaggerated? Consider the data: The overall crime rate in the United States was five times greater in 1992 than in 1960. The United States has long held the distinction of being the most violent and lawless of all industrialized nations in the world. Moreover, in every category of violent crime—rape, murder, robbery, assault—the number of offenses committed by youngsters (children and teenagers) has increased substantially in the past decade. As well, youngsters increasingly are the victims of violent crime.[6]

What is causing this? That is a very good question to put to children in the classroom. As we will see in the next chapter, such an *inquiry* teaches children to hypothesize at the same time that it teaches them to gather relevant data (information) and revise hypotheses as the data require. A planned program of law-related education can help children focus on the problem of lawlessness and the idea of rule by law. Such a program should concern itself with broad goals such as these:

1. Develop an understanding of concepts that are basic to the legal system, such as liberty, justice, fairness, toleration, power, honesty, property, equality, and responsibility.
2. Develop an understanding and appreciation of the constitutional basis of the American legal system.
3. Develop a functional knowledge of how the institutions of the legal and justice systems operate.
4. Develop an understanding of and respect for the need for a system of law and justice as prerequisite for orderly and harmonious living.

In addition to inquiry-oriented units on crime, such simple activities as the following can make a difference in children's attitudes toward and knowledge of this enduring social concern:

Invite a local police officer to talk to the class about law enforcement, drug traffic, youth gangs, or some other real or potential problems in the community.

Bring in news clippings describing acts of vandalism; discuss the effects and costs of such behavior.

Discuss rights versus responsibilities along lines familiar to children such as "Can we go to the movies and talk out loud even if we disturb others?"

Research the latest legislation on drugs (upper grades). Find out if the legal penalties for drug abuse are the same for adults as for juveniles.

Take a field trip to a court, the state legislature, or a city council meeting.

Find out how a jury is selected. Invite someone who has recently served on a jury to speak to the class about the responsibilities and duties of jurors.

Conduct a mock trial in the upper grades.

Discuss citizens' rights and responsibilities in terms of specific cases that appear in the news.

List legal needs of their community at the beginning of the 20th century. List legal needs of their community today. Discuss differences, and have children explain why legal needs have changed.

Study the structure and functions of local community government, and relate them to the daily lives of the people who live there.

Develop appropriate activities in connection with "Law Day USA," observed each year on May 1. Write to Law Day USA, American Bar Association, 541 N. Fairbanks Ct. Chicago, IL 60611, or telephone (312) 988-5735.

A vast number of national, regional, and local projects and centers have dealt with law-related education in recent years. Perhaps the best known are those projects conducted by the following groups:

National Street Law Institute
605 G St., N.W.
Washington, DC 20001

Center for Civic Education
5115 Douglas Fir Dr., Suite 1
Calabasas, CA 91302

Special Committee on Youth for Citizenship
American Bar Association
541 N. Fairbanks Ct.
Chicago, IL 60611

Constitutional Rights Foundation
601 S. Kingsley Dr.
Los Angeles, CA 90005

Peace and Understanding

We live in a world fraught with danger, which is likely to increase as modern instruments of destruction become available to more and more nations. Even a minor power, if armed with modern weapons, constitutes a threat to the entire world. To ignore the real danger that exists or to minimize it could result in disastrous consequences for the entire human population. Perhaps through educational programs directed toward the understanding of others and toward a search for world peace, a more satisfactory method of resolving international disputes can be found than the oldest and least effective method, war. Many believe that a global perspective that engenders worldmindedness, therefore, is essential if humankind is to survive.

Teachers will need to be imaginative in exploring and discovering new avenues to a worldview. For example, when children in the primary grades are studying homes and home life, that is the time to begin developing the understanding that people all over the world need homes and that they build them in a variety of ways. Or when the food market is studied, time might be spent on an examination of food markets around the world. Units on transportation and communication can, likewise, be expanded to famil-iarize the child with these functions on a broader basis than the local community. Almost any topic has within it such possibilities for teaching global relationships.

If a school accepts global perspectives education as one of its primary purposes, it will concern itself with ideas such as these:

1. The interdependence of peoples.
2. The need for peaceful relations among nations.
3. Basic similarities and differences in peoples because of geographical, cultural, and historical considerations.
4. The philosophy and practice of respect for the dignity of the individual, irrespec-tive of race or other factors over which he or she has no control.
5. The need to develop a sensitivity to and respect for the cultures of other people, both within one's community and around the world.

The most productive teaching plan, as suggested earlier, is to extend each social studies unit in such a way that it includes global comparisons. Issue-centered units (see Figure 6–3) have great promise for helping children explore global problems. Such units can be planned on the question, How can war be prevented? or What can the individual do to increase peace and harmony in the world? Many other activities also have been used successfully. A sampling follows:

Use experiences from the everyday lives of children as a springboard for global studies. Take *blue jeans*, for example. Here we have a fashion fad that began in the United States during the 1960s and suddenly spread worldwide. Responding to this demand, blue jeans factories were established in South Korea, Mexico, the Philippines, Hong Kong, and elsewhere.

Keep instruction and experiences for primary grade children simple and child-oriented. A major purpose of global studies in the primary grades is to develop the concepts of friendliness and neighborliness among the "human family." Learning experiences, therefore, should focus on the ways children in other lands live, play, dress, and eat. Social studies textbooks and children's trade books can be of tremendous help here. Jane Cowen-Fletcher's little book, *It Takes a Village* (Scholastic, 1994) offers a lovely story based on the African proverb, "It takes a village to raise a child." A girl must care for her younger sister while her mother sells fruit at the market.

Bulletin board. Expand the classroom's current events bulletin board to include news of "the country of the week."

Guests. Invite foreign-born local residents to the classroom to display photos, flags, and traditional clothes. Former members of the Peace Corps and persons who have lived at least a year abroad also have much to share.

Travel brochure. Have small groups prepare travel brochures on several countries. Children can role play tourists and tour guides discussing a two-week itinerary.

Embassies. Have student committees write to embassies, consulates, airlines, or travel bureaus for material on the countries being studied.

Make direct contact. One of the best learning experiences for children while they are studying the people of other lands is to have direct contact with someone from that country, especially a child their own age, who can answer questions about the clothes they wear, their schools and games, celebrations, and homes. With help from the teacher and their parents, children can correspond with children abroad, exchanging photos, news, and stories. Teachers who wish to have their students correspond with children in other lands may obtain information from local service clubs or write:

Student Letter Exchange   World PenPals
630 Third Ave.   International Institute of Minnesota
New York, NY 10017   1694 Como Ave.
(212) 557-3312   St. Paul, MN 55108
($5.00 for 1–3 names)   (612) 647-0191

Diversity and Prejudice

It is one thing to teach about differences around the world and another to teach about differences right here at home. The latter often is called *ethnic heritage studies* or *multicultural education*. As we saw in Chapter 2, the children in our classrooms come increasingly from diverse home cultures (defined broadly to include ethnicity, race, language, religion, and social class). Thanks to the trend toward inclusion of special-needs children in the regular classroom, the children we teach will become even more diverse. This gives teachers a tremendous opportunity to teach children firsthand about the meaning and value of diversity. Teachers can engage children in projects in which they play and work together and, thereby, develop habits of friendliness, cooperation, and appreciation for one another.

Like anything else we want to do well, multicultural education cannot simply be wished for; it must be planned. Teachers should direct the program of multicultural education toward the goal of improving the quality of human relations in the school, community, and nation. This includes not only educating children about the ethnic and racial heritages of the incredibly diverse people who call themselves Americans; it also means tackling the problem of prejudice head on.

Prejudice means pre-judging people and places; that is, judging them before they are known—before the facts are gathered. It is a type of ignorance. Before we meet someone, we might believe we know quite a bit about him or her based, perhaps, on stereotypes we hold about that person's group membership. Actually, we may know nothing at all about this person. When combined with fear, greed, and anger, prejudice has played a central role in all sorts of social problems, all manner of hate crimes, even the atrocities called "crimes against humanity." Prejudice has made slavery, apartheid, the Holocaust, and the Japanese-American internment possible, for example. It is a deep and pernicious problem that humans historically have had an extremely difficult time avoiding or overcoming. On the bright side, prejudice is a concept that children can learn, and they can learn it well enough to recognize it when they see it or read it. With the help of caring teachers and other adults in their lives, they may learn to courageously take a stand against it.

Experiencing other cultures reduces prejudice.

In the next chapter, strategies for teaching any concept, such as prejudice, are explained. As well, many teaching suggestions related to diversity were given in Chapter 2. Accordingly, we suggest at this point only a few additional activities.

Vocabulary

Teach children the meaning of the terms *prejudice, respect, stereotype, race, customs, religion,* and *tolerance*. Then read selections from newspapers, the textbook, children's trade books, and reference resources in which these terms are used.

Perspectives

The most powerful form of multicultural study for children in the intermediate and middle grades is to compare the perspectives of various cultural groups on a single event, historical or current. The new generation of social studies textbook programs often give multiple views on events. For example, both Native American and European perspectives on land ownership are given. Children's trade books can also be a great help. Three titles are given here, but also see the examples of multiple perspectives given in "Using Children's Trade Books for Multiple Perspectives" in Chapter 11.

Yoshiko Uchida's *The Two Foolish Cats* (Macmillan, 1987) tells the story of two cats, Big Daizo and Little Suki. When they refuse to cooperate, they both lose.

Lori Carlson's *Cool Salsa* (Holt, 1994) is a bilingual anthology of American Latino poetry.

Mary Ray's *Shaker Boy* (Browndeer, 1994) is a Civil War–era book for the primary grades that teaches about history and the Shaker religion.

Cooperative Groupwork

Create small, diverse working groups of children. Each group should contain as much heterogeneity as the composition of the class allows. During groupwork, help children cooperate on a meaningful and challenging task. The task will help take the attention off one another, placing it instead on the work to be done. The children will gradually get to know one another as a side-effect of completing the task. The problems they have working together will be the usual ones of sharing, communicating, participating, listening, keeping agreements, and so forth, each of which is an opportunity to provide instruction on cooperation. Cooperative learning techniques are explained in Chapter 10.

Scrapbooks and Biographies

Make a scrapbook of outstanding individuals in an ethnic group. Include a list of their individual accomplishments *and what they have contributed to the whole society*. Help children build the idea that outstanding members of ethnic groups are good citizens; that is, they identify with and contribute to the whole society, not only their ethnic group. Examples abound: European-American, Eleanor Roosevelt; African-American, Sojourner Truth; Asian-American, Gordon Hirabayashi; Mexican-American, Caesar Chavez.

Bulletin Board

Have the class research its own ethnic origins. Show on a world map where their ancestors came from. These same countries can become the "country of the week" as suggested in the Peace and Understanding section in this chapter.

Demographics

Make charts and graphs displaying the changing population of the United States. Such data is available in social studies textbooks and reference resources in the library.

Guests

Invite representatives of various ethnic and racial groups in the community to your class. Ask them about their cultural roots. Be sure to include European-Americans; otherwise, children might develop the misconception that whites are somehow "neutral" (not members of ethnic groups).

Music and Art

Encourage children and their parents to share music and art that has distinct ethnic origins or particular meaning to the family. Invite an ethnic musicologist to the class to share information about music's cultural roots. Model for children that, regardless of your own ethnic or racial identification, you value many different forms of music and art.

Community History

Study the local community to discover which Native American groups populated that area, if any, and which nonnative ethnic groups first settled there.

Holidays and Festivals

Write a letter or use e-mail to contact the local chamber of commerce. Inquire about the ethnic holidays and festivals that are celebrated locally. Make a classroom calendar of these events.

Languages

Conduct a survey of the school or local area to find out the number of different languages spoken and identify each. To show that multilingualism is valued, develop an award for the person who speaks the greatest number of languages.

Discussion Questions and Suggested Activities

1. What is your opinion of Buckminster Fuller's response to Michael's letter at the beginning of the chapter? Is it true, do you think, that doing what *you* see needs to be done that no one else may see needs to be done naturally brings out and strengthens your gifts?
2. Three purposes were given for current events teaching in the elementary grades. Which of them is the most important? Why?
3. Three approaches to current events teaching were given in the examples involving Ms. Hansen, Mr. Chung, and Ms. Diaz. Compare and contrast them. Which do you prefer, and for what reasons?
4. Select a current event in the news today that you think might be profitably studied by children in a grade of your choice. Also select one of the four strategies given for teaching current events. Apply this strategy to the event you chose, designing a lesson or unit that centers on that event.
5. What is the relationship between public issues and current events?
6. Select from those given in this chapter a public issue other than "Who is responsible for the poor?" Then revise the issue-centered unit plan as needed for teaching that unit.
7. Imagine that the teaching of current events and public issues is being challenged by a parent at a school board meeting as "irrelevant" to the goals of the social studies program. If you were asked to respond to such a concern, what points would you want to make?
8. How can map and globe study be related to the study of current events and public issues? How can history and the social sciences be related?
9. Select a news story from a daily newspaper and develop a four-part decision-making study similar to the one in this chapter concerning the captured whales.
10. What resource persons in your community might be of help in teaching the events and issues included in this chapter?

Notes

1 Buckminster Fuller, *Critical Path* (New York: St. Martin's Press, 1981), xxxviii
2 Ibid.
3 Ibid.

4 The three kinds of disagreements are from Donald W. Oliver and Fred M. Newmann, *Taking A Stand* (Middletown, CT: American Education Publications, 1972).

5 Walter C. Parker, Jane E. McDaniel, and Sheila W. Valencia, "Helping Students Think About Public Issues," *Social Education* 55 (January 1991): 41–44, 67.

6 National Issues Forums, *Kids Who Commit Crimes* (Dubuque, IA: Kendall/Hunt, 1994).

Selected References

Case, Roland. "Key Elements of a Global Perspective," *Social Education* 57 (October 1993): 318–25.

Bennett, Clifford T., Donna Bliss, Marcia S. Defren, William R. Heitzmann, Brenda Holub, and John E. Steinbrink. Contributors to a special section on using political cartoons in the classroom. *The Social Studies* 79 (September/October 1988): 205–27.

Educational Leadership 49 (December 1991/January 1992). The theme of this issue is multicultural education.

Enloe, Walter, and Ken Simon. *Linking Through Diversity: Practical Classroom Methods for Experiencing and Understanding Our Cultures*. Tucson, AZ: Zephyr, 1993.

Green Teacher, a magazine of environmental and global education for teachers published five times a year in Canada. For information, write to P.O. Box 1431, Lewiston, NY 14092.

Hahn, Carole L. "Controversial Issues in Social Studies." In *Handbook of Research on Social Studies Teaching and Learning*, edited by James P. Shaver. New York: Macmillan, 1991, 470–80.

King, Edith W. *Teaching Ethnic and Gender Awareness*. Dubuque, IA: Kendall/Hunt, 1990.

Parker, Walter C., Benjamin Barber, Thomas E. Kelly, JoAnn Shaheen, and others. "Participatory Citizenship: Civics in the Strong Sense," *Social Education* 53 (October 1989).

Social Studies and the Young Learner 3 (September/October 1990). The theme of this issue is Social Studies and the Community.

Wells, James, Edward Reichbach, Sharon Kossack, and Joan Dungey. "Newspapers Facilitate Content Area Learning: Social Studies," *Journal of Reading* 31 (December 1987): 270–72.

Woyach, Robert B., and Richard C. Remy. *Approaches to World Studies* (Boston: Allyn & Bacon, 1989).

PART

3

Planning and Teaching Social Studies

STRATEGIES FOR TEACHING SOCIAL STUDIES SUBJECT MATTER

OVERVIEW

Outstanding schools teach the students to learn. Thus, teaching becomes more effective as the students progress through those schools because, year by year, the students have been taught to be stronger learners.[1]

This chapter presents strategies for teaching the core subject matter of the social studies curriculum. These are strategies for helping children engage in the processes—the intellectual labor—needed to construct important social studies ideas, master key skills, discuss problems and issues, and engage in the inquiry process. These strategies can be thought of as "means of assisting performance,"[2] which is to say powerful *tools* with which teachers can help children to achieve important learning objectives that they probably would not otherwise achieve. This is why skillful teaching matters. Without it, children will not learn as much or as well; they will not be initiated into ways of knowing that will make them stronger learners and more effective workers and citizens; they will not see themselves as capable and successful thinkers and problem solvers.

Just as learning ideas, skills, the art of discussing issues, and the inquiry process increases children's power as learners and citizens, so also does mastering teaching strategies increase teachers' power as instructors on whose shoulders fall the task of teaching all our children. One would not want to attempt this task without effective strategies. It is the confident possession of these strategies that distinguishes *teachers* from others who work with and care for children: day-care workers, physicians, neighbors, social workers, camp counselors, and so forth. Persons who are not educated as teachers are not expected to have the know-how for teaching. Teachers are presumed to have it.

There are more teaching strategies than can be discussed in this chapter, to be sure. Entire books, such as the one from which the opening quotation was taken, are devoted to the matter. Reading about and experimenting continually with a wide range of strategies is one of the minimal expectations for people in the teaching profession. The strategies presented in this chapter add up to a very strong beginning; in fact, teachers who develop these several strategies to a high level of proficiency should be outstanding teachers.

Matching Teaching Strategies to Subject Matter

How one goes about teaching needs to be linked to who the children are and what the subject matter is. As we saw in Chapter 2, good teachers get to know their learners personally and are curious about their cultural identities and language skills; they learn what their children like to do for fun and discover both their talents and learning challenges. Moreover, good teachers are extremely curious about their students' current understanding of the subject matter—their conception of the past, for example, their definitions of "good citizen," and their suppositions about peoples and places near and far. Good teachers are like scientists pursuing knowledge. What they want to ascertain is the understandings their children have developed *already*. Without this knowledge, teachers cannot teach for they cannot connect the social studies curriculum meaningfully to the child.

How one goes about teaching also should be related to the nature of what is to be learned. *Skills*, *ideas*, the *inquiry process*, and *issues*—drawn mainly from history and the social sciences—are the major subject matter of the social studies curriculum (Table 7–1).

Skills

If we want young children to learn a skill, such as how to locate reference materials in a library or at a computer station, no amount of reading about almanacs or electronic databases or hearing someone explain their location will make them proficient in the execution of this skill. Instruction in its component parts is needed, followed by guided practice and role-playing in the classroom, then guided practice in the library followed by paired or independent library practice in the context of a meaningful task.

Ideas

If we want children to construct powerful ideas—concepts and generalizations—then we must supply them with the necessary building blocks: well-chosen examples, effective assistance so that the children can compare and contrast the examples, and good questions that help children summarize examples into ideas.

Inquiry

If we want children to develop critical habits of mind, such as judging whether conclusions are supported by evidence and making sense of competing accounts of historical events, then we must teach them the processes and spirit of inquiry: making and test-

Table 7–1

Matching teaching strategies to the nature of the subject matter

Subject Matter	Teaching Strategies	Exemplars in this Text
Skills	Explain, model, practice, apply	Using a newspaper directory, Figure 7–2
Ideas	Provide examples and help students compare and synthesize them	Forming the idea *democracy*, Figure 7–1
Inquiry	Have students develop, then revise hypotheses as evidence warrants	Inquiring about the *Titanic* tragedy, Lesson Plan 6 (Chapter 7)
Issues	Classroom meetings, discussion, decision making, conflict resolution	Participating in discussions of classroom problems, Mrs. Paley's class, Chapter 3

ing hypotheses, respecting facts rather than prejudices, and disciplining oneself to not jump to conclusions.

Issues

If we want children to become good citizens, they need years of experience wrestling with significant public issues. This experience, and the instruction that must accompany it, should begin in kindergarten. Learning to talk with one another in a civilized and caring way about the controversial public issues that face us, whether a town's proposed curfew laws or the rules regarding lining up for recess, is the essence of citizenship education. Teachers can regularly lead discussions of classroom and playground issues with young children, gradually including community issues in the second and third grade, and national and global issues in the fourth and fifth grades.

In this chapter we explain teaching strategies that help even the youngest children learn ideas, skills, and the inquiry process. Strategies for teaching issues and current events were detailed in Chapters 3 and 6. Before we proceed, however, two points that were raised in earlier chapters must be recalled.

First, children need to learn subject matter, and they can. Prominent African-American educator Lisa Delpit implores teachers to *teach*. She worries about a phenomenon that she calls "teaching less," which she has found especially in the elementary grades. It occurs when teachers plan activities for children, often very elaborate ones, but provide little actual instruction on skills, ideas, issues, or inquiry. There is much *doing*, but little *teaching*, and therefore little *learning*, of the subject matter that will empower children. Delpit is concerned not only about ethnic minority children, who bear the brunt of teaching less, but white, middle-class children as well.

Good teachers do not merely keep children engaged and entertained, and they do not only select and provide environments for learning. They have thoughtful curriculum objectives; they have high expectations that their students will build powerful ideas and abilities; and they teach them these things. The vision statement of the National Council for the Social Studies states that "social studies teaching and learning are powerful when they are *challenging*."[3] Delpit writes, "When teachers do not understand the potential of the students they teach, they will underteach them no matter what the methodology."[4] Of course, subject-matter objectives always need to be matched to the developmental maturity of students, but teachers must be wary of letting this intention express itself as teaching less.

Second, beginning teachers need to start with teaching strategies that they feel they can manage comfortably. There is no need to overreach, and doing so can slow teachers' professional development rather than advance it. To make themselves comfortable, teachers can control the teaching environment sufficiently well to keep management concerns to a minimum. The objectives can be specific, listed on the chalkboard, and explained to students; materials and examples can be preselected by the teacher; and the entire process can be entirely teacher directed. Perhaps most important, the process can be kept short—20 to 30 minute episodes—and involve teaching a single example.

Moreover, initial teaching experiences might be based entirely on the textbook program, with heavy reliance on the suggestions presented in the teacher's manual that accompanies the program: skill explanations to give to students, sections that they should read aloud and silently, comprehension questions to ask them, practice exercises, forms of assistance, and projects to involve them in. After a few experiences of this sort, the novice will have gained some confidence in the teaching role and will know better how to evaluate responses and adjust instruction "on the fly." He or she can begin to add variation, such as small group discussions, cooperative team work, and inquiry, always keeping the activity short at first. Teachers need to be comfortable in the teaching role (they teach better when they are) and, at the same time, push themselves to acquire new, exciting, and more powerful teaching strategies.

Teaching Powerful Ideas: Concepts and Generalizations

In everyday parlance, the term *concept* is used to mean *idea*, as when someone says, "My concept of leisure is not the same as yours." In social studies the meaning is the same: concepts are ideas. Social studies concepts often embody an elaborate meaning that evolves with experience and learning over a period of years. Sometimes a child's initial understanding of a concept includes misconceptions that in later years must be corrected. Consider a kindergartner's concept of *history*, for example, or *freedom* or *money*, compared to an eighth grader's or a twelfth grader's. Let us explore in some detail the meaning and implications of concepts for teaching and learning social studies.

The Nature of Concepts

If asked to tell what a village is, most adults would probably say something along this line: "A village consists of a group of persons living in a rural area in a cluster of homes smaller than a city or a town." For most purposes this is an adequate definition to make communication possible. But *village* had a much more elaborate meaning for the Native Americans of British Columbia, as explained in Margaret Craven's novel *I Heard the Owl Call My Name*. On the boat trip north, the young priest, Mark Brain, recalls what his bishop had told him about the village:

The Indian knows his village and feels for his village as no white man for his country, his town, or even for his own bit of land. His village is not the strip of land four miles long and three miles wide that is his as long as the sun rises and the moon sets. The myths are the village and the winds and the rains. The river is the village, and the black and white killer whales that herd the fish to the end of the inlet the better to gobble them. The village is the salmon who comes up the river to spawn, the seal who follows the salmon and bites off his head, the bluejay whose name is like the sound he makes—"Kwiss-kwiss." The village is the talking bird, the owl, who calls the name of the man who is going to die, and the silver-tipped grizzly who ambles into the village, and the little white speck that is the mountain goat on Whoop-Szo.

The fifty-foot totem by the church is the village, and the Cedar-man who stands at the bottom holding up the eagle, the wolf and the raven! And a voice said to the great cedar tree in Bond Sound, "Come forth, Tzakamayi and be a man," and he came forth to be the Cedar-man, the first man-god of the people and more powerful than all others.[5]

This is a superb example of a concept because it illustrates so well the richness and depth of meaning that can inhere in a single word label. It also illustrates how vital experience is in developing such meanings. It is doubtful if anyone who did not actually grow up in the village culture of these Native Americans could understand and appreciate the full meaning of *village* as they conceptualize it. Yet the novelist does very well in conveying the meaning by skillfully building word images for us of things that are familiar because they come out of our own background of experience.

As we have said, concepts are ideas. But what are ideas? They are abstract categories or classes of meaning. Ideas are abstract because they are removed from specific instances. For example, *island* is the word label for a geographic phenomenon consisting of land completely surrounded by water. Kauai is one specific example of such a set of conditions. There are thousands of other specific examples of the concept *island*. But to know that Kauai is an island (that is, a body of land completely surrounded by water) is not to know very much about that beautiful outcropping of land in the Pacific. To early Hawaiians, *Kauai* had a meaning closely akin to that of *village* to the Pacific Northwest Native Americans. Concept definitions, therefore, tell us only about those qualities or attributes that a group of examples *has in common*. They do not tell us about the unique features of particular examples. The concept—the idea—refers to the attributes shared by all examples.

The human intellect makes use of this system of classifying, categorizing, and organizing the vast amount of specific perceptual data with which it deals. Trees having certain attributes are *evergreen*; others having different attributes are *deciduous*. Some groups of animals are known as *mammals*; others, as *reptiles*; and others, as *birds*. A certain form of government is called a *democracy*; another, an *autocracy*. This ability and inclination to classify perceptions of reality into groups having common qualities is what is meant by conceptual thought. Conceptual thought makes it possible to manipulate reality intellectually; that is, one can figure out complex problems "in one's head." This is a distinctly human quality.

Concepts *always* have to do with meanings; words are simply their labels. Concepts may deal with concrete places, persons, objects, institutions, or events such as these:

mountain	flood	valley
plateau	dairy	ocean
home	island	Chinese
country	famine	harbor
state	community helpers	desert
producer	political party	consumer goods

Concepts may also be more or less abstract ways of thinking, feeling, and behaving, such as these:

adaptation	freedom	responsibility
democracy	justice	cooperation
tolerance	fairness	rights
honesty	liberty	equality
loyalty	interdependence	conflict
free enterprise	legal system	prejudice
ethnic group	hypothesis	ecosystem

Note that each of the ten curriculum standards developed by the National Council for the Social Studies is a concept or a group of two or three concepts:

culture	power, authority, and governance
time, continuity, and change	production, distribution, and consumption
people, places, and environments	science, technology, and society
individual development and identity	global connections
individuals, groups, and institutions	civic ideals and practice[6]

Similarly, the five themes of geography that were described in Chapter 4 are concepts: *location, place, human/environment interaction, movement, region.*[7] Recognizing that these curriculum standards and themes are *concepts* is important: Recognizing them as such, teachers can reach into their toolbox of teaching strategies for that set of strategies that is tailored to concepts per se. Matching strategies to subject matter makes teaching more effective.

The Role of Facts

Before we examine the difference between concepts and generalizations, we should think carefully about facts: What are they? How do they differ from concepts?

Facts are data or information; these terms are synonyms. Facts can be observed using the senses: A child can see that a Pueblo home is made of a pinkish mud, she can feel the adobe brick, she can hear the slow beat of the drum, she can taste the fry bread and smell the burning sage. These are facts. There are millions of facts that students could be asked to learn. Concepts, on the other hand, are ideas that exist "only in the head." This is why we say they are abstractions. They are based on examples, and examples are bundles of facts. The fact that adobe is used to make Pueblo dwellings, that it is made from the soil found in some parts of the southwestern region of what is now the United States, that an adobe home feels remarkably cool inside though the New Mexican sun shines bright and hot overhead—these facts together make one example of the concept *human/environment interaction.* The Lakota Sioux portable shelter made of buffalo hide is another, and the woodland Iroquois' long house is yet another.

Examples of concepts are like magnets that attract facts into meaningful clusters, and concepts do the same for examples. They are "powerful content organizers." Facts provide the supporting detail and the elaboration that make concepts meaningful. Without facts, we cannot help children build concepts. *Human/environment interaction* is a meaningless term without knowledge of multiple examples. Likewise, *village* has no meaning without knowledge of specific villages. Without facts, children can no more build an idea than workers could build a house without materials.

However, instruction on facts *alone* is rarely effective or useful. Facts taught in isolation have "nothing to hang on," so to speak. They have no place to go, no organizer. Consequently, they are difficult to make sense of and difficult to remember. A great many facts, however, can be taught and learned in the context of concept learning. When facts are learned as part of concepts (and, as we shall see, generalizations and inquiry), children can remember them longer and use them more ably in future learning.

The Nature of Generalizations

Let us return to the village concept cited earlier and ask the question, What can we say about the relationship between the village and the people who live there? Several things could be said, of course, but the following will serve our purpose:

> The village embraces the total culture of traditional Pacific Northwest Native Americans.

This statement expresses a relationship between the concepts *village* and *culture*. Such relationships are called *generalizations* and are expressed as declarative statements. Because generalizations are relationships between two or more concepts, they are summarizing statements that have wide applicability. They are generally true—true in many situations. For example, the generalization cited does not apply only to one village but to *all* villages of traditional Pacific Northwest Native Americans. That is what makes it a generalization. The generalization "All human societies have a culture" has even broader applicability. It would apply to *any* human society anywhere in the world.

Generalizations are similar to concepts in that they, too, help the individual order the physical and social environments. Rather than being represented by a single word or expression, however, generalizations are usually expressed as declarative statements. The following are examples of generalizations often found in social studies. Notice how each expresses a relationship between concepts embedded in the statement.

1. New inventions lead to change in ways of living.
2. As human beings interact with the physical environment, both they and it are changed.
3. Because the peoples of the world are interdependent, the behaviors of one group of people affects the lives of the other groups.
4. Families are a primary means of socialization in all cultures.
5. Written laws clarify the rules by which a society operates and promote fair and equal treatment of its members.
6. The survival of a multicultural society relies upon most citizens agreeing to a core of commonly held values (e.g., justice, equality, liberty).
7. Great and small historical events rarely have a single cause.
8. Compromise is necessary in most situations because continuous conflict has severe consequences.

Three different types of generalizations are relevant to social studies education:

> 1. A supermarket sells all food products needed by consumers.

This is a *descriptive* generalization. It could have been a concluding statement made by the children who were using the first strategy described in the next section on concept development. It describes in summary form the relationship between the supermarket and the food needs of consumers.

2. Advertising the price of merchandise results in more comparative shopping by consumers.

This is a *cause-and-effect* generalization. "If-then" statements are usually generalizations of this type.

3. Misleading or false advertising takes unfair advantage of consumers and is illegal.

This generalization is a statement of a *value principle*. Generalizations of this type constitute the guidelines by which individuals govern their actions, and many have been handed down through the ages in the form of proverbs or wise statements for good living.

Again, let us consider the role of facts. Let us say that a child reads the following generalization: "The livelihood of persons in this region depends on the seasonal cycle of rain to make their crops produce as much as possible." This statement has meaning only if one has specific information needed to answer such questions as "Which crop?" "How much rain is needed?" "When does the rain come?" "Is agriculture their only livelihood?" Children need to build the concepts that together compose a generalization, and for that they need to learn the bundles of facts—the examples—on which concepts are based.

Teaching Concepts to Young Learners

Now that we have looked at the nature of concepts and generalizations, we turn to how to teach them. We begin with strategies for teaching concepts.

Social studies concepts can be studied at various levels of complexity. Kindergartners and first-graders often study the family and family life. Yet a graduate student working on a doctorate in sociology or anthropology might take an advanced seminar on the same subject. The United States Supreme Court struggles with the meaning of justice in a complex case, yet children in the elementary school learn about the meaning of "liberty and justice for all." How does a teacher go about setting the complexity of subject matter, concepts, and generalizations and present them in ways that make sense to children? The following are suggested:

1.   Define concepts in terms familiar to young children. For example:

Concept	For a Young Child This Means
Justice	Being or playing fair
Laws	Rules
Equality of opportunity	Seeing that everyone gets a turn
Cooperation	Working with others
Responsibility	Doing your part or duty
Hypothesis	A good guess
Democracy	Majority rule plus civil rights

2.   Select subject matter with which children can identify. This does not mean that topics selected for study must be physically close to them. Children can study about

Helping children build powerful ideas helps them learn forever.

things far away that are psychologically close to them. On the other hand, things that are physically close may be psychologically remote. The life styles of families who live across town, for example, may be as unfamiliar to a child as those of people halfway around the world.

3. Rely on diagnostic approaches to teaching. That is, find out what children already know. It is especially important when teaching concepts to anchor them in a child's experience. Such experience may be direct or vicarious, real or represented in some way, but one way or another, new ideas must be linked to students' prior knowledge. This usually can be accomplished through informal class discussions in which children respond to open-ended questions the teacher has prepared in advance. Remember, children who are culturally different from their teacher will have somewhat different experiences and knowledge, and it is important that the teacher discover this information and relate to it. For any concept, ask students to think of several examples and then tell why they are examples. By listening to the examples students suggest but, more important, to the *reasons* they give, teachers can diagnose children's present knowledge of a concept and plan accordingly.

We assume that students have learned a concept when they can summarize the attributes shared by all of the concept's examples. But there are other indications of learners' understanding of concepts. Teachers should keep these in mind for, as we shall see in the discussion of performance assessment in Chapter 9, they serve as the objectives or targets of instruction. For example, students can distinguish examples from nonexamples (a nonexample is any item that has some but not all of the attributes the concept requires). Students who have learned a concept thoroughly also can produce (find, create, describe) new examples and correct nonexamples. When students have learned the concept *village*, for example, they can:

- summarize what all villages have in common (summarizing)
- distinguish villages from cities and suburbs (distinguishing)
- write a story about a village they invent (producing)
- describe the changes the state capital would have to undergo to become a village (correcting a nonexample)

Concept Learning: Three Strategies

This section describes three strategies for teaching concepts. As you will see, all rely on helping children experience multiple examples of the concept to be learned. This is, in a nutshell, the key to concept teaching and learning. Yet, the three strategies are different from one another in interesting ways. The first two strategies are construction oriented[8]; that is, children *construct* the concept (*build* and *assemble* are good terms, too) using the *building blocks* you provide: a handful of well-selected examples, plus techniques for examining, organizing, and synthesizing them. In the third strategy, more of the "brainwork" is done by the teacher. It is a somewhat easier strategy to use, therefore, and the beginning teacher may wish to try it before the others.

The first strategy, called *concept formation*, has students systematically build the summary in their minds as they compare and contrast three or four examples.[9] The second is the time-honored "list, group, and label" strategy.[10] The third, called "concept attainment," is a deductive version of the first strategy. The teacher tells students the critical attributes of a concept and then helps them work with examples and nonexamples.

Strategy 1: Concept Formation.   A fifth-grade class is studying the concept *democracy*. The teacher, Kenneth Bailey, has asked diagnostic questions such as these: What is democracy? Is the United States a democracy? Why? What persons do you think of when you think of democracy? In this way, Mr. Bailey learns that students have no concept of democracy save vague notions of voting and majority rule. With this information in hand, he builds an introductory concept-formation lesson on *democracy*.

First, he knows he should assemble three or four examples of democracy. These will be the building blocks of the concept. He decides to use the governments of the United States, Mexico, and Canada, because the textbook has information on them. For the fourth example, he wants something less "bookish," more experiential; accordingly, he selects the democratic classroom meeting his students have each Monday afternoon.

Using the concept-formation strategy, students will build an understanding of democracy "from the bottom up" by studying each example and then comparing and contrasting them. Similarities among examples are the critical attributes of the concept *democracy*: In the United States, Mexico, Canada, and Mr. Bailey's classroom meetings, the majority rules (laws are made by all citizens or their representatives), minority rights are protected, and laws are written down. These are the three attributes students eventually should summarize under the name "democracy." Is the resulting concept as complex as the one formed by college political science majors? Of course not, but it would be quite an achievement for fifth grade children. Here is the teacher's plan for achieving this result.

Studying Multiple Examples.   Mr. Bailey creates a data-retrieval chart that contains the four examples down the left and Focus Questions across the top (see Figure 7–1). These questions focus students' attention on the critical attributes.

Mr. Bailey instructs his students to use this chart to record information they find on each example. He gives them some time in class to work with the information in their textbooks and complete the chart. He directs them to finish the chart as homework.

Noting Differences.   The next day, after verifying that all the needed information on the four examples has been gathered and recorded, Mr. Bailey asks students, "In what ways do these four governments differ?"

Noting Similarities.   He then asks, "In what ways are these four governments all alike?" He records their responses on the chalkboard for use in the next step.

Summarizing.   He then instructs students, "Take a few minutes now to jot down a summary of these similarities in one, complete sentence. Let's begin the summary with, 'These are all ways of governing that. . . " Now students compose their own definition of the concept. Mr. Bailey takes time to allow for sharing and gives students feedback. Students then compose a second draft, taking more care to include all the critical attributes of *democracy* in their summaries.

Labeling.   He then asks, "What is a word you might use to describe governments like these? Be creative—invent a word if you like. Make sure it captures the essence of this kind of government." After eliciting several nicknames, Mr. Bailey tells them that the conventional label for this kind of government is *democracy*. He takes some time to examine with his students the etymology of this Greek term.

Guided Application: Classifying.   Now that students have constructed in their minds a rough idea of *democracy*, it is time to reinforce, extend, and refine it through a powerful application activity called *classifying*.

Figure 7–1
A data-retrieval chart for the concept *democracy* as developed by Mr. Bailey for his class.

Focus Questions			
EXAMPLES	Does the majority rule? How?	Are minority rights protected? (Describe.)	Are laws written? Where?
United States			
Canada			
Mexico			
Class meeting			

Classifying requires students to recall the critical attributes of a concept and, moving to higher-order thinking, determine whether those attributes are present in a new situation. The new situation is bound to be different from the examples studied initially to form the concept; accordingly, students need to decide if any of the differences really matter as far as the concept is concerned. In this way, a concept is not formed only to remain unused in the mind. Rather, learners are asked to regard a concept as "portable" knowledge that can be taken with them and used to make sense of new situations. There are several varieties of this time-honored activity. Here we give the basic form and two variations:

1. *Distinguishing examples from nonexamples.* Mr. Bailey gives students information about two or three other governments (China's; Denmark's; Japan's) and asks them to decide which of them, if any, is a democracy. He asks them to write down their reasons and calls on several students to share their decisions and reasons.

2. *Producing examples.* He directs his students to get into teams of four and together create a fictional example of a democracy. He asks them to imagine themselves ship-wrecked on an island with no chance of rescue; hence, they must create a society from scratch. He reminds them to look back at their summaries to be sure the example they create has each of the attributes all examples of democracies must have.

3. *Correcting nonexamples.* Mr. Bailey tells students that he will describe several organizations, all of which are nonexamples of *democracy*. The students' task is to describe the changes that would be needed in order to make each of them into examples of the concept. First, he describes a modern military dictatorship and asks them to make the needed changes that would render it a democracy. After students have accomplished this task satisfactorily, Mr. Bailey describes a little league baseball club and, finally, a monarchy. Students again are asked and helped to make the needed changes.

Incorporating Cooperative Group Work.   At step 1 in concept formation, students can be placed in cooperative teams of four students each. Each member of the group takes responsibility for gathering information on one of the four examples. Sherry takes Mexico, Jamal takes Canada, Mei takes the classroom meetings, and Rena gets the United States. Because one member of every other team is studying the same example, these students get together in an "expert group" to work on their example together. Every team member thus leaves his or her team to work with other students responsible for the same example. Eventually, experts return to their teams where they teach their example to teammates. In this way, everyone studies all examples—which is crucial for concept formation: remember, a concept is a summary of attributes shared by all examples.

For *noting differences* through *labeling*, it is a good idea to work with the whole class as Mr. Bailey did. But for *classifying*, teams can again be convened to work through the three activities.

Strategy 2: Listing, Grouping, and Labeling.   Imagine a primary grade class that has just returned from a field trip to a supermarket. Now, back in the classroom, the teacher asks the children to list as many things as they can remember having seen in the supermarket. As they name items, the teacher writes them on the chalkboard—for example, eggs, bread, beans, meat, butter, checkout person, stock clerk, watermelons, candy, store manager, dog food, ice cream, and so on.

After completing the process of listing what they saw, the teacher asks the children to examine their list to see if certain things on the list seem to go together. That is, can these items be put together in groups that have something in common, as, for example, milk, butter, cheese, cream, and yogurt? They catch on to this activity quickly, and soon they are suggesting which items can be placed in the same group. Having placed items that seem to go together in the same group, children are then asked to think of names or labels for these groups. In the foregoing example, a name for that group would probably be "dairy products." The children should develop a name or label for each of the groups.

This listing-grouping-labeling strategy can be used in many ways to teach concepts in social studies. Here are a few additional examples:

1. Suppose a visitor from another country spent a day at our school; what would he or she see?
2. What did you see on the walk through the neighborhood?
3. What are all the ways goods and people can be moved from one place to another?
4. How many things can you list that are manufactured in our city (or state)?
5. What items are sold in a department store?
6. What are things human beings can do that no other creatures can do?
7. What natural resources do we depend on in our everyday life?

This strategy is particularly useful in situations in which learners have made many observations in a short period of time and need to sort out what they experienced into meaningful categories.

In using this strategy with young children, the teacher may have children find examples of the concept in pictures from old magazines. Or the teacher may have a collection of magazine pictures that illustrate examples of the concept and have children group the ones that seem to "go together." Children can then suggest word labels for these groups.

Strategy 3: Concept Attainment.   A sixth-grade class has been studying the economic development of nations in the Third World. The teacher, Ms. Rush, wants her students to develop the concept *modernization* and helps them do so in the following way. Note that she does not give them examples to study and then lead them to a discovery of the concept based on the examples' shared attributes; rather she *tells* them the attributes and then provides examples and nonexamples. She begins by writing the concept label and critical attributes on the chalkboard:

Modernization involves
1. The application of technology to the control of nature's resources.
2. The use of inanimate sources of power and energy.
3. The use of tools to multiply the effects of human energy expended.
4. A high per capita production output.

The teacher then explains the meaning of each of the four attributes by using large pictures. That is, she shows the class specific examples of modernization—situations in which technology is applied to the control of resources, where inanimate power and energy sources are used, where tools multiply human energy, and where the per capita production is high. As children raise questions, these are discussed and issues are clarified. The teacher then provides the class with a series of pictures in which modernization, as defined by the particular attributes, is *not* evident. Again, these are explained and discussed, and questions raised by children are answered.

Having satisfied herself that the children understand the attributes that indicate modernization, the teacher presents the class with another set of pictures, but this time the *children* must identify examples and nonexamples of modernization and tell why or why not each is an example. These pictures are discussed in detail. The teacher then provides the class with back issues of *National Geographic* and asks them to find picture examples and nonexamples of modernization and to tell why each is or is not an example. Finally, the teacher evaluates the children's ability to understand the concept by having them identify examples and nonexamples from a new set of pictures.

This strategy is less construction oriented than the other two, but it does, nonetheless, present opportunities for search and discovery. In this case, the teacher provides the attributes of the concept in advance rather than having learners build them in the process of study. In summary, Ms. Rush:

1. Identified the label for the concept (modernization).
2. Provided the major attributes (or critical characteristics) of the concept.
3. Provided examples that illustrated the presence of the attributes.
4. Provided nonexamples in which the attributes were missing.
5. Presented examples and nonexamples, had the children identify the attributes, and had them tell why or why not each was an example.
6. Had children find examples and nonexamples on their own.
7. Evaluated their ability to use the attributes in identifying examples and nonexamples.

Concept Extensions

These three concept-learning strategies help learners form initial ideas of all kinds of phenomena—people (e.g., civil rights reformers; explorers), places (continents; countries), events (national holidays; cultural festivals), skills (composing summaries; cooperating in small groups), systems (democracies; civilizations), and so on. The concepts children build as a result of such strategies are necessarily incipient; that is, they are *beginning* understandings because they contain only a small number of examples, and each example may not have been examined in great detail. For this reason, expert teachers have in their repertoire strategies that help students *extend* and elaborate concepts after they have been formed initially. These strategies have the effect of building a second and third layer of understanding atop the first. *Further, they help learners to correct misconceptions formed earlier.*

Return to the Examples.   This is the easiest way to extend the meaning of concepts. It involves having students return to the examples they studied initially to build the idea, only now to learn about them in greater depth. Returning to Mr. Bailey's democracy lesson, three committees might be formed to write biographies on the founders of democracy in the United States, Canada, and Mexico, respectively. A fourth can gather information and stories related to the first town meetings in colonial America and use this information to advise classmates on the conduct of their own democratic classroom meetings.

Additional Experience with Classifying.   Classifying of any sort should strengthen a concept after its initial formation. This is so because classifying requires learners to recall the attributes of the concept again, each time applying them to a slightly different set of facts. This higher-order thinking process should result in a flexible understanding of the concept that can be used in various situations.

Any of the three kinds of classifying explained under the concept-formation strategy (strategy 1) is effective, but perhaps *distinguishing examples from nonexamples* best promotes the elaboration of a concept. When children have formed an initial understanding of modernization, for example, they are ready to apply it to the examination of any country in the world, on any continent, deciding if the society in question is "modern" according to the attributes they have learned.

Teaching Generalizations

Because generalizations are summarizing statements that include two or more concepts, these statements are "generally" true. They can also be called, simply, *conclusions*. It is important to understand the difference between generalizations and stereotypes. Generalizations are rational because they are based on concepts that are, in turn, based on facts. Stereotypes are irrational generalizations—that is, general beliefs that a person holds *in spite of* the facts.

Building a social studies generalization can be a time-consuming and difficult construction project for children and requires skillful guidance from the teacher. By the end of the third grade, children should have formed the following generalization about community life: "Community needs are met by groups of people engaged in many interdependent activities." Much conceptual teaching will need to occur, however, especially on the concepts *community needs* and *interdependence*, and even then several children probably will not form it without additional teaching and practice. "A supermarket sells most of the food products needed by consumers," on the other hand, should be more easily achieved. Why? Because most children will have the necessary experiences on which the latter generalization relies: namely, getting food at supermarkets. Of course even this will depend on the child's proximity to supermarkets. Wealthy and poor urban families alike are more likely to shop in smaller, store-front grocery stores. Likewise, rural village children will have few supermarket experiences.

Generalizations, like concepts, have to be developed out of the experiences of children. Many, but certainly not all, of the experiences will be the examples the teacher has them explore. As with concept teaching, it is the teacher's job to provide well-chosen examples, but also to draw on the out-of-school experiences of his or her children and to provide guidance so that children will think about these experiences in such a way that a rational generalization is formed. It is essential that students understand the concepts in the generalizations in order to grasp the relationship among them, for this relationship *is* the generalization. For this reason, it is not effective for learners simply to memorize generalizations. Generalizations, like concepts, are mental tools that can be taken from subject to subject and from one situation to another. Generalizations that are memorized but not understood cannot be used as tools.

There are two common strategies for helping students build generalizations. One, called summarizing, comes at the end of a sequence of study; the other, hypothesizing, comes at the beginning.

Summarizing

The essence of this approach is asking children to make connections among the items they have studied and experienced. As in concept learning, the differences sometimes seem to overwhelm the similarities. Yet, it is the similarities that connect across the differences, like a bridge, to make an idea. This is true of both concepts and generalizations.

To help children make such connections, they can be guided through this sequence of questions:

1. What is happening in all these situations? (each of the native villages we built, the African societies we studied, the American colonies we studied, the inventors we read about, the migrations we mapped, the conventions we dramatized, the mountain ranges we explored, the historical eras we examined, the civilizations we read about)
2. Where else do we see this happening?
3. How is this alike or different from the problem we discussed before? (during news time, during classroom meeting, during the American Revolution unit)

It is helpful to the children if the various situations, persons, events, or places are clearly listed on the chalkboard or represented on the bulletin board. As well, it may be necessary to ask students to review each item to bring it back to mind if considerable time has passed since it was studied.

Hypothesizing

When generalizations are presented at the beginning of an instructional sequence, they should be treated as hypotheses to be confirmed or rejected by the students in light of the information that will be gathered in the course of study. This way, students learn that statements are not automatically true, but must be investigated. This is the true spirit of inquiry. For example:

Teacher:	"Many people believe in the law of supply and demand, which states, 'Scarcity of goods results in higher prices whereas an oversupply of goods results in lower prices.' How could we go about finding out whether this is true of the things we and our families buy?"
Student 1:	"We could find out if the flood last summer made corn more expensive."
Student 2:	"We could see if orange juice costs more in the morning when everybody wants it."
Student 3:	"We could see if videos cost more when they're new and lots of people want to see them."

In this illustration, the children themselves have named three instances they could examine to determine whether the hypothesis is generally true. The teacher should add other instances drawn from long ago and far away to expand the children's base of experience.

Teaching the Inquiry Process

The inquiry process is also called the *scientific method* or *problem solving*. It is the chief method used by scientists to develop new generalizations and correct old ones. Children who have learned it are able to judge whether generalizations are supported by the evidence. Numerous thinking-skills experts exalt the inquiry process as the highest form of higher-order thinking, what they call *critical thinking*.[11] As part of the inquiry process, students not only evaluate the truthfulness of statements but learn that evidence varies in its quality and that there are usually competing accounts of any one event. Their teacher is forever pestering them with the questions "Where did you read (see; hear) that?" and "How do you know that's true?" and "Do your sources agree?" Gradually, they will come to ask these questions themselves.

Even the youngest children engage in inquiry. Their incessant "why" questions are proof. Teachers can help children to become more skillful inquirers, and therefore more skillful thinkers and better informed citizens, by engaging them in inquiry often, both as part of daily classroom life and as a way of learning social studies skills and ideas.

The general inquiry procedure is this: The teacher has the children pose hypotheses about the probable cause of an event, what is generally true in some area of social life, or what might solve a problem. Then the teacher designs activities in which the children gather information and compare it to these hypotheses. As they do the comparisons, the children learn to discard, add, and revise hypotheses as the facts require.

Here we provide two examples of inquiry teaching. The first concerns an intermediate-grade class that has been studying the concept *advertising*. Notice how this teacher has students assemble many examples, elicits hypotheses about the value of advertising, and then has them search for information that confirms or denies these hypotheses.

Example 1

An intermediate-grade class has been introduced to the the concept *advertising*. Sensing that the children's understanding is still quite weak, the teacher selects the following strategy to extend and strengthen it. First, children are asked to search for as many different examples of advertising as they can find. This search uncovers newspaper and magazine advertisements, classified ads, radio and television commercials, billboards, signs on transit buses, signs in public buildings, direct mailers, catalogs, and others. These various methods of advertising are discussed in terms of their purpose; the audience to which they are directed; the extent to which they are local, regional, or national; and the nature of the appeal. This leads the class to speculate on the value of advertising. Who benefits from advertising, and how do they benefit? Out of this discussion the children develop the following hypotheses:

1. Advertising helps consumers because it informs them about new products and their prices.
2. Effective advertising tries to create wants for products whether they are needed or not.
3. Local advertising has a more direct effect on sales in local stores than does national advertising.

The children begin searching for information that would support or refute these hypotheses. Much of their information gathering is done outside of school by interviewing consumers, local merchants, and representatives of advertising agencies. This process forces them to explore further such related subconcepts as needs and wants, promotion, audience, client, account, market, layout, impact, theme, and sales appeal. In time, they are able to form some tentative conclusions relating to their hypotheses, but their conclusions suggest other hypotheses that need exploration.

Example 2

The teacher has students speculate on the causes of the *Titanic* tragedy in the early 1900s (Lesson Plan 6). Notice that the teacher in this lesson provides the information to students, rather than having them conduct research themselves. Also note that the information is provided a little at a time, in chunks, or data sets. This way, children can be helped to evaluate their hypotheses after each chunk of data. This is a highly effective strategy with younger and older children alike. It is vivid: It gives children a memorable experience of the power of data, for they see hypotheses vanish from the chalkboard as the data roll in.

Children who have participated regularly in the inquiry process display more than skills; they display disciplined ways of thinking, too: a respect for facts, a reluctance to "jump to conclusions," and an eagerness to spot prejudices and root them out. These are habits or dispositions that are among the most valued goals that we have for children's learning. For this reason, even beginning teachers should make it a priority to involve children in inquiry experiences. Children who are denied this are placed at a considerable disadvantage, for they are not empowered to become stronger learners.*

Teaching Social Studies Skills

The systematic and sequential development of skills is of utmost importance to children because skills are the tools with which they continue their learning. Consequently, inadequately developed skills tend to retard learning in many areas of the elementary and middle school curriculum, particularly in the social studies. Inadequate achievement in the social studies can, in many cases, be traced to poorly developed reading skills, inability to handle the vocabulary of the social studies, inability to read maps and globes, poor work-study skills, inability to use reference materials, or underdeveloped language skills. Therefore, a well-balanced program in the social studies needs to provide for systematic and planned instruction to ensure the development of these skills.**

Skill implies proficiency, the capability of doing something well. To have a skill is ordinarily taken to mean that a person is able to respond more or less habitually in an efficient way. Skills are commonly classified as motor, intellectual, and social.

We do not deal with motor skills in this book, but social and intellectual skills are considered throughout. They are fundamental subject matter in social studies. Social skills, for example, include forming small groups for cooperative work and functioning

---

* Readers may wish to skip ahead to Chapter 12 at this point in order to examine the integrated curriculum called *Explore*. It is used with third and fourth grade children in Northglenn, Colorado, and teaches them "the scientific way of learning" or inquiry.

** For an extended list of social studies skills, see National Council for the Social Studies, *Social Studies Curriculum Planning Resources* (Dubuque, IA: Kendall/Hunt, 1990), 36–37.

Lesson Plan 6

Causes of the Titanic Tragedy: Scientific Inquiry

Grade
4–8

Time
Two to four class periods

Objectives
Children will understand that an event can have multiple causes. They will learn to formulate and revise hypotheses as new information is encountered.

Interest Building
Show slides or photos of the *Titanic* gathered from magazine articles about the sinking of the ship and recent expeditions to find it at the bottom of the Atlantic. Tell students the story of the *Titanic*—that it was billed as luxurious and "unsinkable" but hit an iceberg and sank on its first voyage.

Lesson Development
1. Ask students *why* they think a ship this great with a captain so skilled might have hit an iceberg on its maiden voyage. List their reasons on the board under the title *hypotheses.* If needed, suggest some possibilities: captain was asleep, terrorism, lookouts were at a party, crew was not expecting icebergs in those waters at that time of year, captain was overconfident, design flaws in the ship.
2. Ask each student to jot down the hypothesis that he or she thinks might be true.
3. Give students more information, one set (five to ten minutes) at a time. Begin with a set of information on the ship's design, then move to such things as the weather conditions that night, the captain's experience, the *Titanic*'s sister ships, the way ships communicated and received warnings in those days, icebergs, social life aboard the ship, the life boats, the ship's cargo, and so forth. *Between each set of information you provide, pause and ask students to examine the list of hypotheses on the board. Have them remove, add, and revise hypotheses in light of the information they are getting.* This is the core activity of the lesson
4. At some point draw the inquiry to a close and ask students to return to the hypotheses they wrote down at the beginning of the lesson. Have them revise these as needed to reflect what they now believe to be true. These statements are conclusions based on data.

Summary
Tell the class that this process of revising conclusions ("changing our minds") in the light of new data is the essence of science. It is the meaning of *open minded.* Ask students what information they can imagine would cause them to revise their conclusions again.

Assessment
Ask students for the meaning of such common phrases as *jumping to conclusions* and *closed minded.* Then ask them to write down the inquiry sequence they experienced in this lesson. Listen to their responses and provide assistance as needed:

1. Becoming familiar with the problem (viewing slides, reading newspaper reports).
2. Suggesting multiple hypotheses (these were recorded on board).
3. Gathering information.
4. Using information to test each hypothesis.
5. Concluding what is true based on the information gathered.

Follow up

Repeat the inquiry sequence with other problems: What happened to the people in the Lost Colony at Roanoke? Were there witches in Salem? Who were the first Americans? Where does the food on the lunch table come from? Where does garbage go?

Materials

Teacher resources on the *Titanic* (e.g., the textbook, encyclopedia, magazine articles, books on its sinking and the expeditions to find it).

well within them, and giving oral reports. These are the subject of Chapter 10. Social skills also include citizenship skills, such as discussion and decision making, which were examined in Chapter 3. Intellectual skills are dealt with in nearly every chapter of this book. The present chapter alone features several powerful thinking skills that are associated with concept formation:

- Organizing information on data-retrieval charts
- Noting differences and similarities across examples
- Summarizing (or *synthesizing*) similarities
- Naming an idea
- Classifying (applying the concept)

Testing and developing generalizations using the inquiry process requires skillful thinking as well:

- Hypothesizing
- Gathering relevant data/evidence
- Judging whether hypotheses are supported by data
- Drawing conclusions (generalizations) based on data

Thinking skills that are closely related to the development of understandings such as concepts and generalizations should be taught systematically to students. As children become proficient in the use of these, their power as learners can really soar. They find themselves able to master bigger chunks of subject matter, in greater depth, and better able to apply it, too.

Skills Teaching

All skills have two characteristics in common: They are developmental, and they require practice if they are to be mastered. To speak of skills as being developmental means that they are learned gradually over a period of years. They are never really learned to completion although there usually comes a time when the learner has mastered them sufficiently for most purposes. However, one could continue refining these skills throughout one's lifetime. Thus, teachers should not assume that skills are taught and learned only once in some particular grade. All teachers need to assume some responsibility for the teaching and maintenance of social studies skills.

No amount of explanation or meaningful teaching will make children proficient in skills. In the ordinary study of a topic, there will be numerous opportunities to practice skills in the daily work-study activities of the class. In this way, the children improve their skills as they develop their understanding of concepts and subject matter. Skills are learned more effectively when they are closely related to actual situations in which they will be used.

Procedures in skills teaching are fairly clearcut. The learners should first understand what is involved in the skill, how it is used, and what it means. Providing a good model of its use is helpful at this point. Second, the learners need to work through a simple use of the skill under careful teacher guidance. This is essential to verify that they understand what is involved and are making a correct response. Third, they need additional practice in increasingly complex variations of the skill, applied in functional settings. Children need to use the newly learned skill in solving problems, thus demonstrating its value as a learning tool. Finally, they need continued practice in its use over an extended period of time to maintain and improve facility with the skill. These steps, along with an example of their application, are provided in Figure 7–2.

For purposes of focus and clarity of analysis, in the treatment of teaching methods, skills teaching is often discussed in a separate section. This separation should not suggest to the teacher that skills are taught or learned outside a content framework. The content connection is most obvious in the case of work-study skills such as finding information, arranging information in usable forms, using maps, globes, and graphics, and organizing information. Such skills have no purpose outside of a subject-matter setting. But the integration of content and skills applies to intellectual skills and group-work skills as well. Higher-order thinking processes such as problem solving, critical thinking, inquiry, and decision making must have a content framework if they are to be taught with integrity. Teachers should not set out to teach these important processes without giving ample consideration to the subject matter in which they are to be used.

Having said this, we need to be very clear about the need to provide explicit instruction on skills that children are expected to demonstrate. Children *can* learn new skills, and they can improve skills they already possess. They do so all the time. What is required is an effective skill-teaching strategy, such as the one just presented, along with the firm expectation that all students learn them to the highest degree of proficiency of which they are capable. One of the main causes of poor skills among children—whether cooperative skills, thinking skills, reading and writing skills, research and study skills, or whatever—is, not surprisingly, *lack of instruction.* There are many important causes for this lack, but three are outstanding.

Contexts, But No Instruction

First, it is not sufficient to place children in functional contexts in which skillful behavior is required *without also providing instruction on the skills themselves.* Doing so is a good example of what earlier was called "teaching less," and it systematically disadvantages children whose home life is culturally different from school life.[12] What is needed

Figure 7–2
Example of steps in teaching a skill applied to the use of the directory of a newspaper

STEPS IN TEACHING A SKILL:

Step 1 Make sure children understand what is involved in performing the skill. Show them how it is used. Provide them with a good model of the skill in operation.

Step 2 Break the skill into components and arrange them sequentially. Develop the teaching sequence step by step, having the children do each component as it is presented and explained. Supervise carefully to make sure their responses are correct.

Step 3 Have the children perform a simple variation of the skill under your close supervision. This is to ensure that they are performing the skill correctly.

Step 4 After it is established that the children are performing the skill correctly, provide for supervised practice, using simple variations that ensure success.

Step 5 Gradually increase the complexity of the variation of the skill, and begin having children apply the skill in situations in which it is useful. Continue this procedure until the desired level of proficiency is achieved.

Step 6 Continue to practice the skill at regular intervals, largely through functional application, in order to maintain and improve performance.

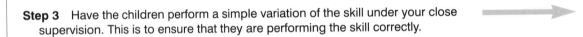

is an artful combination of skills instruction and meaningful contexts for using the skills. The result is that learning occurs and is meaningful. When a third grade teacher is introducing her children to the skill of using a newspaper's directory, she does not merely distribute the newspapers and tell students to find particular items. She also provides explicit instruction on the skill of using the directory. Similarly, she does not simply pass out textbooks and ask children to read the first lesson. She teaches them how to use a textbook, how to read expository material, how to preview the section before beginning, and so forth.

Wishful Thinking

Second, teachers sometimes *wish* their students behaved better rather than getting down to the business of actually teaching students how to behave. Some teachers do

EXAMPLES OF APPLICATION OF EACH STEP:

Step 1   Secure a newspaper, preferably a Sunday edition, and show how difficult and time-consuming it is to find some bit of information if one has to leaf through the entire paper to find it. Have children try their hand at finding items without using the newspaper directory. Show how easily one can find information with the aid of the directory.

Step 2
a. Acquaint children with various sections of the newspaper: general news, classified ads, sports, editorials, letters to the editor, weather, and so on.
b. Teach children the specialized vocabulary associated with the newspaper: vital statistics, obituaries, market quotations, headline, byline, dateline, syndicated, and so on.
c. Teach children what items are included in the various categories listed in the directory, and how they are arranged. For example, what is included in the Arts and Entertainment section? How are the classifieds organized?
d. Provide a newspaper for each member of the class, and have the children locate easy items using the directory. Such items might include the television schedule, sports, and the comics. Supervise to make sure everyone is performing the skill correctly.

Step 3   Follow Step 2 immediately with an exercise requiring children to locate items making use of the directory. Supervise and assist as needed. Check responses.

Step 4   Assign children to find information in the next day's newspaper. This should be done on their own without teacher supervision. Check responses.

Step 5   Bring to class copies of a different newspaper from the one used thus far in which a slightly different directory format appears. Assign children to find information in this paper without teacher assistance to see if they can transfer and modify their skill from one situation to another. Check responses.

Step 6   From time to time have children make use of the directory to locate needed information. Observe the accuracy and extensiveness of use of the directory.

not teach children certain skills because they assume children "at this age" already possess these skills or believe they should have learned them by now. This is wishful thinking. Effective teachers assess their children's skills and performance levels and provide instruction as needed.

Discrimination/Unequal Expectations

Third, some teachers have different expectations for different students: for example expecting girls, but not boys, to learn social skills and manners; prodding boys, but not girls, to learn higher-order reasoning skills; or assuming that racial- or ethnic-minority children are incapable of learning certain skills. Recall from Chapter 2 that teachers who are determined to teach *all* their students provide explicit instruction to *all* children as needed.

Asking Good Questions

Questioning strategies are a favorite topic of teachers. Painters talk about their brushes, plumbers about wrenches, politicians about speeches, and historians about primary documents. For teachers, questions are the constant companion and the handiest and most powerful of tools. We are not suggesting that they replace love, patience, and curiosity; these are not replaceable. But whether the subject matter is a concept, a generalization, the inquiry process, a skill, or, more likely, a combination of these in a unit of study, a toolbox of good questions is arguably the teacher's best friend.

For this reason, beginning teachers should work diligently to develop a fine awareness of the questions they ask as well as those their children ask. "Can I play with you?" a child asks another tentatively. "Why did they wear those hats?" she asks the teacher. And, "Do you like my story?" Teachers, meanwhile, ask two kinds of questions: interrogative statements that end with a question mark and directions. Directions are not actually questions, but they often serve the same purposes as questions. "Please tell us more about that" is a direction, but it is functionally equivalent to "Can you tell us more about that?" Typically, therefore, both forms are considered to be, in effect, questions.

The teaching strategies presented in this chapter all rest squarely on good questions. None of them could help children achieve the objectives without careful questions that are purposefully aimed at eliciting certain kinds of responses.

Purposes of Asking Questions

Questions serve five purposes. They *assess*, they *focus attention*, they *stimulate thinking processes*, they *follow up* on students' responses, and they *direct participation*. A good understanding of these purposes is the first step to asking good questions; therefore, sample questions are given in relationship to each purpose.

Assessment

"In the end, it is more interesting listening to pupils and trying to understand why they see things as they do, than it is to hear one's own voice trying to push them into giving the right answer."[13] Questions help curious teachers listen to students and, thereby, learn how they see things as they do and why. In other words, questions help teachers know children and ascertain their understanding of concepts, generalizations, inquiry, and skills. They also help teachers assess children's comprehension of a message they have heard, read, or viewed; whether they understand what they are to do; and their reactions to demonstrations or explanations. Here is an example of each:

Are playground games *democratic*? Should they be?

What is this photo (story, paragraph, film, art print) saying?

Before beginning, let's review the instructions. What are you to do first? Keesha? Michael?

What did you learn from that demonstration? What would you have done differently?

Focus Attention

"What proves to be effective is not telling the child the right answer, but guiding him or her towards the right considerations."[14] Teachers use questions to focus students' attention on a particular topic—that is, to guide their thinking to these matters, not those. This is done both in a moment-to-moment fashion during instruction and during planning. In the unit planning format that we explain in the next chapter, one or more focus questions are planned for an entire unit so that all the individual lessons relate in a meaningful way to one another and the unit's main focus. Reflecting back on the teaching strategies introduced in this chapter, focus questions played a key role:

Concept teaching: "What is a word you might use to describe governments like these? Be creative—invent a word if you like. Make sure it captures the essence of this kind of government."

Inquiry teaching: "Who benefits from advertising, and how do they benefit?"

Inquiry teaching: "What caused the *Titanic* tragedy? We know it hit an iceberg, but why?"

Skill teaching: "How can the directory be used to locate information in the newspaper?"

Promote Thinking

Questions also promote particular kinds of thinking. Research conducted over the past several decades on classroom questions reveals that teachers use a high percentage of questions that stimulate only recall of information that has been read or discussed in class. These questions are lower-level questions because they involve simple memory rather than higher-order thought processes that require some manipulation of information such as application, analysis, synthesis, interpretation, or evaluation. Lower-order questions can be easily identified because they often begin with *who, what, when,* and *where*. These questions are important, to be sure; we have already discussed the importance of facts. The problem is that they are overused, with a corresponding lessened use of questions that prompt higher-order thinking. Questions that prompt higher-order thinking help children achieve higher levels of understanding and skill: being able to create and test generalizations, construct and apply concepts, distinguish examples from non-examples, and use skills in contexts different from those in which they were initially practiced.

Lower (memory): "Describe majority rule in Canada and Mexico."

Higher (compare and contrast): "How are these governments alike and different?"

Higher still (classifying/application): "Create a fictional democracy that is different from those we've studied, though still possessing all the attributes of a democracy."

Follow Up

Questions elicit responses. What to do with those responses, how best to respond to them, brings us to the fourth use of questions. Generally speaking, the most powerful follow-up questions are those that cause students to go further with their initial response. There are four main types of follow-up questions:

Clarify: "What do you mean by _____?" (a term the student has used)

Elaborate: "Tell us more about _____." (something the student has said)

Variety: "What might be a different explanation?" (or different reason, item, example)

Verify: "How do you know that is true?"

Participation and Inclusion

Questions can help teachers increase student participation in the lesson and include all students.

"Talk with your partner about your response to that question, and in a moment I will ask several of you to share with the whole class." The teacher lets the children know they will be held accountable for responding, thus causing more of them to attend to the task. Also, the sharing technique gets all children involved and allows sufficient time for the children to think, and the teacher can roam around, giving feedback, praise, and correction as needed.

"How many of you think that advertising benefits mainly the consumer? Show one finger if you agree, two if you disagree. Then I'll ask several of you for your reasons." All students are involved in the decision because of the finger-voting technique, and all know they could be asked to give reasons.

"Thanks, Nathaniel. How did some of you others respond?" The teacher uses this question to acknowledge one student's response and invite other children to speak.

Figure 7–3
Use a clipboard to prompt
improved questions.

Focus Questions
1. What goods does our classroom store produce?
2. What services...?
3. What are some similarities and differences between goods & services?

Follow-up Questions:
CLARIFY: What do you mean?
VERIFY: How do you know?
ELABORATE: Tell us more.

Improving Questioning Skills

Once teachers understand that questions, like painters' brushes, serve different purposes and that no one brush can serve them all, they can improve their questions with practice. All skills require practice if proficiency is to be achieved; asking good questions is no exception. A teacher is in a position to practice question asking daily, and colleagues can be invited to observe his or her instruction and provide feedback. One way to begin such practice is to write out the focus questions for a lesson and carry them on a clipboard during class. Also written on the clipboard are the types of follow-up questions (Figure 7–3). They are taped to the clipboard because they are used whatever the focus questions may be. That is, no matter the topic, teachers should encourage students to elaborate and clarify their understandings and be able to back up their conclusions and beliefs with evidence and sound reasoning. Several suggestions for improving the questions teachers ask appear in Figure 7–4.

Figure 7–4
Improving the teacher's questioning skills

1. Consciously reduce the number of factual recall questions and increase the number of questions that require higher-order thinking. Also, use and teach the *vocabulary* of thinking, terms such as *classify, analyze, hypothesize, predict,* and *think*.

2. Don't confuse instructional questions with management directions. When you mean to give a direction, such as "Sit down," say "Sit down." Indirect commands given as questions ("Are you ready to sit down now?") can be confusing to children, especially those who are culturally different from the teacher or not native English speakers. These children may not know that such a question is actually a command.

3. Match the question to the purpose it is to serve. Questions that call for yes-no responses are not appropriate when an elaborate response is desired. Discussion questions should not be used for homework or independent study.

4. State questions in ways that communicate precisely what is being asked. Sometimes children cannot respond to questions, not because they do not know the material but because the question is ambiguous or poorly framed. The vocabulary of the question must be consistent with the vocabulary of the children.

5. Provide adequate time for children to respond. Ask the question *before* calling on a child to respond. This requires all children to form their own response. Asking children to jot down their response before calling on individuals to respond aloud gives everyone time to collect their thoughts.

6. Vary the way you acknowledge responses. In addition to "uh-huh," "all right," and "O.K.," ask a follow-up question. Avoid always acknowledging responses with positive evaluative comments such as "right," "great," or "very good," although these should be used from time to time to encourage participation and help children feel successful.

Resources for Teaching and Learning Social Studies

Children cannot learn ideas, skills, or the inquiry process without valid sources of information. We encourage a multimedia approach. Information sources for the social studies can be grouped into two broad categories: (1) reading materials and resources (textbooks, encyclopedias, references, computer databases using text, electronic mail, magazines, pamphlets, primary documents, newspaper clippings, travel folders, classroom periodicals) and (2) nonreading materials and resources (pictures, films, filmstrips, computer databases of art prints and photos, recordings, field trips, maps, globes, and community resources of all types). Together they provide the information base for social studies programs.

In the selection of *any* instructional resource, the objectives to be achieved should be uppermost in the mind of the teacher. The particular resource or material selected should be the one that will move children most effectively in the direction of those objectives. In short, instructional aids, materials, and resources are used to achieve specific purposes. The teacher is encouraged to use a wide range of instructional media for any or all of the following reasons:

1. Not all children learn in the same way; different media are able to appeal to the learning styles of different learners.
2. The reading range among children who are randomly selected to form classroom groups are great, averaging three to five years in the lower grades and five to ten years in the middle and upper grades.
3. Each of the media has peculiar strengths and limitations in the way it conveys messages.
4. The impact of a message is likely to be stronger if more than one sensory system is involved in receiving it.
5. Material to be learned varies greatly in its abstractness and complexity.
6. The use of a variety of media has motivating and interest-generating qualities.
7. Teaching modes that stress inquiry and problem solving require extensive information searches and sources.
8. Different sources may provide different insights on the same subject; there may be discrepancies or inaccuracies that go undetected if a single source is used.

Instructional materials need to be evaluated carefully before, during, and after they have been used. It is unwise to use any and all materials simply because they are available. The quality of the resource should be a primary consideration in deciding on its use. It might be better if maps that are out of date, films that are of poor quality, pictures that are inaccurate, or field trips that are poorly guided, for example, are not used at all.

The maximum value of any instructional resource requires skillful use on the part of the teacher. No instructional material is entirely self-teaching—all require a teacher to set the stage for learning to take place. A first-rate textbook in the hands of an unimaginative teacher can be devastating to the social studies program. The same book used by another teacher can become one of the most valuable resources available to the class.

Textbooks

The policy of school districts that calls for furnishing free of charge the same basic textbook for every child in a class is based on the legal principles of equal treatment and equality of opportunity. For this reason, textbooks are widely used and will doubtless continue to be widely used for years to come. It is apparent from their widespread acceptance that most teachers, especially those in grades three and above, perceive the textbook as a valuable teaching tool in social studies. It is important, therefore, for the beginning teacher to learn how to make the best use of these books.

Textbook development has tended to be consistent with changes in curriculum and teaching methods. Modern textbooks are attractive and inviting, a pleasure to look at and to read. There are many maps and visual materials; skills are taught in relation to the facts and ideas, not in isolation from them; plays and recordings are routinely included in the teacher's resource materials; anthologies of children's literature are often provided; suggested debates, projects, and assessments are plentiful. Significant improvement is readily apparent in the treatment and inclusion of racial and ethnic groups and women. In general, textbooks contain a wealth of resources that teachers otherwise must gather on their own. (Note: Readers can turn to Chapter 11 for suggestions for using textbooks.)

Yet, clearly, a textbook is *only* a resource. A teacher should be its master, not the reverse. This is the case with any resource, such as computers and community resources, to which we turn next.

Computers in Social Studies

The use of computers in education has been promoted so vigorously that it is estimated that, by the end of this decade, microcomputers will be a part of the instructional media of almost all schools. According to Quality Education Data, a Denver-company that tracks resource use in schools, there was one computer for every seventy-five students in U.S. public schools, on the average, in 1985. Ten years later, in 1995, there was one for every eleven students.[15] Differences from school to school, however, muddle these "average" figures. One researcher found in 1991 that the number of computers in elementary school buildings ranged from 100 in the wealthiest to none in the poorest. Four thousand public schools in the United States had no computers at all in 1991, and half of all schools had fewer than ten.[16] The number is growing, however.

In the social studies, as in other curricular areas, the challenge to the teacher is to adapt the use of this technology to the ongoing instructional program of the classroom. The emphasis should be on using computers to assist teaching and learning of social studies subject matter—ideas and skills drawn from history and the social sciences, citizenship, and the inquiry process.

One of the major differences between the computer and other instructional media is that the computer has the capacity to *interact* with the student. The computer does not simply present the material to be learned as is the case with a film, filmstrip, or a recording. The computer requires the operator to *do something* in order for the process to proceed. This interactive characteristic of computers necessitates the active involvement of the learner.

Students test their hypotheses by gathering data from a CD-ROM.

In the social studies, the contribution of computer-assisted instruction (CAI) falls into the following four categories:

1. *Using the computer to gather and organize information needed to build and test important ideas.* There is a growing number of electronic collections of information, known as *databases*, many of which are relevant to social studies. Databases can be purchased on laser videodiscs and the smaller CD-ROMs (Compact Disc-Read Only Memory). Also, databases can be accessed through various "online" services, which are accessed through computers connected by modems and phone lines.

Electronic databases will one day include much of what is now found in libraries, government document centers, archives, museums, encyclopedias, and other information collections. They place enormous stacks of information at students' fingertips. *Hypertext* goes further. It lets children navigate and interact with those stacks, picking and choosing, creating visuals, and constructing their own software.

2. *Using the computer to practice and apply social studies skills* such as hypothesizing, hypothesis testing, map reading, graph reading, chart making and interpretation, decision making, and problem solving. Simulated "town meetings" are available, too, that engage students in discussion and decision making related to community issues.

3. *Using the computer for tutorial assistance.* Tutorial software provides a sequential program for the development of knowledge and skills. These programs are essentially

courses of study that have been developed for the computer. It would be ideal if such *courseware* were available to supplement each social studies unit a teacher planned, but such is far from the case. However, teachers will find programs on some basic topics, such as the Constitution and the American Revolution.

4. *Using the computer to communicate.* Children in many schools have been using word processing programs for some time to help them revise and edit reports and biographies for the classroom newspaper. They can *scan* photographs of their classroom into the newspaper file with little trouble, if they have the equipment. And in an increasing number of classrooms, they are communicating in *cyberspace*, a term coined by science-fiction writer William Gibson. *Cyber* means part human, part machine. The term *information superhighway* refers to the same space. Both terms refer to an electronic network—actually, a network of networks—that exists worldwide.

The Internet is one such network. It links computer users throughout the world through networks of all sorts: educational, commercial, military, and others. Children can log onto a network and search for information, perhaps using "browsing" and access systems (e.g., Gopher, Mosaic, Prodigy, Netscape, America Online, CompuServe), and they can carry on conversations with other persons on the network.

Electronic mail (e-mail) allows children to have cyberpals or keypals in another community in the state or a sister city across the sea. Using e-mail, children can inform the president of the United States (and probably your state's governor and city's mayor) of decisions they have reached on public problems. *Newsgroups* for children are also part of the "net."

Examples

What follows are several examples of teachers and children using computer resources.

Searching and Charting.   "Search teams" of three children take turns going to the library to use the school's one electronic database—a CD-ROM called *Grolier Multimedia Encyclopedia*. Each team searches for information related to a concept of their unit, Land and Peoples of Asia. Each team creates a simple chart to organize its data, one each on the natural resources of Asia, landforms, farm products, manufactured products, religions, governments, history, arts, and games.

Newsgroup.   The third grade teachers at Cascadia Elementary School gather around the computer before school one morning and "surf the Internet"—that is, explore its online resources. They locate KIDSPHERE, a newsgroup for K–12 teachers. There, they find several activity opportunities. An Alaskan teacher is requesting keypals for village children, and a Detroit student teacher is looking for a conversation with peers in other urban elementary schools. They find two ongoing discussion groups: one on the curriculum standards from the National Council for the Social Studies, another on the issue of multigrade classrooms. Also, they browse the list of announcements of upcoming classroom projects.

Scavenger Hunt.   Three new CD-ROM databases have arrived in the school library plus access to two online databases (the Smithsonian's *Let's Go to the Museum* and

Encyclopedia Britannica Online). To help preview these resources, the teacher creates a list of five questions and hands the list to a team of five students. Each teammate is assigned to one of the databases, and his or her task is to determine how many of the five questions can be answered on this database. The children report their findings back to their teammates, and the team creates a preliminary report describing and reviewing the quality of the new resources. The school librarian serves as judge of these reports, providing feedback and correction as needed.

Exchange.   Second grade children in the Baltimore-Washington, D.C. area learn about one another's schools using e-mail. After asking and answering lots of questions, the children at one school plan and write an article describing their own school and another school, which is published in their classroom newsletter.

Joining the Debate.   Sixth grade children learn in the local newspaper about the city council's debate over whether to establish curfews for children and teenagers. They locate KIDLINK online, a newsgroup for older children, and strike up a conversation with students at other sites about the issue. Then, they e-mail the council members a report of their discussions and recommendations.

Computer Simulations.   The fifth grade teachers at Mapleton school are great fans of *The Oregon Trail*, developed by the Minnesota Educational Computing Consortium (MECC), 3490 Lexington Ave. N., St. Paul, MN 55126. The story line is that of a wagon train party moving westward in the 1800s. Along the way the wagon train has to deal with a number of contingencies such as foul weather, sickness, and native peoples. As each is encountered, a decision has to be made, and a poor decision can have disastrous consequences for the entire party.

Popular simulations involving citizenship education are *Decisions, Decisions* (for grades 5 and above), *Choices, Choices* (K–6), and *Our Town Meeting* (5–8), all from Tom Snyder Productions (123 Mt. Auburn St., Cambridge, MA 02138). The first two can be used with an entire classroom and only one computer; the third is designed for use with up to 15 students and one computer. All promote group interaction and community decision making. In *And If Reelected*, a presidential simulation for grades 7 and up (485 S. Broadway, #12, Hicksville, NY 11801), students grapple with numerous public policy controversies, such as nuclear waste and budget deficits.

Emphasizing geography is the very popular *Where in the World Is Carmen Sandiego?* Produced by Broderbund Software (17 Paul Dr., San Rafael, CA 94903), this exciting game has students play detective as they use geography clues and a reference book (*The World Almanac and Book of Facts*) to solve a crime. Also available are *Where in the U.S.A. Is Carmen Sandiego?* and *Where in Europe Is Carmen Sandiego?*

Other commercially prepared simulations that have been used with success in elementary and middle school grades are (1) *The Market Place* (grades 3–6) produced by MECC, designed to develop economic concepts and relationships as the player is placed in the role of an entrepreneur; (2) *President-Elect* (grades 8 and above), produced by Learning Arts, P.O. Box 179, Wichita, KS 67201, has to do with variables associated with the election of a president of the United States; (3) *Agent USA*, produced by

Scholastic, 730 Broadway, New York, NY 10003, simulates a secret agent traveling around the United States in search of a bomb as students assist in selecting best routes; it is intended to develop map-reading and geography-related skills; and (4) *Stock Market* (grades 4–6) and *Millionaire, The Stock Market Simulation*, both produced by Learning Arts, designed to teach principles of the stock market.

Keeping Up

This is a rapidly evolving field, and there is a confusing array of terms and jargon. Accordingly, teachers need to use the most current lists and reviews of available computer resources. Teachers can rely on the two journals published by the National Council for the Social Studies, *Social Education* and *Social Studies and the Young Learner*. School libraries ought to carry both of these. Another very good resource for keeping up with both the problems and promises of cyberspace is *Electronic Learning—The Magazine for Technology and School Change*. *Multimedia Schools* and *The Computing Teacher* are others. Also, the building principal and librarian should be able to assist, either directly or by marshaling resources in the school district and state. A survey such as the one shown in Figure 7–5 can be used to determine what computer resources are available and being used in a school building, and for what purposes. Teachers who are new to a building are advised to conduct this survey as soon as possible and locate those colleagues who are the school's technology leaders.

Figure 7–5

Computer technology survey

School name _____

Technology resource person _____

	Available? (If so, give location)	Describe use
Computers		
Printers		
Computer Lab		
CD-ROM		
Electronic encyclopedia		
Other databases		
Videodiscs		
Hypertext		
Internet		
Online services		
E-mail		
Electronic card catalog		

Teachers who enjoy conducting literature circles with children should consider forming one with colleagues. They could read books about technology written for adults and preview books written for children. For example:

For children
Invention by L. Bender (New York: Alfred A. Knopf, 1991)
Eureka! It's Television by J. Bendick and R. Bendick (Brookfield, CT: Millbrook, 1993)
Technology by R. Bridgman (London: Dorling Kindersley, 1995)

To help teachers plan
Restructuring Schools with Technology by L. R. Knapp and A. D. Glenn (Boston: Allyn & Bacon, 1996)
Teaching Social Studies with Technology by J. A. Braun, P. F. Fernlund, and C. S. White (Wilsonville, OR: Franklin Beedle, 1996)
Social Studies and the Young Learner, January/February 1995. Theme of this issue: technology and social studies (phone: 202-966-7840).
Children's Software Revue, a bi-monthly newsletter that rates computer programs for children ages three to ten (phone: 312-480-0040).

Community Resources

It is in the local community that the teacher should sow the seeds of a lifetime study of human society. Here the social processes that function a thousand times over in communities around the world may be observed firsthand. In the local community, the child is introduced to geographical concepts, to the problems of group living, to government in operation, to the production and distribution of goods and services, and to the rich historical heritage of the nation. In most American communities, the child can see evidence that it is possible for persons of varied backgrounds, nationalities, religious faiths, and races to live and work together harmoniously.

The teacher may make use of the local community in two basic ways. One is to bring some portion of the community to the classroom; the other is to take the class out of the school to some place or person of importance in the community. Either way, the children are interacting with and gathering information from the community. With guidance from the teacher, children can incorporate this information into investigations (inquiries) they are conducting and concepts they are building.

As a matter of principle, it is advisable to take elementary school children into the community only for the experiences that cannot be duplicated in the classroom. For example, it is usually better to arrange to have a person bring photographs of early life in the community to the school and speak to the children there than it is to take a class of thirty children to a home. On the other hand, the process involved in canning tuna fish or cranberries cannot be observed in the classroom; the children must be taken to the cannery if this process is to be observed firsthand.

Teachers also make use of community resources when children bring materials from home for the bulletin boards or for their construction projects; when parents are asked to assist in any way; when books are obtained from the public library; when the local newspaper is used; or when children bring items from home to share with others in "show and tell." The personal experiences children have in the community and share with the class are likewise a common use of community resources.

The teacher must always select with care the persons who are invited to spend time with the class for instructional purposes. Some people should not be asked to speak to children because they are not able to make themselves understood, they lack an understanding of children, they freely hold and express attitudes or beliefs that may be offensive to members of the group, or they fail to grasp the significance of their visit to the class. The teacher should plan to spend some time with the visitor sufficiently far enough in advance to brief the guest on the activities of the class, the purpose of the visit, and the points to be discussed and stressed. Likewise, the children must be prepared for the visitor, listing questions they would like to ask, and be aware of general courtesies that should be extended to classroom guests. Handled in this way, persons from the community can make a significant contribution to the instructional program in the social studies. Those who might be used either for the purposes of interview or as classroom resource visitors might include:

Persons with special skills: weavers, potters, jewelry makers

Armed forces personnel

Exchange students

Persons with interesting hobbies

Community helpers

Members of the local historical society

Newspaper reporters

Members of service organizations

County agent

Representatives of environmental and conservation groups

4-H and other club leaders

Early inhabitants of the community

Professional persons: ministers, doctors, lawyers

Judges

Legislators

Members of the local business community: bankers, salespersons, shop owners

Local officials

Representatives of local industries

Travelers

Recent immigrants or other newcomers to the community

Authors

Commercial pilots

Whenever children are taken off the school site, the teacher must attend to several exceedingly important details. Adequate planning will help the teacher anticipate some

FIELD TRIPS

Preparing for the Trip

1. Clearly establish the purposes of the trip, and make certain that the children understand the purposes, too. The excursion should provide opportunities for learnings that are not possible in the classroom.

2. Obtain administrative permission for the field trip, and make arrangements for transportation. As a matter of policy, it is better to use a public conveyance or a school bus than it is to use private automobiles. In using private cars, the teacher is never sure if the driver is properly insured, is competent behind the wheel, or even has a valid operator's license.

3. Make all necessary preliminary arrangements at the place of the visit. This should include the time for the group to arrive, where the children are to go, who will guide them, and so forth. It is recommended that the teacher make the excursion prior to the time the children are taken. This will alert the teacher to circumstances and situations that should be discussed with the children before leaving the classroom. Make sure that the field trip guide is aware of the purposes of the field trip.

4. Study the literature on the subject. No teacher should approach a field trip unprepared. This knowledge will later be valuable in helping prepare children for the field trip and in initiating followup and study activities.

5. Obtain written permission from each parent or guardian for the child to go on the trip, and do not take children who cannot or do not return signed permission slips. Although this action does not in itself absolve the teacher of responsibility or liability in the event of an accident, it indicates to the teacher that the parent or guardian knows of the field trip and approves of the child's going. Most schools have forms for this purpose that are filled out by the teacher and sent home with each child for the parent's signature.

6. Prepare the class for the field trip. "What is it that we wish to find out? What hypotheses are we testing? For which concepts do we want to find examples? What questions do we want to ask the guide?" Through careful planning and preparation the teacher helps children to be more observant and makes a genuine research activity out of the field trip. The children probably will be taken to places to which many of them have been before. Most of them have seen trains, many have been to the airport, some have been to the harbor, and all have been to a filling station. Why, then, should the school take children to such places on field trips? The answer is that different purposes exist for the field trip than for incidental visits. The children are prepared to look for things they would not otherwise see. Discuss with the children how they will record the information obtained on their trip. If they are to take notes, teach the needed notetaking skills.

   The class should set up standards of conduct for the trip before leaving the school. Children are quick to accept the challenge that the responsibility for a good trip rests personally with each member of the group. Time spent on this part of the preparation for the excursion will pay dividends when the trip is under way. Nothing is more embarrassing for the teacher, more damaging to school-community relations, or more devastating to the educational purposes of the field trip than a group of rude and unruly children. This often happens when the children have been inadequately prepared for the trip.

7. If the trip is to be long, make arrangements for lunchroom and restroom facilities. Take along a first-aid kit.

8. Have an alternate plan in case the weather turns bad or something interferes with your plans.

Conducting the Trip

9. Take roll before leaving the school grounds, and "count noses" frequently during the trip to make sure that some of the children have not become lost or left in some restroom along the way. With young children it is a good idea to place them in pairs because a child will know and report immediately the absence of a partner. To assist with supervision of the children and to help ensure a safe trip, the teacher should arrange for other adults to accompany the group. Teachers can usually count on parents to assist in this way but should plan to meet with them prior to the trip and explain the purposes, standards of behavior, the route to be followed, and other important details. The adults accompanying the children must be prepared for the excursion also.

10. Arrive at the designated place on time, and have children ready for the guide. Be sure to introduce the guide to the class. Supervise children closely during the tour to prevent accidents or injury. Before leaving, check again to make sure all children are with the group.

11. Make sure that time is allowed for answering children's questions.

12. Make sure that each child can see and hear adequately. Be sure to summarize the experience before the trip is concluded.

Evaluating the Trip

13. Engage the class in appropriate followup activities. This should include writing a thank-you note to the firm and to the adults who accompanied the class. In the primary grades, the children should dictate such a letter to the teacher who writes it on the chalkboard or chart. Individual children then copy the letter, and one may be selected to be sent, or, in some cases, they may all be sent. If the host has an e-mail address, the children's letter also can be sent using this medium.

   The teacher and children will also want to evaluate carefully the extent to which the purposes of the trip have been achieved. "Did we accomplish what we set out to do? Did we get the answers to our questions? What did we learn that we didn't know before? What are some other things we will want to find out?" Finally, the teacher and children will want to evaluate the conduct of the class in terms of the standards set up before the trip was made. This evaluation should always include some favorable reactions as well as ways in which the group might improve on subsequent trips. A list of these suggestions for improvement may be saved for review just before the next trip is undertaken.

14. Discuss enrichment projects in which children may engage for further study, such as construction activities, original stories, reports, dramatic plays, and diaries. Survey other resources available in the community for study.

15. Use opportunities to draw on information and experiences from the field trip in other subjects taught in the classroom.

of the problems that may arise in connection with the field trip and will help make the trip educationally worthwhile. Poorly planned field trips are worse than none at all, for they lack purpose, may jeopardize the safety of the children, may cause poor public relations between the school and community, and can break down learnings the teacher should have been trying to build in the classroom. Although the field trip should be pleasant for everyone including the teacher, it is first of all an educational experience, and its primary objective is not that everyone have a joyous outing. Good planning will ensure that the trip will be both a pleasant as well as an educational experience. The suggestions on pages 223–224 will be helpful in achieving that goal.

Every community has places that can be visited by classes and thereby can contribute to the enrichment of history, geography, and all of social studies. These will differ from place to place, but any of the following could be used:

State historical society displays	Aquarium
Historical sites, monuments	Library
Flood plain, eroded areas, dam sites	Refinery
Razing of a building	Fish hatchery
Hospitals	Museums
Weather bureau	Public health department
Warehouses	Local stores
Airports	Legislative bodies in session
Railway station	Art galleries
Assembly plants	Fire station
Post office	Newspaper printing facilities
Broadcasting or telecasting station	Bakery
Courthouse	Observatory
Factories	Canal locks
Farms	The harbor
Urban planning commission	Police station
Docks	Zoo
Dairy	Parks
	Shopping centers

Experience Summaries

Experience summaries are ordinarily constructed cooperatively by the teacher and the class and are used to record and assess a single or specific experience. For example, when the group returns from its trip to the airport, the children can summarize some of the important things they have learned as a result of the trip and place these on a chart. The chart may then be used to evaluate the extent to which they found out the things they set out to learn. An example of an experience summary is on page 225.

National Council for the Social Studies

We have identified three groups of resources for teaching social studies: textbooks, which we examine in much greater depth in Chapter 11, Reading to Learn Social Studies; computers; and community resources, especially field trips. We close the chapter with what may be the most important resource, the National Council for the Social Studies (NCSS).

EXPERIENCE SUMMARY

What We Learned at the Food Distribution Center:
1. How food is sent to grocery stores.
2. That food we eat comes from all over the world.
3. Certain foods must be kept in temperature-controlled rooms so they do not spoil.
4. It takes many people to handle the food before we see it in our stores.
5. Food is sent by railroad cars, ships, trucks, and sometimes planes before it reaches the store.
6. Grocery stores order the amounts they need each week before it is sent to them.

The curriculum standards adopted by this organization accompany this text, but this organization's usefulness to classroom teachers hardly stops there. Members receive a *monthly newsletter* filled with news of travel opportunities for teachers, special events for the students, workshops and conferences, advanced notice of special television programs, and reviews of award-winning computer software and children's literature. There are also the monthly and quarterly journals for teachers, *Social Education* and *Social Studies and the Young Learner*. Recently, NCSS opened a World Wide Web site, *NCSS Online*. Readers who have access to the web are invited to contact NCSS at the following addresses:

General information: *ncss@ncss.org*
Publications: *publications@ncss.org*
Annual conference: *conference@ncss.org*

Discussion Questions and Suggested Activities

1. Select three unit topics from the following list, and provide examples of five concepts that might be included in such units. Then, using two or more of the concepts you have identified, write a generalization that expresses a valid relationship between them that is relevant to each of the topics you have selected.

   People Change the Earth (K–8)

   School Living (K)

   Families and Their Needs (1)

   The Shopping Center (2)

   Life in the City (3)

   Our Home State (4)

   The American Revolution (5)

   Crossroads of the World: The Middle East (6–7)

   Colonial America (8)

2. Interview individually four or five children from a grade in which you have a special interest to determine their understanding of selected social studies concepts. Use a straightforward procedure and everyday concepts. For example, you might ask, "What does the term *prejudice* mean to you? Can you give me some examples of prejudice?" (or use *history, justice, cooperation, democracy, long ago, the future*, or geographical terms such as *environment, plateau*, or *rain forest*). These interviews will provide you with firsthand knowledge of what it means to transform an otherwise complex idea into a form that is sensible for elementary school children. Write up your findings to share with classmates, parents, or perhaps potential employers.

3. What are the essential differences among how one teaches concepts, skills, and the inquiry process?

4. Use the left side of Figure 7–2 and apply each of the steps to a skill of your choice for a grade in which you have a special interest. Share your examples with others in class.

5. Create a data-retrieval chart like the one in Figure 7–1. On the left list the four subject-matter emphases in social studies: ideas (concepts and generalizations), skills, issues, and the inquiry process. Along the top, write focus questions such as "What are examples of this subject matter for a grade in which I have interest? What strategies can be used to help children learn this?"

6. Read again the three types of generalizations described in the section The Nature of Generalizations. Then, use them to classify the list of eight generalizations in that section.

7. It was suggested at two points in this chapter that teachers sometimes "teach less," to use Lisa Delpit's phrase, and that this practice especially impacts culturally different and LEP students. Reread these sections, one near the beginning of the chapter and one in the Skills Teaching section. What is the meaning of "teaching less?" Do you believe that even very good teachers might provide too little instruction? If so, why?

8. Five purposes of question asking were given in the section Asking Good Questions. Rank order these in terms of importance and add other purposes that you believe are missing from this list.

9. Today the worker, citizen, and family member have access to information sources that are almost unlimited in the scope of knowledge they can provide. Should the availability of such information influence decisions about what is taught in school? Provide examples to support your points.

10. Three kinds of resources were addressed: textbook programs, computer resources, and community resources. Assume that you are going to teach a class of teacher interns about these resources. Create a data-retrieval chart, such as the one given in Figure 7–1, that will help them compare and contrast these resources.

Notes

1 Bruce Joyce and Marsha Weil, with Beverly Showers, *Models of Teaching*, 4th ed. (Boston: Allyn & Bacon, 1992), 2.

2 Ronald G. Tharp and Ronald Gallimore, *Rousing Minds to Life* (Cambridge: Cambridge University Press, 1988), 44.

3 "National Council for Social Studies, A Vision of Powerful Teaching and Learning in the Social Studies: Building Social Understanding and Civic Efficacy," in *Curriculum Standards for Social Studies* (Washington, DC: Author, 1994), 167.

4 Lisa Delpit, *Other People's Children: Cultural Conflict in the Classroom* (New York: New Press, 1995), 175.

5 Margaret Craven, *I Heard the Owl Call My Name* (New York: Doubleday, 1973), 19.

6 NCSS, *Curriculum Standards*.

7 Association of American Geographers and National Council for Geographic Education, *Guidelines for Geographic Education, Elementary and Secondary Schools* (Washington, DC: Authors, 1984).

8 See Jacqueline Grennon Brooks and Martin G. Brooks, *The Case for Constructivist Classrooms* (Alexandria, VA: Association for Supervision and Curriculum Development, 1993).

9 Walter C. Parker, "Thinking to Learn Concepts," *The Social Studies* 79 (March/April 1988): 70–73.

10 The listing-grouping-labeling strategy was developed by the late Hilda Taba and her associates in research related to concept learning in social studies.

11 See Barry K. Beyer, *Critical Thinking* (Bloomington, IN: Phi Delta Kappa, 1995) and Richard Paul, *Critical Thinking* (Rohnert Park, CA: Center for Critical Thinking and Moral Critique, 1990).

12 Delpit, *Other People's Children*.

13 Rosalyn Ashby and Peter Lee, "Children's Concepts of Empathy and Understanding in History," in *The History Curriculum for Teachers*, ed. Christopher Portal (London: Falmer, 1987), 86.

14 Ibid.

15 Quality Education Data, *Technology in Public Schools* (Denver: Author, 1995), 14.

16 Jonathan Kozol, *Savage Inequalities* (New York: Crown, 1991).

• •

Selected References

Banks, James A. *An Introduction to Multicultural Education*. Boston: Allyn & Bacon, 1994. *Chapter 5 contains helpful tips on teaching concepts and generalizations related to multicultural education.*

Beyer, Barry K. *Critical Thinking*. Bloomington, IN: Phi Delta Kappa, 1995.

Braun, Joseph A., Phyllis F. Fernlund, and Charles S. White. *Teaching Social Studies with Technology*. Wilsonville, OR: Franklin Beedle, 1996.

Brooks, Jacqueline Grennon, and Martin G. Brooks. *The Case for Constructivist Classrooms*. Alexandria, VA: Association for Supervision and Curriculum Development, 1993.

Delpit, Lisa. *Other People's Children: Cultural Conflict in the Classroom*. New York: New Press, 1995.

Ehman, Lee H., and Allen D. Glenn. "Interactive Technology in Social Studies." In *Handbook of Research on Social Studies Teaching and Learning*, edited by James P. Shaver. New York: Macmillan, 1991, 513–22.

Hunkins, Francis P. *Teaching Thinking Through Effective Questioning*. Boston: Christopher-Gorden, 1989.

Joyce, Bruce, and Marsha Weil, with Beverly Showers. *Models of Teaching*. 4th ed. Boston: Allyn & Bacon, 1992.

Kozol, Jonathan. *Savage Inequalities*. New York: Crown, 1991.

Martorella, Peter H. "Knowledge and Concept Development in Social Studies." In *Handbook of Research on Social Studies Teaching and Learning*, edited by James P. Shaver. New York: Macmillan, 1991, 370–84.

National Council for the Social Studies. "A Vision of Powerful Teaching and Learning in the Social Studies: Building Social Understanding and Civic Efficacy." In *Curriculum Standards for Social Studies*. Washington, DC: author, 1994, 155–77.

Parker, Walter C. "Teaching an Idea." *Social Studies and the Young Learner* 3 (January/February 1991): 11–13.

Social Studies and the Young Learner, January/February 1995. *The theme of this issue is technology and social studies*.

Taba, Hilda, Mary D. Durkin, Jack E. Fraenkel, and A.H. McNaughton. *A Teacher's Handbook to Elementary Social Studies: An Inductive Approach*. Reading, MA: Addison-Wesley, 1971.

PLANNING UNITS, LESSONS, AND ACTIVITIES

At first we were quite concerned when we found out that Lori was to be placed in Mr. Allison's room the next year. His room had such a relaxed atmosphere about it, and he was very popular with the kids. We just assumed, I guess, that a teacher who was so well liked by all the children could not be very effective in maintaining a disciplined environment for learning. I must say this assumption was wholly unfounded.

Mr. Allison was clearly the most creative, imaginative, and overall the most effective teacher Lori had during the seven years she attended that school. He always had the most unusual things going on in that room that would so hook the kids that they spent hours of unsupervised study on what they were doing. Schoolwork seemed to be a sheer delight, strange as that may seem. They analyzed advertising techniques in a unit on consumerism; they simulated law and justice procedures; they studied the effects of immigrant groups on American life and culture; there were art, poetry, music, and dramatic activities galore. Once they constructed a whole set of authentic models of Indian villages representing various tribes that inhabited this part of North America in pre-Columbian times. This involved the children in an incredible amount of research and information gathering in order to do the constructions. There were always games, puzzles, inquiries— tremendous interest grabbers. It was the only time I can recall that children had literally to be told to go home after school. If not, they would stay until dinnertime.

Mr. Allison convinced my husband and me that disciplined learning did not have to give the appearance of rigidity and drudgery. He seemed to embrace the philosophy that a teacher should obtain "maximum learning with minimum effort." But the "minimum effort" only seemed that way because of the tremendous motivating power of the creative activities he used. Actually, I have not seen children work any harder nor be more productive in their efforts than their year with Mr. Allison.

How does a teacher develop this type of stimulating program for students in social studies? In a word: *planning*. Such planning comes partly from a knowledgeable teacher who is able to select powerful subject matter, such as the inquiry process or an important idea, and match it to powerful teaching strategies. But it also comes from an attentive and imaginative teacher who is able to capitalize on the natural interests, curiosities, and home cultures of children. The teacher selects the objectives of learning from curriculum guides and collections of curriculum standards in combination with his or her own good sense, then encourages the children to raise questions and suggest activities. In this way the child and the curriculum meet.

Tools for Planning

Knowledge of social studies goals, subject matter, the state legislature's curriculum mandates, teaching strategies, and the children in the classroom probably are the most important tools for successful planning. Thoughtful teachers pay attention to national organizations' curriculum guides, too. Granted, some effective teachers ignore these documents, but that strikes us as not much different from the student who completes a research project without using any reference sources. These guidelines can be helpful resources and often were developed by teams of expert teachers who are widely recognized for their talents. Their advice is worth seeking and considering, we believe. In the case of state-mandated curriculum, teachers may be obliged by law to teach particular subject matter.

It is helpful in particular to have access to the national curriculum standards developed for history, geography, civics, and integrated social studies that were discussed in previous chapters. These are rich collections of blue-ribbon advice concerning which subject matter should be emphasized. Also, state curriculum standards are published in virtually every state, and most are now being revised in light of the new (voluntary) national curriculum standards. Of course, the teacher should consult the local school district curriculum guide before the planning process begins. This can be obtained from the school building principal or the school district curriculum coordinator. These persons should also be able to provide a copy of the state curriculum framework.

State governments have the legal responsibility for directing educational programs of public schools. Typically, one finds certain curricular requirements relating to social studies in state education codes. These range from mandating the teaching of United States history and the Constitution to drug and sex education programs. State education agencies often have a state framework for social studies that provides guidance to local districts in developing a philosophy and rationale, selecting subject matter for various grade levels (scope and sequence), recommending teaching procedures, and selecting instructional materials. In practice, state agencies have delegated much of their responsibility for education to local school districts.

Much choice making in curriculum is left to local districts. With site-based management on the rise, more of these decisions are likely to be made at the school level. The feeling that the schools belong to the people of the local community and that schools should serve local needs has long been fundamental to educational planning in this country. Social studies programs must be tailored to the experience and background of children who live in a specific attendance area. State and national influences presumably ensure attention to common societal goals that are necessary for national unity; local influences should ensure that the children living in the area are well served by the social studies program.

Types of Teaching Plans

In most instances, the school district will supply a curriculum guide, a list of suggested topics, a curriculum framework, a textbook, or some directive that provides the teacher with guidance as to which topics or units are to be included in the curriculum. Often teachers can make choices within the established guidelines. It is not uncommon to find some topics required, some optional, and perhaps some to be chosen by the teacher. A teacher must be familiar with district expectations and assessment policies in order to plan appropriately.

Thorough planning will not ensure successful teaching, but it will do much to give the teacher a margin of confidence that will enhance the possibility of more effective teaching. Many experienced teachers make use of three types of plans for the social studies: (1) unit plans; (2) short-range plans focused on a single topic, main idea, or skill; and (3) daily plans. The long-range plan, usually referred to as a *unit* or a *unit of work*, covers a period of six to ten weeks, during which time the class studies some broad topic on an ongoing basis. The unit plan is a way of organizing materials and activities for such an extended study. The following are examples of topics that would be suitable for parcels of work called *units*:

Living in Our Community

Families Around the World

The Exciting World of Lewis and Clark

The World of the Big City

Life in Early America

The Middle East—Crossroads of Cultures

Not all social studies instruction needs to be organized around comprehensive units of the type described. Many topics can be adequately covered within a week or two. These can often be sandwiched in between the larger units. Such topics, which call for short-range plans, might be organized around subject matter that is timely or is of special relevance to a class. They might consist of unconventional subjects or topics on which there is not an abundance of learning resources for children to use. The following are examples of topics suitable for such shorter blocks of work:

Winners and Losers in the Election

Danger Spots in Our Home

Deserts of the World

Getting Information from Maps

Workers and Their Wages

Getting Your Money's Worth

Who Is the Me I See?

It is also possible to plan a large unit of work as a series of sequentially related mini-units of the type described here. When this is done, however, the teacher will want to provide some ongoing activities to give continuity to the larger study.

The third type of teaching plan is that which the teacher actually uses in doing the teaching. It is what is usually called a *daily lesson plan* and is really the teacher's "trip map" through the lesson. Such plans should extend and continue the instruction from one class session to the next. Naturally, these specific teaching plans are developed within the context of the more extended unit of study. Separate and discrete plans that do not tie into some larger framework are not recommended because of the resulting fragmentation of the topics studied. Plans should move the process of learning sequentially and continuously over a period of time.

Textbook-Based Plans

A textbook-based plan is one that is developed in advance by the teacher, who often relies on the textbook or other curriculum documents in determining the nature and content of the program. The textbook program is the prime information and activity source, and all children deal with the same basic subject matter.

If we follow a teacher through the steps in planning and teaching social studies in this way, we would observe that the teacher:

1. Surveys the text to find out which units are included and decides how to apportion the amount of time available to each one. The recommendations of the textbook authors may be used in making these decisions.
2. Studies the teacher's guide accompanying the text to find out how the program is organized and what major goals and objectives are stressed. These goals and objectives may be accepted as appropriate for the program.
3. Uses the teacher's guide for teaching plans, learner activities, and assessments.
4. Uses additional resources and activities for enrichment, extension of learning, and individualizing learning. Some of these are suggested by the teacher's guide, including those provided by the publisher of the textbook program such as plays, music, children's literature, construction activities, and workbook activities or "blackline" masters that can be easily duplicated for students.
5. Assesses learnings as suggested by the text and teacher's guide, focusing mainly on factual knowledge, basic concepts, and related skills.

Theme or Topic-Oriented Plans

A planning approach based on a theme or topic has some of the same characteristics as the one just presented, but the reliance on the text is not as complete, more of the teacher's influence is apparent, and it is not so thoroughly preplanned and teacher directed. Children are more involved in planning—if not of the objectives, then of the focus questions and activities—and there is a wide range of instructional materials and resources.

If we follow a teacher through the steps in planning and teaching in this way, we would observe that the teacher:

1. Examines the curriculum guide and the textbook and talks with colleagues to find out what topics and units are expected to be included in the program.
2. Establishes broad goals and objectives for the year; takes into consideration those suggested by the curriculum guide and the textbook's teacher's guide, but is not wedded to them. *The boundaries between the various school subjects and skills are*

blurred; indeed, the social studies units may serve as the integrating center for the total elementary school curriculum.

3. Tentatively selects topics to be studied; consults the teacher's guide and curriculum guide in this process, selects some that are suggested, omits others, and adds some. These topics may be modified as the program develops and as learner interests and capabilities are better known.
4. Decides on the sequence of units selected and time allotment for each, taking into account holidays, seasons of the year, and so forth.
5. Uses some teaching suggestions from the teacher's guide and curriculum guide but develops many of her or his own ideas for learning activities and teaching procedures.
6. Plans for and uses many instructional resources in addition to the textbook. This includes pictures, packets, learning centers, library books, films, filmstrips, recordings, and artifacts.

Child-Centered Plans

Some teachers prefer to plan the social studies program cooperatively with children, deriving the subject matter from the interests and concerns of the children. Although it requires considerable preplanning by the teacher, the program itself is not structured in advance, as are the other two approaches that have been discussed. Study units and learner experiences are planned jointly by the teacher and the children in terms of their interests and backgrounds. Thus, the unit emerges under the guidance of the teacher, who relies on learner initiative and interest. Children help decide what they will study. They raise questions about the information they are interested in getting and search out relevant sources. They plan ways of working, activities in which they will engage, and ways of sharing ideas with one another. Children are encouraged to become involved in assuming responsibility for what they are to learn and how they will go about learning it.

If we follow a teacher through the steps in planning and teaching in this way, we will observe that the teacher:

1. Formulates broad goals and objectives for the year in terms of anticipated social and intellectual development of the children.
2. Studies learner backgrounds; develops an awareness of the social milieu from which children come.
3. Prepares motivating or facilitating questions dealing with social issues and topics to arouse learner interest.
4. Provides books, artifacts, displays, visuals, construction materials, and other items to generate interest and curiosity.
5. Encourages children to suggest topics for study and to suggest possible questions and problems for exploration.
6. Guides children in exploratory information searches.
7. Assists children in developing an in-depth study of topics and problems selected; plans are refined and/or modified as the study progresses.
8. Individualizes the program in accordance with learner interest and ability using interest centers, individual study contracts, individual study materials, projects, and activities.
9. Closely relates social studies work to reading, language arts, mathematics, science, art, music, and drama.

Planning Instructional Units

The way units are planned and taught varies greatly from one teacher to another. For one, the unit may be no more than a chapter or a section of the textbook that deals with a single topic. For another teacher, the unit may be a comprehensive study that incorporates subjects, skills, and activities from all the rest of the school curriculum. One teacher may structure the unit in advance by thorough preplanning; another may plan the unit as the study evolves. Two teachers working on an identical topic at the same grade level may have their classes deal quite differently with it. The same teacher might handle the same topic differently with different groups of children. What follows is a description of the essential components of a comprehensive unit plan. The reader should understand, however, that a great deal of individual teacher judgment and decision making go into the planning and teaching of social studies units.

Making a Survey of Available Instructional Resources

If a school district includes particular topics in the social studies curriculum, it will ordinarily provide the necessary instructional resources. The amount of such resources that are available will vary, however, from no more than a basic textbook to a generous amount and variety of multimedia. As an initial step in planning, the teacher should inventory the availability and the adequacy of learning resources for the unit to be studied. What the teacher finds will have a direct bearing on how the unit will be planned. Whereas instructional materials should not entirely determine the social studies program, the availability of essential instructional resources necessarily affects the teacher's planning.

Much difficulty is avoided in securing and using instructional materials when teachers plan well in advance what they will need. Books, recordings, pictures, films, and filmstrips must be requested early enough to ensure their arrival at the time they are needed. Usually, instructional resources must be ordered, reserved, or even secured before the unit begins.

Establishing Objectives

Social studies units are almost always concerned with the attainment of multiple objectives: ideas, skills, the inquiry process, citizenship. The individual lessons that compose a unit can deal with one or more of these.* Instructional objectives should be stated in ways that make clear what children are supposed to *learn*. This will enable the teacher and the learners to see more clearly how instructional activities relate to the purposes of the study. Insufficient clarity of objectives is likely to lead to involvement in activities that have neither purpose nor meaning. It makes little sense for teachers and children to try to solve a problem when no one seems to know what the problem is.

Objectives may be framed as broad, general statements that describe what it is the children are expected to learn. The following are examples, selected from several different units, of such descriptive objectives:

---

* Note that the sample lesson plans that are distributed through this book sometimes have two objectives: one concerning the content and another concerning a skill that can be taught meaningfully along with that content.

As a Result of a Study of This Unit Children Will
- Learn the use of simple research skills associated with gathering information.
- Understand that certain basic needs must be satisfied if human life is to be sustained.
- Realize that decisions are based on one's value orientation.
- Learn to work cooperatively in small groups, respecting the rights and feelings of others.
- Understand the interdependent relationship between geographical regions.
- Develop the skill of orienting a map to directions.
- Gain a knowledge of vocabulary associated with the legal system.
- Learn how advertising aids both the consumer and the producer.
- Learn to formulate and test causal hypotheses relating to community development.

These examples would provide purpose and direction for a study. Many teachers are comfortable with descriptive objectives of this type. Although they are general, they are, nonetheless, specific enough to communicate what the main concerns of the study are to be. Such objectives need further clarification, but most teachers prefer to make these statements more specific and explicit at the time the material is actually taught.

Another way to state objectives is in terms of specific observable learner behavior. Such statements are referred to as *behavioral objectives*. Prior to the time the instruction takes place, the teacher frames statements of expected student performances that are predicted to occur as a result of the proposed learning experience. These predicted performances are so precisely stated that their achievement could readily be assessed by an objective observer.

In order to achieve this degree of precision, teachers must use language that leaves no doubt as to what is wanted. Terms such as "to comprehend," "to know," "to realize" are not well suited for this purpose because they do not specify what the learners are *doing* that would convince an impartial observer that the children do, indeed, "comprehend," "know," or "realize." Stems that are more suitable for behavioral objectives are these:

to name	to explain why
to choose	to identify
to illustrate	to cite
to provide examples	to define
to write	to locate
to place in order	to use

Examples of behavioral objectives are these:

As a Result of a Study of This Unit Children Will Be Able to
- Identify four different types of structures people use for homes.
- Provide five examples of consumer fraud.
- Locate a specific reference book in the library.
- List the main ideas in a passage of social studies prose.
- Show that they know how to use the index to find factual material in the textbook.
- Match causes and effects in an exercise relating to labor-management conflicts.
- Define the essential characteristics of the concept *region*.

The use of behavioral objectives has accompanied the growing concern for account-ability in education. Advocates of behavioral objectives claim that such objectives encourage precision in teaching and learning by focusing on observable learner perfor-mance. They would argue that unless the child can actually do something to show what has been learned, one can only speculate about whether learning has taken place. They argue, further, that unless the teacher can define what is to be learned in terms of the child's intellectual or physical behavior, it cannot be assumed that learning has actually occurred.

Those who do not favor the use of behavioral objectives say that many significant outcomes of social studies instruction, or any instruction, for that matter, do not lend themselves well to behavioral definition. For example, who can say precisely what hap-pens to a child while reading an exciting account of life in a rain forest? How does one define such learning behaviorally? Should it be the same for all learners?

Opponents also claim that the use of behavioral objectives tends to fragment the social studies curriculum into bits and pieces of content and skills rather than to encourage the integration of learnings into larger wholes.

There is a midposition that suggests a limited use of behavioral objectives for those components of social studies that lend themselves well to definition in terms of observ-able learner performance. As we will see in Chapter 9 concerning the assessment of student learning, the criteria that describe an exemplary performance are, in effect, behavioral objectives. In this way, the planning of objectives and the planning of per-formance assessments are closely linked. Certain work-study and inquiry skills are of this type: reading maps, making maps, using references, interpreting charts and graphs, forming or testing a hypothesis. Social skills also can be of this type: participating in small-group discussion of a school problem, criticizing ideas rather than persons, mov-ing quickly and quietly to the team tables, sharing the work load.

Some content-related objectives can also be stated behaviorally, such as arranging events in a sequence, relating effects to causes, drawing a conclusion based on data, providing examples and nonexamples of concepts, and so on. In the case of social, intel-lectual, or affective learnings that cannot be easily defined behaviorally, the teacher may want to state instructional objectives in descriptive terms as illustrated previously.

Whatever form the teacher uses to state objectives, it is important to stress that the objectives should indicate clearly what it is the children are *expected to learn*, not what they will do. For example, the following are *not* appropriate instructional objectives because they simply describe procedures and activities that will be used by the chil-dren presumably to learn something that remains undefined:

The children will view a film.

The class will work in small committees.

The children will draw a map of the local area.

The class will discuss individual projects.

Children will make a model of a harbor.

Children will role play workers in a shopping center.

Selecting and Organizing the Subject Matter

When teachers are asked what they are doing in social studies, they often respond by naming the title of the unit or topic under study, as for example, "We are studying Japan (or Canada, Mexico, the Community)." The presumption is that this response will communicate the nature of the study. The fact is, however, that the title or topic of a unit tells us little about the focus of the study, the concepts being developed, the relationships being established, or the conclusions reached, if any. It does not tell us whether students are learning the inquiry process, thinking skills, or any powerful ideas. Any topic can be studied from several different perspectives. Part of the task of organizing subject matter, therefore, deals with establishing the focus of the study and determining which particular ideas and skills will receive priority.

Many social studies programs and most of the modern textbook series organize subject matter around basic ideas from history and the social science disciplines. These are usually called major generalizations, basic concepts, key ideas, or other similar designations. Examples of such ideas are listed in Chapters 3, 4, and 5 of this text as well as in the *Sampler* that accompanies it.

There is some variation in school district policies, but typically elementary and middle school teachers have a limited amount of freedom to select the subjects and topics to be included in the social studies curriculum. Topics and units are either designated by the school district curriculum guide, or the district has adopted a textbook series that pretty much determines the subject matter and skills to be included. Teachers do, however, have a considerable amount of latitude in deciding how those topics will be developed and what *ideas* will be singled out for emphasis. It is those ideas that really determine the specific subject matter. An example will illustrate how this comes about.

Let us say that the fifth-grade curriculum guide calls for a unit on Canada. The guide also indicates what the emphasis is to be and the major generalizations that are to provide a focus for this unit:

Canada: Land Giant of the Western Hemisphere

This unit should provide children with a comprehensive view of Canada as it is today. This does not mean that historical information will be excluded, but simply that the stress is to be interdisciplinary with an emphasis on contemporary life. The unit should treat Canada as a whole rather than focus on a particular small sample of Canadian life and culture. Whereas the similarities between the United States and Canada should be studied, it is important to present Canada as a nation distinguished by its own nationality and culture. Some emphasis must be placed on how it is different from the United States. The longstanding tradition of cordial relations between the United States and Canada should also be stressed. The following generalizations should emerge as a result of the study of Canada:

1. The physical features of an area influence settlement patterns and transportation routes. (geography)
2. Maintaining an ethnic identity is important to most members of a cultural group. (anthropology)
3. The use of available resources depends on the nature of the economic system, the values of people, and their level of technology. (economics)
4. The early history of a country has a definite bearing on the present cultures of its people. (history)

How does the teacher go about selecting subject matter about Canada that will be in accord with the focus suggested by the curriculum guide?

One option available to the teacher is simply to teach whatever is included in the children's textbook. If the textbook treatment is in harmony with the focus suggested and the teacher makes enlightened use of the books, this is not an altogether undesirable procedure. We would like to think, however, that the teacher will be able to develop a more imaginative approach and, in the process, make better use of the text and other learning resources that are available.

The basic question here is this: What is it that children are expected to learn about Canada that is consistent with the suggested emphasis? Or, what are the main ideas about Canada that will receive attention in this unit?

To respond to this question, the teacher should do some self-study with the thought of selecting six to eight major ideas to be included in the unit. The public library, *The World Almanac*, encyclopedias, and the instructional materials in the classroom can be used for this purpose. Let us assume that the teacher has done this research and decides that the following *main ideas* will be developed in the unit:

1. Canada is a country with a unique northern geographic location.
2. Canada is a large, regionally divided, and diverse country.
3. Canada is a highly industrialized and technologically advanced country.
4. Canada is an urbanized country, rapidly becoming a nation of city dwellers.
5. Canada is an exposed country, open to a multitude of external cultural, economic, and political influences.
6. Canada is a multiethnic country with two predominant linguistic groups.[2]

After the teacher has selected the main ideas, such as those listed here, it is possible to identify the essential related concepts and the specific subject matter, as shown in Table 8–1.

Thus far we have discussed subject matter selection only in terms of facts and ideas—that is, cognitive objectives. But what about skills, attitudes, and values? How do they fit into the picture? Objectives that deal with skills, attitudes, and values are developed concurrently with facts and ideas. Unless the curriculum guide specifically indicates which skills, attitudes, and values are to receive attention—and usually it does not—the matter is left to the judgment of the teacher.

In the example of Canada, it is reasonable that map and globe skills would be a necessary part of main ideas numbers 1 and 2. All the main ideas will require information searches that will provide a way to teach and apply research and inquiry skills. The teacher will doubtless plan activities that require the children to use group-work skills. Attitudinal outcomes can hardly be ignored because the curriculum guide states explicitly, "The longstanding tradition of cordial relations between the United States and Canada should also be stressed." Values will come into the study as children begin to examine the tradeoffs involved in Canada's becoming an urbanized country, exploiting its resources, assimilating its native people, and maintaining an official bicultural position. Discussions can be planned, and discussion skills taught, in relation to these controversial issues.

The use of a planning format such as the one shown in Figure 8–1 can be helpful for the coordination of information, skills, attitudes, and values objectives. The essential

Table 8–1

Essential cognitive elements of a unit on Canada

Main Ideas	Essential Concepts	Subject Matter Synopsis
1. Canada is a country with a unique northern geographic location.	Arctic Latitude Coastline Heartland Natural boundary Political boundary	Location and size of Canada along with its dominant physical features, unique natural regions, and climatic characteristics; population distribution; location in terms of other nations of the Northern Hemisphere
2. Canada is a large, regionally divided, and diverse country.	Regionalism Prairie Maritime Offshore Province	Brief history of Canadian development; political and natural regions; occupations of its people; regionalism as a social, economic, and political factor in Canadian life
3. Canada is a highly industrialized and technologically advanced country.	Natural resources Minerals Raw materials Technological change	Development of Canadian resources for export and domestic use; rise of Canadian industry; transportation and communication systems in Canada
4. Canada is an urbanized country, rapidly becoming a nation of city dwellers.	Metropolitan area Trading center Manufacturing center Urban environment	Move toward urbanism with cities gaining in their influence over the lives of all Canadians; problems associated with urban sprawl and urban renewal; Toronto, a case study
5. Canada is an exposed country, open to a multitude of external cultural, economic, and political influences.	Foreign investment Nationalism Cultural influence	Influence of foreign investments in Canadian industry and agriculture; the American presence; cultural influences from the United States; influence of immigration on Canadian development
6. Canada is a multiethnic country with two predominant linguistic groups.	Ethnic group Bilingual Bicultural Heritage Minority Cultural mosaic	Historical background of Canadian bilingualism; effect of bicultural life on social, political, and economic decision making; status of native people in Canada

point is that it is around the basic subject matter that all these objectives are achieved. If a careful job is done in completing the four cells above the middle line (Figure 8–1) *for each of the main ideas included in the unit,* the task of selecting resources and activities will be made easier.

Beginning the Study

Building and sustaining the interest of children in a topic are continuing responsibilities of the teacher, but are especially important when beginning a new unit of study. This involves more than simply getting started. It requires arousing the curiosity of the youngsters, exploring some of the possibilities for study presented by the topic, and, in general, setting the stage for learning to take place. In advance of the time the unit is actually

Figure 8–1

This form can be used in developing unit plans. Notice that it consists of five components: (1) the learnings to be achieved; (2) the references and resources to be used; (3) the activities to be performed; (4) the relationship to the rest of the curriculum; and (5) assessments.

SOCIAL STUDIES UNIT PLANNING

Unit Title _____ Date _____

Main Ideas to Be Developed:	Related Skills:	Related Attitudes and Values:	Questions to Stimulate Higher-Order Thinking:
Key Concepts and Terms:			
Focus Questions:			
Text References:	Oral and Written Language Activities:	Musical and Dramatic Activities:	Simulations and Construction Activities:
Supplementary Resources:			
Multimedia Resources:	Assessment:	Assessment:	Assessment:
Community Resources:			
Summative Assessment:	Related Curriculum Activities (Science, Math, Art, Music):		

Role playing arouses curiosity at the beginning of a unit.

undertaken, the teacher should post material in the room that will arouse interest in the anticipated study, and the relationship of the new topic to previous work should be indicated. There should be books and other appropriate materials in the room through which the children may browse. Materials can be brought to class that stimulate the thinking of the children. All these activities and others, which the imaginative teacher will use, serve to create interest and will help cause the children to want to learn more about the topic. Through procedures such as these, the children have an opportunity to discover the new material gradually and will be ready to engage in productive teacher-guided planning.

Some teachers use dramatic representation successfully in the initial stages of the unit. Let us assume that a primary class is beginning a unit on transportation. The teacher suggests that the children show through creative dramatics what the workers at an airline terminal do. The children become excited about this and want to start immediately, which the teacher allows. Under the teacher's guidance, they begin to plan and to play the representation, but they soon discover that they do not really know enough about the situation to present it accurately. They do not know who the workers are at the terminal, let alone what each worker does. Now they have identified a problem they can understand and can go about their research and problem solving with genuine purpose. The children's purposes have to do with getting information to do the dramatic play whereas the teacher's purpose is to have them learn basic ideas about the airport and to learn important related skills. Although the example given applies to a primary grade, the procedure can be used at any level.

Other activities can be used in a similar way to motivate work, to develop purposes, and to give children reasons for doing the things they do. The projects are important in that they provide a child-oriented vehicle for learning. Construction activities are often used in this way. If an individual or a class is to build something, they have to learn what goes into it, how it functions, and how it is or was used. One has to be careful, of course, to make certain the time taken in such endeavors is justified by the learnings that result. Properly understood, this phase of unit development consists of a *group* or *series* of experiences rather than a single experience.

Developing the Study: Problems, Experiences, or Activities

A distinguishing characteristic of a good elementary or middle school teacher is the ability to engage children in an interested way in activities that help them achieve important learnings. One unfortunate practice in teaching social studies is that of using activities without relating them to social studies purposes. Activities are means to ends—they are used to help children learn something. It is thus imperative that the teacher define the objectives and know clearly what the children are supposed to learn *before* deciding what activities are to be used. If the planning format shown in Figure 8–1 is used as suggested, this will not be a problem because the upper portion dealing with objectives is completed before the activities are selected. As decisions are made concerning activities, the teacher must also select the information sources that will be used by the children. These can be listed in the space provided, as shown in Figure 8–1.

Good unit development always makes provision for the involvement of children in planning instructional activities. This is in keeping with attaining and maintaining student interest. Having them participate in planning can do much to overcome the feeling that they are only "doing assignments for the teacher." Such participation assists in clarifying objectives of learning for the children and allows them to identify psychologically with the unit activities. The many values of such planning have been well documented, and it is now generally recognized as sound teaching procedure by good teachers everywhere.

Teachers should plan with children many of the specific learning tasks undertaken in the unit: listing questions on which information is desired, making charts of what to do, finding and listing sources of information, appointing committees, reporting progress, pooling suggestions, and making plans for a construction activity. A fifth-grade teacher and her class summarized their plans for part of a unit on colonial New England as shown in Jobs in a Colonial New England Town.

In general, the development of a unit consists of a sequence of procedures, each one emerging from the preceding one. In its simplest form, this pattern might be described as follows:

1. *Problem identification* and related information gathering; problem-solving activities such as reading, interviewing, listening, viewing, collecting, using references, doing map work.
2. *Application* through expressive activities such as discussing, illustrating, exhibiting, dramatizing, constructing, drawing, and writing.
3. *Summarizing*, *generalizing*, and *transferring* to new situations resulting in identification of new problems of a more complex nature; the cycle is then repeated.

This procedure includes both data-gathering and data-processing activities. Children not only take in information knowledge but also must act on information so obtained—manipulate it, analyze it, interpret it in play or song. Moreover, they must generalize and apply their knowledge to new problems and situations.

The Development Phase

As the unit moves into the development phase, each class period should provide for three instructional operations: (1) readiness, (2) work-study, and (3) summary and evaluation. Teachers usually begin the social studies instructional period with the entire class in one group. At this time the previous day's progress is reviewed, plans for the day's

JOBS IN A COLONIAL NEW ENGLAND TOWN

Each of us will select a different job from New England town life.

Each of us will find out what skills and responsibilities each person has.

Each of us will share our role with the others in the class by dressing up like the person, showing something one might have created or used, making a bulletin board or diorama, or preparing a dramatization.

Some of the jobs in a colonial New England town are:

candlemaker	homemaker/mother
blacksmith	merchant
weaver	shipbuilder
farmer	minister
school teacher	fisherman
miller	barrister
carpenter	tanner
slave	doctor
watchman	innkeeper
printer	cooper

What We Will Want to Find Out About Our Jobs
1. What skills did the person need?
2. What training was necessary to do the job?
3. How much money did the person make?
4. How was the person paid?
5. How many people will need the services?
6. How does the job relate to other jobs in the community?
7. What special equipment or resources did the people use in their job?
8. Would you like to have done this job or performed this service?

work are outlined, and work objectives are clarified. The children then turn to their various tasks while the teacher moves from one child to the next or from one group to another, guiding, helping, clarifying, encouraging, and suggesting. The teacher will terminate the work period sufficiently early to assemble the entire group once again to discuss progress, to evaluate work, and to identify tasks left undone that must be continued the next day. As the children complete their various work projects and are ready to share them with the class, time will be arranged for them to do so. On some days the children may spend the entire period sharing, presenting reports, discussing, and planning. Other days may be spent entirely in reading and research or on worksheets the teacher has prepared because of a special need of the class. And on other days part of the group may be reading while others are preparing a mural and still others are planning a panel discussion, television news program, or musical.

The need to take time at the end of the work period to summarize what has been learned or to review work that has been accomplished should be underscored. Having a clear understanding of the objective or purpose of a learning activity and having knowledge of the progress go hand in hand. Unless the teacher spends some time crystallizing what has been accomplished or learned, the children may work for days without feeling that they have learned anything or that they are getting anywhere. Some teachers find it worthwhile to place these daily summaries on charts that serve as a log of the unit work as it progresses. Such logs are helpful in the culmination and may also be useful in assessment activities associated with the unit.

The work-study or problem-solving phase of the unit is handled somewhat differently in the primary grades than it is in the middle and upper grades. Although children of all ages need many firsthand experiences to extend their understanding of social studies concepts, the older child has a greater familiarity with the world of things and people and can, therefore, profit from vicarious experiences to a much greater extent than the primary-grade child. Furthermore, the older child can make use of reading as a tool for learning in the social studies whereas the young child is less able to do so. The physiological and psychological makeup of the primary-grade child makes necessary the use of learning activities that involve the child actively in firsthand experiences. (See Table 8–2.)

The following are a few examples of learning activities for all grade levels:

LEARNING ACTIVITIES

Sharing

Mr. Johnson's second-graders were studying their seashore community. Using a sandbox and things that each of them had gathered or collected with their families, they created a model of a seashore. The boys and girls talked about what they had brought and where their items had come from. They discussed whether the items were natural or artificially constructed.

Construction
Ms. Kim's class studied early people and constructed tools and utensils with sticks, rocks, and vines they gathered in nearby wooded areas. Each child demonstrated the use of the implement.

Experimenting
Ms. Womble secured samples of various grains—oats, corn, barley, wheat—while studying agriculture with her class. The children compared the appearance and taste of each type of grain and then planted some to compare germinating time and appearance of the first shoots.

Listening
In Mr. Potts's class, the focus of study was Native Americans. In motivating the children, Mr. Potts read a Native American legend and asked them to decide what the people valued in their lives, using the legend as a clue to their value system.

Discussion
Ms. Montoya's sixth grade class had a current events time, and a child brought an article from the evening paper telling about the sale of United States grain to China. A discussion that weighed the advantages and disadvantages of this action to the American people followed.

Written Language Experience
Ms. Thomas's class had written letters to their grandparents asking them to share their recollections of earlier school days. Those grandparents who lived nearby were asked to visit Ms. Thomas's classroom.

Dramatic Activities
During their study of Indonesia, each of the children in Ms. Monroe's class created a shadow puppet. In small groups they dramatized situations from Indonesian life.

Art Experience
A first grade class made a trip to a farm. On their return they painted a mural showing the animals, equipment, people, and buildings they had observed.

Field Trip
A day was spent at a fair during the study of the state. The children noticed what products were displayed and what their region of the state had contributed.

Processing
During a study of colonial history the class divided into groups to make soap, dip candles, bake bread, churn butter, make dyes, and weave.

Table 8–2

Learning activities for social studies

Type of Learning Activity	Examples	Purposes Served

Research	Reading
	Writing
	Interviewing
	Notetaking
	Collecting
	Map work
	Using references
		To
		  Gather information
		  Practice information-gathering skills
		  Answer questions
		  Test hypotheses

Presentation	Telling
	Demonstrating
	Illustrating
	Dramatizing
	Exhibiting
	Announcing
	Giving directions
	Pantomiming
	Relating events
		To
		  Share ideas with others
		  Practice communication skills
		  Clarify ideas
		  Encourage initiative
		  Apply information
		  Correct misconceptions

Creative and construction experiences	Writing
	Sketching
	Illustrating
	Sewing
	Soap carving
	Manipulating
	Comparing
	Drawing
	Modeling
	Painting
	Building
	Singing
	Dramatizing
	Imagining
		To
		  Express ideas creatively
		  Encourage creative abilities
		  Stimulate interest
		  Extend and/or enrich learning
		  Build on children's talents
		  Provide concrete experiences

Selecting Activities

In selecting a social studies activity, the teacher should consider these criteria:

1. The activity is useful in achieving a definite objective related to social studies.
2. It clarifies, enriches, or extends the meaning of some important concept.
3. It requires children to do careful thinking and planning.
4. It is an accurate and truthful representation.
5. It is within the capabilities of the children.
6. The time and effort expended can be justified by the learnings that occur.
7. It is reasonable in terms of space and expense.
8. The needed materials are available.

Type of Learning Activity	Examples	Purposes Served
Appreciation	Listening Viewing Describing Reading	To Develop attitudes and feelings Provide valuing experiences Extend and/or enrich learning
Observation or listening	Observing Visiting places of interest Viewing pictures or films Listening to recordings Viewing art	To Gather information Building observation and perceptual skills Compare and contrast
Group cooperation	Discussing Sharing Helping one another Doing committee work Asking questions	To Develop group-work skills Make decisions Engage in larger projects Develop citizenship skills
Experimentation	Measuring Demonstrating Conducting experiments Collecting	To Clarify complex procedures Develop inquiry skills Gather information Test hypotheses
Organization	Planning Outlining Holding meetings Discussing Summarizing	To Clarify relationships Prepare a plan of action Organize ideas Develop citizenship skills
Evaluation	Summarizing Criticizing Asking questions Reviewing	To Clarify direction and purpose Assess progress toward goals Modify plans

Assessing Learning

Throughout the study the teacher and the children should make frequent evaluations of how well the unit is progressing. This is *formative* evaluation conducted to diagnose student learning difficulties and to improve teaching and learning. Much of this day-to-day evaluation is, and ought to be, informal. The teacher sees children working well or poorly and adjusts the instruction accordingly. The teacher can also sense whether children are interested in what they are doing. Through observation and feedback, the teacher can gauge the extent to which progress is being made toward the achievement of objectives. An appropriate, short teacher-made test can be used to check how well specific areas of content and skills have been learned.

Much of the informal evaluation that takes place on a day-to-day basis involves the children themselves. They should be encouraged through discussion to take stock of their work individually and as a group. Assessment of learnings, therefore, should not be associated only with the conclusion of a unit, but should be an important part of the ongoing instruction. Of course, the end of a unit provides a time to examine the extent to which the overall objectives have been achieved. This is *summative* evaluation, and both informal and formal evaluation procedures are appropriate for this purpose. As a rule, learning activities should result in some product that can be placed in each child's unit portfolio. In the case of a single product made cooperatively with others, a description of it, perhaps with a photograph, can be used. (Chapter 9 deals extensively with assessing student progress.)

Concluding the Study

As a class nears the end of a unit, the teacher should plan a series of activities that encourage children to summarize what they have learned. This might involve opportunities to show what they have done or to share interesting things they have learned with other classes in the school or with their parents.* What is important about closing a unit of study is the opportunity to discuss conclusions, evaluate what has been learned, identify what children found to be of especial interest to them, and identify areas where additional study is needed. Concluding activities should include a suggestion of various interesting facets of the topic that were left unexplored and about which the children may wish to read and study independently. Concluding activities can and should serve as bridges to new intellectual pursuits.

Planning Short Instructional Sequences

Thus far our discussion has concerned itself only with planning a unit—a parcel of work that might take several weeks to complete. To implement such a plan, teachers must extract from the unit plan ideas that can be converted into shorter instructional sequences that may last anywhere from a single day to a week or more. Usually these are called daily lesson plans. These plans must be complete in every detail, correctly sequenced, contingencies anticipated and accounted for, with as little as possible left to chance. As the teacher prepares such plans, it is helpful to rehearse mentally how the lesson is expected to proceed, step-by-step.

There are four essential components of plans of this type. These are (1) the objective that identifies what children will *learn*; (2) lesson development to include (a) interest-building procedures that indicate how the sequence is to *begin* and (b) work-study activities that indicate what children will *do* to help them learn; (3) summary and assessment that indicate how the sequence will *close*; and (4) a list of the instructional materials and resources needed to teach the sequence. The example in Lesson Plan 7 shows how these plans can be constructed. Other lesson plan samples can be found throughout this text.

---

* The idea of a "sidewalk fair" in a local shopping mall could be a good outlet for sharing what has been learned with others. See Barbara Hatcher and Mary Olson, "Sidewalk Social Studies," *Social Education* 48 (September/October 1984): 473–74, 485.

Lesson Plan 7

Group membership

Grade
2

Time
Two class periods

Objectives
Children will learn to identify human groups and will become aware of reasons why people are grouped together.

Interest Building
Display five pictures of groups. Underneath each write what type of group is represented. (Ideas: soccer team, birthday party, family, class, scout troop)

Lesson Development
Ask class to think of one word that describes all the pictures. Elicit the word *group*.

Generate a simple definition of a human group.

Have children think of the names of several more groups.

Suggest that they include groups to which they belong. Write these on chalkboard.

Focus the class discussion on the reason people are grouped together, and place ideas on a chart as follows:

Human Groups	
What are some groups that we know about?	*Why are these people grouped together?*
family	love, help each other
team	to play games
class	to learn
birthday party	for fun
scout troop	camping, making things, helping others

Discuss ways that groups can be identified. Look at the five original pictures for clues. Some clues might be: clothing/uniforms, symbols/mascots, official names, special songs, distinguishing looks or languages.

Summary
Bring the concept of group into the children's immediate experience by asking the following questions: Is this class a group? How do you know? Why are we grouped together? What are *your* reasons for being a member of this group?

Assessment
Have old magazines available, and ask children to cut out a picture of a group. Have each child tell something about what the group is doing. As they make their presenta-

tion, have them finish this sentence: "I think that these people make a group because. . . . " Use the pictures to make a collage on the bulletin board.

Follow up

Have children bring in personal photos of groups to which they belong and share them with the class.

If possible, take a photo of the class group, and have a print made for each child.

Needed Materials

Five pictures of different groups for display purposes. White butcher paper and felt pen to make chart.

Old magazines or newspapers that have pictures of groups.

Option: Personal camera

Judging the Adequacy of a Lesson Plan

A teacher is never as well prepared as he or she *might* have been, given more time and more resources. Lesson planning is an open-ended process that can go on endlessly. Many teachers can recall, as student teachers, staying up half the night preparing a half-hour lesson to be taught the next day. Although such effort is commendable, it cannot be sustained for any length of time. At some point, the teacher must decide that the lesson is well enough planned and then be able to turn to other matters with a clear conscience.

It is not always easy, especially for the beginning teacher, to know when one has reached the point of diminishing returns in lesson planning. The checklist that follows can be useful in deciding whether all important aspects of the lesson have been given appropriate attention in the planning process.

Lesson Plan Checklist

1. Do the lesson objectives state clearly what it is that the children are expected to *learn*?
2. Do the learner activities for the lesson relate in a direct way to the stated objectives? That is, will the children learn what they are supposed to learn by doing the things they are asked to do?
3. Do you know how the lesson is to begin? What is the very first thing you will do? Say? What next? What third?
4. Have you written down the focus and follow-up questions you plan to ask? Do you have them in the order you plan to ask them? (See Chapter 7.)
5. Do you have all the needed instructional material? Equipment? If you are planning to use a machine, have you arranged to get it? Do you know where the electrical outlets are in the room? Will you need an extension cord? Screen?
6. Are there specific directions you are planning to give the children regarding what they are to do? If so, do you know what they are?
7. If you are going to group the children, do you have productive work planned for *all* the groups, *all* the time?

8. Do you know how much time will be needed for each component of your lesson?
9. Have you provided for differences in rate and level of learning among children? Do you have productive work-study activities planned for those who complete their assignments quickly?
10. Have you considered whether the lesson will require changes in the room environment, movement of furniture, and so forth?
11. Do you know exactly how the lesson is to close—that is: What you will do? What you will say? What you expect the children to do?
12. Have you planned for any followup activity?
13. Have you taken into account how learning is to be assessed?

Enriching Learning Activities

As we have seen, the most important characteristic of learning activities is that they help children achieve curriculum objectives that are deemed essential. We turn now to five ways to enrich learning activities: incorporating thinking skills, construction processes, simulations, music, and drama.

Incorporating Higher-Order Thinking Skills (HOTS)

Higher-order thinking skills (HOTS) do not develop spontaneously. They must be incorporated purposefully into the ongoing work of the class if children are to develop proficiency in their use and, better, the *disposition* to think in these ways. Occasional special lessons on these skills are necessary but not sufficient for their proper development.

As we have seen in previous chapters, several thinking skills are particularly suited to the subject matter of social studies. Any of them can be brought to the heart of social studies learning activities:

- Organizing information on data-retrieval charts
- Comparing and contrasting examples
- Summarizing (or *synthesizing*) similarities
- Classifying (applying a concept to new material)
- Forming hypotheses
- Gathering relevant data/evidence
- Hypothesis testing (judging if hypotheses are warranted)
- Drawing conclusions (generalizations)
- Identifying and weighing alternatives
- Making decisions

Of course, not all skills will appear in social studies lessons every day. During a period of a few weeks, such as that of a unit of study, one should see balanced and systematic attention being given to them. In a unit involving inquiry, children naturally will be raising and testing hypotheses; to extend concepts, they will be classifying; to decide on the fairest classroom procedures, they will be engaged in decision making.

Incorporating Construction Activities

Most children love to make things. They build villages and castles in the sand at the beach; they make boats to float in the pond and creek; they sew clothing for dolls and make birdhouses to hang near a window. These natural sensory-motor play and creative-building activities are valuable for children in and of themselves. They give countless opportunities for thinking and planning as well as for creative expression, use of tools, physical activity, and the development of coordination. Children need many experiences of this type. In social studies, however, these values are only incidental to the chief purpose, which is *to extend and enrich meaning of some aspect of the topic being studied*. The excellence of the final product is, likewise, not a major concern. What is important is the learning that has occurred as a result of the construction activity. This being true, authenticity and accuracy can be included in the criteria by which they are evaluated.

It is possible to use construction activities to motivate children's work and to establish more clearly children's purposes for doing things. For example, the teacher of a primary grade conducting a study of the dairy farm might suggest that the class construct a model farm in the classroom. Naturally, the children will want to make their model as authentic as possible; therefore, a considerable amount of research will be necessary as they proceed with the building of the farm. In fact, they cannot even begin unless they know what it is they want to do. This gives them a genuine need for information. The children's purpose in this case may be to learn about the dairy farm to be able to build a classroom model of it. The teacher's purpose, however, is to have children form accurate concepts and understandings of a dairy farm; the construction activity is being used as a vehicle to achieve that goal. Under this arrangement, both learner objectives and teacher objectives will have been achieved.

There is no limit to the items that children can make in projects related to the social studies. The following have been used successfully by many teachers:

Model furniture

Books

Musical instruments

Simple trucks, airplanes, boats

Puppets, marionettes, and paper bag dolls

"Television set" with paper-roll programs

Looms for weaving

Hats, crowns, headdresses, and wigs

Maps (pictorial, product, relief, floor)

Candles

Soap

Baskets, trays, bowls

Preparation of foods (making tamales, jelly, butter, ice cream)

Ships, harbor, cargo

Retail food market and equipment

Scenery and properties for stage, dioramas, panoramas

Holiday decorations

Jewelry

Pottery, vases, dishes, cups

Covered wagons

Post office

Hospital

Fire station

Dairy farm and buildings

Playhouses

Model Sioux or Pueblo villages

Birdhouses and feeding stations

Seedboxes, planters

Production of visual material needed in the unit, such as pictorial graphs, charts, posters, displays, bulletin boards

Block printing

Storyline

One of the most imaginative construction activities originated in the elementary schools of Scotland and has children create a story together.[3] Called *storyline*, the procedure builds on children's prior experience and their love of story telling, scissors, and glue. There are four interlocking parts. First, a curriculum-related setting for the story is created. The teacher might tell children about a fictitious community in the American Southwest that is facing another year of water rationing. Working with the children, the teacher adds sufficient detail so that a shared visual image of the community is created. Second, characters for the story are created. Children are placed in small groups to cut and paste paper-doll families who live in the community. Responding to the teacher's questions (How large are the families? What are their physical characteristics? What kinds of homes do they live in?), the children decide what kind of families to create. Written descriptions of the families are posted with the paper dolls on the classroom wall, thus creating a vivid and highly personal mural representing the families in this community.

Third, the teacher suggests a number of curriculum-related episodes with which the small groups must cope. The teacher might suggest, for example, that a young child in the community, one the children have created, wants to know what the rules are so that he or she doesn't break any accidentally. Now the small groups deliberate the community's laws and post them on the mural. Next, the teacher might tell the class that an exchange student will be joining each family. The small groups decide where the visitor is coming from, then gather information about that country and decide what the visitor will be most eager to see in their own community. Next comes the water rationing problem. What are the community's priorities? Should larger families get more water? Should the golf course be closed? By whom should these decisions be made? Finally, the teacher might introduce the concept of *trade*, asking the families what goods they will produce and which goods must be imported and purchased with money . . . which is kept in the bank . . . which is robbed . . . and the robber turns out to be a youthful offender . . . and so on. Finally, the children invite an audience, perhaps their own families, to come to class and experience the narrative they have created, with its evolving mural on the classroom wall.

Storyline requires careful planning so that the setting and episodes around which the children build this imaginary world are related directly to challenging curriculum objectives. This is the first criteria, recall, for selecting activities.

The following suggestions are offered to help the teacher use construction activities in teaching social studies.

Discuss the Purpose of the Activity with the Children

The practice of having children make stores or maps without knowing why they are performing these activities is open to serious question. Children may not have any idea of the real purpose or significance of the construction. It is suggested, therefore, that at the beginning of such an activity, the reasons for planning it should be discussed and understood by all. The purposes for the construction should be reviewed from time to time during the activity.

Plan Methods of Work with the Children

Construction activities involve working in groups, using tools, perhaps hammering and sawing or other noisy activities, and somewhat more disorder than is usually found in regular classroom work. This means that unless rules and standards concerning the methods of work are established and understood, there is likely to be much noise, commotion, and general confusion. Therefore, it is recommended that the teacher and the children discuss and decide what the rules of work are to be. Group discussions and decision making about rules, recall, constitute citizenship education at its best. These rules might concern:

1. How to get and return tools and construction materials.
2. Use of tools and equipment, including safe handling.
3. Things to remember during the work period: talking in a conversational voice, good use of materials to avoid waste, sharing tools and materials with others, consideration for others, doing one's share of work, asking for help when needed, and giving everyone a chance to present ideas.
4. Procedures for cleanup time. It is good to establish a "listen" signal to get the attention of the class. It can be playing a chord on the piano, turning off the lights, or ringing a small bell. When the listen signal is given, children should learn to stop whatever they are doing, cease talking, and listen to whatever announcement is to be made. In this way, the teacher can stop the work of the class at any time to call their attention to some detail or get them started at cleanup.

Provide Plenty of Time Each Day for Planning, Assessing, Working, and Cleaning Up

Before work on the construction activity is begun each day, time should be spent in making specific plans. This is to ensure that everyone will have an important job to do and that the children will know their responsibilities. It also is a time when the teacher can go over some of the points the class talked about during its previous day's assessment. "You remember yesterday we had some problem about which group was to use the tools. Which group has the tools today?"

During the work period the teacher will want to move from group to group observing, assisting, suggesting new approaches, helping groups in difficulty, clarifying ideas, helping children find materials, and supervising and guiding the work of the class. Children will be identified who need help in getting started, those who are not working well together, those who seem not to be doing anything, or others who may be having difficulty. The teacher will keep an eye on the time and stop the work of the class in time to ensure a thorough cleanup.

An important part of each period is the assessment that occurs after the work and cleanup. During these times, the teacher will want the class to evaluate the progress it is making on the construction as well as the way children are working with each other.

"Were we able to make progress in building our store today?"

"Did anyone see signs of unsafe handling of tools today?"

"I wonder if the mountains aren't too high on Julie's group's map. Did you check that against the picture in your book?"

Some attention should be given to (1) progress on the construction, (2) methods of working together, and (3) problems that need attention the next day.

Make Use of the Construction in Some Way, Relating It to the Unit under Study

When constructed objects are completed, they should be put to good use. In the primary grades such a project may serve well for dramatic play activities. A market in the classroom, for example, gives the children an ongoing opportunity to play customer, grocer, checkout person, delivery person, and various community officials—health inspectors, fire and safety advisers, and the tax authority. By rotating these roles, every child gets the opportunity to make change, to make decisions about supply and demand, to see firsthand the interdependence of the store and the community, and even to practice interviewing and preparing a resume for different jobs. This brings us to a wonderful way to enrich learning activities: simulations.

Incorporating Simulations and Role Playing

A fifth grade class was studying the concept of *assembly-line production* in its unit on the growth of industry in the United States. In the discussion, the children contrasted assembly-line production with custom-made, individually built products. The class listed the strengths and limitations of each method of production:

Assembly Line

Strengths	*Weaknesses*
1. It is faster.	1. Sameness makes for an uninteresting product.
2. Every product is the same.	2. Production can be slipshod because no one person is responsible for it.
3. Can be produced at low cost.	3. The sameness of the work makes for a boring job.

Custom Built

Strengths	*Weaknesses*
1. "One of a kind" product.	1. Buyers cannot be sure of the product's quality because each is different.
2. Product made to fit needs of buyer.	2. Fewer people can afford to buy the product.
3. Work is less boring to the workers.	3. It takes longer for workers to become skillful in doing all the tasks needed to make the product.

The teacher pointed out to the class that each of the items they listed could serve as a hypothesis that they might be able to test. "Is it really true," she asked, "that assembly-line production is faster? Do workers on an assembly line become bored more quickly than those who make the whole product themselves? Do workers take greater pride in their product if they do it all themselves and sign their name to it? How could we test the truth of the statements?" The teacher and the children decided they could test their hypotheses by using a simple simulation involving the manufacture of envelopes.

The class was divided into two groups: One would be assembly-line workers; the other group would be custom workers. The teacher provided cardboard templates, or patterns, of an outline of an envelope, scissors, paste, and used ditto paper that would be needed to manufacture envelopes. After the pattern was placed on a piece of paper, its outline could be traced and could then be cut, folded, and pasted to make the finished product. The assembly line was arranged according to a division of labor as follows:

ASSEMBLY LINE

Pattern tracer	*Cutters*	*Folders*	*Paster*	*Stacker*
Number of workers: 1	Number of workers: 2	Number of workers: 2	Number of workers: 1	Number of workers: 1
Equipment: pattern pencil paper	Equipment: scissors	Equipment: none	Equipment: paste	Equipment: none

Total workers: 7
Supervisor: 1   SUPERVISOR

The custom workers consisted of seven individuals (the same number as on the assembly line) and a supervisor. Each of the seven workers had his or her own pattern, paper, pencil, scissors, and paste and was required to do all the steps necessary to make an envelope. These children would be required to put their own name on each envelope they produced and were encouraged to personalize their own product.

All children in both groups took turns, and all participated in the activity. The supervisor from each group could make changes and substitutions as needed. Three children served as a quality control panel that would accept or reject finished products in terms of quality of workmanship.

CUSTOM CRAFTSPERSONS

| Worker 1 | Worker 2 | Worker 3 | Worker 4 | Worker 5 | Worker 6 | Worker 7 |

Each worker has:
pattern
paper
pencil
scissors
paste

SUPERVISOR

When all preparations were completed, the teacher gave the signal to start, and both groups began manufacturing envelopes. After a half hour, the production was stopped, and the debriefing took place. Children were able to test their hypotheses in terms of the data they generated through the simulation.

We have here an example of a simple simulation. It is a strategy designed to reconstruct as closely as possible some of the essential characteristics of the real thing. Simulations are enthusiastically accepted by those teachers who pursue innovative approaches to social studies teaching. The simulation may be a simple one devised by the teacher, as described here, or it may be one of the growing number of commercially prepared simulations and games now available.

Sharon Pray Muir provides an annotated list of nearly 200 simulations appropriate for use in grades K–6 and that deal directly with social studies concepts and processes.[4] This collection is a treasure. In order to accommodate the typical classroom, it concentrates on simulations that can be played with large groups. Included are the title, recommended grade levels, and bibliographic information so readers can readily locate or order each simulation. Some appear in journals, newsletters, and magazines, which can be read in libraries for free; others can be purchased. Muir also indicates the social science discipline with which the simulation is associated. Several of the simulations she includes are those we described in Chapter 4, grouped by discipline. For *computer* simulation suggestions, see Chapter 7.

Incorporating Music in the Classroom

Music activities not only enrich social studies learning but contribute to the school's music program itself. Singing, listening, dancing, and playing musical instruments from cultures near and far all add meaning and firsthand experience to social studies learning.

Singing

For almost any social studies unit, the teacher will find appropriate and related songs for children to sing. One of the chief values of singing is its affective quality; it gives the child a *feeling* for the material not likely to be obtained in any other way. Through singing, the child senses the loneliness of the voyageur, the gaiety of a frontier housewarming, or the sadness of a displaced people longing for their homeland. Folk songs can be springboards to the study of a period in history, to the contributions of ethnic groups, to the lifestyles of a group, and to many social studies topics. Singing is an experience that can broaden chil-

Computer-assisted simulations can be involving.

dren's appreciation of people everywhere. In the study of communities around the world, the teacher will want to use the songs of various national groups. This provides opportunities to learn more about a culture through the language of music.

Some educators have recognized the rich learning resource folk music provides, and they have promoted the use of folk songs in social studies classrooms. Contemporary folk songs such as "Little Boxes," "We Shall Overcome," "Detroit City," and "Sittin' on the Dock of the Bay" convey powerful social messages. Cowboy songs such as "I Ride an Old Paint," "Colorado Trail," "The Night Herding Song," and "Git Along Little Dogie" have both lyrics and melodies that are hauntingly reminiscent of the lonely life of this American folk group. "The Yellow Rose of Texas," "When Johnny Comes Marching Home Again," and "Over There" are associated with significant conflicts of this nation (Texas Independence, Civil War, and World War I, respectively). Teachers interested in learning more about the use of folk songs in the classroom should write to John W. Scott, P.O. Box 264, Holyoke, MA 01041, or to Diana Palmer, 433 Leadmine Rd., Fiskdale, MA 01518, for information about the newsletter entitled *Folksong in the Classroom*.

Music Appreciation

"Music from different cultures can offer us information and an entry point to understanding a people who may have lived thousands of years ago or thousands of miles from us."[5] Music in nonwestern cultures may serve many of the same purposes as in North America and Europe: entertainment, religious expression, and relaxation, mainly. But it serves others as well: building community solidarity, struggling against bondage, and relating to nature, for example. The African-American gospel tradition is inseparable from the history of enslavement. "Oh Freedom" and "We Shall Overcome" are synonymous with the civil rights movement. Listening to Native American flute and drumming, children of all backgrounds can appreciate that pitch and harmony are not universally applicable attributes of the concept *music*.

Listening to music should be an imaginative experience for children. The teacher can help them learn about mood in music and contrast what is bright, happy, and lively with music that is quiet and restful. Through listening the child learns to identify the use of music by different groups throughout the world—it provides for another direct cultural contact with people of many lands. The teacher will have no difficulty obtaining recordings for the purposes described.

Incorporating Drama

Dramatic representation in any one of its many forms is a popular activity with children—one in which they have all engaged during their early years. What child has not "been" a firefighter, a cowhand, a jet pilot, or a doctor during the fanciful and imaginative play of early childhood? Dramatic activities have great value in promoting social studies learnings by helping sharpen the child's power of observation; giving purpose to research activities; giving insight into another's feelings; providing experiences in democratic living; helping create and maintain interest, thereby motivating learning; and affording an excellent opportunity for the teacher to observe the behavior of children.

The most structured dramatic activity is the *play*, which requires a script, staging, rehearsal, and an audience. It may be used to show some historical event, to represent the growth of a movement or idea, to represent life in another period, or to demonstrate some problem of living. Children are usually involved in a considerable amount of creative work in productions of this type. They may plan and prepare costumes, do the artwork necessary for staging and properties, plan a program, send invitations, and make all arrangements attendant to the project. This requires that the children do a great deal of planning, working together, evaluating, and participating. Consequently, many social studies objectives are involved.

Less structured dramatizations involve *dramatic play* and *role playing*. When kindergartners and first-graders are playing various roles of mother, father, sister, brother, minister, nurse, and teacher in a corner of the classroom, they are engaging in both. There is no prepared script, rehearsal, or memorization of lines. Props are improvised.

When the teacher directs these informal dramatizations, children can be helped to achieve social studies objectives. The biographies of famous Americans, for example, can be dramatized with great effect. Kindergarten teacher and writer Vivian Paley does this masterfully. In one lesson, she gathered the children at the circle to act out events in the life of Martin Luther King, Jr. "The story of King's struggle evoked strong feelings among the children," she writes. "The indignities of being told where to sit, where to play and with whom, where to go to school, and where to eat seemed to echo some of the children's own complaints."[6] One child, a boy named Wally, wants the class to act out one of

King's speeches in which he describes the feelings of his young daughter, Yoki, when she was told she could not enter an amusement park. "My mother told me to bring you this record," Wally said. "She says you'll like the speech about the little daughter." Mrs. Paley has the children listen then immediately dramatize this scene. After learning of the Montgomery bus boycott, they dramatize it, too, then a scene from King's childhood.

Listening to children's dramatizations, teachers can assess their understandings of events as well as their sense of history and their ability to empathize. "Which character did you like best? Why?" "How do you suppose that character felt? Have you ever felt that way?" "Can you think of another event that is like this one in some way?" "Let's see if we can place these events in order. Which happened first? How long ago was that?"

Discussion Questions and Suggested Activities

1. Locate a copy of your state's curriculum guidelines. In some states, these are now called *curriculum standards*. Compare them to the ten themes of the national curriculum standards developed by the National Council for the Social Studies. Are there "grade bands"? That is, are the standards developed for the fourth, eighth, and eleventh grades or something similar? Keep notes on the ideas for curriculum and instruction you draw from this document.

2. Locate a copy of your school district's curriculum guidelines, and do the same.

3. Select a unit theme or topic that would be appropriate for a grade of your choice, and identify three to eight main ideas that could be developed in such a unit. State these as declarative statements (generalizations) as in Table 8–1. Then complete a unit planning chart such as the one shown in Figure 8–1. Think creatively about incorporating music and drama as well as construction activities and simulations.

4. Develop a lesson plan related to the unit plan you developed in response to question 3. Use the simple format suggested in Lesson Plan 7 and elaborate it as needed.

5. Write one or two behavioral objectives for the lesson you developed in response to question 4.

6. You have probably discovered by now that there is no standard unit or lesson plan format. Discuss teaching plans and how to prepare them with your supervising teacher or another teacher you know. If possible, bring to class a sample of a lesson plan used by that teacher. In class, compare several types of plans.

7. Create a data retrieval chart to compare and contrast the five approaches to enriching learning activities suggested in this chapter. List the approaches down the left. Discuss with classmates what focus questions should run across the top (e.g., relevance to the instructional objective, sensitivity to cultural differences among children, flexibility for children's different strengths).

8. Prepare a lesson plan just as you would teach it to a grade of your choice. Apply the thirteen-point checklist given in the chapter for judging the adequacy of the plan. These are performance criteria you can use to assess your planning. How did you do? Would you revise the checklist? Your plan?

9. Determine by asking numerous student teachers and practicing teachers the degree of freedom allowed teachers in various schools and districts to select subject matter for their classroom. Do you believe children are best served when their teachers have more or less freedom to choose subject matter?

10. Demonstrate for your classmates how you would proceed with a construction activity of some type (e.g., making butter, dipping candles, creating a model Cherokee village).

11. The use of songs and dramatizations was discussed in the chapter. Select a unit theme or topic, identify a few instructional objectives, then brainstorm with classmates a variety of learning activities that would involve songs and drama.

12. Select a piece of children's literature, the reading of which would serve one of the objectives identified for question 11. Make a list of dramatic activities that can be used in conjunction with this literature selection.

Notes

1 National Council for the Social Studies, "A Vision of Powerful Teaching and Learning in the Social Studies: Building Social Understanding and Civic Efficacy," in *Curriculum Standards for Social Studies* (Washington, DC: Author, 1994), 163.

2 CONTACT, No. 60, Canada Studies Foundation, 252 Bloor St. W., Suite 3-390, Toronto, Ontario M5S IV5, Canada. December 1983.

3 Margit E. McGuire, "Conceptual Learning in the Primary Grades: The Storyline Strategy," *Social Studies and the Young Learner* 3 (January/February 1991): 6–8.

4 Sharon Pray Muir, "Simulation Games for Elementary and Primary School Social Studies: An Annotated Bibliography," *Simulation and Gaming: An International Journal of Theory, Practice, and Research* 7 (March 1996): 41–73.

5 Douglas Selwyn, *Living History in the Classroom: Integrative Arts Activities for Making Social Studies Meaningful* (Tucson: Zephyr, 1993), 150.

6 Vivian Gussin Paley, *Wally's Stories* (Cambridge: Harvard University Press, 1981), 108.

Selected References

Airasian, Peter W. *Classroom Assessment.* 2nd ed. New York: McGraw-Hill, 1994.

Brophy, Jere, and Janet Alleman. "Activities as Instructional Tools: A Framework for Analysis and Evaluation." *Educational Researcher* 20 (May 1991): 9–23.

Gronlund, Norman E. *How to Write and Use Instructional Objectives.* 4th ed. New York: Macmillan, 1991.

Jarolimek, John, and Clifford S. Foster, Sr. *Teaching and Learning in the Elementary School.* 6th ed. New York: Macmillan, 1996.

Katz, Lillian G., and Sylvia C. Chard. *Engaging Children's Minds: The Project Approach.* Norwood, NJ: Ablex, 1991.

Muir, Sharon Pray. "Simulations for Elementary and Primary School Social Studies: An Annotated Bibliography." *Simulation and Gaming: An International Journal of Theory, Practice, and Research* 7 (March 1996): 41–73.

Paley, Vivian Gussin. *Wally's Stories.* Cambridge: Harvard University Press, 1981.

Selwyn, Douglas. *Living History in the Classroom: Integrative Arts Activities for Making Social Studies Meaningful.* Tucson: Zephyr, 1993.

Wharton-Boyd, Linda F. "The Significance of Black American Children's Singing Games in an Educational Setting." *Journal of Negro Education* 52 (Winter 1983): 46–56.

Mrs. Rivera is a new fourth grade teacher who plans to teach children to read and make maps of their state and the United States. The school district curriculum guide states that it is the responsibility of fourth grade teachers to achieve the following objectives. The first specifies understandings, the second skills:

> *Knowledge: At the end of the fourth grade, pupils should understand (1) the difference between state and national maps and (2) the differences and similarities among different kinds of maps: political, landform, and shaded relief maps.*
>
> *Skills: Pupils at the end of fourth grade should be able to (1) use map symbols and directions, (2) make different kinds of maps of the school grounds, and (3) locate places on the U.S. map using longitude and latitude.*

Before she begins planning a unit of instruction, she decides to find out what these children presently know about maps. She considers asking the whole class several questions: What is a map? Have you ever used a map? What kinds of information do maps give us? What things make a map a really good map? Who knows what a map legend is? She also considers listing key map terms on the board and asking students to define each of them on a sheet of paper. These are fine ideas. After considering these alternatives, Mrs. Rivera decides to create a brief pencil-and-paper test so that she can maximize the amount of information she obtains from each child. Using ideas from her college methods course, she finds a map skills practice exercise in the students' social studies workbook (Figure 9–1) and makes a copy for each child.

The next day, Mrs. Rivera informs the children that she wants to find out some of the things they know about maps so that she can plan instruction accordingly. She warms them up to the task by asking them about their experiences using and making maps. Then, she directs them to take fifteen minutes or so to answer the ten questions below the map. After they finish, in order to find out their immediate reactions, she asks the class which items were the most and least difficult for them. She jots down a few notes on what they say.

Later that day, she looks over her notes and scores the assessment. She notes that two-thirds of her students marked four or five of the ten items correctly. Two students answered none correctly, and two answered nine of the ten items correctly. No one got all ten. Examining responses item by item, she observes that no students correctly answered the question about "due north," and nearly all the children identified the railroad. This is good information, and she figures it will help her plan instruction on maps.

She goes back to school the next day eager to gather more information. She decides to lead a class discussion of the same ten items. She makes a transparency of the map and questions and displays it on the overhead projector. This time, she asks the class to respond to each question out loud. Her questioning procedure goes something like this: She directs her students' attention to the first question and asks the children which responses they selected yesterday. She uses the "fingers" technique to maximize participation: "Hold up one finger if you said it was a swamp, two if you said it was a desert, and three fingers if you said it was mountainous." Then she calls on a student to give reasons for his or her choice. After listening, she asks another child for his or her reasoning,

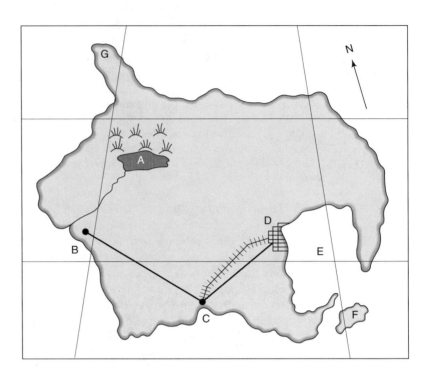

Use the map above to decide the correct answers. Then underline the correct answers.

1. The land north of A is (a swamp), (a desert), (mountainous).
2. The mouth of a river is located near letter (A), (B), (C).
3. The city at D is perhaps a (capital), (seaport), (mining town).
4. The river flows (from southwest to northeast), (from northeast to southwest), (from east to west).
5. An island is marked by the letter (A), (B), (F).
6. A railroad runs between (B and C), (D and B), (D and C).
7. The letter E marks (a bay), (a peninsula), (an island).
8. A peninsula is shown on this map at (B), (G), (C).
9. A delta might be found just north of (C), (A), (B).
10. The letter G is due north of (C), (A), (B).

Figure 9–1
Using map symbols and knowing directions.

then another child. This way, she is able to hear their reasoning—something that yesterday's exercise did not allow. As she moves through the ten items, she is able to hear each student reason aloud at least once. Children are able to hear one another's reasoning, too. Mrs. Rivera is careful to call on as many girls as boys.

Hungry for still more information, she turns to a different kind of assessment procedure on the following day. She places a blank sheet of paper in front of each student and asks them individually to try to draw from memory a map of the United States. She tells them to sketch very roughly the nation's general outline, add the Rocky Mountains and the Mississippi River, and draw in their own state, locating it as best they can. She asks them to indicate compass directions as well and to create a legend/key to explain any symbols used. Her students are nervous and a little embarrassed at the prospect of drawing. Mrs. Rivera calms them with a little humor and impresses upon them how important it is for her to find out what they now can do so that she can plan the very best instruction for them.

She has a hunch, based on the prior assessment, that several children will do very well on this map-drawing exercise, but mainly she is genuinely curious to see what they will draw, where they will draw the Mississippi, whether they will use symbols, and where they will say north is.

After mulling over all the information she has gathered, Mrs. Rivera plans a unit. The learning activities begin with conversations about road maps found in automobile glove compartments, which several students bring from home, and she displays well-worn trail maps that she has used on outings in summers past. During the unit, pairs of children learn to make maps of the classroom and playground, and they search for explorers' routes on CD-ROM programs. Assigned to cooperative teams, the class develops expertise on different regions of the United States, making political and landform maps of each region. Each day, they practice drawing an outline map of the United States from memory, after studying once more the map hanging in the front of the room. Global comparisons are made between each region and a geographically similar region on another continent: the Rockies are compared to the Swiss Alps, Death Valley to the Sahara, the Great Plains to the Steppes of Russia, and so forth.

When introducing the unit, Mrs. Rivera (with great flourish) informs the class that "by winter vacation this year, each of you will be able to place in your portfolio a landform map of the United States drawn from memory, and it will include our own state mapped in correctly."

Assessment Is Natural

Assessment means finding out what students know and are able to do. Like a detective trying to get the facts, assessment's emphasis is on observation of what is happening *now*. *Evaluation*, by contrast, involves value judgment: comparing what is—the facts about the child's present understanding—with what *ought* to be—the desired outcome of instruction. This distinction is often blurred. When teachers assess children's present understanding of *landform map* or *map legend* (or *citizenship* or *immigration*), they usually do so with a desired level of understanding—a standard—in mind. Indeed, assessment and evaluation often occur in one breath. In this chapter, we will follow common practice and use the terms *assessment* and *evaluation* almost interchangeably, making the distinction where necessary for clarity.

Mrs. Rivera's Student Assessments

Mrs. Rivera was assessing her students' map knowledge and skills. For what purpose? To help her plan an effective unit of instruction. Was she doing anything out of the ordinary? Not really. Teachers assess their students almost continually, observing them at their desks, checking their homework, and looking over their shoulders as they make models, paint lakes and mountains, read about deserts of the world, and write stories about historical events. They notice when children raise their hands higher and higher, hoping to be called on, and when they slump down in their chair, avoiding the teacher's gaze. They notice when children are rejected from one another's play and observe how they negotiate tasks in small cooperative groups. Teachers are constantly assessing.

Mrs. Rivera is a model of curiosity. She loves to learn what her children now know and can do. She is able to make them feel comfortable as she gathers information. They know she has much to teach them and that she diagnoses their present knowledge and skills so that she can properly plan instruction.

Note the variety of assessment procedures she used. First, there was the paper-and-pencil assessment. She pulled an activity from the workbook and adapted it to her assessment purpose. This paper-and-pencil assessment was of the *selection* or multiple-choice type because students were asked to choose the best response from several that were given. After that, she asked the whole class which items they found difficult and easy. Informal question asking of this sort is probably the most common kind of assessment conducted by teachers. Mrs. Rivera then placed the same map and questions on the overhead projector and conducted a sort of group interview—using a planned sequence of questions and the "fingers" technique to get all of her children involved—so that she could gather information about how they puzzled their way through these items. She did not provide correction or instruction; these would come later, during the unit. She was only trying to find out how they thought about these things. Finally, she used a *production* (also called *supply*) assessment when she had students sketch the U.S. map. When Mrs. Rivera introduced the unit to students, she informed them of a key performance expectation or *target*.

These are only a few of the kinds of assessment commonly carried on in classrooms, and Mrs. Rivera's purpose—to plan instruction—is only one purpose. We will explore these and other kinds and purposes in this chapter. For now, let us emphasize that assessment goes on continually in classrooms. And it *ought* to. Assessment "ought to become part of the natural learning environment," writes Howard Gardner. "As much as possible it should occur 'on the fly,'" as part of a teacher's or learner's "natural engagement in a learning situation."[2] What is to be avoided is a view of assessment as a formal procedure that occurs only at the end of an instructional unit for the purpose of reporting a score or grade. That is one purpose of assessment, and a necessary one. But it is a narrow purpose and not one that helps teachers plan or children learn.

Purposes of Assessing

In this section and the next, we invite you to think about purposes and principles of assessment. Following this, we provide many examples of assessment techniques, from simple observation to self-assessment checklists and rating scales for historical reasoning. First, consider three general purposes of assessment (Figure 9–2).

Mrs. Rivera's assessments were serving the purpose of diagnosing her students' knowledge and skills, which in turn served the purpose of planning effective instruction. This—*instructional planning*—is the primary purpose of assessment as far as the teacher is concerned. Instructional decision-making without assessment data would be subject to considerable error. Not only does assessment information allow teachers to tailor instruction to individual students, it helps them decide on the instructional objectives themselves and monitor students' progress. If Mrs. Rivera knows, for example, that her children's oral reports on the geographical regions of the United States will be graded on organization, accuracy of information, voice clarity, and use of visual aids and

Figure 9–2
Purposes of assessing student learning

Instructional Planning

Assess in order to
- diagnose students' understanding of maps before developing a map unit
- provide feedback to students on their progress and problems
- decide how to modify a unit plan
- identify cultural differences
- identify ability strengths and weaknesses
- provide evidence of success to students; therefore, motivate them to persevere

Public Accountability

Assess in order to
- report student progress to the community
- compare students across schools, school districts, states, and nations
- discuss students' progress and problems with parents

Student Placement

Assess in order to
- assign students to pairs and cooperative groups or ability groups
- decide which students require an IEP
- place profoundly retarded and extraordinarily gifted children in special programs

music, then these become major performance objectives of the unit. We will discuss this in detail in the next section.

Public accountability and program evaluation is a second important purpose of assessment. Most states in the United States have developed social studies assessments that will be administered to students statewide, and the United States Congress funds assessments of students' knowledge in history, geography, and civics.* Assessments such as these are administered typically to students in grades 4, 8, and 12, and the results are used by parents and public officials to compare education programs and student achievement within districts, across states, and among nations. Assessments designed for this purpose are usually standardized and norm-referenced. *Standardized* means that the test is designed to be administered and scored in the same way wherever it is given. *Norm-referenced* means that the results are going to be used to compare one group of students (e.g., those in your school or state) to another (students in the nation as a whole).

A third purpose of assessment is the *selection of students for particular schools and programs* or, simply, *placement*. IQ tests and the Scholastic Aptitude Test (SAT), introduced in 1926, are perhaps the best known tests used for this purpose. IQ and other similar tests are often used to determine placements of exceptional children. The SAT has determined college and university admission for millions of high school students. In the elementary grades, standardized reading and math tests are often used to determine ability group placement, and other assessments of social competence, intelligence, and language proficiency are used to place students in special programs.

Critics of testing have called attention to some of its abuses, one of which is to sort children into categories from which there may be no escape. As was pointed out in Chapter 2, once a child is labeled, the label often "sticks" long after its supposed benefits to the child have worn off. It may generate negative effects as a *self-fulfilling prophecy*: Teachers' expectations of the child may be lowered in a way that is not warranted, the child's self-perceptions may be lowered accordingly, and, making matters worse, he or she may be permanently (rather than only temporarily) separated from other children. As a result of the separation, the child may experience a less challenging and less empowering curriculum, and as a consequence he or she will know and be able to do less than his or her peers. Labels have been misused especially among racial-, ethnic-, and language-minority children. For these reasons, teachers are urged to use extreme caution when using test results for placement purposes.[3]

Principles of Assessment

When teachers plan an assessment of their students' learning, they should at the same time be thinking about curriculum objectives and alternative ways to provide instruction. The reverse is also true: When teachers plan curriculum objectives and think about how they will teach to them, they need also to think about how they will assess

---

* National assessments are developed and administered by the National Assessment of Educational Progress (NAEP). Information can be obtained by writing to the National Assessment Governing Board, 800 N. Capitol St. NW, Washington, DC 20002.

student achievement of these objectives. They are, in effect, thinking about three things at once. For this reason, it has become popular to say that the boundaries between assessment, curriculum, and instruction are "blurred."[4] This brings us to the first principle of good assessment practice.

Principle 1: Assessment Is an Integral Part of Curriculum and Instruction

Assessment planning should not be tagged onto the *end* of a unit, *after* curriculum has been planned and instruction has been delivered. Good assessment is not an add-on or an afterthought. If assessment is to facilitate student learning, it must be woven into the fabric of curriculum and instruction. It must be done before, during, and after instruction.

Assessments conducted before instruction are *diagnostic assessments*. Mrs. Rivera developed her unit to address the geographic knowledge and skills she found wanting in the assessments she conducted *before* planning the unit. Assessment conducted *during* instruction are *formative* assessments. These assessments help teachers decide what to do next in a lesson or unit. They are called formative because they help teachers "form" or modify instruction to help children achieve the objectives. Often these are nothing more than observations made of students while they are engaged in project or committee work or while they are working independently at their desks, but they also are brief paper-and-pencil tests given periodically through a unit of instruction. Teachers do this to check students' understanding of the topic at hand and then to alter the lesson as needed. They also do it to give students knowledge of the results of their work and a sense of making progress. This can be of tremendous help in motivating learners of all ages to carry on with the task at hand. Frequent formative assessment provides both teachers and students with the feedback they need to teach and learn better.

Assessments conducted *after* instruction are *summative* assessments. These are used to judge students' overall achievement at the end of instruction. They sum up the learning that has taken place and may incorporate many quizzes, work samples, performances, and other evidence of learning. Chapter and unit tests are the most common kinds of summative assessments, along with the grade given at the end of the school term.

Principle 2: Essential Learnings

Teachers should spend their assessment time on a relatively small number of *essential* subject matters or skills. Key themes of citizenship, history, and geography were discussed in Chapters 3 through 6, and the teacher should direct assessment in social studies primarily to these. It is more important, for example, to develop assessments related to ideas such as democracy, cultural pluralism, and human-environment interaction than it is to spend time listing crops produced in Latin America, Civil War battlefields, and hometowns of U.S. presidents. Of course, these latter subjects may have their place in a well-conceived curriculum, but *school time is precious*. Skillful teachers spend most of their instruction and assessment energies on the learnings that matter the most.

Principle 3: Aim Teaching and Learning at High Standards

The minimum competency movement of the 1970s and 1980s was an attempt by the educational community to restore public confidence in American education. Test data indicated a downward trend in scores on tests of basic school subjects over a period of several years. It was widely believed by the public—rightly or wrongly—that the

Good assessment is not an "add on" or an afterthought.

achievement of American school children was falling behind that of their counterparts in other industrialized nations. Out of this concern came the idea that schools should identify minimum levels of competency for basic school subjects that presumably all students would be expected to master. Teaching for these minimum competencies would be followed by minimum competency tests. This movement had great appeal and received strong support from public officials. Several states developed programs to implement minimum competency testing. What was not anticipated in this process was the detrimental effects of foreshortening achievement by focusing on *minimum* requirements. Minimum expectations gave no hint of the kinds of targets toward which students and teachers should put forth their best effort.[5]

"Social studies teaching and learning are powerful when they are challenging," according to the vision statement developed by the National Council for the Social Studies.[6] Assessments, like the curriculum objectives to which they are connected, need to capture the richness and depth of social studies subject matter. Teaching children whether Geronimo was a hero to the Cherokee or Apache people is a far cry from helping them to write and dramatize a biography of his life. Knowing the names of those who signed the U.S. Constitution is important, but it falls short of knowing why the Constitution has the content it does, grasping the principles on which it relies, and knowing what democracy requires of citizens.

To set high standards for children's learning and to assess their attainment in relation to these standards, teachers need to be familiar with the several sets of curriculum standards developed in recent years. These were discussed in Chapters 1, 3, and 4. Consider the two following curriculum standards for social studies learning developed for children in the early grades. By the end of the fourth grade, students should be able to:

- Identify key ideals of the United States' democratic form of government, such as individual human dignity, liberty, justice, equality, and the rule of law, and discuss their application in specific situations.[7]
- Demonstrate understanding of events that celebrate and exemplify fundamental values and principles of American democracy.[8]

Teachers who teach to these standards in the early grades are "aiming high." But there is more. In order to assess student achievement of these standards, it is necessary to envision the levels of achievement that students must reach to receive particular scores, awards, or certificates. These levels are called *performance standards* or *performance criteria*. They define levels of achievement—that is to say, degrees of mastery or proficiency—from high to low. Teachers often define three levels: good, fair, and poor. When a fourth level is added, it usually specifies a higher level still: excellent, superior, commendable, highly proficient, distinguished, and so forth. Sometimes five or six levels are specified.

We present below performance criteria that were developed for use in the fifth grade. They spell out three levels of achievement related to the second of the two curriculum standards given above. They were developed to assess the quality of short essays that students write about important events in American history, such as the signing of the Declaration of Independence or the Emancipation Proclamation.

- *Level 3—Proficient*: Response shows considerable knowledge of the time period and geographic factors, as appropriate, and frequently demonstrates insight. It usually supports ideas and conclusions with specific historical examples. Response is well reasoned and organized and is largely historically accurate.
- *Level 2—Adequate*: Response contains adequate information about the event. It demonstrates some knowledge of the time period and geographic factors, as appropriate. Response demonstrates some understanding, but reasons and evidence are in limited depth.
- *Level 1—Minimal*: Response addresses the question, but shows minimal understanding. It may lack historical and geographical context. It may contain numerous historical errors. It may simply rephrase the question but includes at least a word or phrase showing historical knowledge.[9]

Principle 4: Clarify Targets Early

Teachers need to clarify for students the targeted level of performance early in the instructional unit. In other words, they should "let students in on" the objectives of instruction and try to describe those objectives in performance terms—what students will know and be able to do if they achieve the objective. If teachers want children to develop their skills and knowledge to a high degree of proficiency—in other words, if they want children to hit the target—then the children must know the target well in advance. Just as an archer cannot shoot an arrow to the bull's-eye if she cannot see the target, children cannot become proficient if they have no idea of the level of performance they are striving for. Skillful teachers, therefore, clarify the goals of instruction at the beginning of the year and state specific objectives/performance criteria at the beginning of the unit.

For example, Ms. Paley's kindergartners know in advance that their dramatizations of historical events must be rich in detail. Consequently, each time she repeats to them the story of Rosa Parks's bus ride or of Squanto, the Pilgrims' friend, it is with the expectation that their retellings of the story will evolve. And they do.[10] Likewise, Mr. Smith tells his seventh grade class in September that by June they will draw a world map beautifully from memory on a blank piece of tag board. "When they arrive here, I tell them they'll end up with 150 countries, and they tell me, 'No way.'" But they do, confidently. "I used to hear about countries on television and think they were over there somewhere," admitted one student. "I hadn't heard of half of them. Now I can figure out better what's going on in the world. I'll always know that Angola is in Africa and not just over there somewhere."[11]

Teachers like Ms. Paley and Mr. Smith wisely make clear for children the "destinations" of their efforts. They then assess continuously, in large and small ways, formally and informally, collecting samples of students' work, using teacher-made as well as standardized tests. Such teachers can provide additional instruction and experiences as needed, calibrating them to student progress toward the outcomes.

Principle 5: Towards More Authentic Assessments

Assessments should be geared to finding out students' ability to apply knowledge and skills successfully in meaningful or *authentic* tasks. These tasks are exhibitions of children's ability to *use* what they have learned. Such tasks are meaningful because they are goal directed, and these goals have a real-world quality; hence, they are not "school-bound" tasks that have no bearing on what people do in their lives as citizens, workers, family members, and neighbors. Like all goal-directed activity, these tasks involve reasoning and decision making. Rather than focusing only on what children have memorized, they require children to analyze, manipulate, or interpret information in some way; consequently, higher-order thinking is incorporated into the assessment.

Examples of authentic tasks in social studies are plentiful. Teachers can assess students' ability to:

- Participate in discussions of classroom/community problems as part of maintaining a healthy civic life.
- Use reference books as part of social studies research projects.
- Work cooperatively as part of a team accomplishing a challenging task.
- Display historical judgment by applying knowledge of history to current events.
- Create a museum exhibit of a geographic region (the Southwest), a landform (Salt Lake), or an historical event, era, or person.
- Observe and interpret primary documents, such as speeches, newspaper accounts, photos, and songs.
- Read and make charts and graphs showing food supply, election results, census data, and economic data.

- Explain supply and demand or the relationship between savings accounts and economic growth.
- Make a recommendation for school or community policy on a controversial issue.
- Make picture postcards and travel brochures of the community.

Principle 6: Multiple Indicators of Learning

Teachers should collect multiple indicators of student achievements. A score on a lone chapter test does not go far enough to tell us what a child knows and is able to do. Teachers can have students collect numerous work samples into a *portfolio* that documents their work over the course of a unit. The portfolio might contain a chapter test from the social studies textbook program along with two or three other paper-and-pencil tests. There might also be a team-written biography to which the student contributed a chapter, self-assessments of the student's reading and thinking skills, and several drawings and maps. In this way, students have much to show for their work, and teachers can justify the grades they give by pointing to an array of evidence.

Principle 7: Opportunity to Learn

Students should not be held accountable for learning subject matter on which they have not been provided adequate instruction. This is why schools should not provide only targets for learning, but also the *means* of achieving them—teachers, curriculum materials, classrooms, wall maps, libraries, stimulating environments. Children must be provided *support* or *assistance* if they are to reach the targets. School buildings that are in poor physical condition, curriculum materials that are outdated, school administrators who deny teachers the assistance of knowledgeable curriculum coordinators, citizens who do not support the schools, and teachers who have little professional compe-

If students will be assessed on their knowledge of historical chronology, they should have ample opportunity to learn it.

Figure 9–3
Principles of good assessment

Principle 1: Treat assessment as an integral part of curriculum and instruction

Principle 2: Direct assessments toward essential learnings

Principle 3: Aim teaching and learning toward high standards

Principle 4: Clarify targets early

Principle 5: Assess student performance in authentic tasks

Principle 6: Collect multiple indicators of learning

Principle 7: Provide ample opportunities for students to learn

tence all combine to deny children sufficient opportunity to learn. It is clear that some of these problems are larger than what individual teachers can deal with in their own classrooms. Nonetheless what teachers *can* do is assess what is taught, teach what will be assessed, and assure the community that what is taught and assessed are essential learnings. Figure 9–3 summarizes the seven principles.

Methods of Assessment

We turn now to a variety of methods of assessment. We begin with informal techniques, then turn to the more formal methods of paper-and-pencil tests, performance assessment, and portfolios. The latter are more formal because they require more planning and the development of materials, such as scoring guides.

Informal Assessment Techniques

Much of the evaluation of learning in social studies is done informally by the teacher. Many times each day the teacher observes learners and makes a judgment about the quality of their work. The teacher notices what problems individual children are encountering or what kind of help they need in order to progress. The teacher then makes decisions concerning what deficiencies are apparent in children's work, whether the instruction is proceeding too rapidly or too slowly, what materials are required, how well concepts have been understood, or how proficient children are in their use of skills. Of course, formal tests have a place in this process, but most of the assessments a teacher does involve informal methods and observation. This means that careful records must be kept if the progress of each child is to be reported accurately. Some of the more commonly used informal assessment techniques are described on the pages that follow.

Group Discussion

Group discussion can be used to appraise the progress of the children in terms of previously established plans and standards. Discussion will activate self-evaluative thinking; it helps clarify and remind children of learning objectives; it is useful in establishing an attitude of looking forward to progress and successful achievement. The teacher should reserve some time near the end of every social studies period for the class to discuss its progress and to make plans for the next day's work. This helps children identify concepts needing further study and reminds them of the things they are learning in social studies.

Observation

Observation is among the best techniques the teacher can use in learning about children, appraising their progress, and sensing their needs for improvement. Although all teachers use this method of learner appraisal, not all teachers are skillful in its application. The teacher who makes the most of observation knows what he or she is looking for, systematizes observations, and makes an attempt to objectify the information so obtained. To this end it is suggested that the teacher:

1.   Spell out the traits to be evaluated and state evidence of these traits in terms of child behavior. For example, if the teacher desires to observe whether there is evidence of progress in *consideration for others*, the following would be appropriate:

   Does the child
   a. show respect for the ideas and feelings of classmates?
   b. abstain from causing disturbances that make it impossible for others to do their best work?
   c. carry a fair share of the work load in a small group?
   d. enjoy helping a classmate when needed?
   e. display sensitivity to injustices that may occur in the course of life in and out of the classroom?
   f. return borrowed materials? Obtain permission to use materials that belong to others?
   g. observe rules established by the group?
   h. fulfill responsibilities on time? Avoid doing things that hold up the progress of the class?

2.   Select certain children for intensive observation and study rather than observing "in general." This intensive observation might be limited to certain specific situations. For example, just what happens to David when he is placed on a committee to do some project in connection with a social studies unit? How can the situation be changed to help him develop more responsible habits of work in a group situation? The purpose of observations of this type is to gain insight into the child's behavior in the context of a specific set of circumstances.

3.   Record observations in writing and do not depend on memory. Keep a written record of information obtained through observation, and maintain this record over a period of time to establish a definite pattern in the child's behavior. At best, observation

ANECDOTAL RECORD

Sara Larsen

9/24   Difficulty in getting going in independent choice work; ignored all suggestions of activities. . . . "It's boring."

9/26   Found a fiction book related to unit for Sara. Read during work time. Took it home today.

9/27   Finished book . . . took suggestion to make a poster showing main characters.

10/1   Asked for time to show class the poster and to tell about the story.

10/2   Showed work. Talented artist. Received lots of compliments/support from classmates.

10/3   Sara asked for another book; suggested biography to her, plus suggested she do a map showing the area in which the person lived.

---

is a highly unreliable method of evaluating learner progress, and without a record of the observations, it is of little value indeed.

Anecdotal Records

An *anecdotal record* is a description of some incident or situation in the life of the child. A collection of such descriptions of learner behavior kept over a period of time, therefore, provides the teacher with a documentary account of changes of behavior that have occurred or are in progress. It is another way of systematically recording observations. Anecdotal records should indicate the date and time of the incident, the circumstances under which it occurred, and an objective description of the situation. If an interpretation is made of the incident, it should be kept separate from the description of the actual happening. Above are six entries in one teacher's anecdotal record on a child.

Because this is a time-consuming procedure, the teacher will want to limit its use to those particular children who seem to be exhibiting behavior that the teacher believes requires in-depth study.

Asking Questions

Asking questions is perhaps the most widely used assessment technique of all time. The Socratic method relies on this tool, parents could not get along without it, and skillful teachers turn it into an art form. A few well-chosen questions can assess students' understandings of a difficult concept. The classifying questions discussed in Chapter 7 are beautifully tailored for this purpose:

"Children, I want to ask a few questions about what you think *transportation* (or *immigration* or *citizen*) is."

"Hold up one finger if you think walking from the cafeteria to the playground is an example of transportation. Hold up two fingers if you think it is not an example. Hold up a closed fist if you aren't sure."

"Good. Now let's hear some of your reasons. Rosa? Tom? . . . "

"Let's get lots of examples of *transportation* on the board. Who will give us the first example? (pause) Okay, Lisa? Tran? . . . "

"Good. We have 15 suggestions on the board. Now let's hear the thinking behind them. Nicole, you suggested covered wagons. What makes you think covered wagons are an example of transportation?"

Conferences

Conferences with children should teach them how to assess their own work, thereby leading to increased self-direction. The teacher-learner conference can be of help in discovering particular learning problems and difficulties that children may be having, gaining insight into their feelings about schoolwork, and becoming aware of special personal-social problems the children may be having, as well as being a method of assisting every child individually in a personal way. Teachers need to budget their time to allow regular ten-minute conferences with individual children. Children need the personal contact with their teacher that a conference can give.

A conference will be of little value if the teacher does all the talking and the child all the listening. A friendly, helpful approach is needed, one that results in greater feelings of personal worth on the part of the child along with some constructive and concrete help for improvement. This close working relationship with children is critical to good education, especially in the social studies.

Paper-and-Pencil Tests

Paper-and-pencil tests in the classroom usually are constructed by the teacher or selected from the collection of tests that accompany textbook programs. Even though they can be used successfully with primary-grade children (assuming they are designed accordingly), their value increases as the child moves into the third and fourth grades and beyond. Such tests can help teachers gather data about how well students understand the concepts they are learning, their ability to write and to reason, their ability to recall key information, and their ability to use skills.

Mrs. Rivera's diagnostic exercise relied on a paper-and-pencil test of map symbols and directions (Figure 9–1). It assessed both knowledge and skill. The classifying test shown in Figure 9–4 is a straightforward way to assess students' understanding of economic concepts concerning the theme of *production*. Note that it gives one example, then asks for another. Students' understanding of any concept, from climate to culture, government to market, ecosystem to rain shadow, can be tested in this simple way.

Paper-and-pencil tests also can assess children's grasp of cause and effect relationships. Even as complicated a skill as using the encyclopedia can be assessed, at least somewhat, using a paper-and-pencil format. Figure 9–5 suggests a test in which students find topics in one encyclopedia, then locate the same topics in another. A benefit of this particular test is that children find their way around not one but two encyclopedias. From the standpoint of concept formation, a powerful teaching strategy discussed in Chapter 7, two examples are always better than one. With two comes the possibility of comparing and contrasting, which, in turn, is the gateway to the formation of ideas.

Figure 9–4
Understanding concepts

UNDERSTANDING CONCEPTS

One example is given for each of the terms listed. Your job is to write down *another* example.

1. Raw material   *Wood* is a raw material for making furniture; another raw
                    material is _____

                    used in making _____

2. Fuel   *Oil* is a fuel used for heating; another fuel is _____

                    used for _____

3. Grain   *Corn* is a grain used for feed; another example of a grain is _____

                    used for _____

4. Industry   *Dressmaking* is an industry; another example of industry is _____

                    that makes _____

5. Natural   *Water* is a natural resource necessary for life; another natural
   resource   resource is _____

                    used for _____

6. Manufactured   A *rocket booster* is a manufactured product used for space exploration; another
   product   example of a manufactured product is _____

                    used for _____

Paper-and-pencil tests lend themselves to both formative and summative assessment. Short matching and true-false quizzes can be written and scored quickly, and these can help students feel successful if they are made purposefully to be somewhat easy. A favorite way of ours to give these formative tests is to put children in teams of four. Hand the team *two* copies of the test. One has the questions only, the other has the answers filled in. Of course, the material on the test has been taught to students over the previous one or two days. Explain that the reason you have given students both the questions and the answers is because the team's job is to make sure that each person on the team understands *why* these are the answers. Inform them that they will have twenty to thirty minutes for this review. Appoint a timekeeper and chairperson for each team. Explain that this review will be followed by a quiz on the same material, and that the teams who do well will earn a certificate. After the time has expired, administer the same test to each individual.

Robert Slavin, an expert in cooperative learning, has shown that this assessment technique has many positive benefits, which we will examine in Chapter 10, Cooperative Learning. One of these benefits is that children learn the material on the test.[12] This is good news, reflecting the opening quote of this chapter: The purpose of testing should be to *improve* teaching and learning.

Of course, more challenging assessments are needed as well. Two kinds of paper-and-pencil test items are becoming increasingly popular. Both challenge students in

Directions: Using the ten-volume *Our Own Encyclopedia* shown in this diagram, select the number of the volume in which you would find information about each of the items listed below. Write the number of the volume you select in the spaces on the left side of the sheet. Then list the volume number of *World Book* in which the same items are found in the spaces on the right side of the sheet.

Our Own		*World Book*
1. _____	1. Earthquakes in Japan	1. _____
2. _____	2. The Mexican leader Zapata	2. _____
3. _____	3. The history of rocketry	3. _____
4. _____	4. The People's Republic of China	4. _____
5. _____	5. The U.S. Constitution	5. _____
6. _____	6. Apple-growing in Washington State	6. _____
7. _____	7. The Pony Express	7. _____
8. _____	8. Countries that are members of the United Nations	8. _____
9. _____	9. Confucius	9. _____
10. _____	10. The history of computers	10. _____

Figure 9–5
Using the encyclopedia

interesting ways. Both require higher-order thinking. One uses multiple-choice items; the other requires short essay responses. Remember that multiple-choice tests require students to select the best response of those given. The major shortcoming of such tests is that too often they are not *authentic* tasks; that is, people rarely engage in multiple-choice tasks outside of school settings. But this shortcoming can be offset when the questions (1) deal with essential social studies learnings and (2) require higher-order thinking: analysis, interpretation, application, or manipulation of information. The multiple-choice test items shown in Figure 9–6 accomplish both. How?

Figure 9–6
Multiple-choice with justification

Example #1	**Example #2**
I. Which of these was a cause of the Declaration of Independence?	I. Which of these is an example of the idea *culture*?
a. The Intolerable Acts.	a. The life of the people living in a Lakota Sioux village.
b. The King sent troops to force the colonists to obey.	b. The rules of cooperation and interaction in our classroom.
c. Americans wanted to keep their wealth rather than sharing it with England.	c. The way kittens in a litter are raised by cats.
d. The way the English treated the colonists.	d. The animals and plants living together in a forest.
II. Give your reasons	II. Give your reasons

Note: See Steven L. McCollum, *Performance Assessment in the Social Studies Classroom: A How-To Book for Teachers* (Joplin, MO: Chalk Dust Press, 1994), 26, for additional examples.

Note that these are multiple-choice *with justification* items. Such items present students with more than one reasonably correct answer. The student's task is to choose the response he or she thinks can best be supported with reasons that are based on knowledge. In other words, the child has to justify his or her selection, which requires much higher-order thinking. The emphasis, therefore, is on the reasoning children bring to the choices they make. "By justifying their answers, students must go beyond mere rote learning. The answers they give provide teachers with greater insight into the knowledge and thinking patterns of individual students."[13]

Turning now to short essay assessments, Figure 9–7 shows a short essay item used to assess fifth grade students' understanding of historical events. There are several innovative features of this item. First, note that it assesses an essential learning, events leading to the American Revolution. Second, it presents students with an object—a stimulus—for them to examine, in this case a time line. Other possibilities are a map, photo or artwork, or a brief quote from a primary document, such as Abraham Lincoln's Gettysburg Address or Longfellow's poem depicting Paul Revere's ride.[14] Third, the directions for student writing are given in one very clear sentence. Fourth, assistance or scaffolding is provided in the form of several "be sure to" prompts. These are intended to help students reason with facts: in this case, explain the relationship between two events, rather than only recall facts. Observing these four attributes, teachers can construct similar items for other historical events.

Performance Assessment

Figures 9–6 and 9–7 actually are performance assessments. Why? Performance assessments are assessments that help teachers find out how well students can *translate knowledge into action*. In the multiple-choice justification assessment (Figure 9–6), children are required to use the knowledge they have acquired in order to defend the

EVENTS LEADING TO THE AMERICAN REVOLUTION

(Suggested time: 30 minutes)

In history, important things happen that cause other things to happen. This is very plain when we talk about the events leading to the American Revolution.

Study the timeline below.

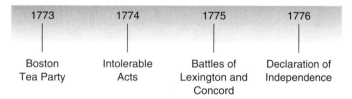

Circle two events on the timeline and write a short essay about them, using your knowledge of history.

Be sure to:

• Describe each event.
• Explain how the two events are related to each other.
• Explain how the events are related to the American Revolution.

Figure 9–7
Short Essay Item

Source: California Department of Education, *A Sampler of History—Social Science Assessment, Elementary* (Sacramento: California Learning Assessment System, Department of Education, January 1994), 35. Reprinted by permission of the California Department of Education.

choice they make. In the short essay assessment using the time line (Figure 9–7), students are required to interpret the time line and to use their knowledge of cause and effect to explain the relationship between two events. Both are *authentic* tasks, too. Using one's knowledge to defend a position or explain a choice one has made is an extremely valuable and necessary life skill; sensing cause-effect relationships is another.

Rating Scales

If students are to aim high in their responses, and if the proficiency of their responses is to be assessed, performance criteria are needed. *These performance criteria serve also as instructional objectives*, and this is why performance assessment truly "blurs the edges" between instruction and assessment. The criteria are the behaviors we want students to learn. On a rating scale (also called scoring *guide* and scoring *rubric*), these criteria are identified and sequenced from high to low proficiency.

As we said in the discussion of the third principle of good assessment, these criteria can be arranged on a three-level rating scale with descriptors such as *proficient, adequate*, and *minimal*. Doing so helps students to aim high. Look again at the short historical essay item (Figure 9–7). A rating scale needs to be created that spells out for students and teachers the criteria that will help them distinguish between a proficient short essay and one that is merely adequate or only minimally competent. Suggested criteria were given earlier in the chapter in discussion of Principle 3. While this three-point scale will be more helpful to students and teachers than a simple "yes/no" checklist, a five- or six-point scale can make for a still more powerful instructional tool and scoring guide.

A six-point rating scale for teaching and assessing short-essay historical writing is reproduced in Table 9–1. California teachers have field-tested this rubric with fourth and fifth grade students. Its advantage over the three-point scale is that is has greater explanatory power: more distinctions are made and, thus, the quality of students' performances can be refined. Just as pianists at a recital or divers at a tournament are not judged merely "good," "fair," and "poor," historical reasoning even in the elementary grades can be advanced beyond the three-point scale. Of course, the six-point rubric is more difficult than the three-point rubric. Teachers can try starting students on the simpler one and graduating them, as they become ready, to the more complex one. As well, different scales can be used with students of different ability. *A good illustration of this difference can be found in Table 3–1 and Figure 3–3 in Chapter 3.* In that chapter the point was made that discussion competence is one of the most important of all citizenship behaviors. Two rating scales were presented for assessing students' discussion abilities: one that might be more appropriate for assessing the abilities of children in the primary grades, the other for students in the fourth grade and higher. The latter was field-tested in the Oakland County, Michigan, schools with sixth grade students.

Creating a Scoring Rubric

Remember, the three-point scale is a terrific place to begin. It is easy to develop because children's work so easily falls into three categories: the good, the bad, and the in-between. Creating a scoring guide, whether three-point or more, is a fairly direct procedure with five steps.

Table 9-1

Short-essay scoring guide for elementary history-social science

Development of Historical Ideas	Historical Accuracy	Organization and Communication
A "6" short essay Always stays on the historical topic. Uses many important historical facts and reasons to support ideas, and makes detailed conclusions. Shows understanding of the historical time period by • comparing and contrasting ideas, events, and people, or • showing cause and effect between events, or how past and present connect.	**A "6" short essay** Has no historical mistakes.	**A "6" short essay** Is very well organized. Has very clear beginning, middle, and end. Makes excellent sense. Responds to all parts of prompt.
A "5" short essay Same as a "6," but doesn't use as many important historical facts and reasons to support ideas.	**A "5" short essay** Has minor historical mistakes.	**A "5" short essay** Is well organized. Has clear beginning, middle, and end. Makes good sense. Responds to all parts of prompt.
A "4" short essay Mostly stays on the historical topic. Uses some important historical facts and reasons to support ideas, and makes conclusions. Shows some understanding of the historical time period and tries to: • compare and contrast ideas, events, or people, or • show cause and effect between events, or how past and present connect.	**A "4" short essay** May have a big historical mistake, but most information is correct.	**A "4" short essay** Is organized. Has beginning, middle, and end. Makes sense. Sometimes responds very well to part of prompt, and not very well to other part of the prompt.
A "3" short essay Sometimes stays on the historical topic. Shows some knowledge of the historical time period with a few facts and reasons. Makes a few connections between events or people. Describes an event but doesn't analyze it.	**A "3" short essay** Has some correct and some incorrect information about history.	**A "3" short essay** Does not have beginning, middle, and end. May respond only to parts of prompt. Makes some sense, but sometimes writing and grammar make it hard to read and understand.
A "2" short essay Often goes off the historical topic and describes events or people that are not correct for the prompt. Lists historical facts with little description.	**A "2" short essay** Has serious historical mistakes.	**A "2" short essay** Has very little organization. Doesn't make much sense, and often writing and grammar make it very hard to read and understand.
A "1" short essay Mentions historical topic with very few facts. Describes mostly events or people that are not correct for the prompt.	**A "1" short essay** Has very little knowledge of history and may have many serious mistakes.	**A "1" short essay** Doesn't make any sense.

Source: California Department of Education, *A Sampler of History-Social Science Assessment, Elementary* (Sacramento: California Learning Assessment System, Department of Education, January 1994), p. 31. Reprinted by permission of the California Department of Education.

Step 1. Objectives/Curriculum Standards.   Determine what students are to learn. Refer to state and school district curriculum guidelines, the curriculum standards published by professional organizations (e.g., the NCSS curriculum standards; the History, Geography, and Civics standards), and to Chapters 3 through 7 in this book. Be sure to think in terms of processes (intellectual and social skills) as well as knowledge (concepts and information). Also consider democratic values and attitudes. Here, for example, is an illustrative list of social studies objectives: By the end of the fifth grade, children should

- know the history, government, and geography of their home town/state
- know why the American colonists declared independence from England
- know the parts and principles of the U.S. Constitution
- understand how and why so many different ethnic groups have come to the United States
- be able to distinguish goods and services, production, and distribution
- be able to compare and contrast the geographic regions of the United States
- be able to develop different kinds of maps to represent the same physical space
- be able to participate competently in discussions of classroom problems

Step 2. Performances.   Determine how children might exhibit or demonstrate what they have learned. Brainstorm performances with colleagues, and ask your students for their ideas. Pianists usually have recitals, artists exhibit their work in galleries, athletes perform in tournaments. What about your students? Above, we discussed two kinds of performances, both using paper-and-pencil formats. Below we will suggest others that do not rely on writing.

Step 3. Criteria/Performance Standards.   Create a relevant scoring rubric. It should provide students, teachers, and parents with indicators, or actual descriptions, of the behaviors at different levels of mastery.

Step 4. Share.   After creating the rubric, discuss it with students. Listen carefully to the questions they raise about these performance criteria and watch for confusion. Typically, teachers will learn enough from this experience to revise the rubric somewhat before trying it. Naturally students will not understand these criteria very well, for they have not yet received instruction on them. The point is to provide students a reasonably clear idea of the target, so they will be able to marshal their efforts accordingly.

Step 5. Try and Revise.   Explain the performance criteria and provide the instruction that should help children develop proficiency. Use what you learn to revise the rubric before using it again.

Checklists

Scoring rubrics come in all sizes and shapes. The simplest are *checklists* that specify how often a desired behavior (the learning target or objective) occurs. A four-point scale might read: "Always," "Usually," "Rarely," "Never." Figures 9–8 and 9–9 present two checklists. The first lists the behaviors called *consideration for others* that were

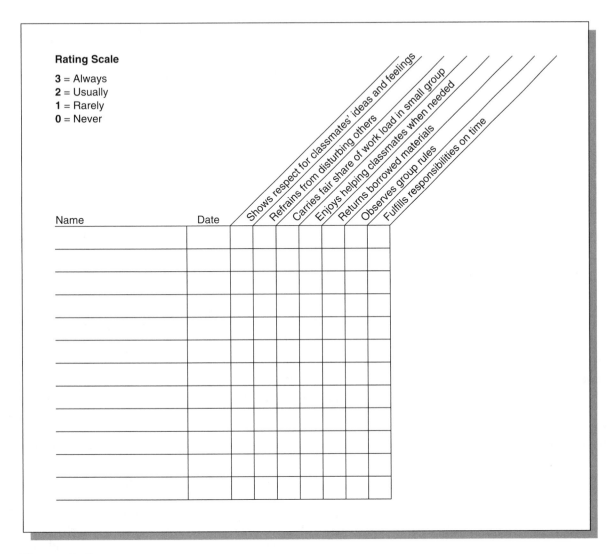

Rating Scale

3 = Always
2 = Usually
1 = Rarely
0 = Never

Figure 9–8
Checklist: Consideration for others

given above under the informal technique "observation." Using a checklist, teachers can assess each student periodically and record the observations directly on the checklist. This is much preferred to relying on memory. At conference time, checklists can be shared with parents.

Children also can be taught to assess their *own* behavior using the same four-point scale. Figure 9–9 shows a self-assessment checklist that can be used during the unit (formatively) as well as at the end (summatively). Both formative and summative assessments can be gathered into the child's portfolio.

Figure 9–9

Student self-assessment checklist

SELF-ASSESSMENT CHECKLIST

DATE _____   NAME _____

In this unit I was able to:	Always	Usually	Rarely	Never
Choose appropriate activities				
Use my work time efficiently				
Work cooperatively with another person				
Use materials from the Resource Center				
Keep my work area clean				
Use suggestions that others gave me				

Comments:

Portfolios

The practice of saving samples of children's work in a portfolio has become popular in recent years.[15] In many schools, it has become the primary means of assessing children's progress both through a single school year and across several years. This practice is similar to that of the parent who cuts notches on the inside of a closet door recording the height of a child at various ages. Both the parent and the teacher know that changes are occurring, but, because of their continuous, day-to-day contact with the child, changes are imperceptible. They need, therefore, a specific example of the child's status at one point to compare with his or her status at a subsequent time. The greater the time interval between the two samples, the greater should be the evidence of change.

Work samples that are saved for this purpose are usually written material and may include a report, a story, a classroom test, an explanation, a booklet, or a research project. The teacher might also want to save a child's map work, artwork done in connection with the social studies, or a small construction project. The tape recorder can also be used to obtain a sample of the child's oral language. For example, children find it revealing and profitable to hear reports privately that they have made to the class at various times during the school year. The same device can be used by the entire class to evaluate their progress in discussions, dramatizations, and similar speaking situations. Care must be taken that the work samples saved are closely related to essential learnings and desired social studies outcomes. There is no need to clutter the portfolio with relatively unimportant work when there are so many learning outcomes that are critically important and in need of continuous assessment.

The portfolio of the child's work can be useful during parent conferences at the regular reporting periods during the school year. Additionally, some teachers send samples of the child's work home from time to time simply to keep the parents informed of the child's progress in school. To make sure the parent has received the material, teachers may want to use a message sheet that asks the parent to comment, sign, and return to the teacher.

We conclude the chapter with two sample portfolios (Figures 9–10 and 9–11). One is a collection of maps the children have made. The collection is tailored to the fourth

Figure 9–10
A map portfolio

Contents of my Map Portfolio   _____

Type of Map	Place	Date/My Comments
landform	our community	_____/_____
landform	North America	_____/_____
political	U.S.	_____/_____
political	counties in our state	_____/_____
shaded relief	playground	_____/_____
shaded relief	state	_____/_____

Figure 9–11

A response to literature portfolio

**Contents of my Social Studies
Literature Response Portfolio**   _____

Response Type	Selection (genre)	Date/My Comments
paraphrase	Paul Revere's Ride (poem)	_____/_____
compose new verse	"Oh Freedom" (song)	_____/_____
memorize	"I Have a Dream" (speech)	_____/_____
book review	*Aekyung's Dream* (book)	_____/_____
explain	The Pledge of Allegiance (oath)	_____/_____
short story	climate of Sahara (textbook)	_____/_____

Figure 9–12
Assessment glossary

Assessment
The process of gathering and interpreting information about students in order to plan instruction and evaluate achievement.

Authentic Assessment
Assessing students' ability to succeed in meaningful (goal-directed, "real-world") tasks. For example, observing students' participation in a discussion of a classroom problem or their use of reference books while drawing maps.

Criteria
The aspects of a performance task that are most important to its successful completion and are used by judges to evaluate the quality of the performance.

Curriculum (or Content) Standards
Statements that describe what students are supposed to learn; they specify the knowledge, skills, and values that students should learn.

Evaluation
The process of making judgments about the quality of a performance.

Grade
A symbol (usually a letter, word, or number) that represents a student's level of achievement of one or more curriculum standards.

Formative Assessment
Assessment conducted during a unit of instruction for the purpose of improving student learning; providing feedback to students to help them improve their performance (see *Summative Assessment*).

Objective
A statement that describes what students are expected to learn; in performance assessment, the behaviors they will learn to perform (see *Criteria*).

(continues)

grade mapping objective that Mrs. Rivera was working with in the vignette at the beginning of this chapter. Mrs. Rivera's children, after much instruction and practice, eventually became proficient at creating three different kinds of maps, and six different places were mapped, ranging from the playground to the North American continent. The second collection contains children's written responses to social studies literature. This collection displays students' ability to integrate literacy skills and social studies subject matter. Note the categories of the students' responsive writing (compose a new verse, paraphrase, etc.) and the variety of social studies literature—from trade books and textbooks to songs.

Finally, we provide an assessment glossary (Figure 9–12) which should assist readers as they work to make sense of the many specialized terms that are used to describe and discuss assessment procedures in social studies.

Figure 9–12, *continued*
Assessment glossary

Performance Assessment
Assessing students' ability to translate knowledge into action—that is, to *demonstrate* their knowledge and skills.

Performance Standards
Levels of attainment that students must reach to receive particular grades, awards, or certificates. They are based on criteria and define what degree of mastery is "good enough."

Portfolio
A collection of a student's school work that can be used to document achievement over time.

Reliability
The extent to which an assessment procedure will produce the same information about a student each time it is used.

Scoring Rubric
A rating scale that describes levels of attainment in relation to an assessment task. Used to score performances and to focus curriculum and instruction.

Summative Assessment
Assessment conducted at the end of a unit of instruction for the purpose of determining a grade (see *Formative Assessment*).

Task
An *authentic* assessment activity within which a student is asked to demonstrate his/her knowledge and skills.

Validity
The extent to which an assessment procedure measures what it claims to measure and is appropriate for making decisions.

Questions for Discussion and Suggested Activities

1. Return to the chapter's opening quote. Select another that in your judgment would be as effective a summary of the chapter, or more so.
2. Determine whether your state has developed a social studies assessment and the grade levels at which it is administered. Find out whether and when individual school districts participate in this assessment and what is done with the results. Also determine whether the school district in which you live or work has developed a social studies assessment.
3. Make a list of each of the assessment samples provided in this chapter. Then discuss how each could be used formatively or summatively.

4. Which two of the seven principles of assessment discussed in this chapter are most important in your judgment?

Principle 1: Assessment is an integral part of curriculum and instruction

Principle 2: Assessments should be directed toward essential learnings

Principle 3: Aim teaching and learning at high standards

Principle 4: Clarify targets early

Principle 5: Gear assessments to authentic tasks

Principle 6: Collect multiple indicators of learning

Principle 7: Teach what is assessed and visa versa

5. Construct a diagram that shows the interaction among the seven principles.
6. Construct two multiple-choice-with-justification items similar to the ones given in Figure 9–6. Focus the first item on an important *event* in American history; focus the second on an important *concept*.
7. Construct a short essay item to assess students' historical reasoning similar to the one in Figure 9–7. Include the four innovative attributes of this assessment that were discussed in the chapter: essential learning, stimulus object, one-sentence directions for writing, and scaffolding prompts.
8. Plan collections of student work (portfolios) similar to the two given at the end of the chapter. Focus one on an important curriculum objective (e.g., valuing diversity; knowing how to use reference books and computer software). Develop another for an entire grade level, for example, "My Second Grade Portfolio." Try to integrate literacy and social studies; that is, help children display their reading and writing *through* social studies subject matter, and visa versa.
9. What advantages and disadvantages can you see in using statewide or even nationwide achievement tests in social studies?
10. Do you think it is fair to evaluate teacher effectiveness on the basis of student achievement? What do you see as the relationship between the two?

Notes

1 National Council for the Social Studies, "A Vision of Powerful Teaching and Learning in the Social Studies: Building Social Understanding and Civic Efficacy." In *Curriculum Standards for Social Studies* (Washington, DC: Author, 1994), 171.
2 Howard Gardner, *Multiple Intelligences: The Theory in Practice* (New York: Basic Books, 1993), 174–5.
3 A good discussion of the three purposes can be found in Lauren Resnick and Daniel P. Resnick, "Assessing the Thinking Curriculum: New Tools for Educational Reform," in *Changing Assessments: Alternative Views of Aptitude, Achievement, and Instruction*, ed. Bernard R. Gifford and Mary C. O'Conner (Boston: Kluwer, 1991), 38–76.
4 Joan Boykoff Baron, "Performance Assessment: Blurring the Edges Among Assessment, Curriculum, and Instruction," in *Assessment in the Service of Instruction*, ed. Audrey B. Champagne, Barbara E. Lovitts, and Betty J. Calinger (Washington, DC: American Association for the Advancement of Science, 1990), 127–48.

5 Grant Wiggins, *Assessing Student Performance: Exploring the Purpose and Limits of Testing* (San Francisco: Jossey-Bass, 1993).

6 National Council for the Social Studies, *Curriculum Standards*, 167.

7 *National Standards for History for Grades K–4: Expanding Children's World in Time and Space* (Los Angeles: National Center for History in the Schools, 1994), 52.

8 Adapted from California Department of Education, *A Sampler of History-Social Science Assessment, Elementary* (Sacramento: California Learning Assessment System, Department of Education, January 1994), 30.

9 Ibid.

10 Vivian Paley, *Wally's Stories* (Cambridge, MA: Harvard University Press, 1981).

11 Sam Allis, "Quick! Name Togo's Capital," *Time* (July 16, 1990): 53.

12 Robert E. Slavin, *Student Team Learning: An Overview and Practical Guide* (Washington, DC: National Education Association, 1986).

13 Steven L. McCollum, *Performance Assessment in the Social Studies Classroom: A How-To Book for Teachers* (Joplin, MO: Chalk Dust Press, 1994), 24.

14 Kristin Palmquist, "Involving Teachers in Elementary History and Social Science Test Development: The California Experiment," *Social Education* 56 (February 1992): 99–101.

15 Dennie Palmer Wolf, "Portfolio Assessment: Sampling Student Work," *Educational Leadership* 46 (April 1989): 4–10; Valencia, Sheila, "A Portfolio Approach to Classroom Reading Assessment: The Whys, Whats, and Hows," *The Reading Teacher* 44 (January 1990): 338–40.

Selected References

Airasian, Peter W. *Classroom Assessment*. 2nd. ed. New York: McGraw-Hill, 1994.

Baron, Joan Boykoff. "Performance Assessment: Blurring the Edges Among Assessment, Curriculum, and Instruction." In *Assessment in the Service of Instruction*, edited by Audrey B. Champagne, Barbara E. Lovitts, and Betty J. Calinger. Washington, DC: American Association for the Advancement of Science, 1990, 127–48.

California Department of Education. *A Sampler of History-Social Science Assessment, Elementary*. Sacramento: California Learning Assessment System, Department of Education, January 1994.

Gardner, Howard. *Multiple Intelligences: The Theory in Practice*. New York: Basic Books, 1993.

McCollum, Steven L. *Performance Assessment in the Social Studies Classroom: A How-To Book for Teachers*. Joplin, MO: Chalk Dust Press, 1994.

National Council for the Social Studies. "A Vision of Powerful Teaching and Learning in the Social Studies: Building Social Understanding and Civic Efficacy." In *Curriculum Standards for Social Studies*. Washington, DC: Author, 1994, 155–77.

Perrone, Vito, ed. *Expanding Student Assessment*. Alexandria, VA: Association for Supervision and Curriculum Development, 1991.

Resnick, Lauren, and Daniel P. Resnick. "Assessing the Thinking Curriculum: New Tools for Educational Reform." In *Changing Assessments: Alternative Views of Aptitude, Achievement, and Instruction*, edited by Bernard R. Gifford and Mary C. O'Conner. Boston: Kluwer, 1991, 38–76.

Social Education, Vol. 56, No. 2, February 1992. This issue has a special section on assessment.

Valencia, Sheila. "A Portfolio Approach to Classroom Reading Assessment: The Whys, Whats, and Hows." *The Reading Teacher* 44 (January 1990): 338–40.

Wiggins, Grant. *Assessing Student Performance: Exploring the Purpose and Limits of Testing*. San Francisco: Jossey-Bass, 1993.

COOPERATIVE LEARNING

If a teacher wants to produce active learning, then groupwork, properly designed, is a powerful tool for providing simultaneous opportunities for all class members.[1]

The process of group interaction is "enormously interesting" to children, observes Elizabeth Cohen. Professor Cohen has learned a great deal about groupwork. She is an acclaimed sociologist and a teacher, and her research projects in schools have centered on managing groupwork in culturally diverse classrooms. There's something about group interaction, she observes, that is almost magical. Yet it is not magic; children can learn procedures that enable them to learn more *and* to cooperate successfully. They act as a team, caring for one another while accomplishing an engaging task.

Students who usually do anything but what they are asked to do become actively involved with their work and are held there by the action of the group.[2]

What causes this dynamic? First, face-to-face interaction helps children pay attention, because it requires a response and other forms of interaction. Second, children care deeply about the judgments of their peers, and this only increases as children move into adolescence. Third, children get assistance from one another in their groups; the teacher, therefore, is not the only "coach" in the classroom. The importance of this last point cannot be overestimated: Students who do not understand the task at hand become quickly disengaged from it, and disengagement from school work is precisely what teachers and parents want very much to avoid. And for good reason: It can be the proverbial straw that breaks the camel's back for a child who is a member of a language or ethnic minority or for any other child who is at risk of school failure.

There are other reasons why groupwork is important, as we shall see in this chapter. Democratic citizenship is certainly one of them. As we saw in Chapter 3, societies that are organized under democratic ideals place special demands on their school systems. Children in these societies need to be educated to be the kind of citizens who can and will share in popular sovereignty. It is not easy work, and it does not appear to come to us naturally. Indeed, our "primary nature" is egocentric.[3] For this reason, all of us to some degree are tempted to let others look after the common good while we tend to our private affairs—to our friends, families, jobs, hobbies, religions, shopping, entertainment, and so on. But the democratic ideal requires people to extend their caring beyond private life to public life—to share in decision making, to join in efforts to reduce crime and poverty, to fight injustice and work for peace, to help prevent delinquency and substance abuse, create public parks and museums, reduce and repair damage to the natural environment, improve public health, and so on. The list is long. Everyone's help is needed. This is the democratic vision.

Most basically, the work of democracy requires citizens who can work well together in task-oriented groups. These may be study groups, such as parents meeting to study the problem of drug selling near schools, or decision-making groups, or both. These are different from play groups, where there is no task *per se*, and they are different from other settings, such as a baseball game or a church service, where people may be physically near one another and may perhaps share materials. Task-oriented groups have work to do, often problem solving, *and their members are mutually dependent on one another for planning the work and getting it done successfully.*

Can a classroom be such a group? It can and it should. Like it or not, classroom life is a social apprenticeship, and the character of that apprenticeship most likely will be carried with the children into later years, especially the work habits that are formed there, the skills and norms of interaction that are fostered, and the attitude toward learning and cooperating that takes shape there. Put differently, children learn by doing, and the kind of doing shapes the kind of learning that will take place. Teachers play the central role in determining the kind of apprenticeship it will be, and there is much they can do to help fashion it to be an apprenticeship for cooperation and democracy. This involves structuring tasks that require students to make decisions on their own, to use one another as resources, and to plan and carry out work.

Consider two additional reasons why people need to learn to work well together. First, the business community in the United States increasingly is demanding employees who can function on teams—together identifying problems worth solving, setting priorities for them, planning, integrating diverse ideas, dividing the work load, and building on one another's contributions. Second, the population of North America is becoming rapidly more diverse racially, ethnically, and linguistically. All of this requires contemporary students—students of the 21st century—to overcome initial prejudices rapidly, to learn to appreciate people who are culturally different, and to build healthy, working relationships.

Creating a Positive Climate for Human Relations

An emotionally supportive atmosphere is one that is characterized by trust and by evidence that individuals care about each other. When a child volunteers, "Robin's group had more to do than the rest of us. They should have more time to finish," the observer senses that he or she is in a caring environment. Or when a minor classroom accident results in damage to material or broken equipment and the teacher treats the incident as an accident, one concludes that the teacher values human beings more than things. Teachers who develop comfortable classroom environments are concerned with a broad range of educational outcomes, including those that relate to the emotional and social development of children, in addition to attending to subject matter and skills goals. The classroom conditions that establish the *setting* in which children learn the basics of human relations is sometimes referred to as the *hidden curriculum*.

A Caring Environment

The most significant characteristic of a desirable classroom climate is the absence of hostility between children and the teacher and among the children themselves. Put positively, a desirable classroom atmosphere is one in which caring, kindness, encouragement, and support are fully present. This means many things, of course, but it includes modeling for children what it looks and sounds like to care for others, children and adults and pets alike. It means helping children to see the origin of classroom rules in caring. As well, it means "attributing the best motive" to children—assuming that a child's intentions were good even when she or he has done something bad. Making this assumption is a basic act of kindness on the teacher's part, and generally it should be communicated to the child directly. For example, the teacher might take aside a student who has cheated, beginning not with a reprimand or punishment, though these may well come, but with caring, saying, "I know you want to do well." Likewise, a student who has called another student a cruel name can be taken aside, and the conversation can begin with, "I know you mean to treat others as you want to be treated yourself."[4]

To clarify these ideas further, consider the eight sets of contrasting teacher behaviors in Figure 10–1.

Getting Started with Cooperative Groups

Committee work or small-group enterprises are effective instructional procedures in the social studies and have many values for children. It is in the small group that the children get experience with and develop skill in group processes. These experiences should begin in a limited way even as early as the kindergarten. In block play, for example, the teacher can let some children choose the things they wish to build with blocks. Some will want to build an airport; some, a house; others, a post office; others, a supermarket; and so on. The teacher can let each of these children choose two other children to help build the project. The children proceed with the building and, when it is completed, tell the class or their teacher a story about their building. Early experiences in such block play will consist mainly of parallel play—three children may be building an airport but each is working independently of the other two. As the year progresses, there will be more evidence of cooperative endeavor. Children become more conscious of what others in their group are doing and will plan their own contribution in terms of the other children and the group goal.

A good way to familiarize primary-grade children with small-group work is to have committees responsible for various housekeeping duties in the classroom. José's committee has the responsibility of keeping the library table neat, Paul's committee is in charge of the game shelf, Long's committee is responsible for the care of the aquarium, and Denisha's committee keeps the coat corner orderly. Membership on these committees can be changed from time to time to include all the children in the class. Such experiences will help prepare children for the committee work that is done as a part of the instructional program.

Small-group enterprises in the primary grades need careful supervision and direction. The goals or purposes of the group should be well defined, concrete, and easily understood. Materials needed for the group to do its work must be immediately at hand. Rules and responsibilities of working on committees should be discussed, explained, and posted conspicuously in the room. Groupwork skills develop slowly and

Figure 10–1

Dimensions of the hidden curriculum

Practices and Procedures that Tend to Increase Hostility in a Classroom

1. *Excessively competitive situations* Fair competition in classrooms is highly desirable. It can stimulate good work, motivate children to do their best, and help children learn the graces associated with winning and losing. It becomes undesirable when it is of the "dog-eat-dog" variety where each child is pitted against every other child whether the competitive situation is fair or unfair.

2. *Negative statements by the teacher*
Ridicule, sarcasm, criticism, and negative and tension-producing statements made by a teacher to children invariably lead to hostility, emotional disturbance, selfishness, fear, and criticism of others. Examples:

> "I wish you would start acting like fourth-graders instead of kindergartners."
>
> "Someone is whispering again, and I guess you all know who it is."
>
> "Most fifth-grade classes could understand this, but I am not sure about you."
>
> "Why don't you listen when I give directions? None of you seems to know how to listen."

3. *Disregard for individual differences*
Classrooms where some children are made to feel "this place is not for me" contribute much toward breeding hostility in children. Such rooms are characterized by one level of acceptable performance applied to all, uniform assignments, one system of reward, and great emphasis on verbal, intellectual performance.

4. *Rigid schedule and pressure* A rigid time schedule and constant pressure associated with "hurry up," "finish your work," "you will be late," or stopping lessons exactly on time whether completed or not can create insecurity in children that leads to hostility. A class that is always "one jump behind the teacher" is likely to be one in which children blame others for their failure to finish, invent excuses for themselves, and seek scapegoats.

Practices and Procedures that Tend to Decrease Hostility in a Classroom

1. *Positive Interdependence* The teacher often structures learning activities so that "students perceive that they can reach their learning goals if and only if the other students in the learning group also reach their goals"*. This is the most basic element of cooperative learning, and it helps children learn to care about and support one another's progress.

2. *Positive statements by the teacher*
Friendly, constructive statements by the teacher tend to reduce tension and hostility in the classroom. Examples:

> "We will all want to listen carefully in order not to miss anything Sue is going to tell us."
>
> "All of us did our work so well yesterday during our work period. Do you suppose we can do as well today?"
>
> "It is really fun for all of us when you bring such interesting things for sharing."
>
> "It's nice to have Jason and Kendra back with us again. The boys and girls were hoping you would come back today."

3. *Recognition of and response to individual differences* In such classrooms, all children are challenged at a level commensurate with their abilities and in ways that are mindful of cultural and linguistic differences. The teacher strives to see *all* children's gifts and talents.

4. *Relaxed, comfortable pace* Good teachers working with young children maintain a flexible schedule and will not place undue pressures on children. They will have a plan and a schedule, yet will not be compulsive in adhering to it. They will deviate from their plan now and then in the interests of the needs of the boys and girls they teach.

* David W. Johnson, Roger T. Johnson, Edythe J. Holubec, and Patricia Roy, *Circles of Learning: Cooperation in the Classroom*, (Alexandria, VA: Association for Supervisions and Curriculum Development, 1984), 2.

5. *Highly directive teaching practices* Teachers who must make every decision themselves, give all the assignments, and allow for very little participation on the part of children in the life of the classroom may encourage feelings of hostility. Such practices usually mean that teachers refer to the class as "my children," or in addressing them, say, "I want you to . . . ," or more subtly, "Miss So-and-so wasn't very proud of her class this morning."

6. *Lack of closeness between teacher and children* Some teachers feel they must "keep children in their places," meaning they must remain socially distant from them. This leads to a cold relationship between the children and the teacher, causing the children to feel that the teacher lacks affection and warmth for them.

7. *Lack of satisfying emotional experiences* Some classrooms do not provide opportunities to express positive affect. Everything is deadly serious business—work, work, work. Even the music, art story time, or dramatic activities are made to seem like work. Little time is spent on teaching children to enjoy one another, feel the inner joy that comes from a good poem or music selection, or express their feelings in some art medium.

8. *Rules are about obeying*—Some teachers have elaborate systems for dealing with violations of classroom rules, but fail to capitalize on them to teach children about caring. Obedience becomes the sole aim, rather than understanding the purpose of the rule.

5. *Student involvement in planning and managing the class* Giving children some opportunity to plan and manage the affairs of the classroom does much to develop feelings of "we-ness" of a democratic community. Children under such circumstances are less inclined to want to think of ways to disrupt the teacher's orderly room but will work hard to make "our" room a good place to work.

6. *Warm and friendly relationship between teacher and children* One of the basic needs of children is that of love and affection. They need it in their homes, in their playgroups, and in their schools. The feeling that children will not respect the teacher who is friendly with them is incorrect. They are likely to respect the teacher more who they feel is a "human being" capable of warm personal relationships with others. This is a professional relationship, however, and teachers are advised *against* trying to develop a peer relationship with the children they teach.

7. *Many opportunities for pleasurable emotional experiences* Teachers can reduce tensions that build up in children during the course of classroom life by providing opportunities for the release of these tensions through various emotional experiences. Children have the opportunity to express their feelings orally, in writing, or through art forms. They talk together and enjoy one another's company. They prepare skits, do creative dramatics, and role play situations to help get the feelings of others. All these activities tend to reduce feelings of hostility.

8. *Rules are about caring*—Teachers can use rule violations to help children appreciate that we have rules because we care for one another. We do not call other children names because it hurts their feelings; we don't write on desks and tables out of respect for others who use them; we tell the truth because others deserve sincerity, not lies; we try to be punctual because we care for those who are waiting.

gradually and require practice, as do any other skills. The skills of groupwork can be learned only by working in groups.

In the middle and upper grades, small-group work becomes an increasingly greater part of the social studies instructional program. At these grade levels, each group member can be given an assigned task to help the group achieve its goal. Small groups are used to prepare reports; discuss issues; plan activities; do construction, art, or dramatic activities; write plays, biographies, and short stories, gather resources for the class; interview community resource persons; and so on. Through instruction and experience, children will learn that the success of the group depends on the initiative and cooperation of individuals within the group.

There will be many occasions when the class will be divided into small work groups. These are task oriented; they are formed to do things that really need doing. In this way, groupwork can avoid artificiality. Groups are not formed merely to have children practice cooperative groupwork; *they are formed to get some sort of work done.* Groupwork therefore can be relatively short lived. A committee may be assigned the task of finding out how bridges are built or to create a map of a nearby river system. When the committee has completed its task and reported to the larger group, it can be dissolved.

When attempting for the first time to organize small-group work, the teacher may find the guidelines in the feature "Forming Academic Committees" helpful. Note that it is not necessary to place all students in small groups at the same time, at least not when the teacher is just learning to manage small-group instruction. Instead, we recommend a gradual, diagnostic approach. This permits the teacher and students to "get their feet wet" little by little, all the while observing group dynamics and strengths and weaknesses in the children's cooperative behaviors.

How might these guidelines look in action? In the following example, a teacher appoints a committee to help introduce and question a classroom guest.

The children in Mr. Shigaki's class have been involved in a career awareness study and are going to have resource persons visit their classroom. The children have indicated careers they would like to have included. Mr. Shigaki has asked four children to meet him in the rear of the classroom and is now speaking to them.

"Because the four of you are particularly interested in learning about computer science careers, I am asking that you take responsibility for introducing Ms. Timms tomorrow. You will have to select one person to do the introducing. The others can help by suggesting things that should be said about her in the introduction. Also, all of you should help develop some questions to ask her after her presentation. Remember one of our objectives is to find out what kind of training and skills computer scientists need and what opportunities there are in that field. Is there anything else you think you will need to prepare to be the host group tomorrow?"

One member of the group asks if they were to thank the visitor for coming.

"Yes. Good point! I'm glad you thought of that, Mark. You will need to select someone to thank Ms. Timms. Anything else?" (No further suggestions are offered.)

"I guess you are ready to begin your work then," says Mr. Shigaki. "Lisa, would you act as the group leader and report to me when your group is finished planning?"

Mr. Shigaki then leaves the group to its task and supervises the remainder of the class who have been working on individual assignments.

FORMING ACADEMIC COMMITTEES

1. Defer small-group work until the management of the class has been well established and until the work habits, interpersonal skills, and special needs of individual children are known.

2. Select children who already have good interpersonal skills for your first academic committee. Keep the group small—never more than five children.

3. Assign the committee an academic task that is simple and well defined, one that the group is certain to accomplish successfully.

4. Have the remainder of the class engage in individual assignments while the teacher is giving guidance and direction to the smaller group. Either designate a leader for the small group or have the children choose a leader. Explain the nature of their assigned task, and begin to discuss some of their special responsibilities when working in a small group.

5. Have resource materials available for the children. Later on, as they become accustomed to working in groups, they will be able to secure needed materials themselves.

6. Meet with the small group every day for a few minutes before they begin work and again at the end of their work period to make sure things are moving along as planned. If possible, have them make a progress report to the other, larger group during the summary and evaluation that should come at the close of each social studies period.

7. Give students specific help and suggestions in how to organize their work and how to report what they are doing.

8. Have their report to the class be short, concise, and interesting. Have members of the group explain to the class how they did their work as a group. Begin calling attention to some of the responsibilities of persons working collaboratively in small groups.

9. Follow the same procedure with another group of children as soon as possible. Gradually include other children, selecting some who have had previous experience in groupwork and some who have not. Observe carefully the children who need close supervision and those who are responsible and work well in groups.

10. After all the children have had an opportunity to work in a small group under close supervision, more than one group can work at one time. Eventually, the entire class should be able to work in small groups simultaneously. When this is attempted, it should be preceded by a review of the standards of groupwork, objectives should be clearly defined beforehand, and a careful evaluation should follow.

Managing Cooperative Groupwork

Let us turn from forming the occasional committee that accomplishes one or more tasks to simultaneous involvement of all children in small-group instruction. First, we consider goals, then group size, group composition, and alternative small-group structures.

Goals

It would be reasonable to assume that if children are given instruction and have many guided experiences in cooperative groups, they are likely to develop group interaction skills and the disposition to be cooperative. But do cooperative learning strategies also affect a child's overall academic achievement? The answer is a confident "Yes": "Results indicate that cooperative learning experiences tend to promote higher achievement than do competitive and individualistic learning experiences."[5] These results apply to all age levels and subject areas, and for all sorts of academic tasks, from simple retention to concept learning and problem solving. Kristin Gruber, a third grade teacher in Minnesota, tells this success story:

Andy, a low-achieving student who received LD services, was failing social studies, health, and language early in the year. He needed constant supervision just to stay on task, paid little attention to classroom discussions, and seldom completed assignments. With a cooperative group to support and encourage him, however, Andy completed many assignments during class and brought back homework consistently. . . . By mid-February, he was passing every subject; and he was able to maintain his grades for the rest of the year.[6]

Why is this so? Researchers provide interesting arguments that center on the main ingredients of cooperative learning: positive interdependence and individual student accountability. Positive interdependence means that group goals cannot be attained unless each member of the group does his or her part; individual accountability means that the group's success depends not only on group members doing their parts but *learning*. Indeed, they will be held accountable for learning: Grades go to individual students, not groups. Add to these another attribute of cooperative learning—discussion. Discussion is a rich stew of face-to-face talking, listening, responding, paraphrasing, and questioning. Positive interdependence makes all this necessary. Putting thoughts into words requires students to think about the task at hand and to clarify what they mean; trying to understand what others mean involves still more talking, thinking, and clarifying. Further, discussion often produces disagreements—healthy social and academic conflicts—which, when managed skillfully by the teacher and students, promote deeper levels of both academic learning and interpersonal development. Skillful teachers do not squelch these disagreements, since they foster higher-order thinking and help to make learning exciting.[7] As well, disagreements flourish in democratic civic life; students must therefore learn to deal with them.

Closely related to discussion and controversy is still another reason why cooperative learning improves academic achievement—it promotes what researchers call *engaged time* or *time on task*. Cooperative groupwork generally helps children to be more engaged in the task (more attentive and involved) than does seatwork. The main drawback of seatwork is that children are working on their own with little or no guidance, and this allows them to drift far from the assigned task or to attempt it without understanding its purpose and without using helpful strategies. This is especially unfortunate when we consider that seatwork often consumes over half the available instructional time in both primary and intermediate grades, and, ironically, is prescribed most often to children who already are doing poorly in school! Elizabeth Cohen sums up this problem:

Positive interdependence means that each member of this team does her part.

Choosing a method of classroom organization that leaves the student who rarely succeeds in schoolwork quite alone may indeed be the root cause of the observed disengagement on the part of low-achieving students in seatwork settings. These students are receiving very little information on the purpose of their assignment, on how to complete it successfully, on how they are doing, or on how they could be more successful. The tasks themselves are rarely sufficiently interesting to hold the students' attention.[8]

Cooperative learning promotes active student involvement in learning and therefore helps teachers to spend wisely the most valuable aid they have—time.

Group Size and Composition

The size of a small group affects its achievement both of academic knowledge and cooperative skills. If groups are too large, there may be duplication of responsibilities, less opportunity for individuals to carry their share of the group effort, difficulty achieving face-to-face interaction, and a tendency for some members to fade out of the group activity. Also, the larger the group, the more skillful group members must be with cooperative behaviors. On the other hand, if groups are too small, there may be insufficient division of labor to warrant groupwork and too few opportunities to cooperate. In general, however, groups should be kept small—from two to five children, with four to five as the optimal size. When teaching groupwork skills, teachers often begin by placing children in pairs to practice particular skills, such as using names, making eye contact with the speaker, and asking for help. Pairs can then be combined into groups of four.

Group size influences the sort of academic work that can be accomplished. Structured Academic Controversy, discussed later in this chapter, requires two pairs of children in groups of four; meanwhile, STAD (also discussed later) has no required group size. The number of students in a Jigsaw group determines the number of topics that can be studied or, when writing original biographies, the number of chapters in the book students produce (see Chapter 12).

Our discussion of goals emphasized learning cooperative behaviors and academic achievement. Let us consider a third goal, which bears particularly on group composition: positive intergroup relations among students of different ethnic and racial backgrounds in integrated classrooms. Anyone who has visited a desegregated school knows that friendships across ethnic groups did not automatically follow putting diverse children together in the same school or classroom. To the contrary, especially in the upper grades, children of the same ethnic group, whatever it is, often stay together, playing together at recess and eating together at lunch.

A good deal of research shows that when diverse groups of youngsters work together to attain a group goal, positive feelings are obtained: they begin to like and trust one another, more often choose to be with one another during free time, and in general grow in their respect for one another. Of course, a teacher cannot expect these results as a consequence only of placing diverse students together in a small group and structuring a cooperative task for them; rather, students must be prepared for groupwork. They must learn the skills and norms of cooperation. But placing them in diverse groups is a precondition—it at least provides the *opportunity* to tackle the goal of positive intergroup understanding.

Thus, the cardinal principle of group composition is to achieve the greatest mix possible given the student population. A teacher should achieve this mix using whatever student variables are available—academic record, interpersonal skill, gender, ethnicity, disability, language, race, and social class. In this way, small groups are as heterogeneous as the whole class. Ability grouping is ruled out because it minimizes rather than maximizes the mix.

The teacher may use one or more of several methods to form heterogeneous student groups:

1. *Work, not play.* Do not allow friends to choose one another for small-group work. Friends tend to play rather than work when placed in the same group, and groupwork should be thought of in terms of work rather than play.[9]

2. *Random assignment.* With a brand-new class, a teacher might randomly assign students to small groups of four to five students each. Forming groups alphabetically is a good way, and it should result in mixed groups. Look over the resulting lists of group members and make any adjustments needed to achieve a greater mix of gender and ethnicity.

3. *Purposeful mixing.* Once a teacher is more familiar with students' work habits, interpersonal skills, and past academic achievement, groups can be purposefully mixed. Some teachers have good success simply by mixing within each group students who are strong and weak on each of these characteristics. Students with poor interpersonal skills and/or poor academic records should not be placed together any more than friends or highly successful students.

4. *Special helper.* A variation on purposeful mixing is to select one or more students for each group who will serve as a special helper. The help needed will depend on the

kind of work the teacher has structured for the groups. For example, if groups are to construct a papier-mâché map of the United States, each working on a different region, the teacher might identify students who are good with paper products (mixing, gluing, painting) or at creating map legends. One of these helpers is placed in each small group. If the teacher has decided that groups of four children each are to write historical fiction about Harriet Tubman or James Madison, with each student working on a different "chapter," it will help to have someone who likes to sketch in each group. It will also help to have a strong planner in each group—someone who can help the group decide on four different chapter topics.

In general, social and academic resources that can come in handy are reading, writing, planning, decision making (comparing alternatives), notetaking, brainstorming, operating tape recorders or cameras, observing detail, using the library, creating time lines, using reference books, creative dramatics, assisting students with disabilities, interviewing, building with cardboard, drawing, taking surveys, and so on.

5. *Index cards*. Write the name of each student on an index card, strip of construction paper, or Popsicle stick. Decide on the task to which groupwork will be devoted and identify the special help that will be needed. Identify the special helpers, putting at least one in each group, and sort the other students into each group aiming for the greatest mix possible with regard to interpersonal skills, ethnicity, language, academic achievement, gender, and so on. (The teacher can use a random method, such as shuffling the deck of name cards, once special helpers have been selected.)

6. *Duration*. A cooperative group exists until the cooperative task is completed. Rather than reforming groups for the next group task, the same group usually remains together for the purpose of further developing its cooperative skills. Groups should stay together long enough to make progress on the interpersonal problems that inevitably arise. While the group remains the same, the task, of course, changes (e.g., from making maps to writing a biography of Rosa Parks). A new task is an opportunity for the teacher to select a different set of special helpers. The teacher should keep searching for everyone's special talents so that different helpers can be used on each new task.

Alternative Frameworks for Cooperative Tasks

There are many different ways to structure groupwork, all with positive interdependence, individual accountability, face-to-face interaction, and discussion. Teachers often invent their own ways and share them with one another. Teachers just beginning to experiment with cooperative learning may prefer STAD (Student Teams Achievement Division). When teacher and students are ready, they may want to experiment with Jigsaw or Structured Academic Controversy. We discuss each in turn.

STAD

STAD has the students listening to the teacher present information—except that a cooperative task is tagged onto the end, thus adding the advantages of cooperative learning to the disadvantages of the teacher talking *at* students.[10] Students are placed in groups before the lesson begins. First, the teacher explains the purpose and rationale of the lesson, then presents needed information. (In a lesson on map legends, for example, the teacher takes thirty minutes or so to display three different maps, explaining the design and function of the legend on each.) Second, the teacher gives the groups one handout with questions *and* another handout with responses. Each group receives only one copy of each so that group members must share materials. Each group is given twenty minutes to accomplish their task: to understand *why* the answers are correct. Third, students are given a short quiz over the questions and answers, and the group with the highest average score (or that shows the greatest improvement over the last quiz average) is rewarded with special certificates and honorable mention in the class newsletter. This constitutes one round of STAD.

Jigsaw

We encountered Jigsaw in Chapter 7 as a method for incorporating cooperative learning into concept formation. In that example, for this is the essence of the Jigsaw method, students are members of two groups—the usual group of four or five students, which in Jigsaw serves as the students' home base, plus an additional "expert group."[11] Typically, the teacher divides the task into four or five parts. In concept formation, each part is an example of the concept children are to form, or the task might simply be to comprehend a chapter on Native Americans in the textbook, and the parts are the chapter's four lessons. Whatever the task, each member of the home team is assigned to work on one of the four parts, but he or she is not alone (Figure 10–2). All students from the different groups who are assigned to the same part join together to work in expert groups. This may require anywhere from thirty minutes to a week or more, depending on the task. Eventually, experts return to their home teams, where they serve as discussion leaders for their teammates. Following this, student understanding of the *whole* task is assessed, and the teacher rewards the home team that has the highest average score, or that has improved the most, or the one that demonstrated the best use of cooperative skills. This is one round of Jigsaw.

Structured Academic Controversy

We would not want to let the opportunities afforded by cooperative learning to restructure the *ways* we teach social studies cause us to ignore the chance it provides to reconsider *what* we teach in social studies.[12] Structured academic controversy, developed by the Johnson brothers, provides just this chance.[13] It asks teachers to perceive the academic controversy in whatever social studies knowledge they are wanting students to learn and to engage students in that controversy. Rather than teaching about the protection of endangered species, for example, as though the topic were devoid of debate, teachers can help their children to participate in that debate. Other examples are the American Revolution, deciding whether a Bill of Rights was necessary, developing cafeteria rules, deciding who is responsible for making new students feel welcome, and current events issues involving public health (such as placing nutritional information on food labels) and advertising on children's television programs. The study of each of these topics can be designed so that the disagreements at their center are made the object of study. Doing so boosts both the intellectual rigor and the excitement of social studies lessons. Structured Academic Controversy makes such study manageable, even for the beginning teacher and for very young students, and it relies on groupwork.

First, the teacher helps students gather background information on the topic; for example, the American Revolution. The textbook itself usually provides at least some of

Figure 10–2
Jigsaw group assignments

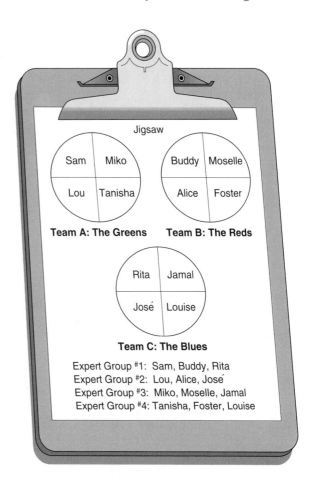

Jigsaw

Team A: The Greens   Team B: The Reds

Sam | Miko
Lou | Tanisha

Buddy | Moselle
Alice | Foster

Team C: The Blues

Rita | Jamal
José | Louise

Expert Group #1: Sam, Buddy, Rita
Expert Group #2: Lou, Alice, José
Expert Group #3: Miko, Moselle, Jamal
Expert Group #4: Tanisha, Foster, Louise

this background. Supplementary resources, such as primary documents and children's literature, can also be assembled. In the second phase, each four-person group is divided into two pairs, and each pair studies one side of the debate. On the American Revolution, one pair would study the arguments that eventually lead to the colonies declaring their independence, and the other would learn loyalist arguments. Third, pairs present their perspectives to one another. Fourth, as a test of their listening and questioning, the pairs reverse perspectives, giving now the argument of the other side. In the fifth phase, genuine discussion begins as the two pairs join together for the purpose of reaching a group consensus.

Identifying and Teaching Cooperative Skills

Teachers who have experimented with small-group instruction and found it frustrating commonly feel that groupwork breaks down either because some children within the groups do most of the work or because the children waste time and accomplish little or nothing. This is an indication that the children have not yet developed the prerequisite

Teachers must teach the cooperative skills they expect students to display.

skills for successful cooperative endeavors. If children are only given the *opportunity* to work in groups without being *prepared* to do so, there is little reason to expect them to function effectively in these groups.

Children need to be taught how to behave during cooperative groupwork so that they can function reasonably well without the teacher's direct supervision. Of course, this is not only a matter of teaching the needed interpersonal skills; group members also need the appropriate academic skills for completing the assigned task. If group members are expected to write a report together, they will require instruction on report writing and have some general writing experience. This instruction does not need to occur in advance; providing it during the action, when it is needed, can be more effective. In summary, the nature of the task assigned to a small group should be consistent with the preparation they have received.

In this section, we offer suggestions on which skills need to be taught and suggest strategies for teaching them. Two kinds of skills are highlighted—skills for getting started as a cooperative group and skills for functioning in a cooperative group.

Getting Started

Tell children both the purpose and rationale for having them learn to work cooperatively in small groups. Teachers have found it helpful to provide examples of real-world situations, both civic and job related, where people need to function well in groups with others who not only are not their friends but may even be strangers (town meetings, fire departments, fast-food restaurants, hospital emergency rooms, and so on), and, whether strangers or not, disagreements are common.

Children typically need to be taught behaviors that help them to do the following:

- move into groups efficiently
- stay with the group during group time
- use quiet voices
- make everyone feel welcome
- state and restate the assignment
- set or call attention to time frame

Functioning

When groups are practicing the skills of getting started, it is especially important that the task be kept short and simple. Once some progress is made in these skills areas, the teacher should instruct the class on some of the behaviors crucial to a group working well together when the task is more complex. These should be posted in the room and referred to often. Examples include:

- plan how best to proceed
- encourage everyone to participate
- use one another's names
- face the speaker and make eye contact
- avoid putdowns
- ask for help when you need it
- ask questions
- be a good sport
- offer to explain, clarify, or summarize
- listen carefully when others are speaking
- paraphrase another's statements
- talk openly about disagreements
- criticize ideas, not people
- cheerfully take the jobs the group wants you to do
- suggest new ideas when the group's motivation is low*

Teaching Cooperative Skills

Practicing any cooperative skill requires that learners understand the skill. Otherwise, they are not really *practicing* anything. An effective skill-teaching procedure was given in Chapter 7.

The T-chart (Figure 10–3), is another popular method for helping children understand a cooperative skill.[14] The teacher writes the name of a skill on the chalkboard and creates two columns beneath it, one for a group of adjectives describing what the skill *looks* like, another for phrases that exemplify what the skill *sounds* like. Children are then asked to generate a list for each.

Once a skill is understood well enough to make practice worthwhile, practice should begin in earnest. Some teachers find role playing to be a valuable technique in teaching the skills needed in small-group work. By selecting four to five children to serve as

---

* See Johnson et al., *Circles of Learning*, for an elaborate list of skills.

Figure 10–3

A sample T-chart used to help children understand a cooperative skill.

SKILL: Encouraging Participation	
Looks Like	*Sounds Like*
smiles	"What is your idea?"
eye contact	"Excellent!"
thumbs up	"That's a good idea!"
pat on the back	"I'd like to hear what you think."

group members, the teacher can demonstrate to the class what it means to "help everyone become a part of the group" or any of the standards that have been discussed. When the role playing is completed, the remainder of the class can analyze the situation to determine why the group was functioning well or poorly. It is helpful to have children observe certain specific elements in the situation to be presented. For example, they might try to answer such questions as these:

1. What did individual members do to help the group do its job? What did members do that did not help the group?
2. What did the leader do to help the group get its job done?
3. How did the group find out exactly what it was to do?
4. Did the group use good resources in solving its problems?
5. Did the group seem to be working together as a team? Why or why not?
6. How could the group be helped to do its job better?

Following the role playing, the class can discuss the situation in terms of the specific points being observed. It may then be helpful to replay all or a portion of the situation to help children appreciate the forces at work in group situations. With young children it may be desirable to have an older group demonstrate such things as a domineering leader, an uncooperative group member, a member who wants only the choice tasks, the noncontributor, the irresponsible leader, the member who must always have his or her own way, the member who talks too much, and so on. In teaching groupwork skills, the teacher will want to do more than talk about what should or should not be done. Children really need an opportunity to see and experience "how it works" as well as an opportunity to experiment and try their hand at doing productive groupwork. Role playing can do much to sensitize them to the various subtleties and forces that come into play in small-group situations.

Increasing numbers of schools have videocassette recorders available for classroom use, and this equipment can be useful in teaching collaborative skills. The teacher can videotape a group role playing certain skills needed for productive small-group work. The tape can then be used for study and analysis of the behavior required if small groups are to be effective in their work. The videotape provides a way to demonstrate over and over again the essential characteristics of groupwork. This teaching procedure is widely used in teaching athletes, and greater use could be made of it in regular classrooms today.

Rewarding Groupwork Appropriately

Part of the reason that groupwork is at times ineffective is because it is not rewarded as generously as are the academic aspects of the classroom work. This stems from the teacher's attitude toward the value of group activities. If the rewards (recognition, praise, value statements, reports to parents, grades) go only to those who do well in paper-and-pencil activities, children rightly conclude that group activities do not count much in the entire scheme of things. Groupwork will be enhanced if the teacher regards it as an important part of the instructional program and rewards appropriately the children who have done commendable work in group endeavors.

Debriefing

While rewarding good skill use is necessary, it is just as important to talk in detail with students about the progress they are making. All groupwork should involve the deliberate practice of one or more cooperative skills; therefore, all groupwork sessions should be followed by a debriefing, in which students are asked to reflect on how often cooperative skills were used, how well they were used, and what skills especially need attention.

Giving Oral Reports

Teams and expert groups will be giving oral reports to the entire class from time to time in the normal course of groupwork. Oral reports also are commonly used to share information obtained through individual research and study. Whether the report represents work done as part of a group or inquiry conducted individually, it serves the purpose of bringing to the group the information and ideas that were acquired, as well as teaching children how to organize, plan, and present a report.

It is the responsibility of the teacher to take an active part in assisting the child with the preparation of the report. This includes helping select a suitable topic, suggesting references, helping with its organization, and suggesting visual devices to use. The teacher should find a few minutes a day or two in advance of the presentation to sit down with the youngster and review what is to be included in the report. Once prepared, the child should be left alone while the report is being given unless help is specifically requested.

Only a few reports should be scheduled on the same day. It is impossible for children to sustain any degree of interest if they must listen to a dozen or fifteen reports consecutively. A better procedure is to have two or three reports given at a time and to spread the reporting over a period of several days.

The following are suggested as alternatives to the traditional oral and written reports.

1. Dramatize an incident, sequence, or situation relating to the topic and incorporate essential data to be communicated in the dramatization.
2. Use children's own drawn illustrations, charts, and graphs as the basis for a presentation or use illustrations found in newspapers, magazines, or other sources.
3. Pretend to be a tour guide taking the class through the area studied.
4. Use the overhead projector for visual aids in a presentation.
5. Role play the part of a newscaster making an on-the-spot report.

6. Interview a classmate who is role playing the part of someone who is an expert on the topic under study.
7. Collect pictures, arrange them in sequence, and use them as the basis for a report.
8. Write a diary or letter that might have been written by someone in an earlier period.
9. Use artifacts or realia as the basis for a report.
10. Prepare and explain a bulletin board display or diorama.
11. Prepare a narration for a filmstrip.
12. Do an original narration for a film or videotape with sound turned off.
13. Write news stories that might have been appropriate to a particular period, or prepare and publish a single issue of a newspaper that might have appeared in some historical period.
14. Tape record a presentation for playback to the class, which frees the speaker to point to parts of a chart or model or to show photos or slides. In this way the child is accompanying him- or herself.

Teaching and Using Discussion Techniques

We saw in Chapter 3 that discussion is a fundamental democratic process. We have seen in the present chapter that discussion is a key ingredient in cooperative learning. Its value lies chiefly in the fact that it represents a type of intellectual teamwork, resting on the principle that the pooled knowledge, ideas, and feelings of several persons have greater merit than those of a single individual. Without discussion a student may never grasp the fact, for example, that there are multiple points of view and opinions on a problem, not just his or her own. Furthermore, this student may never have the opportunity to practice the most fundamental work of popular sovereignty—talking with others about common problems and reaching a decision about what to do. In this section, we look more closely at discussion, concentrating on large-group, roundtable, panel discussions, and buzz groups.

Involving Every Child

Because the strength of discussion is obtained from the information and viewpoint of many members of the group, it is necessary that most members of the class participate. It is a thinking-together process that breaks down if one member or group dominates it. It is the responsibility of the teacher to encourage the more reluctant children to participate. Although there cannot be a single answer to the question of what to do with the child who dominates the discussion, skillful teachers usually take care of the matter with a statement such as "Jack, you have given us so many good ideas today, and I know you have many more good suggestions, but we want to find out what some of the others think would be a good way to. . . . "

Another strategy for dealing with students who dominate discussions is to use student observers. One or two children are asked to observe the day's discussion. Their task is straightforward—to keep track of who talks and how much. Because student observers learn a good deal about discussion, the domineering student can purposefully be placed in this role. One first-grade teacher placed such a student in the role of student observer, instructing him to gather data without talking.

He gathered data on who talked and did a good job, noting that one student had done quite a bit of talking in the group while another had talked very little. The next day when he was back in the group and no longer the observer, he started to talk, clamped his hand over his mouth, and glanced at the new observer. He knew what behavior was being observed, and he didn't want to be the only one with marks for talking. The teacher said he may have listened for the first time all year.[15]

Roundtable Discussions

A *roundtable discussion* usually involves a small number of persons, perhaps no fewer than three and no more than eight. It requires someone to serve as a moderator to introduce the members of the discussion group, present the problem to be discussed, and keep the discussion moving. The leader's role is one of guiding the group rather than one of dominating it. A relaxed atmosphere needs to prevail, and the presentations are conversational rather than oratorical.

Roundtable discussions can be used in the middle and upper grades by having a group of children discuss a problem before the remainder of the class or by dividing the class into several small discussion groups that function without an audience. It is perhaps best to use this procedure with one group at a time, either with or without an audience, until the children have learned how to participate in discussions of this type. It will be necessary for the teacher to introduce the procedure to the class and to explain and demonstrate its purposes and the way it works. Such points as the following need to be emphasized:

1. *Responsibilities of the moderator*—To be informed on the topic to be discussed, introduce the topic, keep the discussion moving, avoid having the group become side-tracked, ask members to explain more fully what they mean, avoid having members argue and quibble over irrelevancies, and summarize and state conclusions.

2. *Responsibilities of members of the discussion group*—To be well informed on the topic to be discussed, especially some phase of it; speak informally while avoiding arguing and quibbling; stay with the topic under discussion; have sources of information available; back up statements with facts; and help the group summarize its conclusions.

3. *Responsibilities of the audience*—To listen attentively, withhold questions until presentation is completed, ask for clarification of ideas, ask for evidence on questionable statements, confine remarks to the topic under discussion, and extend customary audience courtesies to members of the roundtable.

Roundtable discussions may be used for any of the following purposes:

1. To discuss plans for a major class activity.
2. To evaluate the results of a class activity, the merits of a film, school assembly on citizenship, or the decision of a student council.
3. To make specific plans, such as the best way to present the work of the class to the parents.
4. To discuss current events.
5. To present differing views on a community issue or a school problem.

6. To make decisions and recommendations to the class. (The student council wants to know how the class feels about a new play schedule. A committee of five children discusses this matter and presents its findings and recommendations to the class.)

Panel Discussions

A *panel discussion* is similar to a roundtable discussion in many respects, but there are some important differences. The responsibilities of the moderator are approximately the same as they are for the moderator of the roundtable, as are those of the participants. The procedure is more formal than that of the roundtable. It usually begins with a short statement or presentation by each discussant before the panel is opened for free discussion by members. Panels are usually more audience oriented than roundtables, and frequently some provision is made for audience questions or participation at the end of the panel's presentation. A greater responsibility is placed on participants to prepare themselves well for their particular part on the panel, for each panelist is considered to be more or less an "expert."

One teacher made use of a panel discussion format in the following way.

The topic for the panel to discuss was a community problem involving the conversion of a military base into a community resource. Various special-interest groups were competing for the use of the newly acquired property. In class the teacher asked children to volunteer to represent one of the following special-interest groups:

1. city planner
2. golf enthusiast
3. representative of the local community club
4. condominium builder
5. representative of a local Native American tribe
6. moderator

The children were provided planning time in which to prepare a three- to five-minute statement explaining their point of view regarding the future of this property. Time was allowed for questions to clarify points made in the presentations or to raise other issues.

Buzz Groups for Brainstorming

The following is an example of a "buzz" group in operation.

The members of Ms. Kryzinski's class viewed in class a CNN television special dealing with homelessness in the United States. They were anxious to discuss the program and even more anxious to do something about the problem it portrayed.

"What can we do, Ms. K, to help other kids in our school know about some ways they can help the homeless?" a child asked.

"Why don't you decide?" Ms. Kryzinski responded. "You are already arranged in small groups, so why don't you take the next ten minutes and come up with some ideas? Be prepared to give us two or three good ideas that would be possible for us to carry out in our school."

After about ten to fifteen minutes, the children's attention was refocused, and each group presented some ideas. There was no attempt to evaluate suggestions at that time.

All the suggestions were listed on the board and discussed. The class then voted on the list to determine which one they would implement.

We have here a brief description of a *buzz-group* or *brainstorming* technique. It is an informal consideration of ideas or problems where the chief purpose is to solicit the suggestions, feelings, ideas, or consensus of the members participating. In brainstorming for ideas and suggested solutions to problems, it is important *not* to evaluate each one at the time it is offered. If each is discussed, the list will not be very long. The objective of brainstorming is to get as many ideas to the surface as possible, no matter how outlandish they may seem. After the complete list has been generated, time can be taken to evaluate each one and select the best ones by consensus. It is usually best for the group to have a designated leader and recorder.

Talking things over in a buzz session can be helpful in clarifying ideas, getting a wide sampling of opinion and feeling, obtaining suggestions and ideas, and getting children to participate who might be reluctant or fearful in a more structured discussion situation. Likewise, it has some limitations. Buzz sessions can easily get out of hand and become noisy and boisterous where nothing is accomplished except the creation of confusion. There is need, therefore, for the teacher to have firm control of the class before such a procedure is attempted and to establish standards that are clearly understood beforehand. Lesson Plan 8 incorporates buzz groups, individual work, oral reports, and whole-class discussion.

· ·

Discussion Questions and Suggested Activities

1. Under what circumstances might a teacher *not* want to clarify in great detail the objectives of a small group?
2. How might a teacher build readiness for small-group activities with a class that has always worked on a whole-class basis?
3. Develop a role-playing exercise designed to teach groupwork skills.
4. Select a topic that is appropriate for a grade of your choice, and develop questions that could be used to stimulate a discussion with several factual, definitional, and ethical disagreements.
5. For the same topic you selected in item 4, devise two ways to divide it for Jigsaw. Then, create a question and an answer handout for use in STAD, and devise a two-sided approach to the topic for Structured Academic Controversy.
6. Prepare an informal chart that might be used with children to illustrate points to keep in mind when preparing panel discussions, roundtables, and oral reports. Illustrate your chart in a way that you think would appeal to children.
7. In visiting a classroom, what specific things would you look for that would provide an indication of the quality of interaction taking place there?
8. Examine the dimensions of the hidden curriculum given at the beginning of the chapter, and add examples from your own experience that tend to increase or decrease the level of hostility in a classroom.
9. Make a T-chart for several of the skills mentioned in the chapter.
10. Discuss similarities and differences between traditional small-group instruction as used in the teaching of reading, and cooperative learning groups as used in social studies.

Lesson Plan 8

Character Traits of Prominent People

Grade
4–5

Time
Three to five class periods

Objectives
Children will develop an awareness of the traits that characterize persons of prominence and work cooperatively in small groups.

Interest Building
Place children in buzz groups of three to four and ask them to brainstorm as many names of "famous people"—living or dead—as they can think of in five to ten minutes. Then, have the recorder from each group list the names on the chalkboard. Ask the whole class to examine the combined list, and categorize the people on it based on what they did that made them famous (possible categories: musicians, sports figures, politicians, business persons, social activists, television stars). Ask the children to try to think of missing categories, then generate names for them. Have the children discuss why the individuals listed on the chalkboard became well known, whereas most of their contemporaries did not. Tell the class that over the next few days they will study the qualities and character traits of famous people more carefully.

Lesson Development
Have a wide selection of biographies of prominent people available for children. Ask each child to choose one biography to read. The books are to be read in the next week, and children are to write in their response journals answers to the following three questions:

1. What, if anything, do you admire about the person?
2. What qualities did the person have that made him/her come to the attention of others?
3. What did the person do that made him/her famous?

At the completion of the assignment, have children return to their small groups, this time to share their responses. Help each group create a data-retrieval chart (Figure 7–1) with the names of their prominent persons listed down the left side and the three questions across the top. This serves as a guide and organizer for their sharing. After each child has shared, ask the group if there are any *character traits* that were common to each of the persons about whom they read (there may be none). Have each group chose a representative to give a brief oral report on its findings to the entire class.

Summary
Have the class generate a list of character traits that (1) applied to all; (2) applied to some; (3) applied to a few; and (4) applied to none. Ask the children if prominent per-

sons necessarily have admirable character traits and why it might be that they do or do not. Ask them if famous people are necessarily good people, and work to clarify this distinction. Solicit individual reactions in terms of the character traits they wish more famous people exhibited.

Assessment

1. While children are in small groups, assess their behavior using the scoring rubrics in Table 3–1, Figure 3–3, or Figure 9–8.
2. Following the summary, ask the class to take out their response journals. Each child is to identify his/her favorite prominent person, and state the qualities that they believe make this individual prominent. Collect and read the journals.

Materials

Biographies of prominent persons at suitable reading levels for the class, to be secured from the school library.

Notes

1 Elizabeth G. Cohen, *Designing Groupwork*, 2nd ed. (New York: Teachers College Press, 1994), 1.
2 Ibid., 3.
3 Richard Paul, *Critical Thinking* (Rohnert Park, CA: Sonoma State University, 1991).
4 Nel Noddings, *Caring: A Feminine Approach to Ethics and Moral Education* (Berkeley: University of California Press, 1984).
5 David W. Johnson, Roger T. Johnson, and Edythe J. Holubec, *Circles of Learning: Cooperation in the Classroom*, 4th ed. (Edena, MN: Interaction Book Co., 1993), 15.
6 Dianne K. Augustine, Kristin D. Gruber, and Lynda R. Hanson, "Cooperation Works!" *Educational Leadership* 47: 4 (December 1989/January 1990): 4–7.
7 David W. Johnson and Roger T. Johnson, "Conflict in the Classroom: Controversy and Learning," *Review of Educational Research* 49 (Spring 1979): 51–70.
8 Cohen, *Designing Groupwork*, 21.
9 Cohen, *Designing Groupwork*, 71.
10 Robert E. Slavin, *Using Student Team Learning* (Baltimore, MD: Johns Hopkins University, 1986).
11 Elliot Aronson, *The Jigsaw Classroom* (Beverly Hills, CA: Sage, 1978).
12 Mara Sapon-Shevin and Nancy Schniedewind, "Selling Cooperative Learning Without Selling It Short," *Educational Leadership* 47: 4 (December 1989/January 1990): 63–65.
13 David W. Johnson and Roger T. Johnson, "Critical Thinking through Structured Controversy," *Educational Leadership* 45: 8 (May 1988): 58–64.
14 David W. Johnson and Roger T. Johnson, "Social Skills for Successful Group Work," *Educational Leadership* 47: 4 (December 1989/January 1990): 29–33.
15 Johnson et al., *Circles of Learning*, 35.

Selected References

Aronson, Elliot. *The Jigsaw Classroom*. Beverly Hills, CA: Sage, 1978.
Brabeck, Mary. *Who Cares? Theory, Research, and Educational Implications of the Ethic of Care*. New York: Praeger, 1989.

Cohen, Elizabeth G. *Designing Groupwork*, 2nd ed. New York: Teachers College Press, 1994.

Gibbs, Jeanne. *Tribes: A New Way of Learning Together*. Santa Rosa: CA: Center Source, 1994.

Johnson, David W., and Roger T. Johnson. *Learning Together and Alone: Cooperative, Competitive, and Individualistic Learning*. Englewood Cliffs, NJ: Prentice-Hall, 1987.

Johnson, David W., Roger T. Johnson, and Edythe J. Holubec. *Circles of Learning: Cooperation in the Classroom*, 4th ed. Edina, MN: Interaction Book Co., 1993.

Kreidler, William J. *Creative Conflict Resolution*. Chicago: Scott Foresman, 1984.

Noddings, Nel. *Caring: A Feminine Approach to Ethics and Moral Education*. Berkeley: University of California Press, 1984.

Slavin, Robert E. *Student Team Learning: An Overview and Practical Guide*. Washington, DC: National Education Association, 1986.

Stahl, Robert J., ed. *Cooperative Learning in Social Studies: A Handbook for Teachers*. Menlo Park, CA: Addison-Wesley, 1994.

OVERVIEW

If schools are to become "sites for true literary apprenticeships,"[1] reading and writing skills must be taught, used, and refined in the content areas.

Chapters 11 and 12 take up the subject of literacy education in the context of social studies education. We emphasize reading in this chapter, writing in the next. Two principal goals of literacy education will be explored, for both are essential to social studies learning. First, children will accomplish reading and writing tasks efficiently and with care. Second, they will do so mindfully, that is, by selecting and using well the skills they have learned.[2]

In these two chapters, we suggest principles and strategies for accomplishing these goals in a way that accomplishes social studies learning at the same time. Key ideas in both chapters are, first, that reading and writing are best thought of as a common enterprise rather than as distinct endeavors. Readers make meaning when they comprehend text in much the same way that writers make meaning when they compose text.[3] Skillful teachers attend to this similarity by paying special attention to the meaning-making process itself, whether situated in reading or writing. Second, children do not make meaning in a vacuum; children read and write to accomplish goals. In social studies, for example, they read and write to investigate the disappearance of the American buffalo, to follow rivers to the sea, to grasp how the Aztecs could possibly have been conquered, and to figure out why there are homeless people and what can be done about it. They read and write, then, to build and express social studies understandings.

Literacy and the Content Areas

This view of literacy education and content learning sees each situated in the other—mutually dependent. And it sees the central work of the skillful teacher as creating *apprenticeships* for children in which they are gradually helped to achieve expertise in both. By apprenticeship we mean a learning situation with at least three characteristics: (1) learners learn as a consequence of being coached into higher levels of capability by adults and/or more capable peers; (2) practice occurs as learners work to accomplish all or part of a worthwhile task with the guidance and support of the coach or coaches; and (3) the coaching gradually decreases as the learner's capability increases.[4]

In the conventional classroom situation, of course, the coach is the teacher. Sometimes, the teacher will orchestrate situations in which peers who are more capable on the particular task at hand will provide guidance and support to students who are less capable on that task. In the cooperative group work strategy called Jigsaw (Chapter 10), learning is fashioned in such a way that every student serves as a more capable "coach" to other students and is in the same way coached by other students. This should be familiar to every parent who has had the older child teach the younger one to wash dishes.

When social studies curriculum materials are used to teach reading, people take interest.

This kind of literacy learning places less emphasis on traditional "drill and practice" than has been customary in the elementary school. The reason is that drill and practice typically is conducted in isolation from the tasks in which we want children actually to *use* those skills. While not discarding drill and practice, for it surely has its place, the apprenticeship approach strives as a rule of thumb to locate skills instruction in or as close as possible to the very situations where skillful means are needed.

Literacy, properly understood, then, is a cultural practice. Children learn to read and write by being immersed in communities of practitioners who themselves read and write. Three literacy practices deserve the attention of elementary school teachers, and each requires its own form of apprenticeship.[5] The first is the practice of reading or writing written texts in order to function in everyday life. This is *practical* literacy. Examples include reading food labels and bus schedules, following instructions for videotaping a television program or assembling a bookshelf, completing job applications, and writing letters. Most of this apprenticeship occurs within families with the guidance and modeling of parents and older siblings. The second practice is reading or writing to gather data about the world. This is *informational* literacy. Typical examples are reading newspapers and weekly news magazines, studying campaign literature, writing letters to the editor, taking notes at lectures, looking up the location of Iraq in an almanac, and reading about the Vietnam War in a history textbook or on a CD-ROM. For much of this information-driven learning, we depend on the school curricu-

Table 11–1
Literacy apprenticeships in social studies

Practical Literacy	Informational Literacy	Pleasurable Literacy
Reading the ballot	Studying the candidates' positions	Enjoying a biography of Thomas Jefferson
Reading directions to the polls	Reading a political analysis	Reading an absorbing historical novel featuring famous actual persons
Reading the election returns	Reading a news article about a political campaign	Enjoying a nonfiction book about ancient Egypt

lum. The third form of apprenticeship concerns reading for pleasure. *Pleasurable literacy* is the one form of literacy practice that clearly is not a means to an end. It is an end in itself: one picks up and puts down the book or article at will. This apprenticeship often occurs at home, when children are read to by parents, but also at school when literature is read aloud to children and then dramatized, or when children read engaging stories themselves and then discuss them with other children or use them as a springboard for writing an original story.* Table 11–1 shows these three practices, or apprenticeships, in relation to one another.

Schools can become "sites for true literacy apprenticeships," writes Lauren Resnick,[6] but this mandates ample school activities that require students to *use* reading and writing skills in the pursuit of practical and informational goals, as well as for pleasure. Among other things, *this means that reading and writing skills must be taught and used and refined in the content areas*, such as social studies, science, and mathematics. This chapter is focused primarily on these skills.

Reading Skills Essential to Social Studies Learning

Reading remains the chief avenue to information needed in learning social studies, yet children are often unable to read well enough to secure that information. Inability to read well, therefore, is a major cause of poor achievement in social studies, and, unfortunately, the problem becomes worse each year the child is in school.

The usual recommendations for attending to the wide range of reading abilities among learners are these: (1) use multiple texts, (2) rewrite the material at a simpler level, (3) use a nonreading approach to social studies, and (4) secure simpler nontext materials for slower readers. But teachers on the job find these recommendations require resources, time, or skills that they do not have. The college methods courses in reading generally focus on the "basal" program or a whole-language approach. Either

---

* For wonderful examples of dramatization, see Vivian G. Paley, *Wally's Stories* (Cambridge, MA: Harvard University Press, 1981).

way, too little attention is paid to reading in the content fields. Here we will examine in detail the relationship between reading and social studies.

Most elementary schools provide time during the school day when a major effort is made to teach basic reading skills. In this developmental reading program, children acquire a basic reading vocabulary and learn to use various word recognition techniques along with other skills and abilities that characterize the flexible, independent reader. For example, they learn to identify words, create hypotheses about the meaning of a selection, and revise their hypotheses as they read and reread. But even a strong basic reading program will not be able to meet all the reading needs of children because each area of the school curriculum requires reading tasks that are somewhat unique to that special area.

The special reading skills needed to make sense of social studies material may be identified by examining the sorts of reading tasks children will confront. An examination of textbooks, historical fiction, biographies, primary documents, maps, and reference books will suggest reading skills such as those given in Figure 11–1.

The teacher's responsibility regarding reading instruction in the social studies is twofold. First, those special reading skills unique to social studies must be taught simultaneously with the subject matter under study. These include the skills listed in Figure 11–1. The teacher's second responsibility is to help children learn how to use reading as a tool in gaining needed information. Of course, reading should not be the only means through which children encounter new social studies information. Throughout this text, the idea is stressed repeatedly that a multimedia approach is vital to inspired teaching of social studies. But in that broad spectrum of media and activities that is at least potentially available to children today, reading remains undoubtedly the most important and, in the long run, the most critical to their success in learning social studies.

Figure 11–1
Social studies reading skills

In social studies, the capable reader

- Reads flexibly
- Uses chapter and section headings as aids to reading
- Uses context clues to gain meaning
- Adjusts reading speed to purpose
- Hypothesizes cause-effect relationships
- Uses reference material when necessary to understand essential terms and vocabulary
- Seeks data in maps, charts, pictures, and illustrations and interprets data found there
- Uses various sections of a book (index, table of contents, introduction, etc.) as aids to reading
- Previews the selection to become familiar with text structure and to hypothesize general meaning
- Skims to locate facts and hypothesize main ideas
- Compares one account with another
- Recognizes topic sentences
- Uses library skills to find needed material

Using Textbooks and Study Aids

In contrast to reading a storybook simply for enjoyment, much of the reading in social studies involves a search for information. Social studies textbooks are written to be used as information sourcebooks and are not intended to become the social studies curriculum. They can be used in a variety of ways, and individual children may make different uses of the same book. For one child it may constitute a reading resource, for another child the illustrations may be more valuable, for a third child the map materials may be needed, and for a fourth child it may be a source of ideas for additional study. Similarly, different teachers may choose to make different uses of the same book, depending on their skill, experience, or method of teaching. Teachers are encouraged to make such differential use of textbooks rather than to "cover" the content uniformly and require children to "master" all the facts presented.

If the teacher keeps in mind that no single book can meet adequately the reading needs of all children in the class, the textbook can be a useful tool in teaching social studies. Four of the most common uses of the textbook are for (1) exploratory reading; (2) gathering data related to an inquiry the class is undertaking together or a concept or generalization students are constructing; (3) map, chart, graph, or picture study; and (4) summarization of learning.

Social studies textbooks almost always present problems of reading difficulty even though they are written at a level that is suitable for the average reader. The reason for this is that these books are designed to deal with substantive content, and this means that the terms and concepts relating to that subject matter must be used in explaining the ideas presented. For example, a book may be treating a topic such as *trade and commerce*. This subject cannot be meaningfully presented without including at least some of the following concepts and terms: *cargo, tariff, import, duty, international markets, ports, interdependence, hold, tonnage, freight, shipping, stevedore, merchant, commercial, barge.* If these terms are eliminated from the selection to simplify the reading task, it is no longer an essay on trade and commerce. It is the complexity and frequency of concepts that often make reading social studies textbooks difficult, and there is no way this problem can be overcome entirely. An easy-to-read textbook is probably not a good social studies text because its purpose should be to provide information rather than be a simple storybook.

It is important not to try to overcome this inherent difficulty of reading content-oriented textbooks by changing the content. As we saw in Chapter 2, this is what happens again and again to children who are already at risk of school failure. This is what causes some Hispanic and African-American children and children whose home language is not English to fall behind their same-age peers. It is a *lowering* of expectations. The answer to the problem is not changing from Our Nation's Government, or whatever the topic is, to What I Did Over Summer Vacation, Sports Heroes, Circuses, or some other content that is easier because the terms and content are not new. The answer instead is to apprentice children into this sort of reading—make it a goal of the classroom community and help them do it successfully. At the same, it is important that the purposes for reading are important to the children: They are reading to answer questions that strike them as important and to gather data on hypotheses they have formulated, for example. Complementing this work on reading, of course, and interspersed throughout it should be ample dramatizations, music, simulations, and construction activities. These will build comprehension through other channels and resonate with children's multiple strengths.

The design of a social studies textbook provides many aids to make the job of reading easier. The teacher cannot assume, however, that children will make use of such aids unless they are taught to do so. The skills associated with the use of study aids must be taught, reviewed, and retaught each year throughout the elementary and middle school grades. Here are a few teaching suggestions, each of which is discussed in turn:

1. Using various parts of a book.
2. Using the organization of the book.
3. Using pictures to aid comprehension.

Using Various Parts of a Book

The parts of a book should be taught as aids in getting information. For example, if a fifth grade child, Sara, in her study of famous women in American history, wanted to know the name of the Native American woman who assisted Lewis and Clark, how would she find it? She might find a reference to the Lewis and Clark Expedition in the Table of Contents, but that would be less likely than finding the names of these two explorers in the Index. She looks in the Index and finds

Legislative branch, 345, 356–357

Leirich, Julie, 253, 571

Lewis, Meriwether, 371–372

Lexington, Massachusetts, 300

Liberator, The, 420[7]

She turns to page 371 and notes a boldfaced section heading near the bottom of the page that reads, "The Lewis and Clark Expedition." She skims the sentences that follow it. Nothing. She turns the page, skimming quickly, and finds it. In the second column on page 372 she reads,

The expedition spent the winter with the Mandan Indians beside the great bend of the Missouri River. There Lewis and Clark hired a French-Canadian fur trapper as their guide. They also invited the trapper's wife, **Sacajawea**, a Shoshone, and her newborn son to accompany them. Lewis and Clark believed that if they traveled with this woman and her baby, the Indians whom they met would understand that the explorers were a peaceful group.[8]

Thus, in a matter of moments, Sara is able to find precisely the information she seeks. Contrast this with the girl sitting next to her who needs the same information, but, lacking an efficient way of finding it, goes through the book page by page looking for a picture or a clue that will reveal the name of that famous Shoshone woman. She may never find what she is looking for.

Rather than teaching parts of a book in an expository mode, the teacher should use exercises that require children to apply these skills. Often such exercises are included in the book itself. "Learning the Parts of a Book," on page 329, is an example.

Other more complex variations of this exercise are possible. For example, the right-hand column can be omitted, and the child can be asked to find and supply the information. Or the child can be asked to indicate the specific page on which the information appears. Once learned, many of these skills can be transferred to many other situations. If the children can use an alphabetical arrangement, as in the case of an index, they should also be able to use the dictionary, the encyclopedia, and the card catalog. Also, if they develop the habit of knowing exactly what information they seek before beginning the search, information gathering will be more efficient.

Naturally, the complexity of activities of this type should be appropriate to the age and maturity of the learners. Even in the first grade, children learn that books have titles and that pages are numbered. They also learn that sections of their books and stories have titles. In the second and third grades, they can begin to make use of the table of contents to find a particular story. In the third and fourth grades they can learn simple variations of alphabetical arrangements that assist them in using an index.

Using the Organization of the Book

Units, chapters, section heads, and subheads; ends of section, chapter, or unit study aids; maps, charts, or picture captions; introductory questions—all of these make sense to the mature reader who uses them as valuable aids in understanding the organization of a book. But left unguided, a child is not likely to make good use of them as aids to reading. Even teachers may not be familiar with the way a particular book is organized. Figure 11–2 illustrates organizational components that are commonly found in social studies textbooks. Research indicates that knowledge of text *structure* is a significant variable in children being able to recall information.[9]

LEARNING THE PARTS OF A BOOK

In the right-hand column are listed the parts of your book. In the left-hand column are listed some things you might want to find out. For each item in the left-hand column, tell what part of the book you would turn to *first* in order to get the information.

You Want to Know	Parts of Your Book
the number of chapters in the book	title page
the meaning of *treaty*	copyright page
how to say the word *bauxite*	preface
when the book was published	table of contents
the population of various states	list of maps
the date the Dutch bought Manhattan Island	list of illustrations
what a sod house looks like	glossary
the route of the first railroad to the west coast	atlas
whether the book tells anything about Canada	index

USING YOUR TEXTBOOK

Your textbook contains many special features that will help you read, understand, and remember the people, geography, and history of the United States.

TABLE OF CONTENTS
Lists all parts of your book and tells you where to find them

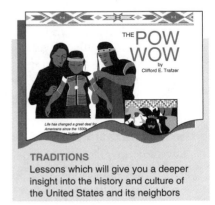

TRADITIONS
Lessons which will give you a deeper insight into the history and culture of the United States and its neighbors

REVIEWING MAPS AND GLOBES
Reviews skills that will help you use the maps in your book

FIVE FUNDAMENTAL THEMES OF GEOGRAPHY
Introduces important themes of geography that will help you to compare, to contrast, and to understand the regions and people you will study

LESSON OPENER

Important vocabulary, people, and places introduced in the lesson

Lesson introduction

Asks you to think about what you already know from previous lessons or your own experience

Question you should keep in mind as you read the lesson

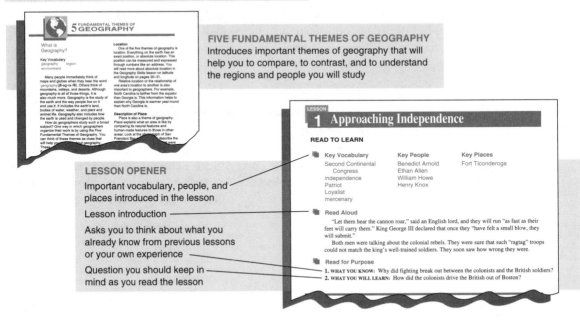

Figure 11-2
Organizational structure of social studies textbooks

Source: United States and Its Neighbors (New York: Macmillan/McGraw-Hill, 1995): 2–3. Reprinted by permission of Macmillan/McGraw Hill School Publishing.

REFERENCE SECTION

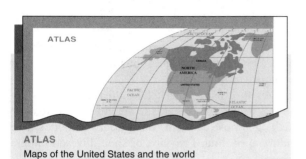

ATLAS

Maps of the United States and the world

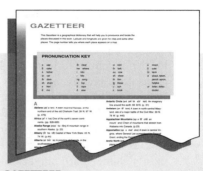

GAZETTEER

Location and pronunciation of the major places discussed in your book and page where each is shown on a map

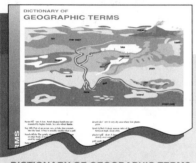

DICTIONARY OF GEOGRAPHIC TERMS

Definition and pronunciation of major geographic features

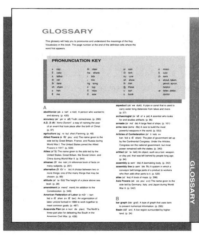

GLOSSARY

Definition and pronunciation of all Key Vocabulary and page where each is introduced

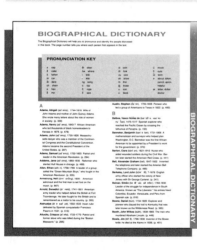

BIOGRAPHICAL DICTIONARY

Identification and pronunciation of important people discussed in your book and page where each is introduced

INDEX

Alphabetical list of important people, places, events, and subjects in your book and pages where information is found

Using Pictures to Aid Comprehension

The most widely used of all visual aids are pictures, photographs, and illustrations. These are used to obtain realism, to clarify ideas, to recall the real object, and, in short, to give meaning to learning. It is well known that words cannot convey meanings as accurately, vividly, or quickly as pictures. Pictures can also be helpful in promoting inquiry skills. For this reason, textbooks sometimes use questions for captions instead of a description of the content of the picture or illustration.

Publishers invest huge sums of money to provide instructive illustrations for social studies textbooks. Unfortunately, the full value of these aids to reading is not realized unless children are taught how to make good use of them. Illustrations are not simply cosmetic touches to make the book more appealing. They are, or should be, an integral part of the message system of the text.

Pictures and illustrations elaborate concepts presented in the narrative but usually do not repeat exactly what is said in the text. Neither do picture captions simply tell what would be obvious to the reader only by looking at the picture. Thus, captions should call attention to some element or relationship in the picture or illustration that might be missed by the casual viewer. Often this is done by using a question or series of questions. In this way pictures and illustrations can provide the reader with a wealth of information. In teaching children how to use pictures and illustrations, teachers will find questions such as these appropriate:

1. What is being shown in the picture?
2. When was this picture taken? (recently, years ago, time of day, and so on)
3. Does the picture illustrate something we discussed in class?
4. What causes or effects can be detected in the picture?
5. How does the picture illustrate something valued by people?
6. How does the picture show conflicts between traditional and modern ways of doing things?
7. What does the picture show that illustrates the roles of men, women, and children in that society?
8. What can you say about the geography of the area shown by the picture?
9. What conversation might be going on between the persons in the picture?
10. Do you think the people use most of what they produce or sell their products outside their community? What makes you think so?

Locating and Using Reference Materials

Children should make use of a wide variety of reference material in studying social studies topics. The value of such references depends not only on their availability but also on the ability of the children to make use of them. The teacher's responsibility in this respect is, therefore, twofold: teaching children (1) which references to use for various purposes and (2) how to use the reference efficiently once it is found. These are continuing responsibilities of the social studies program and cannot be completely taught in any one grade or any one year. A beginning will be made in the primary grades, but the child will continue to extend and refine the ability to use references throughout high school, college, and in later life. Instruction usually will begin as soon as the child develops a degree of independence in reading. The reference materials used in the social studies may be grouped meaningfully as shown in Figure 11–3.

Much of the instruction given on the use of references will have to be specific to the particular resource used. For example, one uses the *World Almanac* differently from the way one uses an atlas or a tour book. Moreover, the references may be used at varying levels of sophistication. The library may be used by primary-grade children under teacher guidance to check out books and CD-ROMs, to look at magazines, or to have stories read to them, whereas upper-grade children should be able to use the library independently, making use of the card catalog and locating references themselves. The use of the various references should be taught as the need for them arises in the social studies.

Skills needed to use references can be practiced and learned on an individual basis or by children in pairs using *task cards*, as is illustrated in Figure 11–4.

Figure 11–3
Types of social studies reference materials

Books
Textbooks
Supplementary reading books
Picture books
Biographies
Historical fiction

Special References (paper and electronic)
Encyclopedias
Maps and globes
Atlases
Dictionaries
World Almanac
Charts and graphs
Constitution of the United States
Yearbooks
Legislative manuals
Primary documents
Internet
CSPAN
Channel One
CNN

Reference Aids (paper and electronic)
Card catalog
The Reader's Guide
Bibliographies
COMCATS

Miscellaneous Materials
Advertisements
Magazines and periodicals
City and telephone directories
Labels
Guidebooks and tour books
Letters, diaries, and journals
Travel folders
Postcards
Newspapers and news clippings
Comic books
Pictures
Schedules and timetables
Pamphlets and booklets (such as those from the information services of foreign countries, superintendent of documents, conservation departments, historical societies, art galleries)
Weather reports
Manufacturers' guarantees and warranties
Money, checks, coupons for premiums, receipts
Reviews
Government documents

Figure 11–4
An example of teacher-prepared task cards

SIDE ONE

Find Out for Yourself

(If you cannot do any one of these, look for a clue on SIDE TWO of this card.)

1. Find the article on "Safety" in the *World Book*.
2. Into how many sections is the article divided? _____
3. Skim through the article to find these two facts:
   a. Where do most accidents happen? _____
   b. What do the letters *UL* on electrical wiring and appliances stand for?
   _____
4. Suppose you heard that someone had been killed in an accident in his or her home but you did not know what kind of an accident it was. You would be right most of the time if you guessed that the accident was a
   _____ or _____ or _____
5. Suppose you questioned the accuracy of this article. What is there about the article that might renew your confidence in its authority?
   _____

SIDE TWO

CLUES

1. Select volume S–Sn. Look for the article according to the alphabet.
2. See the "Outline" at the end of the article.
3. a. Look under the section "Safety/Home."
   b. Look under "Safety with Electricity."
4. What does the article say about the major causes of accidental deaths in the home?
   _____
   _____
   _____
5. What group critically reviewed the article?
   _____
   _____
   _____
   _____
   _____

If teachers regard the teaching of reading as something that is done in three small groups during the reading period and ignore the reading needs of children during the remainder of the school day, they may expect children, especially those who are not native English speakers, to have many disappointing experiences reading social studies material. The feeling that children learn to read in the basic reading program and read to learn in the social studies, for example, is not an entirely correct concept of the relationship between these two processes. Actually, the two occur simultaneously; children improve their reading ability *as they read to learn.* Children can extend and improve their reading skills and abilities quite apart from the basic reading program as they use reading for a variety of purposes.

Lesson Plan 9 shows how one teacher organized a research project for a sixth grade class.

Building Social Studies Vocabulary

The vocabulary load of social studies reading material is one of the major causes of poor comprehension and faulty reading in social studies. Even with the more careful attention that contemporary authors give to word difficulties, the social studies vocabulary remains a stumbling block for many children. Although a degree of simplification is possible, it is true that there are limits beyond which the use of a specialized vocabulary cannot be avoided. If one is speaking or writing about social studies concepts, appropriate vocabulary must be used. This is not altogether undesirable if the teacher accepts vocabulary development as one of the goals of the total social studies program. The same situation exists in other areas of the curriculum; the child must learn the language associated with mathematics, science, art, music—all of which have their own peculiar words, terms, or phrases. Figure 11–5 shows some of the types of words and terms that are peculiar to social studies.

The teacher should anticipate likely word difficulties *before* children are asked to read a social studies selection. Two types of word problems must be expected. One is the inability to recognize the word in print; the other is not knowing the meaning of the word once it is recognized. Therefore, new words and terms should be presented and developed in the context of a phrase or a sentence rather than in isolation.

Vocabulary development should be conducted in relatively short, highly motivated settings. Having children look up a long list of terms in the dictionary prior to reading a selection is not productive. No expert reader does this. A better strategy is to write the key terms in a sentence on the chalkboard and discuss their meanings. These should be the few terms that, in the teacher's judgment, are critical to student comprehension of the selection. Better still, the sentence in the text in which the word or term appears can be selected for directed study.

It is essential for the teacher to model a sensitivity to, and interest in, new words and terms. Curiosity about words and a genuine interest in good communication, after all, are central features of a successful apprenticeship in reading and writing. Teachers should encourage children to use the specialized social studies vocabulary in their discussions and writing. They should also, from time to time, encourage children to create

Lesson Plan 9

China Today

Grade
6 or 7

Time
Ten class periods

Objectives
Students will learn basic information about the People's Republic of China. Students will refine research and small-group work skills.

Interest Building
For several days as the class is reading the text's overview of China, invite students to bring to school other recently published materials about China (books, magazines, travel brochures). Display these in a learning center.

Lesson Development

Preview the resources.

Using the text and other resources for inspiration, brainstorm a list of topics that would be suitable for small-group information-gathering projects.

Have a member of the class list the topics on a chart in the learning center (see Sample Chart).

Divide the class into teams of five children each.

Team assignment: Elect a leader. Meet, discuss, agree on, and sign up for a topic.

Decide on subtopics to study.

Give students a copy of each assessment form. Discuss expectations (see Sample Assessment form).

Use outline format for taking notes.

Organize report into an introduction, main body, and conclusion.

Prepare visuals. Some ideas include charts, graphs, time lines, and illustrations from resources.

Practice giving the oral report.

Assign report dates.

Summary
Groups give their oral reports with each member contributing to the presentation. They field questions and comments from their audience.

Sample Chart: China Today Reports

Topics	Names of Group Members	Report Date
Family life and education		
Geography and natural resources		
Economy: Agriculture and industry		
Political system: Leaders and history		
Holidays and festivals		
Cities		
Tourism and transportation		
Arts and athletics		
Science and technology		

Assessment

China Today Report: Sample Assessment

	Exemplary	Adequate	Minimal	Unacceptable
Was an introduction used?				
Were the main ideas presented?				
Were supporting details given?				
Was there a clear conclusion?				
Were visuals used?				
Was teamwork evident?				

Resources

Text: *World Regions*, Macmillan/McGraw-Hill

Recommended trade books:

China, Here We Come! Tang Yungmei

Two Chinese Families, Catherine Edwards Sadler

Red Star & Green Dragon: Looking at New China, Lila Perl

The People's Republic of China: Red Star of the East, Jane Werner Watson

Dragonwings, Lawrence Yep

Figure 11–5
Terms needing special attention in social studies

Technical terms—Words, terms, and expressions peculiar to social studies and usually not encountered when reading selections from other fields of knowledge. *Examples:* veto, meridian, frontier, latitude, longitude, legislature, polls, franchise, temperate, plateau, hemisphere, mountainous, balance of power, capitalism, democracy, nationalism, civilization, century, ancient, decade, pueblo, fjord, iceberg.

Figurative terms—Expressions that are metaphorical; having a different connotation from the literal meaning usually associated with the word. *Examples:* political platform, cold war, closed shop, Iron Curtain, pork barrel, open door, hat in the ring, domino theory, Sunbelt.

Words with multiple meanings—Words that have identical spelling but whose meaning is derived from context. *Examples:* cabinet, belt, bill, chamber, mouth, bank, revolution, fork, court, assembly, range.

Terms peculiar to a locality—Expressions peculiar to a specific part of the country that are not commonly used elsewhere. *Examples:* truck, meeting, borough, gandy, draw, coulee, right, prairie, section, run, butte, arroyo, geoduck, goobers, grits, potlatch, bayou, haul cane road.

Words easily confused with other words—Words that are closely similar in general configuration. *Examples:* continent for country, alien for allies, principal for principle, longitude for latitude, executive for execution, conversation for conservation.

Acronyms—Words that are abbreviated expressions. *Examples:* NATO, NASA, OPEC, SALT, NOW, UNICEF, AIDS, MADD.

Quantitative terms—Words and terms signifying amounts of time, space, or objects. *Examples:* shortly after, century, fortnight, several years later, score, 150 tons.

new words or nicknames for old ideas. During a concept-formation lesson (see Chapter 7) on *culture*, the children may be encouraged to think of a term other than *culture* that might more powerfully convey the meaning of the concept—*lifeway*, for example. Creating new words puts children at the inventing end of language, rather than the receiving end, which can be an enlightening change of vantage point.[10]

Moreover, the teacher may want to involve them in word games. Devising riddles, providing synonyms or antonyms, making or completing crossword puzzles, or constructing variants of words are helpful in maintaining an awareness of new terms. Bulletin board displays and other classroom exhibits can feature new words encountered in social studies.

Teaching how known words can be used to construct new words can be of help in recognizing new words and understanding their meanings. Among the simplest variations are compound words or the addition of prefixes or suffixes. Some examples are these: construct, construc*ted*, construc*ting*, construc*tion*; consume, consum*er*, consum*ed*, consum*ing*; loyal, *dis*loyal, loya*list*; dictate, dictat*or*, dictator*ship*.

It is often helpful to keep a special social studies vocabulary list posted in the classroom. Lists can be developed by individual children, too, and made into a social studies picture dictionary. If a word is likely to be used frequently in writing, the word might be added to an individualized spelling list. However, many social studies words are not often used by children in their writing and, therefore, do not make good selections for spelling lists. They are more likely to be a part of children's reading vocabulary than their writing vocabulary.

Most social studies texts provide extensive study aids to assist with vocabulary development, including any or all of the following:

1. Contextual definition of words and terms. *Examples*:

   Thousands of persons in this city earn their living by *processing* food. Processing means preparing food for marketing.

   In recent years people have become concerned about *pollution*. Pollution comes about when something harmful is placed into the water or air.

2. End of unit, chapter, or section exercises. *Examples*:

   Matching exercises.

   Selecting terms for incomplete sentences.

   Finding definitions of key terms in the text.

3. Glossaries. *Examples*:

   Pig iron: melted iron that hardens into bars

   Pilgrim: a person who travels to holy places to worship

   Plantation: a large farm that specializes in one crop

   Polar regions: areas in the high latitudes

Improving Reading Comprehension: Making Sense

Reading with comprehension means that readers are able to make sense of what they are reading, that is, to come away from the selection with mental pictures of essential facts and understandings. Through discussion with the teacher and classmates, writing, dramatizations, discussions, and returning to the selection perhaps numerous times, children can check the sense they made with the sense made by others, perhaps revise their interpretation, and, in this trial-and-error way, come to some negotiated understanding about what the author meant to say.

It is obvious that the child who brings the most to a reading situation—whether practical, informational, or strictly for pleasure—will receive the most in return. What the child brings that will enhance social studies reading the most are intellectual aptitude, a storehouse of experience and ideas (put simply, prior knowledge), knowledge about reading, and motivation or will. There is not much a teacher can do to increase children's intellectual aptitude, but a great deal can be done about the other three: Teachers can capitalize on the knowledge and cultural experience children bring to the reading situation, they can build children's knowledge of important components of the reading process itself, and they can establish clear purposes for reading tasks. In order to help children *want* to comprehend, teachers can make connections to students' interests and goals, and they can make sure that the reading tasks they give students to accomplish are authentic—that is, they are not mere "busywork," nor are they the sort of thing that has no larger purpose. ("Drill and practice" activities often are off the mark on both counts.) Rather, tasks are related to a worthy and larger challenge. Children are not just practicing writing sentences, for example, but they are writing sentences in the biographies they are producing about people who work to protect the environment from polluters. In these ways, children can be helped to perform at or near their full potential.

Perhaps the most important general rule of thumb used by good readers is the one that seems so mundane: *read flexibly*. This means that readers should vary their speed and the skills they use depending on the selection at hand. Expert readers do this routinely; poor readers do it rarely; mediocre readers do it unevenly. Apprenticing children into the routine practice of flexible reading should be a daily goal in social studies teaching and learning.

Because reading comprehension varies according to the particular topic and selection at hand, *previewing* may be the most important single comprehension strategy. It means, essentially, looking before you leap. Good readers use it because it tells them what lies ahead, providing a general picture of the terrain. Looking ahead indicates whether familiar or strange material is at hand and, consequently, which additional strategies, such as skimming, may be required. Previewing in this way builds prior knowledge "on the spot."

The simple narrative account of an African-American girl who must survive on her own during the American Revolution, for example, may be relatively easy to understand for many children.[11] They can read accounts of this type without difficulty because they rely on motivating storylines, familiar story structures (e.g., problem-solution), and well-known words. On the other hand the child may encounter in the textbook an expository selection on the topic Democracy and Dictatorship. This is a complex idea that may be difficult for many young children. Not only is its vocabulary specialized (separation of powers, civil rights, limited government, and so on), its place in children's experience will be marginal. Yet, it is easily one of the most important topics in the social studies curriculum.

What's to be done? Several strategies have been shown to be effective in improving reading comprehension. We briefly consider three:

1. Activate prior knowledge
2. Preview
3. Skim for ideas and related details

Activate Prior Knowledge

Just as the rich get richer, the knowledgeable get more knowledgeable. What we know before coming to a learning task influences, often greatly, the kind and amount of learning we will accomplish once we get there. Learners who have more background knowledge about the topic of the text selection they are about to read, all things being equal, will better comprehend that chapter than learners who know little or nothing about it. Minimally, they will comprehend it differently, making different sense of it than their less knowledgeable counterparts. Such is the influence of prior knowledge on comprehending text. Over the long term, therefore, schools should do everything possible to contribute to the prior knowledge of students. Extensive use of field trips to construction sites and factories, study trips to museums, exposure to films of historical events and far away places, assemblies, plays and pageants, projects, pictures, guest speakers, displays, artifacts—all will assist the child in comprehending the ideas encountered in reading.

But there is a problem. When the next learning task is here, staring them in the face, learners will not necessarily use the prior knowledge they have. Ask any teacher! The knowledge they have built up over the years, even in last week's lesson, may lay dormant and untapped in today's lesson. How can a teacher "activate" this prior knowledge so that students can use it to make sense of the coming reading? Our favorite strategy is helping children make a visually vivid *semantic map*.

Semantic mapping provides a graphic representation of a key concept that the teacher (or student) has chosen from the reading selection. Consider a teacher who has chosen Exploring North America as the central theme for a fourth grade social studies/language arts curriculum. Developing in-depth knowledge of each region of the United States is the content focus, and the Lewis and Clark expedition has been selected as the first unit. Before having students read a selection from the textbook on Lewis and Clark, the teacher decides to activate the whole array of ideas and information students associate with the concept *exploration*. The procedure follows.[12]

1.   The teacher places the term *exploration* on the chalkboard and asks students to jot down individually any words they can think of related to this theme. They may think of words such as Columbus, Marco Polo, past, future, time machine, explorers, ships, astronauts, underwater exploration, and so on.

2.   Next the teacher identifies or elicits from students major category labels related to the theme, prompting students to think of categories they may overlook. These are arrayed graphically around the concept term, which serves as a hub (see Figure 11–6).

3.   Now the teacher asks students to generate additional ideas under each category. As well, the teacher can suggest items and ask students to decide under which category label they belong. Figure 11–7 shows two sample categorization exercises.

Figure 11–6
A simple semantic map on the theme "exploration"

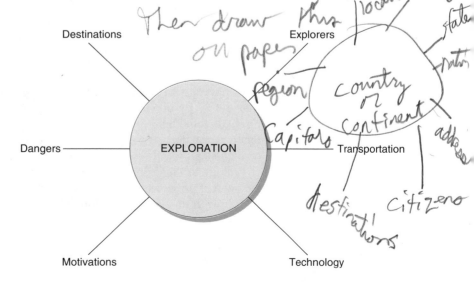

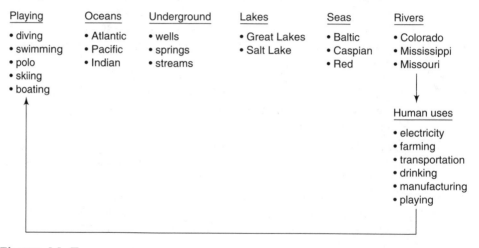

Figure 11–7
Expanded semantic maps on the themes "exploration" and "water"

Preview

Good readers have a general idea of what material is about *before* starting to read it. How do they get it? By previewing. Comprehension is significantly increased because previewing sheds some light on the subject; consequently, the reader does not have to proceed totally in the dark. It is a method for acquiring prior knowledge "on the spot."

Previewing generally will be directed by the teacher, and the teacher typically introduces this strategy to children and helps them initially learn it. But children should develop the habit of previewing material themselves; if instruction goes as planned, the teacher's coaching gradually should diminish as students begin to assume responsibility for previewing. Indeed, this is the goal of instruction on all reading strategies. Let us say that a class is about to read *part* of a new unit entitled The World of Carmelita and José. The teacher speaks to the class:

Teacher: Boys and girls, for the next few days we will be reading from our social studies books. I would like to introduce you to two children we will visit in this unit whose names are Carmelita and José. Please open your books to page 86. (The children take time to find the page.) Notice that the large print says "The World of Carmelita and José." Just looking at this page, what do you think this unit is about?

Frieda: Mexico.

Teacher: Why did you say Mexico, Frieda?

Frieda: Because Carmelita and José are Mexican names. Besides, it shows their pictures and they are dressed in Mexican clothes. . . . We learned that when we studied the community in Texas. . . .

David: That doesn't mean they are from Mexico. They could be from *New* Mexico and have names like that.

Teacher: Those are both good ideas. Perhaps if we page through this unit, we can discover the country it talks about. Turn to the map on page 88. . . .

It is established that the unit is, indeed, about Mexico, and the teacher continues:

Teacher: As you look at these pages, what do you suppose you will be reading about in the world of Carmelita and José?

Eric: Well, it looks like . . . uh . . . it tells like . . . you know . . . what they do every day . . . in school . . . at home.

Lisa: It shows how they do many of the same things we do.

Teacher: What do you mean?

Lisa: Well, we have homes and families, we go to school, we go shopping, and things like that, and they do, too.

The discussion concludes after the teacher is satisfied that the children are oriented to the material to be read. Previews should do the following:

1. Help the reader get the general idea of the selection.
2. Help the reader understand how the material is organized and understand the nature of the narrative.
3. Help the reader see how the subject matter to be read relates to prior studies or experiences.
4. Help the reader understand how illustrations relate to the subject matter to be read.

Skim for Ideas and Related Details

Once children have previewed the selection of text they intend to read, it is a good idea to skim it for ideas and related details. The teacher begins:

Teacher: Now that you have some general ideas about what you will be reading, let's take some time to become still more familiar with it. We will be using a strategy good readers use called *skimming*. What do you think skimming means?

Social studies researchers learn to skim for main ideas.

Mei:	It means taking something off the top, like skimming off the bugs at the swimming pool in the park. I see them do it because we go early in the morning.
Eddy:	Yeah, and it means going really fast.

The teacher helps the children define *skimming* and then directs them as follows:

1. Students are given thirty seconds to thumb through the selection, noticing as best they can what is on every page.
2. The teacher asks what they noticed and takes responses.
3. The teacher directs students to read the questions under the last heading, *Review*. Students are asked if, based on those questions, they want to revise what they earlier said the selection was about. The teacher elicits revisions. For example, a student responds:

Lisa:	Well, it must not be only about Carmelita and José. I mean, it's also about the country because the second question asks about the climate.

4. The teacher directs students' attention to the other section headings and asks students to skim again to find out the number of sections and the topic of each.
5. Next, students are directed to quickly read the first few sentences under each section head. After just one minute or so, the teacher asks them what they found.

Using Children's Trade Books for Multiple Perspectives

Children's trade books have always been popular curriculum resources in elementary social studies education. For twenty-five years, one of the most interesting and active committees of the National Council for the Social Studies has been a joint committee of the NCSS and the Children's Book Council, called the NCSS-CBC Joint Committee. One project of the committee is the annual production of an annotated bibliography, "Notable Children's Trade Books in the Field of Social Studies." The list is eagerly awaited, appearing each spring in an issue of the NCSS journal, *Social Education*.

The Joint Committee has always been clear about one very important point: If teachers are to teach social studies effectively, they need to "be familiar with children's books *and* know how to use them purposefully."[13] The books selected for these bibliographies "(1) are written for children in grades K–8, (2) emphasize human relations, (3) represent a diversity of groups and are sensitive to a broad range of cultural experiences, (4) present an original theme or a fresh slant on a traditional topic, (5) are easily readable and of high literary quality, and (6) have a pleasing format and, when appropriate, illustrations that enrich the text."[14]

This emphasis on the purposeful use of children's trade books is consistent with this chapter's main idea: Literacy learning is most successful when placed in the context of meaningful, which is to say purposeful, work and play. In the social studies, this goal-oriented activity often is geared to an information search of one sort or another, an inquiry. The excitement of searching for wanted information injects positive feelings and motivation into the effort; the importance of the search—its purpose—makes the effort worthwhile.

Perhaps the most important purpose to which children's trade books can be put in social studies, and to which these books are so well suited, is helping children gather information from multiple perspectives. By multiple perspectives we mean multiple interpretations: Children are helped to see events, both historical and current, from more than one angle, more than one vantage point or bias. When multiple perspectives are examined routinely, as part of studying any event, a compare-and-contrast method of teaching and learning becomes a common classroom experience. Encouraged in this way, children will form the habit of looking at events from more than one angle. Hopefully, they will become students who regularly ask, without prompting, "Have we examined all the relevant viewpoints? Is there a perspective we are ignoring?"

This strategy has at least two important advantages over the single-perspective approach. First, any one perspective is prevented from being put forward, uncritically, as "neutral." ("Perspective? *What* perspective? This is just how it happened!" one teacher said, tongue in cheek.) When the English colonists' perspective on the American West is the only viewpoint that is studied, then it does not seem to children like a perspective at all; rather, it seems to them to be simply the truth—the way it happened. Actually, however, different things happened, depending on who we talk with. If we were to talk to the Apache warrior, Geronimo, or the Spanish conquistador, Coronado, we would get quite a different perspective on the same event. This is true of *any* event, from the landing at Plymouth to Paul Revere's ride, from a fight on the playground to the battle at Gettysburg.

A second, closely related advantage is that children are brought into the actual work of historians: making sense of competing accounts. When children are apprenticed into this form of historical inquiry, they, as the NCSS *Curriculum Standards* say, "begin to understand and appreciate differences in historical perspectives, recognizing that interpretations are influenced by individual experiences, societal values, and cultural traditions."[15] This is a valued form of higher-order thinking, and all our children should be helped to engage in it.

Children's trade books are helpful in the following way. One of these books often represents one perspective quite well, sometimes brilliantly, going into considerable detail and providing rich contextual information. When teachers use two (or even three) of these books, in combination with the background information and maps provided in the textbook, multiple perspectives can easily be brought to bear on the event. Using a data retrieval chart (Chapter 7), the perspectives can be organized for careful study and comparison. Through creative activities such as role playing, readers' theater, construction activities, simulation games, and the cooperative learning technique called Structured Academic Controversy (Chapter 10), children will deepen their understanding of the perspectives.

A teacher who wishes to use trade books in this way might implement the following procedure. The teacher:

- Selects a historical or current event that is related clearly to curriculum goals.
- Browses trade books and other resources in order to assemble two or three perspectives on the event.
- Reads aloud or assists students in reading the resources.
- Incorporates dramatizations and other activities to help children comprehend the perspectives.
- Uses a data retrieval chart or other scheme to help children compare and contrast the perspectives on the event.
- Uses roundtables, panel discussions, or other techniques to help children come to a conclusion, based on evidence, as to what happened, its meaning, and its consequences.

Three brief examples of the multiple-perspectives approach are provided on these next few pages. Example A concerns immigration, now and long ago; B compares two perspectives on the American Revolution; and C involves European and Native American perspectives.

Discussion Questions and Suggested Activities

1. If social studies textbooks are written for the average reader, why do all good social studies textbooks tend to be difficult for the average reader?
2. Select a children's social studies textbook, and examine it to find examples of instruction on the reading skills listed in Figure 11–1. On what other skills is instruction provided in the textbook?
3. Using the same textbook, provide sample exercises based on the points made in the section entitled Using Textbooks and Study Aids.
4. Using the same textbook, find examples of the social studies concept labels (terms) listed in Figure 11–5.
5. What reference materials, whether paper or electronic, do you believe are the most useful to children? Why?

Example A

Immigration: Then and Now, Grade 3

Materials

Social studies text: *Communities Then and Now*

Trade books: Laurence Yep's *Dragonwings*; Ann Morris's *Dancing to America*

Primary document: U.S. Constitution

Cultural Perspectives

Immigration is a popular and important social studies topic. Since immigrants come from all over the world to the U.S., and for diverse reasons, it is not difficult to help children study this phenomenon from multiple perspectives.

Activity

This teacher spends an entire year on the theme Immigration: Then and Now with her third grade class. The children learn from the textbook program about European and Asian immigrant communities. They build replicas of the Plymouth and Jamestown colonies but also Santa Fe, New Mexico. They compare and contrast the New York Harbor to the San Francisco Bay, to which Europeans and Asians, respectively, have come for entry to the United States. They read the citizenship rules in the Constitution. They focus especially on the Chinese men who immigrated to work the railroads, listening to their teacher read *Dragonwings*, and a family that recently came to American from the Soviet Union, listening to *Dancing to America*. They create a data-retrieval chart to compare Ellis Island and Angel Island immigrants' stories.

Note

Local immigrant communities may have organized speakers' bureaus. In any event, people who have immigrated are often quite pleased to be invited to share their stories, foods, and photos with the class. One of the children's parents might be willing to help.

6. Select a social studies topic, and sketch a semantic map that displays your own prior knowledge of this topic.

7. Choose one of the references materials listed in Figure 11–3. What skills should a child have in order to use that reference effectively? Then, look back at the skill-teaching strategy suggested in Chapter 7 (Figure 7–2). Will that strategy be appropriate for teaching these skills? Are revisions needed?

8. Examine Lesson Plan 9, then select another nation and determine what revisions, if any, the plan will require.

9. Create a data-retrieval chart for the three lesson plans using trade books given at the end of the chapter. Down the left, list the three plans. Across the top, write these questions: What event is taught in this plan? What perspectives on that event are represented? How are trade books used in this plan? How are other resources used?

10. Select an era of United States history, and identify two or three trade books that bring different perspectives to bear on that era.

Example B

The American Revolution, Grade 5

Materials

Historical fiction. The Collier brothers' *My Brother Sam Is Dead* and *War Comes to Willy Freeman*.

Cultural Perspectives

These two pieces of historical fiction present very different perspectives on the American Revolution. Sam's story is told by his brother Tim. Both Sam and Tim are European American males. Their father is against Sam joining with the American rebels to drive out the British. Younger Tim is torn between his father and Sam. Willy, on the other hand, is a young female who has to disguise herself as a male because she is alone and separated from her family. Soldiers are everywhere. Also, she is African American. It doesn't make much difference to her which side wins. Both enslave Africans. Her father, unlike Tim's, joins with the rebels and, before many pages are turned, is killed defending a rebel fort.

Activity

Children write in their journals while reading these books. The culminating activity is to write a new story in which Tim and Willy meet and learn of one another's experiences and perspectives on this war.

Note

These stories should be combined with data gathered from the textbook, maps, and other informational sources so that students are not left only with narrative, fictionalized treatments of the war for independence.

Notes

1 Lauren B. Resnick, "Literacy in School and Out," *Daedalus* 119 (Spring 1990): 183.

2 Annemarie Sullivan Palinscar and Ann L. Brown, "Instruction for Self-Regulated Reading," in *Toward the Thinking Curriculum Current Cognitive Research*, ed. Lauren B. Resnick and Leopold E. Klopfer (Alexandria, VA: Association for Supervision and Curriculum Development, 1989), 19–39.

3 Marjorie Y. Lipson and Karen K. Wixson, *Assessment and Instruction of Reading Disability* (New York: HarperCollins, 1991).

4 See the influential study of coached practice, also known as "scaffolding," by Annemarie Sullivan Palinscar and Ann L. Brown, "Reciprocal Teaching of Comprehension Fostering and Monitoring Activities," *Cognition and Instruction* 1: 2 (1984): 117–75.

5 Lauren B. Resnick, "Literacy in School and Out," *Daedalus* 119 (Spring 1990): 169–85.

6 Resnick, "Literacy in School and Out," 183.

7 *The United States and Its Neighbors* (New York: Macmillan/McGraw-Hill, 1995), 672.

8 *The United States and Its Neighbors*, 372.

Example C

European/Native American Encounters, Grade 1

Materials
Speare's *Sign of the Beaver* and Bulla's *Squanto: Friend of the Pilgrims*.

Cultural Perspectives
European colonists arriving on the east coast of North America encountered not a new world but a very old one inhabited by millions of people belonging to many different cultures. Children's tendency to stereotype Native Americans—that is, to gloss over the differences among them—can be countered by presenting the differences straightforwardly, using historical fiction. In this activity, the class contrasts two native men: the legendary *Squanto: Friend of the Pilgrims*, and the Native American at the center of Elizabeth George Speare's *Sign of the Beaver*. The latter is neither "savage" nor "friendly," and children learn something of his culture.

Activity
The teacher reads these stories aloud, stopping occasionally to have the children retell what they have heard so far. This lets the teacher diagnose their understanding and watch for what catches their interest. Eventually, students dramatize imaginary meetings between the two men in which they share stories of their respective cultures.

Note
Consider using both books as springboards for in-depth study on the two native cultures presented. Where exactly did they live? What kind of a place was it? How did they interact with the natural environment? Were they different from other Native American groups in the same geographical regions? What was their language? religion? law? medicine? family structure? shelter? food? education? economy?

9   Barbara M. Taylor and S. Jay Samuels, "Children's Use of Text Structure in the Recall of Expository Material," *American Educational Research Journal* 20 (Winter 1983): 517–28.

10 Walter C. Parker and Samuel A. Perez, "Beyond the Rattle of Empty Wagons," *Social Education* 51 (March 1987): 164–66.

11 James Lincoln Collier and Christopher Collier, *War Comes to Willy Freeman* (New York: Dell, 1983).

12 William E. Nagy, *Teaching Vocabulary to Improve Reading Comprehension* (Urbana, IL: ERIC Clearinghouse on Reading and Communication Skills, National Council of Teachers of English, and International Reading Association, 1988).

13 Myra Zarnowski and Arlene F. Gallagher (eds.), *Children's Literature and Social Studies: Selecting and Using Notable Books in the Classroom* (Washington, DC: National Council for the Social Studies, 1993), vii.

14 "Notable Children's Trade Books," *Social Education* 59 (April/May 1995): 212.

15 National Council for the Social Studies, *Curriculum Standards for Social Studies* (Washington, DC: Author: 1994), 22.

● ●

Selected References

Au, Kathryn H. *Literacy Instruction in Multicultural Settings*. Fort Worth: Harcourt Brace, 1993.

Au, Kathryn H., Jana M. Mason, and Judith A. Scheu. *Literacy Instruction for Today*. New York: HarperCollins, 1995.

Brem, Jane. "Books in Brief Bolster Learning." In *Children's Literature and Social Studies: Selecting and Using Notable Books in the Classroom*, edited by Myra Zarnowski and Arlene F. Gallagher. Washington, DC: National Council for the Social Studies, 1993, 46–50.

Campbell, Kay, and Richard S. Knight. "Reading Research and Social Studies." In *Handbook of Research on Social Studies Teaching and Learning*, edited by James P. Shaver. New York: Macmillan, 1991, 578–88.

Goodman, Kenneth. *What's Whole in Whole Language?* Richmond Hill, Ontario: Scholastic, 1986.

Lipson, Marjorie Y., and Karen K. Wixson. *Assessment and Instruction of Reading Disability*. New York: HarperCollins, 1991.

Nagy, William E. *Teaching Vocabulary to Improve Reading Comprehension*. Urbana, IL: ERIC Clearinghouse on Reading and Communication Skills, the National Council of Teachers of English, and the International Reading Association, 1988.

Notable Children's Trade Books, *Social Education* 59 (April/May 1995): 212.

Pappas, Christine C., Barbara Z. Kiefer, and Linda S. Levstik. *An Integrated Language Perspective in the Elementary School*. White Plains, NY: Longman, 1990.

Resnick, Lauren B. "Literacy in School and Out," *Daedalus* 119 (Spring 1990): 169–85.

Tchudi, Stephen. *Planning and Assessing the Curriculum in English Language Arts*. Alexandria, VA: Association for Supervision and Curriculum Development, 1991.

Wineburg, Samuel S. "Probing the Depths of Students' Historical Knowledge," *Perspectives* 30 (1990): 459–76.

Winterowd, W. Ross. *The Culture and Politics of Literacy*. New York: Oxford University Press, 1989.

Zarnowski, Myra, and Arlene F. Gallagher (eds.). *Children's Literature and Social Studies: Selecting and Using Notable Books in the Classroom*. Washington, DC: National Council for the Social Studies, 1993.

SOCIAL STUDIES AS THE
INTEGRATING CORE

OVERVIEW

In Part I of this book, social studies education was defined as the integrated study of the social sciences to promote civic competence. Helping children construct powerful social understandings and take seriously the responsibilities of democratic citizenship are the basic goals of social studies education. A vision this important to society and this basic to the well-being of the children we teach can easily serve as a unifying goal for much of the teaching and learning that goes on in elementary and middle schools.

The reading and writing curriculum can most easily be brought to the service of social studies goals. Children cannot read *reading* or write *writing*, after all; these are means, not ends. Skillful teachers of social studies link literacy instruction to social studies goals and, in this way, give literacy skills purpose and meaning. Meanwhile, because reading and writing are among the most powerful of learning tools, children use them to achieve social studies curriculum objectives. Thus, two things are accomplished. Skills are used to help achieve valued content goals, and the skills themselves are strengthened by being engaged with content. This reasoning stands on firm ground. As research on reading and writing makes abundantly clear, "one does not simply learn to read and write: one learns to read and write about particular things in particular ways."[2]

Two Approaches: Infusion and Fusion

The first approach to curriculum integration is the *infusion* approach. Aspects of one subject area, such as language arts, are inserted or infused into another in such a way that the learner's grasp of both is enhanced. One subject area is in the role of helper, and the other is being enriched. One or more objectives from the latter subject area are being achieved thanks to tools borrowed from the former. Examples of infusion are:

- Using the concepts *plot* and *character* from children's literature to analyze a social event such as the American Revolution, the Underground Railroad, the civil rights movement, or a current event in the children's hometown.
- Using historical paintings along with concepts drawn from the fine arts to study major events in American history, such as Howard Chandler Christy's depiction of the signing of the U.S. Constitution; Marcia Sewall's illustrations of the native people, the Wampanoag, whom the Pilgrims encountered at Plymouth, in her book *People of the Breaking Day* (Antheneum); and Jacob Lawrence's paintings of the migration of African Americans from the South to the North after World War I in *The Great Migration* (HarperCollins).
- Using ideas and skills from mathematics, such as estimation and figuring proportions, to project population trends at the time when the children in the class will graduate from high school.
- Using acting techniques from theater arts to help children dramatize the Underground Railroad, Paul Revere's ride, or the journey of Lewis and Clark.

Reading, writing, literature, music, art, drama, history, geography, and civics: These children loved the unit on ancient Greece.

An alternative approach to curriculum integration is the *fusion* model. Now, two or more subject matters are joined together in such a way that a new, unified understanding is achieved. There is no sense, as in the infusion model, that subject matter A is serving subject matter B, or visa versa; rather A and B are fused to produce C. C is a powerful idea (a concept or generalization) that requires for its proper development in children's minds information from more than one subject area. Consider, for example, the concept *living things*. This idea is made more powerful when it includes *human beings* as well as what the science curriculum will call *flora* and *fauna*. Similarly, the concept *communities* is strengthened when comprised not only of human communities around the world but plant and animal communities as well (such as old growth forests, ant colonies, and schools of fish). The generalization *The decisions of human beings influence the survival of other living things*, also requires the fusion of subject matter drawn from social studies and science. Below are additional examples of fusion:

- American literature and American history are really two dimensions of the same topic. Their fusion will enrich students' knowledge of each dimension and help them build a unified understanding that encompasses both fields. Reading and dramatizing Esther Forbes's *Johnny Tremain* and the Colliers' *War Comes to Willy Freeman* along with reading historical narratives of the American Revolution found in the textbook and primary documents should help children form a better understanding of the American Revolution than if these fields were never brought together.

- Fusing social studies and science subject matter should help children learn the procedures and dispositions of the *scientific method*—that is to say, the *inquiry process*. Two powerful concepts included in the scientific method are *hypothesis-testing* and *evidence*. To form either concept and to learn the inquiry process, children will require examples from the social sciences (e.g., geography, history, anthropology) as well as the natural sciences (biology, geology, chemistry).
- A unified understanding of the voyages of Columbus can help children understand this as a turning point in human history that is far more complex and important than the story of a single explorer and his conquests. The exchange of plant life, animal life, and disease between the Eastern and Western Hemispheres that resulted from these voyages changed the world forever.

As these examples show, the objective of the fusion approach is to help children build ideas that cannot be built adequately without the joining together of two or more subject areas. In other words, the idea children are helped to construct is a *unifying whole* that has a character and significance different from the sum of its parts; conversely, the parts gain a meaning and significance that they otherwise lack.[3] An old-growth forest, with its precious interdependence of community members—human residents, commercial loggers, birds and mammals, ancient trees, moss, beetles, and so forth—becomes comprehendable in a new and insightful way when integrated with the study of the children's hometown, a pod of whales, and people of Mesa Verde. The big ideas that might be built from this fusion have depth and complexity that otherwise would not be possible.

Still, the fusion approach is not superior to the infusion approach. More is not better. Some ideas, whether concepts such as prejudice or community helpers or generalizations such as "scarcity limits people's ability to have all they want and need," may not be strengthened, and may only be muddled, by fusion. Just because subject areas *can* be integrated on a topic or idea is not in itself a reason to do so.

In this chapter the infusion and fusion approaches to integrating the social studies curriculum with other curriculum areas are further explored. We provide two examples in considerable depth so that readers can appreciate that integrated education requires careful planning and that it can enrich learning. The example of infusion is a popular one that is used successfully by teachers across the United States and Canada to help children write, with teammates, original biographies of major historical figures: great citizens, social activists, heroes, villains, scientists, environmentalists, writers, inventors, government leaders, kings and queens, explorers, labor leaders, religious figures, entrepreneurs and the like. The essence of this approach is that reading and writing skills are applied within social studies subject matter, in this case the life and times of a significant historical figure. The fusion example provided next is a unit that joins social studies and science curricula along the lines described above. Children build a rich understanding of the concept *living things* and the generalization *living things depend on one another for their survival*. The unit is taught today by third-grade teachers in Northglenn, Colorado.

Making Sense of Curricular Integration

Before proceeding to these examples, it should be helpful to clarify the concept of *integrated* or, as it is often called, *interdisciplinary education*. These terms have become slogans that are uttered to support nearly any proposal; therefore, the terms have little meaning. Roughly the same thing occurred in the 1950s and, earlier, in the 1930s when curriculum integration was propelled to the "top of the charts" as a popular solution to whatever people at the time thought was wrong with education.*

One reason for the popularity of the idea, no doubt, is that the term *integrated* itself connotes positive things. One is hard pressed to think of a similarly positive alternative. One expert puts it this way:

That curriculum integration is regarded as a good thing is not surprising. Who after all is in favor of non-integration or disintegration with their intimations of disorder and decay?[4]

Definitions

To understand integrated or interdisciplinary education, one must first understand the idea of academic disciplines. These are fairly distinct bodies of knowledge, each with its own preferred method of study. Anthropology, for example, is concerned with accumulating a body of knowledge (facts, concepts, generalizations, issues) about culture and customs; anthropologists' preferred method of accumulating this knowledge is ethnographic field work. Biology, sociology, political science, literature, history, and archeology are other distinct bodies of knowledge and methods. The school subject called *social studies* is itself an interdisciplinary field. It draws on history and the social sciences—geography, political science, economics, anthropology, sociology, and psychology. The school subject called *science* is also interdisciplinary, drawing on biology, chemistry, physics, physiology, and other natural sciences. *Art*, too, is interdisciplinary, combining drawing, painting, sculpting, writing, and other skills.

Interdisciplinary education, however, usually refers not to integrated work *within* these school subjects but *between* and *among* them—between and among social studies, science, literature, art, music, math, and so on. As well, it refers to the development of literacy—reading and writing competence—within these school subjects. Compare these definitions:[5]

Discipline: An integrated body of teachable knowledge with its own key concepts and generalizations, methods of inquiry, and issues.

Interdisciplinary or Integrated: A knowledge view and curriculum approach that purposefully draws together knowledge, perspectives, and methods of inquiry from more than one discipline to develop a more powerful understanding of a central idea, issue, person, or event.

---

* Readers interested in the earlier integrated education movements are referred to *The Integration of Educational Experiences*, The 57th Yearbook of the National Society for the Study of Education, ed. Nelson B. Henry (Chicago: University of Chicago Press, 1958); and Charles W. Knudsen, "What Do Educators Mean by 'Integration?'" *Harvard Educational Review* 7 (1937): 15–26.

Integrated or interdisciplinary education brings several categories of knowledge together for the purpose of helping children more fully understand the object of study. Note that the purpose is not to eliminate the individual disciplines but to use them as tools or resources. Wise teachers do not hide the disciplines from children any more than farmers hide their seeds, shovels, or plows. To the contrary, they call the disciplines by their proper names and help children to become more aware of their ideas and methods of inquiry. Numerous experts are worried that the current trend toward integrated education may cause teachers to withhold disciplinary knowledge from their students. Psychologist Howard Gardner, for example, argues that the disciplines:

represent the formidable achievements of talented human beings, toiling over the centuries, to approach and explain issues of enduring importance. . . . [W]e find the disciplines to be indispensable in any quality education, and we urge individuals not to throw away the "disciplinary baby" with the "subject matter" bathwater.[6]

Pitfalls

Integrated education has numerous pitfalls that must be understood if they are to be avoided. These range from confusion to treating integrated education as an ends rather than a means to an end. What follows is a list of pitfalls and guidelines for dealing with them.

Ends and Means

The greatest pitfall regarding curriculum integration is to treat it as a goal. As this chapter's opening quotation states succinctly, curriculum integration is a strategy, not a goal. In other words, curriculum integration is not an end in itself; it is neither good nor bad on its own. It *may* be good, but this depends on the worthiness of the goal toward which it is directed. It may be a skill or process goal, such as learning and applying the scientific method. It may be a content goal, such as learning that the decisions made by human beings influence the survival of other living things. "The most basic of all principles is goal relevance," write two scholars who have closely examined social studies learning activities. "Each activity should have at least one primary goal that, if achieved, will represent progress toward one of the major social education goals that underlie and justify the social studies curriculum."[7]

Either/or Thinking ("Putting All the Eggs in One Basket")

This error involves the assumption that either a discipline-based curriculum or an interdisciplinary curriculum is always the right thing to do. Neither is true. Both are needed at different times and for different purposes. It is important to exercise professional judgment, using each when appropriate. This is the eclectic approach, and for thoughtful teachers, it is usually the best course.

Trivializing Learning

While discipline-based education sometimes fragments knowledge, thoughtful teachers recognize that interdisciplinary education can create its own problems. It is particularly susceptible to trivializing the curriculum. This occurs when unimportant content is selected for instruction simply because it easily can be integrated with other content. Meanwhile, important content goes untaught. Just because a learning activity crosses disciplinary boundaries does not make it worthwhile. What makes an activity worthwhile is that students are forming or extending a powerful understanding or skill. As psychologist Jerome Bruner put it years ago, "The first object of any act of learning, over and beyond the pleasure it may give, is that it should serve us in the future. Learning should not only take us somewhere; it should allow us later to go further more easily."[8] Here is the point: Teachers need to be sure that learning activities are significant and that they contribute to the accomplishment of major curriculum goals.

Confusion

Interdisciplinary education needlessly confuses learners when teachers require them to study simultaneously topics that more fruitfully could be examined separately. Imagine students trying to study three cultures' customs, literature, art, and scientific achievements all at the same time. The loss in analytic clarity and the increased difficulty would not justify the gains hoped for by integrating social studies, literature, art, and science. Experts in any field do not attempt to tackle a problem by focusing their attention on all its parts at once. John Dewey advised, wisely, that we limit a topic for study in such a way as to avoid what he called "the great bad." This is "the mixing of things which need to be kept distinct."[9] Experts limit the problem they are working on; they analyze it, break it into its component parts. They do this to understand the big picture better and, therefore, to know where they most profitably might begin chipping away at the problem.

We should not train students to study a topic by making a jumbled mess of it. Readers may remember the helpful, clear plastic illustrations often found in a biology textbook. These made it possible to achieve a sort of layered understanding of the human body. Readers are permitted to focus only on the skeletal system, or only on muscle tissue or major organs, and then to lay these systems on top of one another to examine the whole picture and the interaction of parts.

*Dis*integration, then, can be helpful. It also can be needlessly fragmenting. Knowing how and when to separate topics to discern them and make them meaningful and knowing, on the other hand, when to integrate them is a major achievement of skillful teaching.

A Little of This, a Little of That

Closely related to the pitfall of trivializing learning is what one expert calls "the potpourri problem."[10] This occurs when a unit is composed of bits of information from each discipline. If the subject is the Mayan civilization, for example, we could find a bit of history, a bit of art, a bit of science, a bit of math, but not the proper depth in any of these to make the study meaningful and coherent. Better to help children dig into Mayan history in depth than to "superficialize" learning in the name of integrated education.

An Infusion Example: Producing Original Biographies

Infusing literacy education into social studies education gives the former the functional setting—the context—it needs if it is to flourish. Of course, reading and writing instruction, and instruction on other skills as well, sometimes needs to occur in isolation from functional settings so that particular aspects of the skills can be clarified and sharpened. By way of analogy, good musicians have always practiced scales hour upon hour, just as basketball players practice dribbling and shooting baskets. In these endeavors, the usefulness of isolated skills work is widely appreciated because it is known to contribute to the proficiency that is displayed in the functional setting—the concert or ball game. Likewise, teachers should not only provide opportunities for children to infuse skills, but to learn and practice them in the first place. In Lesson Plan 10, children learn to locate references in the library. A teacher might provide this instruction in preparation for an upcoming project in which the ability will be required. By teaching it, rather than assuming children have developed it, the teacher is laying the groundwork for the class's eventual success in the project.

Below we present such a project as an example of the infusion approach to integrated education. In this project, children compose, with teammates, an original biography of an important historical figure.[11] Our example will feature Sojourner Truth, the 19th-century social activist who fought against the institution of slavery, then for women's rights. Ample biographical material about Ms. Truth can be found in most school libraries and social studies textbooks, making it feasible for teachers to teach children about her and help them to write original, brief narratives of her life and times.

Sojourner Truth was first sold when she was nine years old, probably in the year 1807. She was born a slave in New York State to a Dutch man named Hardenbergh, so that was her name, too—Belle Hardenbergh. When she was nine, John Neely became Belle's new owner. He paid $50 and got both the Dutch-speaking African girl and 100 sheep. Two years later, after learning some English and suffering beatings at the hands of the Neely family, she was sold again, this time for $105 to Martin Schryver, who had a farm near the Hudson River. In 1810, Belle was sold yet again. Her new master, Mr. Dumont, wrote in his ledger, "For $300, Belle, about 13 years old, six feet tall." Years later, with the help of Quakers, Belle won her freedom and took the name Sojourner Truth. It was a good handle for the life she was about to live: a seeker and speaker of truth.

Her speeches attracted great crowds and are today among school children's favorites. For example, in May of 1851, she addressed a women's rights convention in Akron, Ohio. Before she or any of the other women could speak, Protestant ministers—all male—dominated the proceedings, deriding the women who wanted social reform. Francis Gage later wrote what happened after the ministers were through:

Then, slowly from her seat in the corner rose Sojourner Truth, who, till now, had scarcely lifted her head. She moved solemnly to the front, laid her old bonnet at her feet, and turned her great speaking eyes on me.

There was a hissing sound of disapprobation above and below. I rose and announced, "Sojourner Truth," and begged the audience keep silence for a few moments.

The tumult subsided at once, and every eye was fixed on this almost Amazon form, which stood nearly six feet high, head erect and eyes piercing the upper air like one in a dream. At her first word there was a profound hush. She spoke in deep tones, which, though not loud, reached every ear in the house and away through the doors and windows:

"Well, children, where there is so much racket, there must be something out of kilter. That man over there says women need to be helped into carriages and lifted over ditches—and to have the best place everywhere. Nobody ever helps me into carriages or over mud-puddles—or gives me the best place at the table!"

Locating References in the Library

Grade

2 or 3

Time

Three class periods

Objectives

To orient children to the school library.

To practice interacting with the librarian.

To group and label some of the contents of the school library.

Interest Building

Ask the children to share incidents of trying to find something—a toy, a book, a hat—but not knowing where to look. Then ask questions to assess their knowledge of the contents and organization of a library.

Lesson Development

Brief the librarian on the following activity and make an appointment to bring the class to the library.

Divide the class into teams. Ask each team to choose an interviewer who will ask questions to the librarian. Have them also decide on two questions for the interviewer to ask: one "where question" about the *location* of something in the library (e.g., Where is the biggest dictionary? Where is information about the Pony Express?) and one "how question" about *how to locate something without asking the librarian* (e.g., How can we find out where Pony Express information is located without asking you?). Then have the interviewers practice asking the two questions with teammates playing the role of the librarian.

Take the class to the library at the appointed time. Have the children sit in teams. Direct each interviewer to ask the team's questions. After all the questions have been answered, provide the teams the opportunity to actively experience the answers they received (e.g., go to the dictionary and open it up; load the CD-ROM with the Pony Express information).

Back in the classroom, lead the class in a list-group-and-label activity (see Chapter 7, Concept Learning: Three Strategies) dealing with the information provided by the librarian. If there were five teams with two questions each, there will be a list of ten answers. Ask the children to group this information together based on similarities they see (e.g., electronic databases, biographies, books on the north wall).

Assessment/Summary ~~Map Game~~

Distribute grid paper and ask students to sketch from memory a map of the library showing the locations of various references. Collect and observe these: On the next day, hand the maps back unmarked and take the class to the library to revise the maps as needed. Then, distribute new grid paper on which students draw a revised map of the library to place in their map portfolios. *This in itself teaches them comprehension when they compare the two grid papers. One from memo & the revised one.*

Materials

Grid paper

Raising herself to her full height, and lifting her voice to a pitch like rolling thunder, Sojourner asked, "And ain't I a woman? Look at me! Look at my arm!" She bared her right arm to the shoulder, showing her tremendous muscular power. "I have ploughed and planted and gathered into barns, and no man could get ahead of me! And ain't I a woman?

"I could work as much and eat as much as a man—when I could get it—and bear the lash as well! And ain't I a woman?

"My mother bore ten children and saw them sold off to slavery, and when I cried with my mother's grief, none but Jesus heard me! And ain't I a woman?

"Then that little man in black says women can't have as many rights as men. If the first woman God ever made was strong enough to turn the world upside down all alone, these women together" (and she glanced over the platform) "ought to be able to turn it back and get it right side up again! And now that the women are asking to do it, the men better let 'em."

Long cheering greeted this. "I'm obliged to you for hearing me," she concluded, "and now old Sojourner hasn't got nothing more to say."[12]

Sojourner had much more to say. When she wasn't speaking for women's rights, she was speaking against slavery. And after President Lincoln ended slavery, Sojourner worked in Washington, D.C.—"Mr. Lincoln's city"—to overcome the remnants of slavery: racism and deeply entrenched prejudice. She tried to help freed Africans find work and homes, and she worked for a time as a nurse in Freedman's Hospital. These were chaotic, heartbreaking times. The Civil War, in which her son fought in the famous 54th Massachusetts Regiment, became a slaughter on both sides. And just as it ended, Lincoln, whom she had met and much admired, was killed by an assassin.

Still, she was not defeated. One of our favorite biographers for children, Jeri Ferris, writes of yet another of Sojourner's efforts to right wrongs:

One afternoon as Sojourner walked back to the hospital with an armful of blankets, she was so tired she just couldn't walk any more. Horsedrawn streetcars clanged up and down the road, filled with white folks. Sojourner waited for a car to stop, but none did. Finally, as yet another car passed her, she called out, "I want to ride!" People crowded around, the horses stopped, and Sojourner got on. The conductor was furious and demanded she get off. Sojourner settled back in her seat. "I'm not from the South," she said firmly, "I'm from the Empire State of New York, and I know the law as well as you do."

The next day she tried to ride another streetcar. Again the conductor would not stop. Sojourner ran after the car and caught up with it. When the horses stopped, she jumped on. "What a shame," she panted, "to make a lady run so." The Conductor threatened to throw her off. "If you try," she said, "it will cost you more than your car and horses are worth." He didn't.

The third time Sojourner tried to ride a streetcar, she was with a white friend. "Stand back," shouted the conductor to Sojourner, "and let that lady on."

"*I* am a lady too," said Sojourner, and she stepped aboard with her friend.[13]

Writing About Historical Figures

We provide this brief sketch of the life and times of Sojourner Truth so that readers can better follow the procedure we now outline for helping children to produce biographies themselves. The creation of an original biography is a splendid way to invite children to read, write, and discuss their way into an in-depth understanding of a historical figure. Not only are their horizons expanded and their historical reasoning encouraged by this exposure to lives different from their own, but their skills in reading, writing, revising, planning, and cooperating are developed along the way.

The names of the historical figures on the list that follows are a small sample of the persons whose lives and times warrant in-depth study by elementary and middle school children. Readers might notice that the persons listed could all serve as examples of *democratic citizens*. In the spirit of the teaching strategy called concept formation (Chapter 7), teachers can select three or four persons who together would help children to form the concept of *democratic citizen*. The class could write three or four biographies during the school year, all the while keeping track of the similarities among these citizens—similarities that make them all examples of democratic citizens:

- They knew that popular sovereignty is the bedrock of democracy and that this means taking personal responsibility for the common good.
- They took time from their private lives to be active in civic life.
- They understood the difference between complaining and proposing solutions.
- They understood, within the constraints of their times, that democracy means majority rule *and* minority rights.
- They exhibited courage on behalf of these principles.

Biographies of Democratic Citizens

James Madison	Abraham Lincoln
Susan B. Anthony	Jane Adams
Thomas Jefferson	Mary McLeod Bethune
Benjamin Franklin	Gordon Hirabayashi
Eleanor Roosevelt	Patrick Henry
George Washington	Martin Luther King, Jr.

Democratic citizen is not the only concept around which subjects can be selected for biographies, though it is one of the most important. Other central ideas are *explorers, inventors and scientists, champions of the poor, friends of nature, leaders, dictators, revolutionaries, and heroes.* Recall that the discussion of concept learning in Chapter 7 emphasized multiple examples. Here this means that a teacher might orchestrate children's biographical studies around one of these themes, having them produce over the year three or four biographies on that theme rather than one each on different themes. This approach should help children to build an in-depth understanding of that theme. On the other hand, teachers might, to cover more ground, mix the kinds of subjects about whom their children write, for example, choosing a hero (Crazy Horse or Harriet Tubman), an inventor (Benjamin Franklin or Eli Whitney), a scientist (Galileo or Newton), and a great citizen (Sojourner Truth or James Madison). Figure 12–1 suggests several themes and related subjects.

Procedure for Producing Biographies

The teacher will need to plan the several phases of the biography project:

1. Decide on the learning objectives.
2. Select the person about whom children will write their biographies.

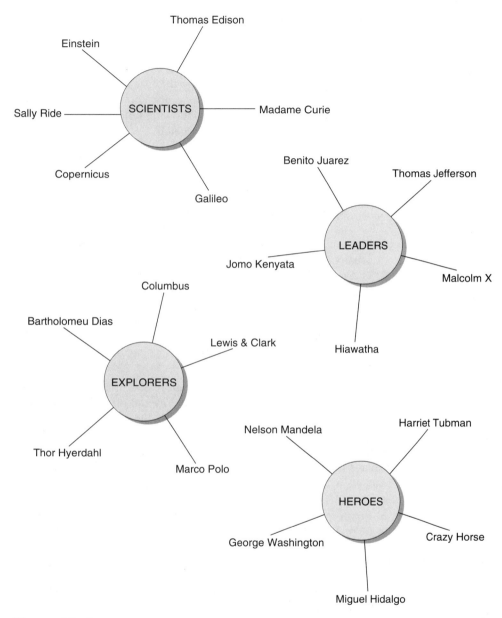

Figure 12–1

Examples of thematic clusters of persons of prominence suitable for biographical study

3. Introduce the project to students, clarifying the objectives, rationale, and audience.
4. Help the children learn about the person and keep track of what they are learning.
5. Help children reflect on the person's life and times and identify key events in the person's life.

6. Orchestrate the cooperative production of biographies in small groups.
7. Conclude the project.

Learning Objectives

The learning objectives or targets for this project will vary with the curriculum, the teacher, the students, the local community, and the person about whom the children will write. Generally, however, the following objectives are pertinent. Note that skills, knowledge, and habits of mind are targeted.

As a result of producing a historical biography with teammates, the children will:

1. Learn that individuals' lives are shaped by history and, sometimes, shape the history into which the next generation is born.
2. Learn to use the writing process to compose and publish a biography.
3. Learn about the genre of literature called *biography* and the way biographies are usually organized and presented.
4. Learn to work cooperatively in small groups to which they have been assigned
5. Read a variety of reference sources for the purpose of constructing and understanding the life and times of a person.
6. Learn to make sense of competing accounts of an event that they find in diverse resources and to compose a fair-minded account of that event.
7. Learn to construct time lines of a person's life.

Not all of these objectives need to be addressed or addressed to the same extent. Some may have been achieved by the class before the project begins and need mainly refinement; others may come in a subsequent biography project. Objectives should be selected that are developmentally appropriate for the children in the class and that can feasibly be achieved given the constraints of time and available materials. Still, this list displays the impressive array of objectives for which the biography project is suitable. Teachers may wish to include other objectives as well:

8. Learn to determine which events in a person's life are turning points (milestones, pivotal events).
9. Learn how a person's geographical setting(s) may have influenced his or her life.
10. Learn to examine character traits in a historical figure's life and draw lessons for one's own life.
11. Learn to empathize with others' dilemmas and struggles.
12. Learn to make books.
13. Learn the art of illustrating a section of narrative using charcoal pencil.

Selecting a Subject

Several criteria guide the selection of subjects for children's biographies. Most important is that the person chosen brings children into contact with powerful ideas of history, government, geography, economics, and/or other social studies disciplines. Individuals who can help children build understandings will not only bring children to the heart of social studies but also build firm foundations for further learning.

Another criterion for subject selection is the likelihood that children will be captivated by this life. It may help some children become more interested in the person if information is available on his or her childhood. Ben Franklin's early troubles with his brother James, for example, James Madison's illnesses as a child, and Sojourner Truth's harrowing childhood all seem to fascinate children, broadening them by giving them access to *other* children's lives—lives that are different but reassuringly similar, too. Learning a great deal about a person can itself make that person captivating to the young biographer. As this third grade student quite wisely reported, one cannot know for certain what makes a subject interesting. He seems to conclude, however, that familiarity breeds interest, not contempt:

Everyone else was real interested in Hiawatha but I wasn't because, well, the things I knew about him just were boring. But the more I found out, the way they learned to hunt and stuff in the long house, and all the magic, well it got real interesting. Now I know him a lot.

A third key criterion is the availability of materials. The "snapshot biography" method we outline here requires students to learn a great deal about the subject.[14] If the subject is obscure, chances are good that neither the textbook nor the school library will have ample books, primary documents, narrative biographies, or other materials.

Consider how Ms. Brem, a fourth grade teacher, selects biographical subjects. She has decided to weave a yearlong study of *leadership* through the state history curriculum her school district requires in that grade. She wants her pupils to study and eventually write biographies of three state leaders. She wants the leaders to be culturally diverse, and she wants them to expose students to different historical periods and geographical areas of the state. Now Ms. Brem begins her materials search. A booklet she received last year from the state arm of the League of Women Voters provides information on several civic leaders, and she asks a committee of students to select one of these for the class to study. The social studies education office at the state capital publishes material on the state's governors; Ms. Brem selects the state's first governor. Now she has selected two of the three subjects she needs. Since they are both European Americans, Ms. Brem wants the third leader to belong to an ethnic minority.

Unaware of who this might be or where materials can be obtained she appoints another committee of students to go to the school librarian for help. The librarian refers them to information on a civic leader who helped to organize the early Chinese-American community in the state. Now the class has a set of three leaders and is ready for the reading-and-writing approach to biographical study.

Introducing the Project

On the day the biography project is introduced to students, the teacher should have in mind five purposes: assess, activate prior knowledge, provide purpose, provide rationale, and identify the audience. First, the teacher will need to assess what the children already know about biographies and what sense they make of the notion of a person's "life and times." A few informal questions should accomplish this task (see Chapter 9). It is assumed here that the teacher has assessed previously the children's reading and writing ability and has come to know something of their home cultures, special needs, and prior experiences. Second, based on what the teacher learns during this brief diagnostic assessment, he or she can further draw out the children's knowledge and experience. A semantic map might be created on the chalkboard (see Chapter 11), and the school librarian can be invited to discuss biographies with the children.

Third, the teacher should reveal clearly the objectives or targets of the project. These may be posted on the bulletin board and explained. Fourth, the teacher should help the children understand why these targets need to be reached—why they are important. For example, it is important to study historical biographies because doing so can introduce us to amazing new worlds and help us avoid mistakes that were made in the past. It is important to learn to cooperate in small groups to which one has been assigned because this mirrors realities in the workplace and civic life. Finally, the teacher should help the children identify an audience for their biographies. For example, if they have recently visited the residents of a rehabilitation center, they may wish to write the biographies for this audience and take them personally to the center. Or they may wish to write them to members of the city council, encouraging them to be wise and fair-minded leaders.

Learning About the Subject of a Biography

Before children can begin to write about a biographical subject, they need to learn something about him or her. Let us be clear, however, that the learning sequence is not read, then write. Rather, it is write a little, drawing on prior experience, then find out a little by reading, viewing a film, or listening to taped speeches. Write some, learn a little more, write some more, and so on. One of the major advances in the science of instruction in the past ten years is that teachers do not have to provide all of the facts before asking students to think. The advice instead is to integrate data gathering and reflection. The teacher should concentrate student attention on the higher-order task, in this case production of the biography, which in turn motivates gathering facts about the subject and interpreting his or her life.

Accordingly, students begin learning about the subject, such as Sojourner Truth, by finding out a little something about her. Perhaps the teacher begins by reading aloud for just twenty minutes from Jeri Ferris's book, concentrating on the beginning of the story when Sojourner is taken from her mother and sold to Mr. Neely at the age of nine. Then the teacher asks the children to discuss this passage—the idea of buying and selling persons, in this case a child. She asks them to imagine the feelings of Belle on the auction block and the feelings of her mother and father. She may ask them what they have learned elsewhere about the enslavement of people. Perhaps some of them will talk about the Jews in Egypt in biblical times. Some may have seen the old movie about Spartacus; perhaps some will talk about the Holocaust. Some children may know quite a bit about the capture and subsequent ownership of Africans through books they have read or lessons they have had in prior grades or in church. The discussion will provide the teacher with diagnostic information about children's current knowledge of slavery while activating the students' prior knowledge.

Now the teacher can ask students to bring out their journals and begin to write. She may ask them to write about the same things she previously asked them to talk about, which should be the easiest for them. Then she might ask them to predict what will happen to Sojourner in her new master's home. This should make them want to gather more information. Where will they get it?

The teacher knows that Sojourner's life with Mr. Neely is documented in the textbook. So, the next day she has children take out their journals to remind themselves of the predictions they wrote yesterday. Then, they are given twenty minutes to read the pertinent section in the text and return to their journal to write what really happened. Next, the teacher turns student attention to the map of the Northeast in the textbook and, based on clues given in the passage read aloud yesterday and the text passage today, helps them to find the state where Sojourner first was bought and sold (New York). In their journals, she has them enter the date and sketch a map of New York under the title, Where Sojourner Truth's Story Begins.

Now that they know where the story began (the geographic theme *location*), students are helped to get a feel for New York (the geographic theme *place*). Their teacher has them go to their cooperative teams and, working with the textbook, answer these questions:

1. What states, countries, and bodies of water border New York?
2. Is the geography of New York all the same, or are there different landforms? If so, what are they?
3. If Sojourner was able to fly away from the Neely farm, which route would have the fewest mountains to fly over?

The teacher then tells students to sketch all of this on a blank handout map of New York, including a legend so readers can understand their symbols.

The next day, the teacher reads aloud Virginia Hamilton's retelling of the folk tale, *The People Could Fly*. A wonderfully hopeful tale, though at the same time tragic, it tells of enslaved Africans literally flying from bondage to freedom:

They say the people could fly. Say that long ago in Africa, some of the people knew magic. And they would walk up on the air like climbin' up on a gate. And they flew like blackbirds over the fields.

But when the people were captured for slavery, we learn in the tale, they shed their wings. The slave ships were too crowded for wings. A few, however, kept the power. Toby did, and he used it to help the others to escape. One day Sarah was hoeing and chopping as fast as she could, a hungry baby on her back, but the baby "started up bawling too loud." The Overseer hollered at Sarah to keep the baby quiet, but Sarah fell under the babe's weight and her own weakness. The Overseer began to whip her. "Get up, you black cow," he called. Sarah looked to Toby: "Now, before it's too late," she panted. "Now." Toby raised his arms and whispered the magic words to her. "Kum . . . yali, kum buba tambe."

Sarah lifted one foot on the air. Then the other. She flew clumsily at first, with the child now held tightly in her arms. Then she felt the magic, the African mystery. Say she rose just as free as a bird. As light as a feather.[15]

Afterward, students return to their journals to reflect on this new material. The teacher continues over the next two or three weeks to read aloud from biographies and other accounts of Sojourner Truth, as well as from related stories and reference material. Student committees are sent to the library to gather data on people, places, events, and issues raised in the teacher's readings that students want to find out more about. As well, the teacher assembles some material for the students to read themselves—material in the textbook on Lincoln's decision to free the slaves and material on influential abolitionists: Frederick Douglass, who escaped from slavery in the South; William Lloyd Garrison, who published *The Liberator*, an abolitionist newspaper; and the Grimké sisters, Angelina and Sarah, who moved north after having been raised with captive Africans on a South Carolina plantation. This information helps to elaborate the children's understanding of Sojourner's life, as well as her civic missions, and should lead to their producing much stronger, richer biographies.

For this reason, information on the women's movement of the 1800s needs also to be gathered, such as the Seneca Falls Convention convened by Lucretia Mott and Elizabeth Cady Stanton in 1848. This is the same movement Sojourner jolted with her "Ain't I A Woman?" speech, delivered three years later at a second women's rights convention.

The setting for all this information needs also to be grasped; consequently, students should study the geography of New York, Ohio, and Michigan—the three states where Sojourner spent much time working, speaking, and living. In this way, students learn about the subject of their biography and gradually piece together in their minds a model of Sojourner's life and times.

Reflection and Setting Priorities

After several weeks of reading, writing, and mapping their biographical subject's life, children are ready to reflect on this life and its times and places, and to select key events. A few of these events will become the focal points of the chapters in the book students will write together. The following procedure is recommended.[16]

1. *Opening.* The teacher announces that today is the day the class begins to pull together all that has been learned about the subject and informs students of what is to come.

2. *Brainstorming.* The teacher asks students to brainstorm all the events in the subject's life that they found interesting, all the events they believe were pivotal in the subject's life, all the events they figure made the subject the most and least proud, and so on. The point here is to get a long list of varied events in the subject's life. Here are just a few of the events in Sojourner's life that students have suggested.

- the time she was separated from her mother
- the second time she was sold
- the third time she was sold
- confronting Mr. Dumont
- rescued by Quakers
- names herself Sojourner Truth
- "Ain't I A Woman?" speech
- meeting President Lincoln
- working as a nurse in Washington, D.C.
- confronting the trolley conductor
- meetings with Garrison and Douglass

When the brainstorming slows, the teacher has students take a break—go to recess, clean the room, do something physically active. When they return, they open their journals and search for other events to add to the list. They come up with more:

- being born in captivity
- speaking out for women's rights
- becoming an abolitionist
- living in New York
- traveling by buggy in Ohio

3. *Selecting.* The class is now asked to select four or five of the key events brainstormed earlier. These might be the four events that interested students the most, or the teacher might direct them to use other criteria. For example, if the teacher previously has worked with children on the meaning of time lines, she or he might have them divide Sojourner's life into four equal segments and choose one event from each segment. Or, the teacher might have them choose one event in each of three categories: meetings with remarkable people, life as a slave, life as an abolitionist. Still another criterion would have students select events that are turning points—pivotal events.

Once the key events have been selected, the children are placed in cooperative groups of four or five members. Each group is directed to divide the events among themselves, each choosing one event. Dividing the events—and thus the labor—is crucial to the coming task: producing an original biography.

Writing and Illustrating

The students are now ready to write and illustrate a biography of their subject. Each cooperative group will produce a biography on the same subject, in this case Sojourner Truth. Some teachers have each group use the same biography title, *The Life and Times of (Sojourner Truth)*. Others let each group create its own variation on this title.

Each person on the team is responsible for one chapter. The chapter's topic is the key event selected before. If the teacher wishes, he or she can use the cooperative groupwork technique called Jigsaw.[17] One member of each small group is working on the same key event as one child on each of the other groups; consequently, these children can meet together to work on their chapter, discussing, sharing, and revising one another's drafts (see Chapter 10). Thus, the book may shape up like this:

> title: *The Courage and Conviction of Sojourner Truth*
> chapter 1: "Sold for 50 Dollars!"
> chapter 2: "New Name, New Life"
> chapter 3: "Ain't I A Woman?"
> chapter 4: "The Trolley Incident"

The child on each team who is responsible for chapter 1 joins with other children from other teams also working on "Sold for 50 Dollars!" Meanwhile, the child on each team responsible for chapter 2 joins with the other "2s," and so on. These are *expert groups*. Together they discuss what they will write and draw, read one another's drafts, and provide feedback. This is advisable with younger children who are just beginning to write early versions of paragraphs; the group support is helpful, and the teacher can more easily monitor and coach the four expert groups than if every child in the room were writing on a different topic.

Whether the teacher uses the Jigsaw technique or not, the children's work has two parts: They write a description of the key event for which they are responsible, and they draw an accompanying illustration. The least experienced writers may produce only a one- or two-paragraph description and may fit their illustration on the same page. The teacher may press more experienced writers, however, to produce a two- or three-page description. The illustration is embedded in the text somewhere as in "real" biographies. Skillful teachers are able to boost their children's confidence about both the writing and the drawing by encouraging them to "just get started, get something on paper, pull something together from your journal, whatever; we'll go back and polish it later." (Teachers and children who play the board game *Pictionary* understand that illustrating is very different from producing realistic drawings. Virtually anyone can illustrate.)

Each team thus produces the rudiments of a biography: a title page and four chapters. But real biographies have more, and so should these. The following parts of a book make a more complete biography, and they generally can all be done even by the youngest children:

Title Page. Title plus complete publication information, for example: The Life and Times of Sojourner Truth (see Figure 12–2).

Foreword. Written by someone other than the four authors; for example, a parent, another teacher, the mayor, a school board member, a bus driver. Instruct the Foreword writer to write no more than one page and to address two matters:

1. Tell readers some ways you feel you can relate personally to the person about whom the biography was written.
2. Tell readers something about the book.

Introduction with Time Line and Map. The introduction should contain a brief message to readers telling them the subject of the book: Who is its subject? Where and when did he or she live? What, in a nutshell, did he or she do? Why? It is also considerate to tell readers the topic of each chapter. A helpful way to portray the *when* is to sketch a time line of the subject's life. The *where* statement should be illustrated with a map, either physical or political, or both, with a legend to help readers understand the symbols.

Chapters 1–4. Each chapter needs a title and author name. Its body is a written description of a key event in the subject's life with an illustration that captures the key event.

About the Authors Page. Ask each child to write a sentence or paragraph about her- or himself. The teacher might ask each group to decide how long the author statement should be. Children can be prompted to tell readers their full name, the name of the city or town where they live, their age, and something they like to do:

Wing Luke lives in Denver, Colorado, with his family. He is 9 years old and loves to play soccer. He wrote chapter 4, "The Trolley Incident."

Figure 12–2

An example of a biography written by students as a cooperative learning project

The Life and Times
of
Sojourner Truth

Amy Redling, Shana Williams,
Eddie Garcia, Wing Luke
1996
Briarcrest Elementary

Concluding the Project

Time should be set aside for drawing the biography project to a close after the books have been completed. The biographies need to be copied so that one can be placed in each child's portfolio. A self-assessment checklist, similar to the one shown in Figure 9–9, might be completed by each child and clipped to his or her copy. Details concerning the delivery of the books to the audience identified at the beginning of the project need to be discussed. A committee could be appointed for this purpose. A concluding discussion focusing on the objectives of the project should follow. Focus questions such as the following, each matched to an objective, will be helpful:

1. What have you learned about how history shaped (*Sojourner Truth's*) life, and about how her life shaped the history into which the next generation was born?
2. What have you learned about writing?
3. What is a biography? Who would you like to read about next?
4. At which cooperative skill do you excel?
5. What have you learned about locating resources in the library?
6. What was difficult about writing a fair-minded account?
7. How would you describe a time line to a younger student?

Summing Up: The Changing Concept of Literacy

Biography writing integrates portions of the literacy and social studies curricula by infusing the former into the latter. By embedding literacy instruction in social studies content *and* cooperative groupwork, the teacher creates the kind of social context that can support in-depth learning. Reading comprehension and writing instruction become much more than plodding through new vocabulary and learning sentences and paragraphs in a vacuum; literacy comes to mean problem solving, interpretation, competing interpretations, conversation, provocation, writing and rewriting to find out what one thinks is true and what one believes ought to be done, and experimenting with new possibilities that exist now only in the imagination. This is "high" literacy.

Reading and writing are processes—more precisely, *crafts*—that evolve through trial, error, and support from those more accomplished. This process-oriented notion of literacy learning is different from what research told us only twenty years ago.[18] Then, it was quite common to define literacy as a finished product: You either had it or you didn't; you were "literate" or "illiterate" (see Figure 12–3).

This emphasis on process is changing the way highly skilled teachers orchestrate literacy instruction. They understand that an individual's reading and writing skills grow and change over time. One's literacy is not static; it evolves, and its evolution depends on the individual's social context, that is, his or her "literacy community." All of us belong to one sort of discourse community or another, and that membership functions to socialize us into one or more patterns of using our minds—of reading, writing, and

Artwork and social studies are inseparable.

Figure 12–3
Literacy research emphases

Early Research Emphasis:	Current Research Emphasis:
Reading and writing instruction are separated.	Reading and writing instruction are integrated.
Both are separated from content learning.	Both are developed within content learning.
Reading and writing are fixed abilities that, like muscles, are the same everywhere.	Reading and writing ability evolves like a craft and mirrors the local literacy community.
Reading and writing are finished products.	Reading and writing are complex processes.

talking. We might be socialized into a literacy community that expects and rewards no more than minimal language use—say, for reading street signs, a ballot, and directions on a medicine label; for "filling out" job applications and worksheets. This is the vocabulary of low literacy. On the other hand, we might be socialized into a literacy community that has a higher vision of literacy and, consequently, expects and encourages something quite different.[19] Here, language is used in the service of higher-order tasks; for example, to plan research on civic problems with an eye toward improving social life, as an avenue to satisfying aesthetic experiences in literature and the arts, and as a means of lively conversation and, hence, conflict resolution and mutual understanding.

When literacy is defined in this more empowering way, literacy instruction cannot remain the same. It, too, needs to change. Now practice and coaching, focused on the *processes* of reading and writing, become the centerpieces of instruction. Learning by doing is the path, *and the doing overlaps important content goals*. Content, whether the parts of the United States Constitution or the cultures of Asia and Africa, is the landscape on which the path is laid. Continuous feedback and guidance, both from the teacher and from more accomplished peers, makes success possible. The biographical approach is, of course, only one vehicle, but it is a powerful and feasible one. The noted biographer Milton Meltzer observed that the biography approach is a vehicle for developing children's natural curiosity about people and the world around them to the point where they themselves investigate a particular life and, through the artful use of language, tell that human story to others.[20]

A Fusion Example: Understanding Living Things

We turn to an example of another approach to curriculum integration, the fusion model. Now two subject areas are tapped because doing so will help children construct an idea that could not otherwise be built. The idea in the following example is that living things are interdependent. Put differently, *the decisions made by human beings influence the survival of other living things*. Recall that this idea is a generalization: a statement that meaningfully links two or more concepts. The main concepts here are decision making, living things, and what they need to survive. Both the generalization and the concepts that compose it are made stronger by reference to subject matter that is conventionally found in the science curriculum and other subject matter found typically in the social studies curriculum. These subject matters are fused in this unit so that the big idea can more richly be developed.

This unit is part of an integrated social studies/science curriculum called *Explore*.[21] It is a K–6 program; accordingly, there are many units like the one featured here—similar, that is, in the way that subject matters are fused to help children build a powerful idea. *Explore* was developed by curriculum specialists and teachers working in Northglenn, Colorado, along with the late Sydelle Seiger-Ehrenberg, a renowned curriculum planner and specialist in higher-order thinking. Working with Seiger-Ehrenberg was elementary school principal Pat Willsey. The two believe that integrated units must not only help children form "big ideas," but engage them in higher-order thinking *without which children will not be able to integrate the information, thereby forming the big idea*. "There is no choice to be made between a content emphasis and a thinking skills emphasis. No depth in either is possible without the other."[22] The general goal statement for the entire K–6 *Explore* program makes explicit this interdependence of curriculum integration and higher-order thinking:

As a result of using thinking strategies and other relevant skills, K–6 students will develop an understanding of the orderliness, diversity, relationships, and changes that exist and are created in the natural world and in human experience. Further, they will learn to make intelligent, responsible decisions and plans in light of each understanding.

Planning a Fusion Unit: Ingredients and Procedure

Teachers who wish to plan a fusion unit should find this unit from *Explore* a helpful model. Its ingredients include many of the most important material in the prior chapters of this book:

- Sets high expectations for achievement
- Engages children in inquiry and concept formation so that content and higher-order thinking are blended
- Assessments are challenging and geared to what was taught
- Citizenship education—decision making, values, and community action—is incorporated
- Children are expected to use the textbook as a data source
- Focus and follow-up questions are carefully planned
- Important material from two subject areas is fused in order to help children construct a powerful and unifying idea

The procedure for planning a fusion unit is not etched in stone. Indeed, there are as many approaches as there are creative teachers. What follows is a procedure that should help beginning teachers get started. The planning form shown in Figure 8–1 may be helpful.

1. *Identify a unifying generalization that is also important and powerful.* "Kites are colorful and ride the wind" is a unifying generalization that could potentially integrate science (aerodynamics) and social studies (production, consumption, and distribution), but it is not important or powerful enough to warrant much school time. The prior chapters of this book, the work of curriculum standards committees, and teachers' own subject matter expertise will suggest generalizations that are critically important for children to develop. *In the following unit, the unifying generalization is: The decisions made by human beings influence the survival of other living things.*

2. *Identify the component concepts.* The teacher needs to examine the unifying generalization and identify the concepts that compose it. *In the following unit, the key concepts are* decision making, living things, *and* survival *(i.e., the needs of living things). Another key concept is the* scientific method *(inquiry process), because this is how children will build the unifying idea.*

3. *Plan a sequence of learning activities that will help children construct the unifying generalization.* Each learning activity (lesson) plan should have an objective and a focus question that anchor the activity to the overall unit goal, which is to help children build the generalization. *In the following unit, the focus question and objective are given at the beginning of each of the four lessons.*

4. *Select teaching strategies that will help children achieve lesson objectives.* Concepts are sure to be the focus of one or more lessons, because generalizations are composed of concepts. Therefore, one or more concept teaching strategies will be relevant (see Chapter 7). Likewise, because the scientific method is featured, strategies for teaching children to inquire scientifically will be relevant (again, Chapter 7). *In the following unit, the concept-formation strategy is the chief, though not the sole, teaching strategy.*

What follows are the four lessons that compose Unit 1 of the third-grade *Explore* curriculum.

- The first lesson introduces children to "the scientific way of learning"—that is, the inquiry method. Note that the assessment asks children to classify a number of activities, selecting the ones that represent the scientific method.
- The second lesson helps children form the concept of "living things." Note the use of the data-retrieval chart, the concept formation procedure, and classifying.
- The third lesson helps children form the concept of the "survival needs" of living things.
- The fourth develops the decision making and social action component of the unit: Students become aware of and committed to individual and group actions that help living things meet their needs and reach their potential. The result should be that children have constructed an initial understanding of the unifying idea, *The decisions made by human beings influence the survival of other living things.*

Explore: Unit 1, Lesson 1

Introduction

Objective

Students will be aware of the general procedures they will be following this year to study science and social studies topics.

Focus Question

What is the scientific way of learning?

Students are told that this year they will be studying science and social studies "as if all of you were scientists." They are then placed in pairs to discuss the question, "From what you know, what does it mean to be a 'scientist'? What does a scientist do?"

As students share their responses, the teacher often asks *verification* questions, especially the central question of science, *How do you know that's true?* This becomes a common question in *Explore* classrooms. Eventually, the teacher presents the following four-step procedure on a chart.

The Scientific Way of Learning

Step 1—Question

Step 2—Hypothesize, Predict

Step 3—Investigate

Step 4—Analyze/Evaluate Data, Conclude

The teacher then puts the following list on the board:

Some Things Scientists Investigate

What plants need to grow

What the stars and planets are made of

How people in communities get along with each other

What the dinosaurs looked like

How people lived long ago

How people live now

What happens when you mix certain chemicals

How we know about weather and climate

After making sure that the class understands each item on the list, the teacher asks students what they know about each topic *as a result of scientists investigating it*.

The teacher then asks the students to go back over the list and name the kind of scientist that investigates some of these things. For example, "What do people call a scientist who investigates stars and planets? life in human communities? how people lived long ago? dinosaurs?" It is not important that students learn all the names of scientists, but that they realize, first, that there are different types of scientists and, second, that social studies stems from the work of *social* scientists.

To review, the teacher then says, "As you study science and social studies this year, you will be working just like the scientists we have been talking about. What does that mean? What will you be doing? What are the four things we said all scientists do?"

Assessment 1

The teacher displays a list of activities related to airplanes and says to students: "Suppose we were going to study airplanes and how they fly, and I told you that you would be working like real scientists. Which of the things on this list would you expect to be doing?"

a. Make up a story about airplanes.
b. Find some facts about airplanes and how they fly.
c. Ask questions about airplanes and how they fly.
d. Draw a picture of an airplane.
e. Describe a trip you took on an airplane.
f. Try to think of possible answers to your questions about airplanes and how they fly.
g. Build a model of an airport.
h. Keep looking for more facts about airplanes to see if the answers to your questions are right.

Assessment 2/Homework

The teacher reviews the four-step procedure, then shows students a rock, leaf, shell, or similar item, giving them this task: "Suppose you were a scientist and had never seen anything like this before. What would you do to investigate it? Be prepared to tell us what you would do, how, and why."

Explore: Unit 1, Lesson 2

Living Things

Objective

Students will develop a concept of living things in terms of both the characteristics common to all living things and those that distinguish living things from nonliving things.

Focus Question

What is true of all living things that distinguishes them from nonliving things?

Step 1: Question

The teacher introduces the lesson: "First we are going to study living things and how they are *alike*. Since we're going to work as *scientists*, what is the first thing we need to do to study living things?" The teacher then reviews the chart, The Scientific Way of Learning, now focusing on the topic, Living Things and How They Are Alike.

Step 2: Hypothesize

Student attention is focused on the question, "How do we know whether something is or is not alive?" The teacher points to the second step in the four-step procedure and asks students what they need to do after they have asked a question: come up with possible answers. Then the teacher repeats the question, and students hypothesize. The teacher elicits responses, helping students to explain what they mean, and writes them on a chart:

We *think* something is alive if it has these characteristics:

_____

_____

_____

_____

_____

_____

The teacher emphasizes that students should give the information they *think* is true. Later they will investigate to find out which of their present ideas are correct. After a few characteristics are placed on the chart, students work in pairs to come up with additional responses.

Step 3: Investigate

The teacher helps children to move into step 3 of the scientific procedure: "As scientists, what is our next step?" Students should respond that they need to *investigate*, that is, find new information to check the accuracy of what they have put on the chart, and find out what else belongs on it. They may ask, "How can we find the kind of information we need?" At this point *Explore* takes students through a detailed introduction to their textbooks and other references where relevant information might be found. This

Figure 12–4
Data-retrieval chart

LIVING THINGS					
List from chart	bird	tree	fish	cactus	person
Moves? How?					
Grows? For how long?					
Changes? In what ways?					
Reproduces others like self?					
Needs food? What kind? From where?					
Needs air?					
Needs water?					

amounts to teaching students how to *use* their textbooks as an information source. (See Chapter 11.)

Once students are familiar with information sources, they are ready to investigate, to test the characteristics they have listed on their charts. *Explore* uses the concept formation strategy, discussed in Chapter 7. The teacher says, "To test our ideas, let's investigate several living things and find out whether the things we have listed are true of all of them." Each child is given a data-retrieval chart (see Figure 12–4).

In pairs, using the reference books they just studied, students gather the information each question requires for each living thing on the chart. Pairs then report their work to the whole class, and the teacher uses a class-size retrieval chart to record their work. A transparency of the student chart placed on an overhead projector works well.

Step 4: Analyze Data/Conclude
The teacher guides students through the concept-formation strategy as a way of making sense of all the data by drawing it together into a concept. "Let's see what all this information tells us about all living things. First, what do you see is true of some living things but not of others?" Here the teacher is eliciting *differences* among the examples. Then students are directed to focus on *similarities*. "What do you find is true of *all* living things, regardless of what kind?" After this, students are asked to compose a conclusion, or *summary*:

We know something is a living thing if it:

_____

_____

Writing a Conclusion

Students write a paragraph explaining what living things are, giving examples and telling how they differ from nonliving things.

Classifying

Continuing the fourth step in The Scientific Way of Learning, students are helped to push their understanding of the concept still further. The teacher has them test their conclusion and at the same time identify the characteristics that distinguish living from nonliving things by having students inspect a nonliving thing—a cloud, an airplane, popcorn, fire, or a balloon.

The teacher says, "Let's consider something nonliving, like a cloud. What answers do we get to each of the questions on our chart when we ask it about a cloud?" Later, "Based on the information we now have about a cloud, what about it could make it *seem* like a living thing?" and, "What is true of all living things that is not true of a cloud and proves it is not a living thing even if it moves?"

Labeling

Students should be introduced to the term scientists use as a synonym for a living thing: *organism*.

Review

Students are helped to review *how* they learned what distinguishes living from non-living things.

Assessment

The teacher prepares a bulletin board with two sections, one marked LIVING THINGS, the other NONLIVING THINGS. Students are directed to bring in a magazine picture or drawing of something that belongs in each section. Each student should be prepared to tell the class the characteristics that make each item belong in one category or another.

Explore: Unit 1, Lesson 3

Survival Needs

Objective
Students will develop a concept of the needs of all organisms.

Focus Question
What do all living things need to survive and develop as they should?

Now that the children have developed the concept *living things*, Lesson Plan 3 is designed to help them build another idea at the heart of the unit generalization: the *needs* of living things. Again, the concept-formation strategy and a data-retrieval chart are used. The same living things are listed across the top of the chart as in the prior lesson. The questions running down the left side of the chart are the following:

1. Does the organism need *food* to live? What kind? Where and how does it get its food?
2. Does the organism need *water* to live? What has to be true of the water? Where and how does it get water?
3. Does the organism need *air* to live? What has to be true of the air? Where does it get air?
4. Where does the organism usually *live*? What other organisms live there? How do the organisms live together?
5. What can *harm* the organism? How does the organism stay safe from harm and disease?
6. What is the organism *able to do*? What sometimes prevents the organism from doing this? What helps the organism do all that it is able to do?

Numerous library resources and the science and social studies textbooks are used by children to gather this information. Using the concept-formation strategy, the teacher helps them conclude that the needs of living things include:

- proper nutrition
- clean air and water
- sufficient light and warmth
- protection from enemies and disease
- opportunity for the organism to reach its potential

Decision-making/Human Action

Objective
Students will develop an awareness of and commitment to individual and group action that ensures that living things can meet their needs for survival and development.

Focus Question
What decisions and plans do people have to make to see to it that living things have what they need to survive and develop?

This lesson moves children from conceptualizing the attributes of living things (Lesson Plan 2) and what they need to thrive (Lesson Plan 3) to human action on their behalf.

attributes of living things ⇒ needs of living things ⇒ human action

There are two learning activities in this lesson.

Learning Activity A: Planning Human Action
The first learning activity in Lesson 4 has students consider cases where threatening conditions are putting living things at risk by making it difficult or impossible for them to get what they need. Students are then helped to suggest courses of action that might improve the situation.

Sample situations:

1. There has been a very heavy snowfall. All the food and water for birds and deer has been covered with snow for several days and the animals can't get to any.
2. It has not rained for weeks. The farmers are worried because their crops are not getting enough water.
3. People who picnic near the lake have been throwing junk into it for years. Much of this junk is harmful to the fish, insects, birds, and plants that live in or near the lake.

Students discuss these situations in small groups of three and recommend courses of action. Two focus questions guide their work on each case:

1. Which living things would have trouble surviving if no one did anything to change the situation? Explain why they would have trouble surviving.
2. What could people like you and me do so that the living things in this situation could survive? Explain how each suggestion would help the living things survive.

Learning Activity B: People Who Make a Difference
The second learning activity has children gather data on situations in which the needs of living things are threatened *and* in which people took specific actions that helped living things meet their needs. The teacher assembles reading materials about such people and/or invites them to class from the community. After gathering and recording data about them, students use the concept-formation strategy to compare and contrast these people and their specific actions. Finally, they return to the courses of action they suggested in the first part of the lesson, revising and adding ideas for action based on the information they gathered about real situations.

Summing Up: Building a Unifying Idea

The fusion model of curricular integration does not simply join two or more subject matters, taking "a little of this and a little of that." The joining of subject matters is not even the goal. Rather, as the *Explore* example from Northglenn, Colorado, illustrates, the goal is to help children build a powerful and unifying generalization. This generalization cannot be constructed without the joining of material that is traditionally assigned to separate subject areas. In this way, curricular integration is made goal-relevant, and that goal concerns something vitally important and empowering for children: the development of a big idea. In the above unit, that big idea or generalization was *the decisions made by human beings influence the survival of other living things*. By the third lesson, the children had constructed a rudimentary notion of two of the constituent concepts (*living things* and *survival needs*), and they were ready to explore what humans can do and are doing to help other living things thrive.

With the two approaches to curricular integration presented in this chapter, infusion and fusion, teachers have two promising tools with which they can launch integrated units of their own.

Discussion Questions and Suggested Activities

1. Discuss the meaning of the chapter's opening quote, "Curriculum integration is a strategy, not a goal."
2. Compare and contrast the infusion and fusion approaches to curriculum integration. Which seems the better way for beginning teachers? Of what other approaches are you aware?
3. Examine the list of learning objectives given in the Procedure for Producing Biographies section for the sample biography on Sojourner Truth. What kinds of subject matter are represented—information, ideas, skills, issues, the inquiry process? To review these concepts, see Chapter 7.
4. The chief guideline for curriculum integration offered in the chapter was goal-relevance. Do you agree? Why or why not?
5. Ask the librarian in two different elementary/middle school libraries to give you a tour of the biography sections. Ask the librarian to identify several of the more popular biographies. As you examine them, consider these questions: (a) What conceptual themes are suggested by these subjects? (b) Could any three or four of them be woven through a school year, all related to a single theme (e.g., leadership)? (c) Which eras of American history are not represented by biographies in either library?
6. Design an array of biography "book" formats. What forms could kindergartners' books take? How about fifth-graders'?
7. In the infusion example—the biography writing project—which literacy skills probably will need to be taught explicitly to children? Will they already be familiar enough, for example, with *writing process* techniques such as *revision* that these will not require direct instruction? Should such instruction be planned? It is important in the infusion approach that children know how to use the skills they are expected to "infuse."

8. The same issue raised in question 7 is relevant to the fusion example—*Explore*. What skills might need to be taught explicitly to children if they are to move successfully through the four lessons and develop the unifying generalization?

9. With classmates, generate additional examples of the infusion and fusion approaches. Be careful to avoid the pitfalls discussed in the Pitfalls section early in this chapter.

10. Review the *Explore* curriculum. Then add a fifth lesson to the four-lesson unit that was described. Select one of the following topics for its focus, then write an *objective* and a *focus question*.

- Careers involving the study and/or protection of living things
- International comparison of living things and their needs
- An organism's "potential"
- Biographies of one or more people studied in Lesson Plan 4
- Community service related to actions suggested in Lesson Plan 4

Notes

1   Roland Case, *The Anatomy of Curricular Integration* (Simon Fraser University, Burnaby, British Columbia: Tri-University Integration Project, 1991): 5.

2   Judith A. Langer and Arthur N. Applebee, "Reading and Writing Instruction: Toward a Theory of Teaching and Learning," in *Review of Research in Education*, vol. 13, ed. Ernest Z. Rothkopf (Washington, DC: American Educational Research Association, 1986), 173.

3   Jerrold Coombs, *Thinking Seriously about Curriculum Integration* (Simon Fraser University, Burnaby, British Columbia: Tri-University Integration Project, 1991), 2.

4   Jerrold Coombs, *Curriculum Integration*, 1.

5   Adapted from Heidi Hayes Jacobs, "The Growing Need for Interdisciplinary Curriculum Content," in *Interdisciplinary Curriculum: Design and Implementation*, ed. Heidi Hayes Jacobs (Alexandria, VA: Association for Supervision and Curriculum Development, 1989), 1–12. See also Nathalie J. Gehrke, "Explorations of Teachers' Development of Integrative Curriculums," *Journal of Curriculum and Supervision* 6:2 (Winter 1991): 107–17.

6   Howard Gardner and Veronica Boix-Mansilla, "Teaching for Understanding in the Disciplines—and Beyond," *Teachers College Record* 96 (Winter 1994): 199.

7   Janet Alleman and Jere Brophy, "Is Curriculum Integration a Boon or a Threat to Social Studies?" *Social Education* 57 (October 1993): 290.

8   Jerome Bruner, *The Process of Education* (Cambridge, MA: Harvard University Press, 1960), 17.

9   John Dewey, *The Public and Its Problems* (Chicago: Swallow, 1927), 83.

10 Jacobs, "The Growing Need," 2.

11 Myra Zarnowski, *Learning with Biographies: A Reading and Writing Approach* (Washington, DC: National Council for the Social Studies/National Council of Teachers of English, 1990).

12 Francis Gage's account was published in an antislavery journal and reproduced in Edward Beecher Claflin's biography, *Sojourner Truth and the Struggle for Freedom* (New York: Barron, 1987), 81–82.

13 Jeri Ferris, *Walking the Road to Freedom: A Story About Sojourner Truth* (Minneapolis: Carolrhoda Books, 1988), 53, 55.

14 Zarnowski, *Learning with Biographies*, Chapter 4.

15 From *The People Could Fly*, retold by Virginia Hamilton. In *Cricket* 15: 6 (February 1988): 21–26.

16 Adapted from Zarnowski, *Learning with Biographies*, Chapter 4.

17 Elliot Aronson, *The Jigsaw Classroom* (Beverley Hills, CA: Sage, 1978).

18 Glynda Ann Hull, "Building an Understanding of Composing," in *Toward the Thinking Curriculum: Current Cognitive Research*, ed. Lauren B. Resnick and Leopold E. Klopfer, 1989 ASCD Yearbook (Alexandria, VA: Association for Supervision and Curriculum Development, 1989), 104–28.

19 See Carl Bereiter and Marlene Scardamalia, "An Attainable Version of High Literacy: Approaches to Teaching Higher-Order Skills in Reading and Writing," *Curriculum Inquiry* 17: 1 (1987): 9–30.

20 Milton Meltzer, Foreword to Zarnowski, *Learning About Biographies*, x.

21 *Explore Curriculum*, developed and written jointly by Sydelle Seiger-Ehrenberg and School District no. 12, Adams County, Northglenn, Colorado, 1990. The material in this section is quoted or adapted from *Explore* curriculum documents.

22 Lauren B. Resnick and Leopold E. Klopfer, eds. *Toward the Thinking Curriculum: Current Cognitive Research*, 1989 ASCD Yearbook (Alexandria, VA: Association for Supervision and Curriculum Development, 1989), 6.

Selected References

Alleman, Janet, and Jere Brophy. "Is Curriculum Integration a Boon or a Threat to Social Studies?" *Social Education* 57 (October 1993): 287–91.

Calkins, Lucy McCormick. *The Art of Teaching Writing* (Portsmouth, NH: Heinemann, 1994).

Case, Roland. "Our Crude Handling of Educational Reforms: The Case of Curricular Integration," *Canadian Journal of Education* 19 (Winter 1994): 80–93.

Erickson, H. Lynn. *Stirring the Head, Heart, and Soul*. Thousand Oaks, CA: Corwin, 1995.

Heath, Shirley Brice. *Ways with Words*. New York: Cambridge University Press, 1983.

Hull, Glynda Ann. "Building an Understanding of Composing." In *Toward the Thinking Curriculum: Current Cognitive Research*, edited by Lauren B. Resnick and Leopold E. Klopfer, 1989 ASCD Yearbook. Alexandria, VA: Association for Supervision and Curriculum Development, 1989, 104–28.

Jacobs, Heidi Hayes. *Interdisciplinary Curriculum: Design and Development*. Alexandria, VA: Association for Supervision and Curriculum Development, 1989.

Lindquist, Tarry. *Seeing the Whole Through Social Studies*. Portsmouth, NH: Heinemann, 1995.

Lockledge, Ann, Pricilla Porter, and others. Articles on the integration of mathematics and social studies in *Social Studies and the Young Learner* 6 (September/October 1993).

Rutherford, F. James, and Andrew Ahlgren. *Science for All Americans*. New York: Oxford University Press, 1990.

Wilton, Shirley. "Newer Biographies Are Better than Before." In *Children's Literature and Social Studies: Selecting and Using Notable Books in the Classroom*, edited by Myra Zarnowski and Arlene F. Gallagher. Washington, DC: National Council for the Social Studies, 1993, 16–19.

Zarnowski, Myra. *Learning with Biographies: A Reading and Writing Approach*. Washington, DC: National Council for the Social Studies/National Council of Teachers of English, 1990.

INDEX